Beyond Structural Listening?

University Cooperative Society Subvention Grant
awarded by The University of Texas at Austin.

Beyond Structural Listening?

Postmodern Modes of Hearing

EDITED BY

Andrew Dell'Antonio

UNIVERSITY OF CALIFORNIA PRESS

Berkeley   Los Angeles   London

University of California Press
Berkeley and Los Angeles, California

University of California Press, Ltd.
London, England

Library of Congress Cataloging-in-Publication Data

Beyond structural listening? : postmodern modes of hearing / edited by
Andrew Dell'Antonio.
    p.   cm.
  Includes bibliographical references and index.
  ISBN 0-520-23757-9 (cloth : alk. paper)
  ISBN 0-520-23760-9 (pbk. : alk. paper)
1. Musical criticism.   2. Musical analysis.   3. Music—Philosophy and
aesthetics.   4. Music—Social aspects.   5. Postmodernism.
I. Dell'Antonio, Andrew.
  ML3880.B49 2004   2004001751
  781.1'7—dc22   MN

Manufactured in the United States of America

13   12   11   10   09   08   07   06   05   04
10 9 8 7 6 5 4 3 2 1

CONTENTS

PREFACE

This project probably has its roots in a long conversation I had with Rose Rosengard Subotnik at the 1990 AMS/SMT/SEM meeting in Oakland, California. Through the ensuing decade and a half, other conversations with many friends and colleagues—among them the authors of this collection— brought about a collective interest in exploring the formulations on structural listening that Rose had first articulated in the Meyer Festschrift. When the essay was republished in Rose's second collection, *Deconstructive Variations*, the topic took on new urgency; shortly thereafter, my conversations intensified, and eventually led to my approaching the University of California Press with a proposal for a collection of essays.

In the process of its formation, the collection has changed (developed?): the cast of characters is slightly different than that originally envisioned, the title—and even the content—of more than one of the essays has metamorphosed beyond the expectations of its author... or its editor. These are probably consequences of the dialogical (dare one say dialectical?) nature of the project, of which this collection is one synchronic manifestation. Most gratifying to me is the fact that our collective dialogue has expanded beyond the boundaries of these essays—we have learned from each other, and have found much common ground, and many fruitful points of disagreement. In the process, I have gained even more respect for my fellow authors than I had before, and I thank them again for their articulateness and willingness to engage in this continuing discussion.

In a collection such as this, it is most appropriate to let the authors make their own acknowledgments, and we have done so in each individual essay. However, I will take the editor's prerogative to give some much-deserved overall thanks.

The University of Texas Cooperative Society provided a crucial subvention grant, without which the collection could not have been published in this form. Mary Francis supplied unwavering editorial guidance and invaluable support in navigating the shoals that invariably face editors of complex collections such as this one. Ruth Solie and Nicholas Cook took time to offer detailed and constructive suggestions on an earlier version of the typescript, and much credit for the resulting improvements goes to them. Without Rob Walser's backing and enthusiasm for the project, the collection would not have come to fruition as you see it today. Adam Krims's wise counsel and insight carried me through many a rough spot. My colleagues' encouragement—especially that of Elizabeth Crist, David Neumeyer, Jim Buhler, Sarah Reichardt, and Dennis Rathnaw—made balancing this venture with other professional duties a pleasure. And the contribution of my family—Lella, Lester, Gianfausto, Ian, Barbara, and especially Susan and Miriam—to my emotional and intellectual balance can never be quantified.

None of this would have been possible without Rose Rosengard Subotnik. This collection is not the Festschrift she still amply deserves, but perhaps its dialectical spirit—and, yes, unresolved conflicts—are a worthy tribute to the influence she has had on us, and on the discipline of musicology.

Andrew Dell'Antonio
Austin, Texas
December 2003

Beyond Structural Listening?

Postmodern Modes of Hearing

ANDREW DELL'ANTONIO

Beyond structural listening? It may not be entirely to our advantage to idealize a listening stance that leaves structure in its wake, as Martin Scherzinger observes at the close of his essay. Yet inasmuch as the "structural listening" model—as described by Rose Subotnik first in the Meyer Festschrift and later in her *Deconstructive Variations*—is a disciplinary commonplace in the academic study of Western art music, and a pedagogical staple of undergraduate education in music history and theory, the essays in this collection follow Subotnik's lead in questioning the universality of that model as a yardstick of aesthetic (and moral) value; we believe that our explorations have taken us "beyond" the structural parameters outlined by Subotnik.

Postmodern modes of hearing? How do our essays, with their diversity of target repertories, critical stances, and theoretical frameworks, all fit into a "postmodern" approach—and in what way do they all represent "modes of hearing"? Several common threads in these essays mark them as proceeding from a common perspective, one that is incommensurate with modernist interpretations of the status of knowledge (hence potentially postmodern); each essay is also concerned with the act of close engagement with specific musical "works" (though several of the essays address the potential pitfalls inherent in associating a textual notion of "work" with musical phenomena), and with the problems that arise when the process of hearing is approached through alternative paradigms.

We should in any case begin with our collective starting point: for while these essays reflect a multiplicity of critical and analytical agendas, rhetorical stances, and repertories chosen for analytical inquiry, we all share an intellectual flashpoint: the notion of "structural listening" as developed by Rose Rosengard Subotnik (1996).[1] Subotnik critiques what she calls the historical tradition of structural listening, which she sees as originating primarily with

Schoenberg and Adorno, and becoming the prevalent aesthetic paradigm in Germanic and Anglo-American musical scholarship. In her usage, the term designates an approach to listening that considers musical works as autonomous structures defined "wholly through some implicit and intelligible principle of unity."[2] Structural listeners who believe in the autonomous art work believe also in the "possibility of reasoned musical discourse," and thus seek to find "objectively determinable" "interconnectedness of structure" based on "concretely unfolding logic" and on the "self-developing capacity of a motivic-thematic kernel" (Subotnik 1996, 154; 156). This leads them to "end by locating musical value wholly within some formal sort of parameter, to which it is the listener's business to attend" (153). In that they "look upon the ability of a unifying principle to establish the internal 'necessity' of a structure as tantamount to a guarantee of musical value" (159), they have been able to use structural listening as a means to judge not only the value of musical works, but also their place in the musical canon. Such a place is guaranteed not only by artistic value but also by moral value, considered as inextricably linked: "The more a musical structure approximates the self-contained intelligibility characteristic of logic, the more it can and does free itself from what Adorno sees as the deceptions or falsehoods inevitably fostered through social ideology in order to maintain the power of existing institutions" (154).

Ultimately, intellectual rigor and discipline are at the heart of the "contract" between composer and listener that Subotnik identifies at the core of the structural listening paradigm; and here it is apropos to quote Subotnik at some length:

> The concept of structural value offered by Schoenberg and Adorno, like their concept of the structural listening that can discern such value, is at once exacting and generous. Demanding an unflagging intelligent concentration on the part of the listener, these men require of the composer, and more generally of themselves, a no less stringent standard of discipline. For Schoenberg these two [structural rigor and expressive capacity] are virtually synonymous: the deepest emotional satisfaction in music arises precisely through the achievement of an intensely expressive structural integrity (which is "independent of style and flourish" and communicable at least to those whose "artistic and ethical culture is on a high level"). (155)

The ethical dimension of structural listening is thus deeply enmeshed within its ideal of organic necessity: music that is "good" (both ethically and aesthetically) will reveal its quality to a disciplined listener who is prepared and willing to receive the composer's coherent structural message in its full detail. As Subotnik points out, this mandate requires a very specific notion of listening, one that can only be gained through technical training and serious self-discipline; such training and self-discipline, in their turn, are the mark of an aesthetically prepared and culturally elevated individual.

But, as Subotnik observes, the notion of "listening" that emerges from this paradigm is potentially detachable from the sense of hearing:

> Even more important, perhaps, is the secondary status that [structural] listen-ing accords to the musical parameter of sound . . . Certainly, to an important extent, structural listening can take place in the mind through intelligent score-reading, without the physical presence of an external sound-source . . . By Adorno's account, in fact, "mature music," which concerns itself with that "subcutaneous" structure where individual integrity can hope to resist or even transcend social ideology, "becomes suspicious of sound as such." [Adorno imagines] a time when "the silent, imaginative reading of music could render actual playing as superfluous as speaking is made by the reading of written material." (161–62)

[margin note: — primacy of speech V.: written word]

Structural listening thus seeks to transcend the potential sloppiness and impreciseness inherent in the physical manifestations of sound; the written score is seen (!) as having more integrity than any sonic realization of the musical work, and as more indicative of the creative process of the composer, which manifests itself through the structural necessity and organic com-pleteness of the musical ideas that unfold from the beginning to the end of a musical work.

[margin note: intentionality]

Indeed, structural listening is closely linked with legitimacy through com-positional intent, since "structural listening is an active mode that, when suc-cessful, gives the listener the sense of composing the piece as it actualizes itself in time" (150). Paradoxically, however, compositional intent is under-played; the suggestion instead is that meaning is immanent in the composi-tional structure itself. "Both Schoenberg and Stravinsky celebrate the activ-ity of musical construction," suggests Subotnik, "and would confine musical meaning within the boundaries of the individual composition, exclusive of contextual relationships and (at least in theory) of intent" (152). The com-position is here conceived of as a "readable text," one that is stable and iden-tifiable and—when properly constructed—creates its own internal necessity through structure.

Subotnik is highly critical of the tradition of structural listening she thus defines. In the spirit of the subject of her study, Adorno, she voices her cri-tique in the preliminary terms of what at first seems to be a dialectic, by defining the abstract, rational structures of structural listening in opposition to what she calls "sound" or "style," which she equates with aspects of music as diverse as "medium," "history," and corporeality (149, 162, 168). Setting up this polarity allows Subotnik not only to link her arguments to historical debates over form and content in art, but also to situate her structural lis-teners in opposition to the most historically and ethically meaningful aspects of music. Subotnik maintains, for example, that structural listeners ignored the "massive evidence of the degree to which the communication of ideas depends on concrete cultural knowledge, and on the power of signs to convey a richly concrete open-endedness of meaning through a variety of cultural relationships" (167). She concludes that the damage wrought by half a century of structural listening can be corrected only through the development of "critical methods or . . . a critical language" for investigating the neglected dialectical pole of sound or style, with which musicologists will finally be able to determine "the social and moral significance of the values discerned in music" (171).

Subotnik's analysis of structural listening is largely aimed at defining the broad philosophical terms of engagement that have motivated discourse about music in the twentieth century. In order to make her readers aware of the key binarisms operative in modern musicological thought, she rejects close readings of historical and theoretical texts in favor of a broad overview of concepts established by summarizing the common denominators in the work of Schoenberg, Adorno, and Stravinsky. As our readers will discover, the authors of this collection do not necessarily concur with Subotnik's conclusions about "stylistic listening," or the necessity of a polar binarism between "structure" and "style" (see especially the essays by Levitz and Scherzinger). The presence of such a binarism in Anglo-American musical discourse is, however, one of Subotnik's central insights; and it is one that has proved crucial for our collective forays in directions "beyond" Subotnik's formulation of the structural listening paradigm.

Subotnik suggests that structural listening is a deeply modernist phenomenon. How might we start identifying the traits of some specifically "postmodern" alternatives? Jean-François Lyotard has pointed to the "erosion of the legitimacy principle of knowledge" as one of the key features of a stage in the systems of communication that he characterizes as "postmodern" (Lyotard 1984, 39). Postmodern models of knowledge, according to Lyotard, question the modernist concept of "knowledge for its own sake," inherently aimed at the understanding of deep and enduring truth-content; rather, such models are *dialogic*, based on constant negotiations (which Lyotard calls "language-games") around the definition and legitimacy of knowledge-systems. Lyotard underlines that the goal of the postmodern dialogic ideal of knowledge is not consensus (under one "legitimate" interpretation with clear truth-value) but constant negotiation between different and sometimes incommensurate models, each of which is defined by its historical/social/cultural context. Thus one of the key principles underlying theories of postmodern knowledge is the impossibility of stable truth; Slavoj Žižek finds the idea of a "central impossibility" of knowledge through the psychoanalytical theories of Lacan, and Lyotard locates it in the proliferation of information in the post-industrial age, but both concur on the destabilizing effects this new perspective can have on established notions of subjectivity, objectivity, and the possibilities of intellectual control or mastery (Žižek 1991b, 141 ff.; Lyotard 1984, esp. 65 ff.).

Some common threads in our essays seem to resonate strongly with these "postmodern" approaches to knowledge (and our readers will doubtless find other threads when reading these essays as a group):

CONTROL 1: QUESTIONING MASTERY. [Maus, Morris, Levitz, Dubiel, Scherzinger; strong resonances in Fink, Attinello] What is our goal when we listen, structurally or otherwise? Echoing Subotnik's characterization of the "ideal structural listener," Maus offers us a snapshot of Allen Forte self-consciously "modeling" the ideal theorist, who organizes time though analysis in much the same way that a composer organizes time through music; music and analysis are both "the product of a controlled, rational, masterful agency," and in this way working through an analytical chart "feels like" composing, helping us connect to the truth of the compositional process and the persona of the composer (see also Power and Personas, below). As Maus observes, mastery is key for Forte since the field of music theory must present itself as scientifically valid and deserving of high estimation during its formative period, a time when high modernist valuing of science was still at a peak. As Morris points out, the mastery of structural listening and/or analysis has a clear moral value: such a practice reflects autonomy and internal development, but also originality and expressivity, drawing explicit parallels with two of the ideals of modernist selfhood: "atomistic individualism" and "disengaged instrumental reason." According to Morris (who is drawing on Subotnik's characterizations), in the modernist structural model "music occupies itself with moral thought and action in ways that strongly resemble the ways in which human beings occupy themselves with thought and action" (see p. 51). Levitz comes to similar conclusions about the importance of static models and comprehensive explanatory gestures in analyses of the *danse sacrale* from Stravinsky's *Sacre du printemps* by Boulez, Forte, and van den Toorn. Departing from Subotnik's characterization of structural listening as score-bound, Dubiel argues that the most productive way to approach structure is through the listening experience itself, rather than through fulfillment of pre-existing organicist models; he finds that listening for structural events is not about mastery, but about "responsiveness along unforeseen lines," or "elusiveness of perception" (see p. 176). Rather than following the established tradition of placing high value and emphasis on musical details that are developed or "fulfilled" in the unfolding of the musical work, Dubiel tries dwelling on "unfulfilled" or unexplainable musical events, and his analyses reflect his experiments with the release of intellectual mastery in the analytical process. The notion of "structural listening," Dubiel suggests, can best be thought of as a way of *thinking about* listening rather than a way of listening; he examines examples in which he has difficulty "hearing" specific details despite his ability to recognize them on the musical score, and pointedly questions what it might mean to "hear" or to "listen" given these paradoxical circumstances; indeed, listening for specific details might result in confusion or disorientation rather than mastery, and this might be a valuable interpretative strategy to learn to deploy. In any case, the lack of coherence in an analytical endeavor should not be seen as a weakness, but rather as a potential opening for new insights. Scherzinger comes to a similar conclusion; seeing Subotnik's definition as too limiting, and wanting to define musical structure more broadly as the "opening of possibilities," he suggests that "open-ended" approaches to structure can be effectively used in destabilizing established notions of the canon "from within"; he suggests that such critiques are no less politically progressive than critiques "from without" that dismiss structure as a progressive tool.

CONTROL 2: PLEASURE, PAIN, AND THE SUBLIME. [Fink, Attinello; strong resonances in Dubiel, Maus] Like Dubiel, Fink specifically challenges the notion of control, finding potential in the pleasure-through-pain of the sublime, and specifically in the potential for the "revelation of unspeakable content" behind the moments when a formal process can be perceived as hurtling toward failure; returning to the now-infamous image evoked by Susan McClary of the recapitulation of the first movement in Beethoven's Ninth Symphony as akin to a "rage of a rapist incapable of attaining release," Fink traces a long tradition of controversy surrounding that musical episode, and argues that the "beautifiers" who wish to hear that moment as non-problematic are at least matched, and perhaps out-argued, by those "sublimators" who feel the frustration and pain of the musical gestures as inherent in the sublime power of Beethoven's approach. We can hear the passage as unproblematic, Fink suggests, but what do we lose by such a decision? Has modernist criticism, in its search for organic solutions, dismissed the power of disruption that many listeners experience as supremely meaningful in this and other music? Attinello argues that the disruptive power of the sonic sublime is a key component of much postwar avant-garde music, and suggests that the scientific metaphors of control and organization deployed by Boulez and composers of the Darmstadt school can mask the crucial preoccupation in this music with the power of the "violent ineffable"—of sound that threatens to "crack open the sky." He proposes that listeners try to focus on the sonic disruption that is created by such ostensibly detached procedures, and to dwell on the paradox created by those two apparently opposed affective states, rather than on the more explicit rhetoric of compositional mastery.

Maus traces the aesthetic implications of an analytical discourse of control, finding parallels between the language of self-abnegation and submission used by musical analysts and the pleasure/pain dynamics of sadomasochistic sensuality; what is missing in analytical discourse, Maus suggests, is the flexibility and power-sharing that sadomasochistic role-playing offers within its (sometimes extreme) discourse of control and submission (see also Negotiations of Power 2, below).

NEGOTIATIONS OF POWER 1: POLITICAL/SOCIAL CONTEXTS OF ANALYTICAL POWER. [Levitz, Dell'Antonio, Scherzinger] Theories of postmodern knowledge (see, for example, Žižek 1991b, 144–45) suggest that the significance of an artistic work or phenomenon is not simply inherent in that work, but strongly shaped by the individuals who are using that phenomenon as a means to gain power/prestige (moral, intellectual, or otherwise). Levitz unpacks the "erasure" of the subjectivity of the Chosen One in Stravinsky's *Sacre*, examining the analytical apparatus that effectively allowed Stravinsky and his historiographers to rewrite the creative process of the *Sacre*, eliminating the role played by the dancer and choreographer Nijinsky, and leading to a misogynistic vision that distorts the impact of the work as a ballet. Dell'Antonio draws on Gramsci's cultural critique and on Jameson's perspective of postmodern aesthetics, and sees potential in the symbolic as viable context of contestation in post-industrial society, specifically through its reflection in the development of an ideal of "collective listening" (relying on immersion rather than critical distance, negotiation rather than stability of meaning) in the context of music videos and MTV. Scherzinger rejects a "turn against the aesthetic" that he sees in much contemporary critique of formal analysis, observing that formalist analyses can be used as the starting point for progressive political projects, and that the "business of analysis" is not a transcendent process (despite its characterization as such by both proponents and detractors) but a social activity, potentially value-neutral and thus not inherently suspect.

NEGOTIATIONS OF POWER 2: POWER AND PERSONAS. [Maus, Morris, Dell'Antonio, Attinello] To his investigation of Forte's strategies (see Questioning Mastery above), Maus counterposes the perspective of Edward Cone, who argues that active listening requires absorption/identification into an outside persona (generally perceived as a creation of the composer). While these may seem to be two opposite approaches—Forte's model of working through an analytical chart "feels like composing," Cone's model of listening abandons control in ultimate passivity—both cases, Maus suggests, invoke an "eroticized power relationship between personas and listeners"; but while both models seem to imply a fixed relationship of mastery and subservience, could the power relationship be made fluid/negotiable, and if so, how? For Morris, this is the specific value in thinking of "musical virtues." Virtues, Morris suggests, assist us in negotiating our place within an authority-based social configuration. If absorption into a controlling persona is achieved through structural listening, with the goal of taking on or "being the same as" the compositional agency, focusing on the inconsistencies, lacks, or contradictions in the music can help locate the *difference* between the listener and a putative homogeneous "composer's voice," which Morris sees as a more compelling "musical virtue" for the twenty-first century; he provides three examples (from Brahms, Reich, and Nine Inch Nails) of analytical "moments" to illustrate his suggestion. Dell'Antonio takes a different perspective, approaching the issue from the collective reception practices modeled by MTV: the dialogues that are inherent in such practices permit negotiations about musical and multimedia meanings that allow changing identifications with the musical and broader cultural message perceived through the videos. In a wider frame, Attinello asks: why do we feel compelled to echo the notion of mastery in our own writings about music? Is it still a "virtue" to deny that academic inquiry arises from personal, subjective passion? How can we justify giving a scientific/modernist tinge to writing that is subjectively crafted, given the illusory nature of objectivity in any analysis, if any description of music that is designed to guide an interpretative process is going to provide more than "just facts"? Can we learn to distinguish, in our subjective descriptions, the "generalizable" from the "private"?

RECLAIMING THE BODY. [Levitz, Morris, Maus, Attinello, Le Guin; resonances in Dell'Antonio] Structural listening highlights intellectual response to music to the almost total exclusion of human physical presence—whether that of the performer or that of the listener; several of the essays in this collection purposefully address the physicality of musical experience. Levitz considers the physicality inherent in Nijinsky's choreographic creation of the Chosen One, and how that physicality creates a "dialogue" with Stravinsky's musical characterization of the Sacrifice; an erasure of that physicality changes not only the ballet's message but also the implications of the *Rite of Spring* as "absolute music." Morris chooses to highlight physical components in his analyses to underline the importance of embodiment to his notion of musical "virtues"; he argues that such physicality is crucial for a critical approach that values individuals over totalizing models. Attinello dwells on the physicality of the modernist sublime, and further reflects on the essential component of physical subjectivity that musical scholarship may well continue to ignore at its own peril; and indeed, Maus remarks on the implicit but intense physicality underlying the language of twentieth-century analysis (see also Control 2, above). In reporting on her listening experiment, Le Guin specifically addresses her awareness of physical responses that is made possible—or certainly more intense—by the withdrawal of the score or other written material as a structuring aide-mémoire; she draws on

Bergson in exploring the usefulness and limitations of kinesthetic responses to musical immediacy, and their influence on synoptic models of musical experience.

LISTENING AND THE MUSICAL "TEXT". [Levitz, Le Guin, Dell'Antonio; resonances in Dubiel, Maus] Can we separate "listening" from other modes of experience? While structural listening appears to rely on a musical "object" that can be "read" in its organic linear unfolding, and conventional analytical practice likewise relies on a fixed musical "text" that can be read either in whole or in part (and even non-linearly) like a literary text, conflicts can arise between the process of hearing/listening and a thus-characterized musical "text": Musical notation can offer information that cannot be heard; musical performance (and multimedia) can provide more than just sonic experience; music can be heard only linearly; and musical works or performances are often experienced partially or incompletely. Levitz observes that the removal of the choreographic element from critical commentary on the *Sacre* allowed Adorno (and the long tradition of analysis that follows him) to dismiss the "chosen one" as an ego-less creature, a powerless victim of the musical necessity of the work. It was precisely the notion of listening as detachable from other forms of information-gathering about the *Sacre* that created the impression of powerlessness that allowed critics to dismiss the work as "fascist." Confronting the notion of a work of music as a "text," Le Guin examines the common analytical trope of "faith in description"—the notion that verbal description can provide a useful account to focus listening practice—and by restricting her experiments to listening (without the visual stimulus of the score or of a live performer) outlines her failures and frustrations, as well as her tendencies to create both physical and visual associations that make her experience no longer one of "pure listening." Le Guin also explores how description and aesthetic immediacy may undermine each other, asking whether "accounting for" all musical details is even desirable (let alone possible), and suggesting that it may be the analyst/critic's job to "rejoice in the incompleteness" of the analysis, since "complete description is . . . fundamentally unsuited to how people think, and remember, and understand" (see p. 250). Dell'Antonio, also examining a repertory and listening practice that is grounded in immediacy, dwells on the specific multimedia character of MTV videos, and the challenge that such works present to the notion of "text," both from the perspective of performance and from the perspective of structural completeness or coherence. He broadens his critical scope to explore the possibility that the "element of the 'structural listening' dyad most susceptible to deconstruction may not be the adjective, but the gerund" (see p. 222)—that "listening" itself may be a concept worth contesting, since notions of primacy of the autonomous and organically structured musical work depend on the desirability of perceiving a musical work as autonomous, a desirability that is strongly dependent on historically contingent (perhaps specifically modernist) notions of subjectivity and objectivity.

In our analyses, we find that structure can often be immanently meaningful: to give just one example, Levitz describes the musical organization of the *danse sacrale* as crucial—once the physicality of Nijinsky's dance is reinstated—to the historical and aesthetic meaning of the work. But if (per Fink's discussion, see p. 113ff.) the standard modernist approach is to "explain away" inconsistencies, revealing the organic unity of the stable masterwork, our approach is fairly uniformly to dwell on the impossibility (and undesirability) of complete integration—as Dubiel describes it, "disorientation and loss"—or even the "death of description," the actual impossibility of the descriptive endeavor. In this "gap" (what Žižek [1991b] might describe as a Lacanian "blot," the unknowable Real making its presence felt while simultaneously revealing its inaccessibility to human understanding) the authors of this collection find various facets of what Fink describes as the "postmodern sublime": the expressive, emotional, and semiotic power sparked by the realization that structural coherence is an impossibility. In several of our essays, the awareness of such an impossibility intersects with a questioning of subjective insight: Attinello confronts the postmodern divide explicitly (even bluntly) through the self-conscious "gap" and the self-reflecting "mirrors" in his essay, but other authors—most notably Dubiel and Le Guin, but several others as well—present reflections on the deceptive nature of perception and knowledge that resonate strongly with postmodern philosophical and epistemological theories within which, as Thomas Docherty puts it, "rather than knowing the stable essence of a thing, we begin to tell the story of the event of judging it, and to enact the narrative of how it changes consciousness and thus produces a new knowledge" (Docherty 1993, 25). Indeed, if structural listening is most suited (as Subotnik suggests) for the aesthetic validation of a limited set of coherent and stable musical texts, our essays attempt to capture a more fluid process of assessment that might avoid the canonic circularity inscribed by structural listening, opening possibilities for new parameters in the aesthetic and cultural/social valuation of music.

If postmodernism has been seen as questioning metanarratives (not only those connected with "enlightenment progress," but also Marxist, Freudian, Darwinist teleologies) then our essays are "postmodern" through their common suspicion of organic unity as a characteristic immanent in a musical work, and thus a rejection of the structural listening that Subotnik describes, as a possible, or even a desirable, paradigm of fruition. For some—indeed most—of us this means not rejecting the possibility of structural perception, but rather reassessing the potential for structure to signify outside models of organic unity—indeed, to signify most powerfully when it creates uncertainties or contradictions. We have no grand project to offer—save perhaps our collective conviction that listening *is* a political and ethical act, and that an awareness of the diversity of interpretative strategies that we have suggested in these pages can mitigate the hegemony—and the hubris—of the totalist/organicist listening project unpacked by Subotnik. Explicitly invoked by Dell'Antonio, evoked by Morris in his call for "musical virtues," the politics of listening are implicit throughout this volume, for the acknowledgment of manipulation of power contains within it an implicit demand for justice. But how can we achieve this justice? In each of our essays there are calls for alternative political/ethical strategies of listening, criticism, or analysis. We will consider ourselves successful to the extent that our suggestions will encourage others to continue expanding the possibilities of perception in the critical study and evaluation of musical repertories.

Several chroniclers of the postmodern have suggested that postmodernism is not a chronologically separate "way of knowing" from modernism; Lyotard opines that postmodernism is "modernism in its nascent state," while Žižek suggests that postmodernism precedes modernism, the latter being an attempt to establish a coherent symbolic order as a response to the potential disruptiveness of the central impossibility of knowledge that the postmodern perspective would imply (Lyotard 1984, 79; Žižek 1991b, 145 and *passim*). Indeed, Dell'Antonio argues that the rhetoric of Schumann's pioneering musical criticism resonates strongly with contemporary postmodern strategies, and Fink suggests that the sublime-focused aesthetics of the "nascent modernism" of the early nineteenth century were dismissed by the beauty-focused "full-blown modernist" critics of the following generations. Given that these two approaches to knowledge are complementary and rely on their mutual opposition for their power, we can now come full circle and read our proposed "beyond" of structural listening not as a chronological displacement but as a multi-dimensional reconfiguration. Seeping outside modernist parameters of organic structure and mastery of coherence, overflowing the plane of objectivity and artistic autonomy, the essays in this collection experiment with incoherence, discontinuity, situatedness, alienation, and subjectivity as features of the listening experience—but perhaps these features can be seen as "structural" after all. Indeed, it is our hope that these excursions "beyond" can inform a broader understanding of musical structure, one that allows direct engagement with the musical event/work without relying on teleological or totalizing models.

NOTES

1. Rose Rosengard Subotnik, "Toward a Deconstruction of Structural Listening: A Critique of Schoenberg, Adorno, and Stravinsky," in Subotnik 1996, 148–76; a pre-

vious version of this essay appeared in Narmour and Solie 1988. Much of the discussion of Subotnik's argument that follows owes its articulation to an earlier version of Tamara Levitz's article for this collection; I would like to thank her for her incisiveness and insight.

2. Subotnik 1996, 158. Subotnik traces the principle of work autonomy so essential to structural listening back to a passionate eighteenth-century debate that found its most influential resonance in Kant's *Kritik der Urteilskraft*. She believes that it was Kant who convinced scholars for over two hundred years of the importance of judging the art work in itself, according to its own *Zweckmäßigkeit* and independently of other realms of knowledge. This led to what is often almost casually, and sometimes incorrectly, labeled "formalism" in music theory in the twentieth century. See also Subotnik 1991.

ONE

The Disciplined Subject of Musical Analysis

FRED EVERETT MAUS

*[Schenker's achievement] may be likened to a particular kind of high-level achieve-
ment in science: the discovery or development of a fundamental principle which then
opens the way for the disclosure of further new relationships, new meanings. Regarded
in this way, Schenker's achievement invites comparison with that of Freud. Just as
Freud opened the way for a deeper understanding of the human personality with his
discovery that the diverse patterns of overt behavior are controlled by certain underlying factors, so Schenker opened the way for a deeper understanding of musical structure with his discovery that the manifold of surface events in a given composition is
related in specific ways to a fundamental organization.*

ALLEN FORTE

STRANGE ECHO

Allen Forte's essay "Schenker's Conception of Musical Structure" comments
on a graphic analysis by Heinrich Schenker, in order to exemplify
Schenker's approach to tonal music. In a typical remark, he paraphrases
Schenker's sketch: "Schenker then shows how this initial prolongation is followed by a restatement."

Then he does something odd. In the next sentence, Forte writes: "To recapitulate, there are two prolongational classes shown in this background
sketch" (12–13). The odd part is the echo between "restatement" and "recapitulation," and the way the words resonate across the obvious distinction
between the music and Forte's own text. The music, interpreted by Schenker,
restates; immediately after, Forte the theorist recapitulates. The words have
almost the same meaning, though they refer to different things—one a musical event, the other an event in Forte's text. Curiously, Forte applies the concept "restatement" to the music and "recapitulation" to his own words. This
reverses the more natural pairing, as though to emphasize (through the
rhetorical figure of chiasmus) a symmetry or mirroring between media.

Why would this echo or mirroring occur? Many people, reading the essay,
might not be puzzled by this: it is easy to ignore such a detail of language,

not allowing it to distract from the "content" of the essay. You might not register it consciously or, perhaps, you might enjoy it as a rather subdued form of wit, as decoration. But what if you want to take that bit of matching more seriously, rather than setting it aside? What if you want to include it as part of the message of the essay? What context of other passages in Forte's essay, and of broader considerations about music theory, could make this play of "restatement" and "recapitulation" more than a mishap or a small joke?

IDENTIFYING THE MUSIC THEORIST

From the late 1950s on, the field of music theory and analysis enjoyed rapid professionalization and growth in North America. The *Journal of Music Theory*, first published in 1957, and *Perspectives of New Music*, appearing in 1962, promoted the image of a sophisticated scholarly field devoted to technical theory and analysis, with its main focus on tonal and post-tonal music. In 1977, formation of the Society for Music Theory embodied this image in a distinct professional society, now for many scholars the primary professional affiliation just as other scholars affiliate primarily with the American Musicological Society, the Society for Ethnomusicology, and so on. For about half a century, "music theorist" has been a professional identity. Schools, journals, and scholarly societies seem to agree that a theory specialization constitutes one way of being professional about music.

What is a music theorist—specifically, what is a later twentieth-century North American professional music theorist? What is this identity, and why might someone identify with it? I want to suggest a partial answer through close attention to a classic of mid-century writing, the famous Forte essay from which I just quoted. First published in 1959, it holds a strategic position near the beginning of the recent professionalization of scholarly theory. It offers to inaugurate responsible, informed discussion of the early twentieth-century theorist Heinrich Schenker's ideas, in place of the disorganized, inadequately informed polemical writings of the past. It proposes, therefore, to create and circulate an image of a particular kind of person, a responsible, intelligent music theorist. In framing an identity, proposing a role model, this text not only says "Read and evaluate the following claims," but also: "Be like me. Do as I do." And, of course, "Write like this." What is the rhetoric of this performative, inaugural essay?

One remarkable, even breathtaking aspect of the essay is the calm assurance with which Forte refers to the discipline of music theory, evoking a coherent, purposeful area of research at a time when almost none of the present institutional structures of music theory existed. Many of Forte's references to music theory are abstract. There are exceptions; in several passages at the beginning of the essay, he writes as though music theorists are a social group of actual people, interacting in shared discourse. He mentions the need to find criteria for "intelligent public discussion" (4), and he expresses hope that, "as Schenker's work becomes more widely recognized, serious music theorists will make further applications of his ideas" (23). These passages evoke music theorists as people who reflect and converse. But in many other passages, a reified music theory floats free from any particular social embodiment. Forte writes of "certain problems which stand before *music theory* today" (4); he identifies "five unsolved problems in *music theory*" (24); he suggests that "*music theory* is responsible for developing new concepts and new analytical procedures" for contemporary music (33). (Here and in subsequent quotations throughout, I add italics to draw attention to wording.) Music theory itself. Is anybody home?

Yes: at several points Forte invokes an abstract, generalized figure, "the music theorist," whose behavior contributes to this field. "From the viewpoint of *the present-day music theorist*," he suggests, Schenker's achievement "may be likened to a particular kind of high-level achievement in science" (7). Extant writings on rhythm, he claims, "have little significance to *the theorist* whose proper concern is with the structural role of what we ordinarily designate as 'rhythmic' " (24). His concluding paragraph states that "in many respects Schenker's work provides us with a model of what the work of *the music theorist* should be" (34). This last sentence lays some of Forte's cards on the table: the essay is not merely about some interesting ideas of an intriguing historical figure, Heinrich Schenker; rather, it is meant to articulate a particular model of a normative subjectivity, a way to be a musician. By following the model, you can discipline and transform your existing self to become a specimen of "the music theorist."

Of course, as I already suggested, Forte's own writing contributes to the model. While admiring and emulating the repetitiously named Schenker, a reader should also want to emulate the agent or self constructed in Forte's essay, the subject of its many first-person pronouns. Given the common conception of professional music theory as impersonal and science-like, you might not expect to see so much self-reference, so many first-person pronouns, but there they are. Surely this personal self-referring subject offers an exemplary instance of "the music theorist," the agent of music theory.

So who is this music theorist—who, in Forte's essay, says "I"?

The music theorist of Forte's essay is conspicuously a writer, concerned to dispose the words of the essay in the allotted time or space. Sometimes the presence of these words, these items that the writer disposes, becomes reflexively explicit. Introducing an account of Schenker's musical activities outside music theory, Forte writes that "I should like to devote a *few words* to a description of them" (7). In suggesting possible applications of Schenker's views, he writes that "I should like to devote *the following paragraphs* to a discussion of five unsolved problems in music theory" (23–24). From the words on the page, you construct a voice or a subjectivity, and then you find that this subjectivity is addressing you about the acts of arranging those very words.

More broadly, temporal references conjoined to the first person pronoun are common in this text, and they almost all refer to the "time" (or "space") within the essay, the ordering and pacing of the essay's materials. For instance: "*Before* describing the content of Schenker's work in greater detail, *I* should like to survey his achievement in general terms" (7). "*I shall first* make a quick survey of this analytic sketch *and then* give a more detailed explanation" (10). "Schenker invented a special vocabulary and devised a unique representational means. *I will* explain these *further on*" (7). "*I* shall attempt to answer this question *as concisely as possible*" (5). "*I* wish to emphasize *at this point* that . . ." (7). "*Further on I* shall provide a commentary . . ." (9). "*First,* however, *I* should like to *complete* this brief survey . . ." (9). "*I shall first* make a quick survey . . ." (10). "criteria which *I shall* explain *further on*" (10). "*As I have already mentioned,* he shows . . ." (15). "However, because of space limitations *I shall not* undertake a summary *here* . . ." (17). "*I* turn *now* to the development of Schenker's theory . . ." (18). Such marks of organizational control are common in academic writing, but their density in Forte's essay is impressive. They exhibit the writer, but almost as though the subjectivity of the writer exists only within the confines of the essay: as though the writer is a special creature existing purely to arrange and display the materials of this text.

There is a moment of pathos near the beginning of the essay, where, for once, the theorist of the essay imagines a time outside the span of the essay, and an encounter with a diverse world in which incomprehension is likely: "I hope that this review of [Schenker's] work, by providing accurate information to those who are unfamiliar with it, will serve to place future discussions on a somewhat more rational basis than they have been in the past. Yet, *even as I write these words,* I prepare myself to be misunderstood—such is the price of disputation long conducted in an atmosphere of general misunderstanding" (4). It's a delicate, sad passage, and strangely concrete: you see before your eyes the very words that this writer, in an uncharacteristically tremulous moment, braces himself to send to an uncertain fate. (Does this make you feel protective, as though you, for one, should try to appreciate these endangered words? Or perhaps it makes you a little anxious, as though you are about to have your intelligence tested?) This isolated moment, associating the future fate of the essay with the writer's vulnerability to misunderstanding, creates, by contrast, a sense that the continuous, enclosed temporality of most of the essay offers a kind of shelter.

MIRRORING

Indeed, within much of the essay, as you read the confident account of Schenker's thought and of the structure of a song ("Aus meinen Thränen spriessen," from the Schumann/Heine *Dichterliebe*), misunderstanding does not seem to be a live possibility. The sense of rapport among Forte,

Schenker, and the music results partly from an extraordinary feature of the essay, the same feature I pointed out in my opening comments: repeatedly, details of language create patterns in which the behavior of Schumann's music, as depicted by Schenker, and the behavior of Forte's essay mirror one another within the space of a sentence or two. The relationship seems undeniable, but bizarre—not just the broad relation of mimicry, but the placement of musical and textual mirror-images in such close proximity. Here are more examples:

(1) Forte expands a point: "In *amplification* of this, example 1.9 shows how the inner-voice component A is stated at the beginning of the song, prolonged by the lower adjacent 7 tone, G-sharp, in the middle section, then in m. 12 begins the descent to C-sharp." And in the next sentence, Forte continues: "In Schenker's terms, this linear progression is the *composing-out* of an interval" (28). The theorist amplifies a point, the piece composes out an interval.

(2) Commenting on Schenker's sketch, Forte writes that "the adjacent-tone D *recurs* in m. 14, where Schenker assigns more structural weight to it, as indicated by the stem. I *reiterate* that conventional durational values are used in the analytic sketches to indicate the relative position of a given component or configuration in the tonal hierarchy" (14). A tone in Schumann's piece recurs, and the theorist reiterates.

(3) Forte discusses the Schumann song's use of a particular secondary dominant. He indicates parenthetically that this point does not continue his explication of Schenker's analysis: "(To avoid misunderstanding, I point out that this discussion is not directly related to Schenker's sketch.)" After breaking continuity to offer this special explanation, he writes that "the A7 chord seems abrupt, has the effect of a *discontinuous* element, and therefore requires special explanation" (27).

(4) Writing about the notion of interruption, Forte comments that "the idea of the interrupted fundamental line provides the basis for Schenker's concept of form." After a few sentences of explanation, Forte continues: "Before explaining the middleground, I should like to direct attention again to the diminution which spans the third below C-sharp" (13). Like a composition, the theorist proceeds by interrupting his structure, delaying the continuation.

Indeed, such interruptions or delays, basic to Schenker's conception of musical time, occasion many of Forte's first-person pronouns: "*I shall return* to this often neglected facet of Schenker's work later" (7); "*further on I shall provide* a commentary upon an analytic sketch" (9); "*I shall explain* the black noteheads *shortly*"(12); "*I shall return* to this *further on* when I consider the general problem of constructing a theory of rhythm for tonal music" (15).

(5) Forte completes his account of the Schumann sketch by showing the form of the complete song: "One final aspect of the foreground sketch

deserves mention: the form" (17). Closure and completeness in song, sketch, and Forte's commentary align.

(6) At several points Schenker is also drawn into this pattern of matching. Forte identifies a passing chord, and writes: "it belongs only to the foreground and therefore is to be distinguished from the initial tonic chord, *a background element.* Two of Schenker's most important convictions *underlie* this treatment of detail" (15). Convictions underlie a particular analytical treatment, as background elements underlie a foreground chord.

(7) Writing of Schenker's motivic thought, Forte notes that "throughout his writings he demonstrates *again and again* that tonal compositions abound in hidden *repetitions* of this kind" (14). Schenker repeatedly identifies musical repetitions.

(8) A more complex transfer of qualities, brought about by a conjunction of temporal references involving Schenker, the composition, and the writer of Forte's essay, appears in the following sentences: "Here we have an example of the careful distinction which Schenker *always* draws between major bass components, or *Stufen,* which belong to the background level, and more *transient,* contrapuntal-melodic events at the foreground and middleground levels. A *brief* consideration of three additional events will complete our examination of the middleground level" (14). "Always," "transient," "brief": the distinction between endurance and transience appears in dazzling succession for Schenker's thought, musical structure, and Forte's exposition.

How strange that Forte's essay, beyond making assertions about musical structure, should also mimic procedures of Schenkerian musical structure. I doubt that Forte consciously formulated such a project, or that his readers have typically perceived the pattern consciously. Nonetheless it adds to the sense of authority in the essay: music theory seems to find something like a musical voice. Or perhaps the essay, and the theory it promotes, gives music the prosaic, reasonable, well-organized voice of an academic essay, placing music within comfortable reach of Forte's writing and concepts.[1]

CONTROL

Beyond the specific moments where Forte's language creates parallels between music and theoretical discourse, there is a more general resemblance between the theorist and the composition in the essay. At the beginning of the explication of Schenker's analysis of Schumann's song, Forte identifies the foreground, middleground, and background levels of the sketch, and meanwhile employs the terms "subordination" and "control." Indicating the middleground level, he states that "it should be evident now that the analytic procedure is one of reduction; details which are *subordinate* with respect to larger patterns are gradually eliminated." And he continues: "Finally, on the upper staff, [Schenker] has represented the fundamental structural level, or background, which *controls* the entire work" (10). These terms imply an anthropomorphic construal of the composition as organized by a kind of behavior: certain actions, acts of subordinating and controlling, give shape and order to the musical events.

This construal continues in details of his analysis, with particular emphasis on the notion of control: he refers to "the triadic third which *controls* the upper-voice motion of the entire song" (28); he identifies the "prolongational motion from 3 to 2" as "the *controlling* melodic pattern of the first phrase" (13); he explains that Schenker, "by slurring E to. . . . indicates that he considers that motion to be the *controlling* bass motion" (14). In one passage, "the lowest voice . . . is *subordinate* to the voice which lies immediately above it" (17). A slur connecting two tonic chords "indicates that the IV and V chords lie within the *control* of that chord" (16).

Forte's drama of control and subordination features one preeminent structure, "the background, which *controls* the entire work," along with subordinate structures which, in turn, exert more local forms of control. In Schenkerian reduction, "detail is gradually eliminated . . . so that the underlying, *controlling* structure is revealed" (18).

It would be accurate to summarize the theorist's activity in this essay, dramatized by the first-person pronouns, as the controlling of verbal material. As agents who control material, arranging it within a particular time or space, repeating, delaying, returning, interrupting, the theorist and the agency of the music are well suited to achieve understanding. Such a theorist can identify with such music. And you, too, could learn the discipline of writing about music in this controlled, mirror-like way.

The more specific, localized instances of mimicry that I pointed out earlier are moments when the broad similarity of theorist and musical agency creates little bubbles on the surface of the prose. Of course, the point of Forte's essay is not that others should imitate this particular play of first-person pronouns and momentary mirroring. But these features display a subject position that you can also occupy less explicitly. I suggest that a similar pattern of matching is present whenever someone writes in a controlled, rational, masterful way, and depicts music as the product of a controlled, rational, masterful agency. Perhaps the desire to write a lucid, coherent account of the lucid coherence of a composition typically derives from the hope of structuring one's writing as a meeting of like minds, from a kind of identification between theoretical and musical agency. In such writing, the music theorist and the music share the strengths and limitations of a rational, controlling mind, and it is no wonder they get along so well. The theorist and the music are made for each other. Tidy, isn't it?

But there is more: another, different resemblance between song and essay.

SUPPLICATION

Forte's essay describes the patterning of musical sound in time, and mirrors it with a patterning of words in the essay. Forte offers the essay to his readers, and permits himself an isolated moment of pathos near the beginning, when Forte steels himself for anticipated incomprehension. Now let's turn to Heinrich Heine's text for Schumann's song. You will not learn from Forte's essay that the famous poet has anything to do with this music—the word "Heine" is absent (the word "Schumann" barely appears).[2] Nonetheless Heine's text is apposite:

> From my tears spring up
> many blooming flowers,
> and my sighs become
> a chorus of nightingales.
>
> And if you love me, child,
> I give you all the flowers,
> and before your window shall sound
> the song of the nightingale.[3]

Heine writes of metaphorical transformations, just as Forte maintains a pattern of matching between musical and linguistic phenomena. The persona in the poem and the writer in the essay offer the products of their transformation to an audience, an addressee of these texts. And both are uncertain about the response of the audience. Here is a diagram to show the shared structure:

	Heine	*Forte*
Starting point	tears, sighs	Schenker's graph, Schumann's notes
	transformed into/symbolized by	
Result	flowers, birds	Forte's words
Addressee	beloved	readers (theorists)
Uncertainty	Will you love me?	Will you understand me?

Obviously this relationship between song and essay is different in its effect from the mirroring that I described before. I suggested that the mirroring creates matched images of music and theorist and, however subliminally, enhances the authority of the theorist. But Forte's structural rhyme with Heine's text occurs in an essay that omits any mention of the poem. It is as though, rather than showing the parallel, Forte prefers to substitute his own new text to go with the music of the song, concocting a loose translation of the original.

But after all, what advantage would Forte's stance derive from attention to the words of the song? As Forte depicts it (drawing upon Schenker), Schumann's song is a display of structural mastery, a disciplined deployment of repetition, delay, interruption, and so on, all subordinated to the background that controls everything. In contrast, Heine's character is mostly out of control, in the grip of strong emotions, the symptoms of which turn miraculously into beautiful natural objects, useful perhaps as gifts; and this lover is dependent, asking for reciprocity, hoping for the mutuality of shared love. The hope for love brings a need for response from the interlocutor, whereas Forte, in his essay, seems secure in his knowledge of Schenker: he doesn't need the readers, though he hopes to benefit them by sharing his knowledge.[4]

It is intriguing to find, a generation later, another Schenkerian analyst, Arthur Komar, directly expressing his disdain for Heine's protagonist: "The words [of *Dichterliebe*] actually impede my enjoyment of the whole cycle—to the extent that I heed them. The moping, distraught lover portrayed in German song cycles bores me, but this feeling in no way detracts from my enthusiasm for the music of the great song cycles of Beethoven, Schubert, and Schumann" (Komar 1971, 11, note 20). As this implies, Komar's extended essay analyzes the music of *Dichterliebe* while disregarding the words. Asking in what way the whole cycle is "an integrated musical whole" (63), he replies by identifying a "tonal plan" and "modal plan" established in the first five songs; taken together, these plans "essentially *control* the remaining course of the cycle" (78). Once that mopey lover is out of the picture, Komar can display the control that gives wholeness to the cycle and purpose to his own analytical writing. I suppose Forte's evasion of Heine's poem has a similar point.[5]

Heine's lover addresses the second half of the poem to the beloved, ending in suspense as the lover awaits a reply. Forte's essay uses the second person pronoun twice, with uniform rhetoric: Forte anticipates a question, which he promptly answers. "But, you ask, what about the books and articles . . ." (5). "You may ask how one accounts for a motion of this kind . . ." (22). Forte ventriloquizes the reader, creating a dependent interlocutor who elicits his own authoritative responses. Rather than "I need your love," we read that "I know what you need to know just now, and here it is." In these approaches—of Heine's lover to the beloved, of Forte to his readers—the trajectories of need and potential satisfaction are opposite. Heine's lover supplicates the beloved, who might return his love; the projected reader supplicates Forte, who offers satisfaction promptly.

The song text is about erotic desire and the transformation of feeling into symbols. Psychoanalysis specializes in such topics. It is interesting, given the omission of such a text, that Forte's essay mentions psychoanalysis prominently. While Forte does not say that music theory is a science, he seems to think it benefits from an increasingly scientific attitude, or an attitude influenced by science. To illustrate the point (which remains rather vague), he compares Schenkerian theory to psychoanalysis: they represent the same kind of achievement. How can Forte praise psychoanalysis, identifying it as an exemplary science and associating it with his own favored style of music theory, while showing no interest in the erotic concerns and symbolic substitutions of Heine's text?

But in fact, Forte's way of evoking psychoanalysis is precisely (if quietly) a refusal of psychoanalysis as a critical tool for understanding music. In likening psychoanalysis and Schenkerian theory, Forte indicates that psychoanalysis is "a particular kind of high-level achievement in science" (7), and that music theory is a parallel achievement for music. Psychoanalysis is a successful scientific approach to the human mind, and Schenkerian theory has a similar success with music. Built into the comparison is a distinction between the mind and music as separate objects of study, each with its own theory (even while the comparison implies, attractively if indeterminately, that studying a composition might resemble, somehow, the study of a person).

Forte uses a specific and limited conception of psychoanalysis, pertinent to the comparison he offers. "Freud opened the way for a deeper understanding of the human personality with his discovery that the diverse patterns of overt behavior are *controlled by certain underlying factors*" (7), and this is similar to Schenker's achievement. As you can see, Forte's analogy is precise, because Schenkerian theory, on Forte's account, also identifies the "underlying factors" that "control" other events. Like Schenker, Freud shows how to master the diversity of "overt" or "surface" phenomena by identifying the underlying, controlling factors. In a mind or a composition, certain factors are in control, and by recognizing and understanding those factors, the psychoanalyst or music theorist attains cognitive control.

What about psychoanalysis as therapy? as a style of conversation between therapist and patient, shaped by conscious and unconscious processes on both sides? as a tool for altering sensibility and experience? What about its depiction of the mind, not simply as an orderly configuration of control and subordination, but as a site of conflicting desires, many of them sexual, many of them unsatisfied? These are aspects of psychoanalysis that do not help Forte's analogy, issues that do not resonate with his conception of music theory, and they go unmentioned.[6]

The essay conjoins identification between Forte and the music with silence about the poetic text—and therefore, of course, silence about any relation between Forte and the poetic text. Someone influenced by psychoanalysis might wonder whether Forte's omission of the text is disavowal, that is, refusal of a recognition or identification that would be threatening in some way. But what would Forte disavow, and why?

IDENTIFICATION AND DOMINATION

The features I have noted in Forte's essay are not easy to interpret on the basis of that essay alone. It will be helpful, now, to turn to a more explicit account of the issues of control and identification that have emerged, inexplicit and untheorized, from Forte's writing. Edward T. Cone's book *The Composer's Voice* (1974) offers such an account. The use of Cone to interpret Forte might be surprising: many musicologists regard Cone's writing as an important alternative to technical theory like Forte's, articulating a contrasting perspective. *The Composer's Voice,* some of Cone's least technical work, is about the imaginary personae and agents with which composers, performers, and listeners populate musical compositions, and that emphasis might seem quite different from a technical Schenkerian concern with pitch hierarchy. Nonetheless, there are shared concerns between Cone's book and Forte's essay. Cone shares some basic assumptions with Forte, but develops the ideas in a different direction. The difference between the two writers will be useful in interpreting Forte: specifically, it will be useful to ask why Forte might wish to avoid certain ideas that appear in Cone's writing.

Cone's book insists at many points that the multiple personae or agents of a composition should be understood in terms of a single encompassing persona, and here he theorizes about issues that recall Forte's essay. According to Cone, a single persona (named in various ways, as "the complete musical persona," "the composer's persona," or "the composer's voice") controls everything in the composition: "It is to be posited as an intelligence *embracing and controlling* all the elements of musical thought that comprise a work" (1974, 109). The notion of a single controlling presence recalls, of course, Forte's account of the "background, which controls the entire work." Though a piece of instrumental music may create a sense of many interacting agents, embodied by the instrumental parts, Cone affirms that "in the last analysis all roles are aspects of one *controlling* persona, which in turn is the projection of one creative human consciousness—that of the composer" (114). Similarly, in vocal music "the composer's persona *governs* words as well as music" (18). The unity of opera, too, "forces us to look for a wider intelligence at work and hence to assume *the constant presence of a single musical persona.*" No real opera could be "free from this persona's *hegemony*" (14).

Unlike Forte, Cone sidesteps issues of technical analysis, and instead offers an account of listening, along with related accounts of composition and performance. Appropriate listening, according to Cone, seeks identification with the controlling persona. "The goal of participation [as a listener] must be *identification* with the complete musical persona *by making its utterance one's own*" (122). "To listen to music . . . is *to make the composer's voice our own*" (157). These formulations are not immediately clear: what do you do, while listening silently, to make the persona's utterance, or the composer's voice, your own? But, despite obscurity, to make the persona's utterance your own must be, somehow, to feel the persona's power and control as your own, and this idea has, one might feel, a general affinity with Forte's procedure of mirroring between the controlling musical forces and his own linguistic control.

Cone's account is complex. Alongside descriptions of identification, other passages emphasize the domination of listeners by music. I already indicated a flow of power within the music, depicted in both Cone's and Forte's accounts: some powerful force, the background or the persona, controls all the subordinate events of the composition. To this, Cone adds that the music exerts control over the listener.[7]

Elaborating the psychology of listeners' experiences, Cone cites the fact that many people have imaginary musical sound in their minds much of the time, involuntarily, and he defines composing and listening in relation to this musical stream of consciousness. "To compose is to *control* this inner voice, to shape it into new forms, to make it speak for us. To listen to music is to *yield* our inner voice to the composer's *domination*" (157). You might have an ongoing stream of musical thoughts, in which case you can simply let it continue. As a composer, you might take your existing stream of musical thoughts and exert conscious control over it: composers make a distinctive use of control in their own mental lives. As a listener, you can yield the stream to the influence of something outside, letting the composer's control (or, as Cone might put it at his most precise, the persona's control) extend to your own mental life.[8]

I want to reflect a bit on this interesting idea of an inner musical voice, offering a more differentiated description than Cone provides. The inner activity can vary widely, ranging from aimless sonic doodling, to full-fledged inner performance of familiar music, to vivid inner improvisation; it can fluctuate from periphery to focus of one's awareness; it can be uncontrolled and spontaneous, or one can shape it in various respects. And, beyond Cone's alternatives of the composer's and listener's roles, the inner stream can flow out into performance, solo improvisation, or musical interaction, and can also emerge in such half-externalized forms as humming, rhythmic fidgeting, finger-tapping, and so on. For me and, I assume, for many people, this ongoing musical stream, and the various fluctuations in its character, are important aspects of what it is to be conscious! Cone's descriptions of the composer, who forcefully directs this inner stream with the goal of producing a score, and the listener, who completely relinquishes control and allows someone else's music to take over, are extremes in a complex range of possibilities. Perhaps Cone's selective account reveals that, despite the calm, affable surface of his writing, he is drawn in some way to these extremes of control and domination. Or, at least, he has not developed the account beyond what he needs to give his description of the classical concert setting.

Cone's conception, in which we experience music by encountering powerful forces that control everything in the piece, and that also control our own inner musical voice, has a complex relationship to his other idea about identification. The listener is dominated by, and also identifies with, the persona, seeming to maintain relations of subordination and identification simultaneously. Listeners are, on Cone's account, at once subjected to control that comes from outside, and empowered by taking on that control as though it were their own. Here is Cone's way of putting it, in sentences that conclude the main argument of the book: "To listen to music is *to yield* our inner voice to the composer's *domination*. Or better: it is *to make* the composer's voice *our own*" (157). These sentences conjoin the two aspects of domination and identification, without clarifying their relationship.[9]

This account of listening reminds me of a useful general concept formulated by the psychoanalyst Christopher Bollas. Bollas (1987) writes of a phenomenon that he calls "extractive introjection": sometimes two people interact so that some mental content or process, originally belonging to one person, seems to be taken away from that person, subsequently belonging only to the other one. Bollas illustrates the concept through a series of anecdotes. For instance, he describes a four-year-old, B, at play, "engaged in a private drama that is nonetheless realized through actual objects. The space is entered by A, who creates such distraction that B loses his playfulness." A might be a parent, who "appropriates the playing by telling the child what the play is about and then prematurely engages in playfulness." With repetition of such interruptions, the child's "sense of spontaneity would diminish" and B "will come to experience an extraction of that element of himself: his capacity to play" (1987, 159). Something that was in the child, an ongoing activity, is now gone, replaced by something outside; the playfulness has been extracted from the child and introjected into the adult. Bollas describes a number of similar interactions, many of them between adults. He goes on to suggest that "a child who is the victim of consistent extractive introjection may choose to identify with the aggressive parent and install in his personality this identification, which then functions as a false self" (164). That is, the response to a theft of part of oneself might be, not exactly a recovery of what was taken, but an imagined identification with the other person and the act of theft.

Similarly, in Cone's account of listening, many people usually have music passing through their minds; but when you listen attentively, you experience a displacement or extraction of the source of musical thought, from your own stream of inner music to the activities of external sound sources. In performance settings that strictly limit sonic participation, such as modern classical concerts, the musical source is entirely outside the listener. However, as Cone describes it, this "extraction" leads immediately to an act of identification, in which the listener somehow identifies herself with the external source of musical activity.

The vocabulary of "theft" and "aggression" may seem melodramatic for ordinary musical listening. Reading Bollas's story about the four-year-old, it is easy to regard the child's play as valuable, and the adult's "extraction" as intrusive. But we are not used to thinking much about the ongoing inner musical lives of most people, and may not have much sense of how to value them: Cone's treatment is helpful in drawing attention to this pervasive music activity. Disruption of a listener's inner voice may or may not strike you as intrusive. Perhaps the slight sense of strain in moving from Bollas's concept to the musical case reflects a useful stretching of concepts. Maybe the process of "extraction" that Bollas describes is not as determinate in its value as his uniformly negative examples suggest; maybe, on the other hand, an alignment of his examples with Cone's account of listening hints at unnerving evaluative possibilities for routine aspects of contemporary musical life.

At any rate, we have reached a tantalizing congruence and gap between Cone's and Forte's writings. The two men agree that a single controlling force governs each composition, and that recognition of this force is central to musical understanding. And both texts suggest some kind of emulation as a proper way of relating to that force. But Cone's account of listening gives a central role to musical domination of the listener, for which there is no clear counterpart in Forte's essay. And, while an element of emulation is present in both writers, the specific forms of mimicry—identification while listening, mirror-like control of a written text—are different.

LISTENING, SCORE-READING, AND "FANTASY RECOMPOSITION"

At this point, a certain speculation becomes attractive. Perhaps Cone gives a prominent role to domination because he writes about the experience of listening, which has obvious aspects of receptivity or passivity in relation to musical sound. And perhaps Forte, in contrast, can sidestep issues about listening, because he writes about professional analysis.

But can Forte really sidestep issues about listening? Listening is relevant to analysis, isn't it?

Actually, the typical practices of analysis can raise questions about the role of listening. As students of musical analysis know well, academic courses in analysis usually proceed with every participant looking at a musical score; discussions that derive exclusively from listening, without ongoing reference to scores, are rare, and often the listening takes place outside the classroom altogether, as private class preparation. Similarly, the activity of making an analysis normally involves continuous consultation of a score; much academic analysis is created in a silent room, by an analyst who stares thoughtfully at pages of musical notation.

I've sometimes encountered a rather simple objection to the primacy of scores in theory and analysis, on the grounds that they distract from, or replace, musical sound—as though analysts are, in some way, thinking about scores *rather than* musical sound. Such a blunt criticism seems ill founded or, at best, undeveloped. The idea that score-readers replace sound with sight is too simple. Experienced score-readers do not just look at visual symbols; we use them as a starting point for remembering or imagining sound. *The Composer's Voice* gives a more helpful point of departure for thinking about score-reading, by considering scores in light of power relations and subject positions.

A score contains the composer's instructions. Therefore, Cone suggests that it can serve as a symbol of the all-powerful persona, and this can give value to its visible presence in live performance settings. "The physical presence of the score (or of its parts) is a constant reminder—for both performers and audience—of the *control* of the complete musical persona" (64). And Cone describes score-reading in terms of identification: "Score-reading . . . permits a musician (the reader) to *identify himself fully and intimately* with the complete persona, and . . . gives him *total control* over the direction of the persona's musical activity" (136). Score-reading, it seems, is the best way to feel like the persona. It even, somehow, gives you control over the persona's activity! How can this be?

As Cone explains, score-reading is "a kind of abstract performance" (136); a performer has the task of bringing musical events into being, and a score-reader does this too, at least in imagination. Performance and score-reading occupy complex positions, neither fully creative nor fully receptive. The performer or score-reader must respect the composer's instructions but, by so doing, can assume responsibility for the creation of musical events, in actual or imagined sound.

In fact, the score opens a wider range of subject-positions for a score-reader than Cone indicates. (Again, as in his account of "our inner voice," Cone seems drawn to a somewhat simplified account.) You can use the score to imagine hearing a performance, in a kind of imaginative listening. Or you can imagine yourself following the composer's notated instructions in a performance, taking the role of an imaginary performer. Or you can imagine choosing the symbols that constitute the score, as though making the decisions that compose the music. Or, less literally, you might imagine creating all the musical gestures of the piece from your own musical initiative, like a composer, but in the ordering and time of a performance; this is probably closest to Cone's conception of identifying with the persona. And of course your imagination might do things that remain a little vague about these distinctions. The most powerful positions, identifying with the composer or his imaginary reconfiguration as the persona, are readily available to a score-reader, probably more available than to a listener. But also, even if you imagine yourself in the least powerful role, as a listener, your own imagination has to conjure up the musical sounds that you imagine yourself hearing. Imagining oneself listening is different, in that way, from just listening. In general, it seems that an emphasis on score-reading is likely to diminish the subordination that listening may bring. So, to the extent that analysis is based on score-reading rather than listening, it may be able to evade issues about the dependency or receptiveness of listening.

But, whatever you think about the general tendencies of analytical practice, it would be too simple to say that Forte's essay emphasizes score-reading and ignores listening. The truth is stranger and more complex: Forte places very strong emphasis on listening experience, but does so at just five scattered points, with no perceptible effect on the rest of the essay. There is a pattern: each reference to listening occurs within a single sentence, after which he drops the topic immediately.

Forte cites Schenker's belief that a performer could play well only "if he had developed *an aural sensitivity* to the hierarchy of tonal values which [the score] expressed" (8). Forte also mentions Furtwängler's emphasis on Schenker's discovery of "*Fernhören* (literally, 'distance-hearing')" (19), and he explains Brahms's curiosity about parallel fifths and octaves by the "contradiction" between pre-Schenkerian theory and Brahms's "own highly-refined sense of hearing, which encompassed large spans" (30). Apart from their paradoxical combination of emphasis, brevity, and lack of consequences, these remarks about listening share other traits. They are all about someone else's hearing, not Forte's. And they concern the listening experiences of good performers, or of those imposing authorities Furtwängler and Brahms, not the experiences of mere listeners as such.

Forte's most important reference to listening comes in a general discussion of methodology. He asserts that Schenker's theory derives from "the organization of the music itself," and explains: "Schenker consistently *derived* his theoretical formulations from *aural experiences* with actual musical compositions, and *verified* them at the same source" (7). Evidently, for Forte, the appropriateness of Schenker's theoretical work depends on the foundational role of those listening experiences. Schenker's valuable contributions rest on his listening. Can we discuss and ponder his listening experiences? No: they are not otherwise acknowledged in Forte's essay, and consequently they occupy a curious position as something crucial that, nonetheless, one barely mentions. In the essay, Schenker's experiences as a listener are both the source of his musical wisdom and, it seems, something private. Schenker's secret life.

In one more passage, Forte suggests that Schenker teaches a particular kind of hearing. Someone who encounters Schenker's thought must learn many new things—"a new terminology, a new set of visual symbols, and, *most important, a new way of hearing music*" (6). As you might expect from the other examples, this assertion of the importance of listening is laconic, tight-lipped.

The whole essay reveals nothing about Forte's personal listening experiences, except insofar as he is included within the generalization that Schenker teaches a "way of hearing." For all the proliferation of first-person pronouns, and the terse assertions of the centrality of listening, the essay never depicts Forte as a listener.

How does Forte propose to teach Schenkerian thought, if not through a direct exploration of listening experiences? He approaches Schenker through an activity that closely resembles shared score-reading: the reading of an analytical sketch. Not only does the contemplation of analytical sketches resemble score-reading, it also includes, almost always, a reading of the actual score along with the sketches; studying the sketches shapes a particular relation to that score.

Following the typical practice of Schenker's analytical essays, Forte begins with the background level and moves to the foreground. That is, he begins by allowing his readers to understand the "underlying, controlling structure." In the process of moving from the background toward the foreground, you move from something generalized toward the familiar "surface" of the actual piece.[10]

Such analyses do not claim to reproduce the sequence of thoughts of the actual composer, but the analogy with composition is hard to miss. Forte's essay brings out the analogy obliquely: he writes that "reduction is approximately the reverse of variation . . . Reduction accomplishes the reverse; detail is gradually eliminated" (18). If reduction, which yields the set of sketches, is like the reverse of variation, then the musical process one follows in reading the sketches from background to foreground must resemble variation.

William Benjamin, two decades later, makes a related point about the process of writing Schenkerian graphic analyses.[11] He emphasizes "the demand [Schenkerian analysis] places on its users of *total creative involvement* with pieces of music" (Benjamin 1981, 159). To create a middleground graph, according to Benjamin, is to compose a piece: he offers this claim as literal truth. The middleground is at once a commentary on an existing composition and, itself, a new composition, a "work of art or, more specifically, . . . anti-variation" (160).[12]

My point is different from Benjamin's but they can work together to confirm a general "compositional" quality in Schenkerian analysis. Benjamin distinguishes between the familiar interpretive or explanatory aspect of analysis and the less-remarked creative aspect, the analyst's artistic composition of middlegrounds. To this, I add that the interpretive aspect also has a compositional quality, though now in an imaginative rather than literal sense: the process of reading a series of graphs feels like composing, as one shares the step-by-step work process of an imaginary composer. The score, which by itself does not determine a reader's subject-position as imaginary creator, performer, or listener, now becomes a prop in a game of make-believe: you imagine, of the score, that it is the goal and result of the quasi-compositional thought-process that you follow.[13] Joseph Dubiel summarizes this elegantly in referring to Schenker's "fantasy recompositions of the 'masterworks'" (Dubiel 1990, 327).[14]

The idea that you can understand music by taking on the perspective of a fictionalized creator brings Schenkerian thought, and Forte's essay, especially close to the ideas of *The Composer's Voice*—close enough that one can refer to the "persona" of a Schenkerian analysis, the imaginary intelligence who creates the music through a kind of variation technique. A Schenker essay, then, might be understood as a novella that narrates the activity of this persona.[15]

Nonetheless, for Cone the persona and identification with it are important aspects of *listening experience,* while in Forte's essay, and Schenkerian practice generally, the analytical understanding that brings you close to the persona is, in a certain way, *incompatible with listening.* Schenker's "fantasy recompositions" present two kinds of musical time, the familiar exoteric time of the music in performance, moving from beginning to end, and the esoteric time of the music as it develops from the background structure by variation, gradually becoming more complex. When you identify most closely with the Schenkerian persona, following its thoughtful decisions step by step, you must occupy the esoteric time of imaginary composition, and this necessarily takes you out of a listener's swifter, less meditative temporality. The two kinds of time dramatize the distinction between a listener's perspective and that of the creative persona. The two perspectives eclipse each other.[16]

A broad pattern begins to emerge. Forte's essay identifies with the persona: it both mimics the creative activity of a musical persona through its depiction of an active, controlling author and also, more directly, encourages the theorist and reader to share an imagined process through which a persona creates a song. On the other hand, his essay avoids any detailed account of listening, despite a few assertions that give listening a kind of abstract importance, and I want to link this to Forte's decision to analyze a song and neglect the text of the song, with its supplicating lover who awaits a response. Perhaps musical listening and Heine's erotic need share qualities of sensuality and dependence.

It seems ever more plausible that the essay's emphasis on control and creative activity is a way of disavowing dependence, receptivity, sensuality, or passivity—disavowing what Cone calls the "domination" of listeners by music. If Forte's essay downplays certain aspects of musical experience, you can't expect it to give a helpful account of those experiential possibilities. For further insight into the dynamic of identification and domination, I'll return once more to Cone's book.

SEDUCTION

In using Cone's writing to interpret Forte's, I have treated Cone as, in certain ways, the more explicit of the two writers. I have looked to his text for relatively direct statements of ideas that can then be read back into Forte's essay. In particular, while Forte does not do much to describe listeners, I have suggested that Cone's account provides an account of listening that works well with Forte's account of control and subordination.

Now, though, I want to change tactics and start teasing out some less explicit aspects of Cone's position. In particular, I want to identify an implicit eroticization of musical experience in *The Composer's Voice.* Just as I have used Cone's views to fill in gaps in Forte's account, now I want to interpret Cone's 1974 book by drawing on a more recent musicological tradition, from about 1990 on, that directly explores relations between musical experience and sexuality.[17] In *The Composer's Voice,* an eroticization of musical experience sometimes comes close to the surface, but Cone's habitual discretion normally keeps sexual issues in the realm of implication and connotation.

Recently, Philip Brett has drawn attention to passages in *The Composer's Voice* about four-hand piano performance, passages that evoke, not quite directly, the eroticism (and, in male–male performance, homoeroticism) of that ensemble. Brett (1997, 154) observes how close Cone's writing comes to raciness, and asserts that "This is surely as close as musicology of a perfectly respectable kind can come to exploring the (deviant) sexuality surrounding music without advertising what it is doing." A few years after *The Composer's Voice,* Cone published "Schubert's Promissory Note" (1982), his most direct treatment of music and sexuality, linking certain passages in Schubert to sensuous pleasures and their horrifying consequence of syphilis. That essay confirms my sense that Cone himself sometimes experiences music as sensual or seductive, and also shows that he is likely to be circumspect in his descriptions.[18]

Closer to the main concerns of this paper, an intriguing passage implies an eroticized power relation between personas and their listeners. In order to clarify his account of identification, Cone contrasts a listener's relation to music with a reader's or listener's relation to language. The contrast concerns the separation between the musical or linguistic "voice" and its audience: according to Cone, it is far easier for an addressee to maintain a sense of independence in perceiving linguistic communication. Music has an invasive aspect, a way of dissolving a listener's control, that distinguishes it from language. After emphasizing this "extraordinary power that music seems to exert over our inner life," and stating that "music can speak *to* us only as it speaks *through* us," Cone offers a model, stating that Zerlina, in the duet "Là ci darem la mano" from Mozart's *Don Giovanni,* "admirably symbolizes the situation" (155). Who is Zerlina, and how might she symbolize you, or me, as a music-listener?

In "Là ci darem la mano" Don Giovanni approaches the peasant girl Zerlina, drawing her away from her impending wedding to suggest that he, rather than her fiancé, the peasant Masetto, will marry her. The duet shows his seduction of her—his wooing, her initial resistance, and her eventual assent just before the two start off for Don Giovanni's house. Though the opera is all about Don Giovanni's successes and failures in seduction and rape, this is the only seduction depicted onstage.[19] The subject matter of the duet—Don Giovanni's destructive, manipulative use of his prestige and charm—is unpleasant, but the duet is widely known and loved, a favorite bit of the opera.

Cone mentions this familiar duet in order to make a specific, delimited point. He brings out a subtle contradiction between textual and musical patterning at the beginning of the duet. Don Giovanni addresses Zerlina invitingly. Zerlina replies by describing her indecisiveness, but while her words seem to resist his invitation, she sings them to the melody of Don Giovanni's invitation. According to Cone, "her melody, her subconscious reaction, reflects his. Already, long before she gives in verbally, she has identified herself with his music" (155). Zerlina's words can keep their distance from the content of Don Giovanni's words. She does not reply by saying back to him what he just said to her (it would be odd if she did!), but that is exactly what happens musically. Cone goes further, interpreting her use of his music as a sign that a part of her, which Cone identifies as her "subconscious," is already beginning to give in to the attempted seduction.[20] It is clever of Cone to cite this example where the musical repetition and the verbal non-repetition seem equally natural, and where the onstage interaction can model a relation between musical persona and audience.

But, while Cone cites this duet to illustrate that music creates identification more irresistibly than words, the example overflows the boundaries of his explicit purpose, in a manner typical of indirect, connotative communication. For one thing, it complicates the politics of identification. In identifying with Don Giovanni by repeating his music, Zerlina models her behavior on his, but the sense of equality or participation that she gains from this mimicry is delusive. By the end of the duet, she feels that she is choosing Don Giovanni, electing to share his prestige and power, but in fact the sensation of choice is part of his snare. Her identification with Don Giovanni's purposes is the mechanism through which Don Giovanni achieves domination. How much of this could one carry into Cone's account of musical identification? Does musical identification, rather than countering the persona's domination of the listener, instead somehow deepen and disguise that domination? "Là ci darem la mano" has sinister implications as a model of musical identification.

The example also raises issues about gender. Cone's analogy offers a banal, predictable alignment between gender and the persona/listener opposition: the active, powerful persona resembles the masculine Don Giovanni, the more passive listener the feminine Zerlina. Cone's use of the duet brings closer to the surface the potential association between listening and femininity.

Cone's analogy also draws in the notion of seduction. If listeners resemble Zerlina, does that mean that music acts as a lover to its listeners, seducing them in some way? In fact, the choice of example makes it hard to avoid thoughts of musical seduction, for this duet that depicts seduction is itself quite beautiful, an especially seductive composition. You don't need to take my word for it; analogies between Don Giovanni's seduction of Zerlina and Mozart's seduction of the listener recur in commentaries on the duet. Critics often notice that the duet delights its listeners into a suspension of their better judgment, just as Don Giovanni's flattery delights, confuses, and persuades Zerlina.

For instance, Nino Pirrotta (1994, 127) emphasizes the music's capacity to persuade listeners of the reality of the seduction: "Up to this point the recitative dialogue has been convincing in its declamation but not in the seduction, even if we grant that Zerlina needs little convincing; the magic of the duettino that follows convinces us." Like Zerlina, we succumb to a magic that produces the effect of conviction. Wye Jamison Allanbrook (1983, 262) emphasizes that listeners enjoy the depicted seduction, rather than judging it sternly: "'Là ci darem la mano' is the sweetest imaginable of love duets . . . all irony and cynicism must be suspended in the fact of the sheer beauty of this dialogue of seduction and acquiescence." Allanbrook's account brings a listener's cognitive condition especially close to Zerlina's: intellectual resistance, one's conscious evaluation of the situation, is undone by the pull of sensuous attraction. Paul Henry Lang (1971, 87), again, spreads the seductive qualities from Don Giovanni to Mozart: he asks, "Was there ever set to music a more delightful, a more tender, a more ravishing and enticing acquiescence to a tryst than 'Là ci darem la mano'?" Zerlina's acquiescence, as Mozart shows it, ravishes and entices the audience. Otto Jahn's version of the same idea is more graphic (1882, 3:187): "[Don Giovanni's] seductive powers are first practised towards Zerlina . . . that which can neither be analysed nor reproduced is the effect of the tender intensity of the simple notes, which penetrate the soul like the glance of a loving eye." Mozart's notes penetrate you, as though someone were gazing at you in just the right way. The vocabulary of these passages—magic, sweetest, sheer beauty, delightful, ravishing, enticing, tender intensity—shows clearly the non-rational allure that, for these critics, undoes any more distanced or reflective judgment.

So Cone is not the only critic to sense, in the relation between Don Giovanni and Zerlina, a model for the relation between the music (or some creative force, a persona or composer) and its listener. But these other writers make the analogy specifically in terms of seduction. Cone's discussion of "Là ci darem la mano" is characteristically reticent about sex and sensuality, but I think his choice of this outstandingly seductive example as the basis for a general model almost inevitably evokes questions of whether musical power is seductive, whether personas seduce their listeners.

If Cone does not comment on the seductive qualities of Mozart's music, I think he *deploys* its gorgeousness instead: surely the duet appears at the conclusion of Cone's argument partly because of its beauty. Incorporating the duet into his presentation, Cone can count on it to add a special glow to the relation between him and his audience. Part of Cone's charm is his deft, timely use of such charming music. Perhaps he would weaken his own seductiveness if he became too analytical about the issue of musical seduction. But if Cone is reticent about any sexual quality in the persona's approach to the listener, his choice of example speaks sweetly enough, giving his account of music a delicately sexy tinge.

BATTI, BATTI

Nonetheless, if "Là ci darem la mano" implicitly eroticizes the relationship between persona and listener, the notion of seduction still does not offer the most precise account of the erotic qualities of that relationship. In "Là ci darem la mano," Don Giovanni talks Zerlina into going away to have sex; subsequently, were they not interrupted, they would move along to his house and do the act. But Cone's analogy likens Don Giovanni's and Zerlina's preparatory conversation to the act of listening, which is itself, for a listener, a consummation, not a negotiation about some future event. Listening, then, would resemble both seduction and sex act, the two occurring simultaneously. But a more exact sexual analogy is possible, one that matches many aspects of Cone's account of listening.

To see this other analogy, let's begin by remembering embodiment: in sexual activities, bodies interact, and so one might ask how the bodies of listeners affect these analogies. As it happens, Cone's book—which really is remarkably comprehensive—addresses the embodiment of listeners. In suggesting that a listener "mentally performs the work he is hearing," Cone specifies that a literal performer shapes the course of musical events, while "the listener has no such opportunity: he must *submit* to the direction of others." This submission includes a suppression of bodily movements. Some listeners might "hum, or beat time, or make other physical gestures," but "most sophisticated music lovers . . . frankly recognize the limitations of their roles and *sublimate their desires for physical activity*" (136–37). A simpler account of listening might deny the relevance of embodiment; Cone's account, on the contrary, identifies a particular bodily experience—an inhibited or "sublimated" desire for movement, linked to submission—as a constituent of sophisticated musical love. As one might expect, Cone complicates this sub-

mission by adding an aspect of identification: "At the same time, an *imaginary physical involvement* underlies the listener's successful *identification* with
the musical persona. For this reason, the visual stimulation of watching a performance is important" (137).

Now what is going on in a musical performance, according to Cone? *Literally,* the performers are moving to make sounds, in part through their own
choices, in part under the direction of the composer's score; various listeners sit in a group, silent and immobile, and pay attention, receiving and
responding to the sounds that performers direct at them. *Imaginatively*—that
is, in the imagination of Cone's normative listener—there is an intense interaction between a persona and a listener, both understood as individuals. The
persona, embodied in the notated music and the actions of the performers,
dominates the musical sounds and the listeners. Holding still, and knowing
that she is not permitted to make any sounds, the listener submits to the persona's will, accepting the distinction between the roles of active, willful persona and passive, receptive listener. At the same time, while the listener is
inhibited and dominated by the persona, she also identifies with the persona's power and activity.

A listener's imaginative experience, then, has a strange multiple consciousness, conjoining an awareness of submission (the persona's power over
her) with a thrill of identification with power (even though that power takes
effect, in part, by domination of herself). To this doubled experience is
added, I suppose, a third aspect, a listener's awareness that the whole configuration is, to some extent, fictional and consensual, a chosen style of imaginative submission rather than a literal subjection to force. And the whole
complex configuration seems to be itself an object of desire. *The Composer's
Voice* describes, as normative, a type of listener who seeks out such experiences. She approaches each new musical encounter with the desire to find,
submit to, and identify with an all-powerful persona who will "embrace and
control" the musical material and the listener herself.

This is starting to sound kinky. It is easy to nudge Cone's account toward
the range of sexual activities known as sadomasochism, or bondage and discipline, those activities where partners agree that one partner will relinquish
overt control and activity to the other. Indeed, Cone's text provides us with
the words "bound," "domination," "submit," "power," and of course "control."

Sadists and masochists eroticize physical pain, and I am not suggesting
that musical experience shares in that. But classical concerts render listeners still and silent, as though bound and gagged. There may also be elements
of humiliation in accepting the restricted role of listener; as Henry Kingsbury (1988, 76–80) points out, becoming a listener instead of a performer
or composer often results from a series of failed or discouraged attempts at
musical production. More generally, sadomasochists, and the music-lovers

that Cone describes, find intense pleasure in experiences structured by an extreme dichotomy between active and passive roles. The classical concert, like the S&M session, depends on different people assuming, for the moment, clearly-defined roles as "tops" and "bottoms."[21] To fill out this account, one could say that musical performers and listeners enjoy and perhaps eroticize the "extractive introjection" that I described before: rather than physical pain, the listener feels, and enjoys, the depletion of her own inner musical initiative, the exclusive assignment of music-making to the persona's activity, and the concurrent identification with a power that originates outside herself.

Now I want to quote a pertinent, experience-based account of masochistic identification. In Dossie Easton's and Catherine A. Liszt's *The Bottoming Book,* a well-received self-help manual, the authors indicate that S&M might be understood as an exercise of "power-over," of one person exerting power at the expense of another. But, they emphasize, it is better to understand the interaction in terms of "power-with." "Power-with is based on the idea that we can all become more powerful by supporting each other in being more powerful" (Easton and Liszt 1995, 19). Or, less obscurely:

> when we [acting as bottoms] give up our power, we feel more powerful. When we give up control, we feel freer (27). When we bottom we feel fabulously powerful . . . When I'm being flogged, . . . I struggle and wonder if I can take it all. That struggle seems to make me stronger, and soon I feel intense energy running through me, as if all the force with which the whip is thrown at me is injected into me, becomes my energy to play with. While my tops throw the whips at me as hard as they can, I take in their power and dance in the center of their storm (17).

These violent images are, of course, outside the range of *The Composer's Voice;* it is remarkable that they replicate Cone's psychology of listening so closely. As Cone might have put it, to listen to music is to grant the persona "power-over" our inner voice; or better, it is to make the persona's power into the "power-with" that we share.

In relation to my present argument, the match between Cone's account of listening and this account of masochistic subjectivity suggests, at the least, that Cone has developed his views in a plausible, non-arbitrary way. Starting with an extreme contrast between the power of the persona and the submission of the listener, Cone attributes to listeners the same mingling of subordination and identification that some S&M bottoms report in their own, similarly-structured experiences, and in a way this confirms Cone's account.[22]

I have argued that Forte and Cone share a starting point in treating each composition as the product of a powerful controlling force, and I observed that Forte's text has little to say about listening, despite proclaiming its importance. If you want to add an account of listening to the shared conception of musical compositions, *The Composer's Voice* offers such an account. Cone describes sharply contrasting roles. The powerful agency of the compositional persona finds its complement in the submission of the listener; simultaneous identification with the persona complicates that submission. Given the shared starting point, Cone's book shows where Forte might end up if he gave direct, sustained attention to the listener's role. In particular, Cone's account describes a passivity, perhaps masochism, in listening, bringing out traits that are commonly devalued and associated with femininity. They are traits that some writers would surely wish to deny or disavow.

FORT/DA

In a well-known formulation, Anna Freud describes a common "defensive mechanism": someone who experiences aggression from outside may respond by imitating the aggressive behavior. For instance, she tells the story of a little boy who had been hurt by the dentist. He came to Freud's home and tried to cut various items—a piece of rubber, a ball of string, some pencils (Anna Freud 1966, 111–12). As Anna Freud puts it, "by impersonating the aggressor, assuming his attributes or imitating his aggression, the child transforms himself from the person threatened into the person making the threat" (113). One active/passive pairing gives way to another; in the first, the subject is passive and then, repudiating the passive role, the same subject becomes active instead. This account resembles Sigmund Freud's description of the game of "fort" and "da" that a small boy played. As Sigmund Freud interprets it, the child responded to his inability to control the disappearance of his mother by inventing a game in which he threw away his toys, saying "fort" ("gone"); with one toy on a string, he was able afterward to pull it back and say "da" ("there"). He was "staging the disappearance and return of the objects within his reach . . . At the outset he was in a passive situation—he was overpowered by the experience; but, by repeating it . . . as a game, he took on an active role" (Sigmund Freud 1961, 8–11). More broadly, Freud identifies the active/passive antithesis as one of three basic "polarities" of mental life. The goal of avoiding passivity is central to masculinity, which routinely seeks the active role in active/passive complementary relationships (Sigmund Freud 1963, 97).

These narratives, in which mastery comes through reversal of active and passive roles, give a helpful model for understanding Forte's essay. Forte's conception of a masterful, controlling force at the heart of each composition tends to imply a subordinate, submissive role for listeners. The event of listening seems to bring together an active, controlling, perhaps aggressive composition and a submissive, receptive listener. Cone writes about listeners

FRED EVERETT MAUS

who accept this submission as part of their listening experience, while adding an identification with the active position. But a listener who is unwilling to accept or acknowledge such passivity might react defensively: he might want, through reversal, to escape or deny the passive role, occupying instead a purely active role in a new pairing. Becoming a theorist or analyst could accomplish that reversal. Listening experiences, with their passive qualities, would be the starting point and motivation for a narrative of reversal that ultimately places the theorist in active roles, as both the fantasy composer in an act of imagined re-composition and the writer who displays control over verbal material.

Listening, in such a conception, is the excessively passive and, therefore, disturbing or problematic moment in a normative progression from a composition to its analysis. If the motivation for analysis is to replace passivity with a display of activity, then analysis would owe its existence to the very experiences that it tries to disguise or displace. It seems that Forte's essay teaches its reader how to be a bottom in the sheets, a top on the streets.

Beyond reformulating some of Forte's and Cone's ideas, as I have done, tasks of interpretation and evaluation are important but tricky.

It is natural to wonder what alternatives can be found to Forte's and Cone's shared preoccupation with control—that is, discursive alternatives, other accounts of classical music, listening, or the concert setting.[23] When I first started thinking about alternatives, I remembered my own use of *The Composer's Voice,* in the article "Music as Drama" and elsewhere (Maus 1988, 1991). I drew upon Cone's ideas about agency and anthropomorphism, but replaced the single imaginary persona with a play of indeterminate agents. This makes it harder to tell a story about the all-powerful persona and the submissive listener. Still, I am not sure that this difference somehow increases the power or independence of listeners; unlike Cone, I didn't develop my views to include listeners in the dramatic interactions I described.

I also thought of Suzanne Cusick, who writes of "the choice I cherish, which is to attend or not, to let the music 'do it' to me (which the musics I love can only do if I have paid the most careful, intense, co-creative attention) . . . or not" (Cusick 1994, 76). On one hand, Cusick seems to value an element of choice, a possibility of refusal, in a way that goes beyond a simple notion of submission. On the other hand, it seems that the basic relationship is still one of musical power over the listener; if Cusick values a particular sense that power is continuously offered and accepted, rather than deployed in an overwhelming way, she still seems to position the listener as either submitting or opting out.

In general, what would constitute a convincing alternative to the active/passive complementarities that I have been describing? Here is one line of thought. Psychoanalyst Jessica Benjamin (1988) argues that participants in S&M adopt fixed roles as a way of avoiding the continuous negotiations, tensions, and uncertainties of intersubjectivity between equals.[24] It is not easy for two people to recognize each other as distinct and equal; it is easier, and in a way more relaxing, to place one person in the position of power and agency. How could one draw on Benjamin's ideas about interaction, uncertainty, and tension in relation to experiences of classical music?

Her ideas apply nicely to musical performance: that is, you can think of performers and composers as, at best, entering into a tense, complex relation of shared agency and responsibility in the production of music, and you can think of more authority-based or work-based concepts of performance as attempts to evade the complexities of joint creativity. But it is harder to apply this positive model of shared creation to the relation between performed music and a concert audience.[25] Perhaps Forte's and Cone's preoccupation with power, even if simple and exaggerated, derives from important aspects of classical music culture.

It may be appropriate to accept and develop an account that likens a certain normative type of musical listening to masochistic submission. An extended consideration could draw on a rich literature about sado-masochism, with some very distinguished recent contributions.[26] Recent discussions suggest that one should not be quick to condemn sado-masochistic practices, and the same goes for potential musical analogs: to compare normative listening to masochism is not necessarily a way of denigrating concert institutions. In this essay, I hope to have shown the relevance of such issues for, among other things, the contemporary discipline of musical analysis. As with concert life, I have tried to reach a better understanding of analytical experience and motivation. It would be premature to offer negative general conclusions about analysis. However, I have suggested that professional analysis involves the formation of identities around a defensive response to musical experience: conscious recognition of this defense and disavowal may be incompatible with the perpetuation of current analytical styles.[27]

NOTES

I presented versions of this paper at New York University (November 2000) and the University of Virginia (February 2001), and benefited from stimulating discussion on those occasions. I am especially grateful to Suzanne G. Cusick, Andrew Dell'Antonio, Nadine Hubbs, and Katharine Eisaman Maus for reading drafts and responding with insightful comments. Epigraph: Forte 1977, 7. The article appeared first in *Journal of Music Theory* 3, no. 1 (April 1959): 1–30. I give page references to the 1977 version.

1. It is important, here and throughout, that I am writing about Forte's essay, rather than directly addressing Schenker's ideas. Study of Schenker's self-conception and positioning of music theory is a separate, demanding enterprise, with a growing literature. See, for instance, Dubiel 1990 or Snarrenberg 1997.

2. Snarrenberg (1994, 53), in his interesting treatment of the essay, notes that

Forte mentions Schumann only once. For another discussion of Forte's essay see
Kerman 1980. Marion A. Guck (1994) offers pertinent comments on another essay
by Forte.

3. Translation from Komar 1971, 16.

4. My description of the poem simplifies a little. Heine's poem shows the lover's
passivity and dependence but also shows, by describing the beloved as a "child" with
whom one might bargain (trading love for flowers and birds), a defensive attempt to
reverse roles, making the beloved seem dependent instead. Near the end of this essay
I will place such reversals at the center of my account of Forte. If my interpretation
of Forte's essay is correct, the depiction of such a defensive reversal in the poem
would hardly make it more appealing to him.

5. Of course, I understand that Forte is commenting on a sketch by Schenker, and
that the omission of text is already present in the original analysis. Still, I think it is
fair to ask why he repeats this omission, especially since the music of this particular
song is odd and, in certain ways, mysterious without the words. Kerman (1980)
emphasizes the role of the poem in understanding the music. It is interesting, too, that
Forte chooses a song as his main example to introduce Schenker's theories, as though
making a special point of Schenker's, and his own, willingness to disregard verbal text.

6. Snarrenberg (1994, 51) states succinctly that Forte's "reading of Freud seems
more colored by his reading of Schenker than vice versa." However, ideas of psychoanalysis in the 1950s were often scientistic, and Forte's general conception of psychoanalysis as, ideally, an objective, impersonal science would have been widely
shared. Much later twentieth-century psychoanalytic thought has worked to diminish this scientific allure.

7. A third kind of control comes from the obligatory nature of music's power.
Cone is not content to say just that someone might choose to yield control to the composer, as one possible relation to music: obscurely but insistently, he states that you
must yield control. (Must? Why? What if you don't?) "When we listen to music, whether
with words or not, we *must* follow it as if it were our own thought. We are *bound* to it"
(156). His account of performance is similar: "The 'convincing' interpretation is the
one that *forces* its listener to follow it, no matter whether he knows the piece by heart
or has never heard it before" (138–39). And, in a passage I already quoted, Cone
asserts that operatic unity "*forces us* to look for a wider intelligence at work."

8. It is not quite clear in Cone's text whether the persona is the force that acts on
listeners: various passages seem to identify the music (145), the performers (137), or
the composer (in the passages just cited) as exerting this control. On the other hand,
Cone disparages listeners who experience music through imaginary relationships to
real performers rather than fictional agents or personae (119–21). An interesting
account emerges if you think of the imaginary persona as dominating the listener,
but the text leaves Cone's intentions unclear, and perhaps he did not think the issue
through. A more intricate account, with which I shall not burden the present essay,
can acknowledge and interpret Cone's unclarity on this issue.

9. The lack of clarity comes partly from verbal ambiguity: "domination. *Or better* . . . to make the composer's voice our own." What does Cone mean when he
says that the second alternative is "better"? Does he mean that the formulation in
terms of identification is more accurate? Should it replace the formulation in
terms of domination? Or is Cone describing two different possibilities, two rela-

tionships to the composer's voice, and saying that the second is preferable? Or should the two relationships be taken together somehow? In this essay I suggest that domination and identification co-exist in the experiences Cone describes, but exploration of alternative readings would be fruitful, in ways I have set aside for present purposes.

10. The background-to-foreground approach, characteristic of Schenker's essays, is less characteristic of Forte's pedagogical writings. The textbook *Introduction to Schenkerian Analysis* by Forte and Steven E. Gilbert (New York: W. W. Norton, 1982) emphasizes reduction, the elimination of detail to move toward middleground and background levels. The review by Dubiel (*Musical Quarterly* 70, no. 2 [Spring 1984]: 269–78) notes this departure from Schenker's procedures.

11. Recently Benjamin has offered an alterative to this view; see W. E. Benjamin 1999, 112.

12. And Benjamin, in the heat of anti-modernist polemic, suggests that the composition of middlegrounds satisfies an otherwise frustrated desire for tonal composition: "If one subscribes to the notion of Schenkerian analysis as a kind of traditional composition, it follows that many creative musicians will turn to it as a way of gratifying their impulses to work in a language which is natural to them" (168).

13. I am drawing on the useful vocabulary of Walton 1990.

14. Notice, by the way, that this conception of imaginary composition is in tension with another aspect of Forte's language that I emphasized before, the specification of certain musical elements as controlling or subordinating others. That is, one conception treats musical elements as fictional characters, the other describes a fictional creator who stands outside, and controls, all the musical material. I have identified similar tolerance of apparently contradictory descriptions in Maus 1988; Guck (1994) also makes this point about imaginative language in analytical writing.

15. In referring to the persona in a Schenkerian analysis, then, I am not referring to that other all too audible voice, Schenker's own violent, vivid self-depiction—a creature that could also be referred to, in a different usage, as the "persona" of a Schenkerian text.

16. Cone (1989) acknowledges that analysis takes you out of the fast-paced, sequential time of listening. But he emphasizes that the goal of analysis lies in the return to an enhanced experience of music in real time. Unlike Cone, Schenkerian analysts seldom try to tell this story to the end.

17. The crucial contributions are McClary 1991 and Brett, Wood, and Thomas 1994.

18. Cone's own abstract of the essay in RILM is chastely technical, and summarizes the sexual content thus: "As a final conjecture, an attempt is made to connect this meaning with specific events of Schubert's life" (RILM No. 82–01540-ap).

19. Curtis 2000 is valuable for its unusually direct and politically committed account of Don Giovanni's relation to the women in the opera.

20. There is a bit more in Cone's interpretation. The interaction continues as the two characters trade inconclusive, briefer phrases in a middle section. Then, when they return to the opening material, they trade material back and forth rapidly, completing each other's musical thoughts, while the text shows Zerlina on the verge of assent. At the same time, when either one falls silent, an instrument continues in the same vocal register, a subtle touch. "When the flute doubles Don Giovanni's voice . . .

can we not take it as an audible representation of her whole-hearted participation in his vocal line, just as the bassoon that doubles her answer can be assumed to reveal the extent of his identification with hers?" (155). When the flute and bassoon play, it is as though the audience can hear the "inner singing" of the characters.

21. For other discussions of listening, analysis, and sexual positions, see Cusick 1994; Maus 1992, 1993, 1996; and Cusick 1999. The last essay also uses the vocabulary of "tops" and "bottoms," but in the gay male sense of, roughly, "inserter" and "insertee," rather than the S&M usage. Cusick also suggests that the "top/bottom" vocabulary, in its relative lack of gender specificity, may improve on the vocabulary of "feminine" and "masculine" roles in musical interaction (Cusick 1999, 494–95). The bottom role, in either usage, has strong associations with femininity or diminished masculinity but also with male practitioners.

Rosen's eroticized account of Mozart attributes to his music a mingling of pleasure and pain (in expressive content rather than in the relation between music and audience—though one should not hope for too clear a distinction here). He refers to "the violence and the sensuality at the center of Mozart's work," claiming that "in all of Mozart's supreme expressions of suffering and terror . . . there is something shockingly voluptuous . . . the grief and the sensuality strengthen each other, and end by becoming indivisible, indistinguishable one from the other" (1972, 324–25). It is difficult not to read this as a knowledgeable, thinly-veiled reference to sadomasochism.

22. Sigmund Freud, in "Instincts and Their Vicissitudes," also emphasizes the identification of masochists with the sadist's position. He suggests that masochism develops out of an earlier sadism, through reversal from an active to a passive position. "Whether there is . . . a more direct masochistic satisfaction is highly doubtful. A primary masochism, not derived from sadism in the manner I have described, seems not to be met with" (Sigmund Freud 1963, 83–103). (Subsequent attempts to integrate the "death instinct" into his theories led to changes in Freud's account of masochism.)

While this passage seems to support Easton's and Liszt's more experiential account, it also suggests caution. Accounts of masochism that stress identification with the sadist may reflect a sense that sadistic behavior is more intelligible, by itself, than the masochist's—that is, such accounts may result from incomprehension, or intolerance, of masochistic subjectivity. The same may be true of Cone's emphasis on identification with the persona.

23. Another kind of alternative would be *practical* rather than *discursive:* rather than seeking alternative descriptions of normative classical music behaviors, one could contrast those norms with, for instance, traditional musical practices that are more participatory, or recent creations such as Pauline Oliveros's *Sonic Meditations* that break down audience/performer distinctions.

24. Benjamin is in the tradition of feminist thought that disparages sadomasochism. Alternative accounts are possible, giving an important role to mutual understanding and support between sadomasochistic partners. My goal in this essay is not to choose among accounts of S&M, but at most to show a way that such accounts might be pertinent to musicology.

25. This may help explain why "On a Lesbian Relation with Music" (Cusick 1994) moves from a relatively brief account of listening to a more extended account of performance, in which Cusick construes performance as an erotic interaction between

performer and music (with no clear role for the audience). Marion Guck makes a similar shift. She writes eloquently of the power of music: "Experience of music's power is definitive of music loving. The powers I've described seem to me genuinely part of close involvement with music. I can understand intellectually how they might seem so disturbing that one would want to deny them. However, I cannot say that these experiences feel dangerous to me, nor can I endorse denying them" (1997, 347–48). But, in moving to a sustained example, a passage from a Mozart piano concerto, Guck suddenly places herself in the role of pianist, thereby taking on agency in the production of the music (1997, 348–50). Again, as in Cusick, the audience disappears from this scene of performance.

26. Recent publications cover an enormous methodological range, including psychological and psychoanalytical theory, ethnography, social history, literary criticism, political advocacy (pro and con), and fiction. Hanly 1995 includes a selection of important psychoanalytical papers. The volume *Masochism,* trans. Jean McNeil (1989), joins Leopold von Sacher-Masoch's short novel *Venus in Furs* and an influential essay, "Coldness and Cruelty," by Gilles Deleuze. Other recent work includes Califia 1988; Stoller 1991; "A Poem is Being Written," in Sedgwick 1993, 177–214; Noyes 1997; Hart 1998; Savran 1998; and much more. It is an especially active area of research and writing.

27. I presented early versions of the interpretation of Forte (the origin of the first four sections of this essay) at the joint meeting of the American Musicological Society, Society for Music Theory, and Society for Ethnomusicology, Oakland, 1990, and at the conference Feminist Theory and Music, Minneapolis, 1991. Other material dates from 2000–2001.

TWO

Musical Virtues

MITCHELL MORRIS

I

"Lamah ragashu goyim?"

Musicological tempers were short in the '90s, and only recently seem to have settled into a sullenness that still occasionally flares into rancor. Many thoughtful and serious scholars hold incommensurate points of view with great conviction and vehemence, and find little success in persuading opponents or often even in eliminating smaller disagreements between their own positions and those of their philosophical allies. Journals, newsletters, internet sites, even some of the (quasi-)mass media, all register this intellectual conflict, and AMS presidents and others have frequently spoken out in attempts to reconcile the various segments of the field, or at least to establish more moderate tones of discussion. As society has gone, so has the Society: everyone's feelings, it seems, are especially delicate around the turn of the millennium.

But why should it be that disagreements in musicology (not to mention many other fields and areas of cultural endeavor) are so often vexed and vexing? Sociologist of philosophy Randall Collins (1999) has argued that conflict in intellectual domains is a necessary stimulus to creativity, and organized by particular structural features of that intellectual field: the composition and history of institutions; cultural capital derived from earlier intellectual work; ideological and personal ties (friendly or hostile) among scholars; a necessarily limited attention-field within which competition takes place; and the contingencies of the larger history that itself defines the course and prospects of intellectual fields. This model is enormously instructive and leads to fascinating and productive ways of thinking about the history and shape of musical scholarship—and of particular interest is its assumption that the divergent stances upon which sustained disagreement is grounded arise inevitably (by the fissioning of dominant positions) in the field of attention that defines a given discipline. But Collins's model does not seek to explain the causes of irreconcilable intellectual differences, nor to offer any ways that reconciliation and synthesis might come about. Debates grow unproductively hot, scholars retreat in the face of discouragingly high levels of repetition, and radical skepticism, though it begins to seem the only way out of intractable argument, will most likely in the end prove merely to be the most secure of tombs for thought. It is incumbent upon us as scholars to seek some way out of this dilemma.

In conversations with assorted musicologists over the last decade, I have occasionally suggested that our discipline would benefit from deliberate attempts to invent (or at least revive) some varieties of moral criticism that have relevance to music. Most often, my suggestion has been met with some combination of skepticism, dismissal, and even disgust. To some of my interlocutors, I seem suddenly to have unmasked myself as a musicological Savonarola, ready to make arguments that would in the end consign innumerable pieces (not to mention articles) to some academic bonfire of vanities. It is as if in the minds of a number of serious and committed scholars, to the extent that a desire for an ethical criticism of music isn't a quaint affectation on my part, it must be terribly dangerous. This in spite of the fact that it is easy enough to identify much of the work that has gone on within musicology as containing powerful, if mostly implicit, ethical assumptions. Occasionally, these assumptions break the surface of texts; but I suggest that musicology in all respects would be better if this happened more often and with greater self-awareness.

Consider, for instance, the intense arguments that have gone on over the interpretation of aspects of Beethoven's Ninth Symphony (see, for example, Robert Fink's essay in this collection), or those about political messages and effects in the works of Igor Stravinsky. Much ink has flowed over both cases, some of it interesting and effective, some of it less so; what has usually disappeared in more general discussions of such debates is the degree to which the clash of arguments significantly registers a conflict between deeply grounded ethical assumptions. Most of the writers who have enlisted in support of one or another point of view in these debates hold strong views about the nature of music and of the knowledge of music, and (in part consequently) about the acceptable range of things that may or may not be said.

These conflicts do not reduce to some parties holding that music is susceptible to kinds of verbal description or can be the object of ostensive speech as opposed to other parties denying any genuine or efficacious connection between music and regions of verbal discourse and action. We can all hear at least some things in particular musical works. But what claims are entailed in the things that we hear, and how are we to judge between competing claims? If Beethoven's Ninth works through musical representations of violence from some points of audition, then how are we to understand such violence in relation to our own lives and the lives of others? Is the music so concrete that we can begin to imagine that it is "like" a particular situation drawn in terms of human lives? Is music on the other hand pointing toward and in part constituting something ineffable, not to say noumenal? How are the various assumptions underlying such potentially incompatible viewpoints to be reconciled or decided between? If Schubert's affectional ties were most characteristically and powerfully to other men such that we are entitled to call him homosexual, and if his music incorporates gestures that resonate with the kinds of histories and attitudes characteristic of particular homosexual people, then what is the relationship of those particularities to those that are characteristic of other kinds of people? Often within musicology we imagine such arguments to be epistemologically directed; the questions we ask reduce to questions about what it is possible to know permanently and (at least provisionally) demonstrably un-falsifiably about the object of perception. But the fire behind these arguments seems to me to derive primarily from the way most apparently epistemological arguments about music contain indirect arguments about morality. Why don't we recognize this?

I think that part of our trouble imagining a moral criticism that would be relevant to music arises from our understanding—the normative understanding of Western European-derived modernity—of what morality is supposed to be. When we think of morals, of moralizing, of immorality, and so on, we imagine that most of our attention is directed toward rules and principles. Morality or ethics is a matter of what it is good to do, and why. But it is at least as plausible, and in fact much more characteristic of moral systems outside those of our kind of modernism, to imagine morality or ethics as dealing with other questions as well, such as what it is good to be and why, or what it is good to love and why.

Or what it is good to hear, and why.

If there is to be any productive way of establishing ways of thinking about music and ethics—whether we are considering music as a kind of moral action or moral reasoning, or our ethical position as performers, listeners, composers, or scholars, or how the institutions that support music in our worlds might necessarily entail an ethical dimension—then we must reflect on the ways that moral claims are already instantiated in some of the things we do, and to propose alternatives that we find helpful and rewarding. Plainly, a single essay can at most begin to sketch out the rudiments of such a project, and even then only for one small segment of a potential musical-ethical domain. I will consider some of the problems entailed by this project through a discussion of structural listening as a moral position, and what I believe to be a way of imagining alternatives. Let me emphasize, as well, that in this essay I do not discuss in any detail the ways that my project inevitably resonates with those ongoing in the work of a number of other scholars, in both philosophy and in music; aside from a very few notes that gesture toward work with which my own project must in the future engage, I will proceed as if from relatively bare discursive ground. By way of a conclusion, I will move to several short discussions that lay out some examples of the starting places from which the kinds of criticism I have in mind might begin to flourish.

The Subject of Structural Listening

In her important article, "Toward a Deconstruction of Structural Listening: A Critique of Schoenberg, Adorno, and Stravinsky," Rose Rosengard Subotnik has taken issue with uncritically maintained musical formalism, particularly embodied in what she calls "structural listening," on a number of grounds. "Structural listening," as Subotnik understands it, exists in a number of variants maintained especially in assorted institutions of Western music-making and education. In one of its most powerful versions, promulgated by Adorno and Schoenberg, it tries

> to describe a process wherein the listener follows and comprehends the unfolding realization, with all its detailed inner relationships, of a generating musical conception, or what Schoenberg calls an "idea." . . . Based on an assumption that valid structural logic is accessible to any reasoning person, such structural listening discourages kinds of understanding that require culturally specific knowledge of things external to the compositional structure, such as conventional associations or theoretical systems.[1]

Subotnik, who locates this notion as a variant of late Enlightenment ideas about art, observes that the autonomy strongly asserted in the definition—music's freedom from cultural contingencies that interfere with the purity of the abstract musical argument—was nevertheless from its inception interwoven with a congeries of ideas about spirituality, poetics, and other important sources of human expressivity and significance. It is important to be clear about the difficulties that arise from such a position. If music is autonomous in this way, then what is the relationship between the meanings that are imagined to arise out of the purity of its internal structures, and those that arise out of the interaction of that structure with the materials of the world around it? Subotnik sees these two poles as dialectical; presumably, therefore, it would be at least theoretically possible to find a way of reconciling their contradictions at a more abstract level. This was clearly a sore point from early on in the history of structural listening, and one which Subotnik questions further in the later versions of the position taken by Stravinsky, Adorno, and Schoenberg.

Hanslick attempted to control the unruliness of historical and cultural concerns by reliance on near-exclusive attention to the formal-technical matters of music. This strategy seemed plausible because the philosophical attitudes of German Idealism, in which the apparent autonomy of music from the world was directly related to music's connection to the noumenal, offered a way to make formal technical details into signposts toward the Absolute. (This is true for Schenker as well.) In Subotnik's view, Stravinsky, in seeking to divorce Hanslick's formalism from its Idealist background, chose to ground it in overridingly quotidian concerns. But it is the very combination of music as an "object" at once aesthetic and prosaic, and composition as an empirical activity, that leads to a view of music that is wholly utilitarian and resistant to considerations of historical and geographical difference (Subotnik 1996, 153). This obsession with immediate purposes, Subotnik argues, completely vitiates our ability to understand musical works in terms of rationality. Specifically, Stravinsky "forfeits the claim of music to validation by any universal principle of rational necessity. At most, he allows the composition to project a plausible rationale, which suggests no necessary basis for its own validity" (153). This means that music as understood from Stravinsky's position cannot possibly have anything to do with genuine rationality (in the Kantian and post-Kantian sense), and thus by extension music cannot have anything to do with genuine moral reasoning.

Subotnik's presentation of this argument works from the observation that rationality in this specific sense is established only by universalizable principles. She takes this to be a central part of the argument for structural listening, and in fact it is crucial to such an argument as it is made by Adorno, who understands moral and structural value to be part of a complex identity. Only to the extent that music operates by universalizable principles of logic can it be said to be free of the moral failures of the social world within which it operates. Universalizability is important as well for both Adorno and Schoenberg when they consider the role of the listener. Music that would fall under the rubric of this concept would necessarily be accessible to any reasonably intelligent educated person, and would make claims on us precisely by its capacity to ground expressivity in the principles of musical logic. The dream of such a musical logic is fulfilled for both men through what Subotnik calls "structural substance," observed above all through "the principle of 'nonredundancy' in music." This entails a number of features,

> including a rationale for chromaticism and dissonance, which they explore in detail . . . the renunciation of preexisting, externally determined conventions, such as symmetrical phrasing and refrains (which in fact often entail redundancy), as foreign to the generating idea of a composition . . . [and] the self-developing capacity of a motivic kernel . . . what they call 'developing variation,' a process they often though not exclusively associate with Brahms. (Subotnik 1996, 154–55)

Subotnik, while acknowledging the power and interest of the concept of structural listening, nevertheless points out that it is very weak on a number of grounds. I cannot summarize all of her discussion here, so let me take a few points upon which I will then expand. First, structural listening

> imagines both composition and listening to be governed by a quasi-Kantian structure of reasoning that, by virtue of its universal validity, makes possible, at least ideally, the (presumed) ideological neutrality and, hence, something like the epistemological transparency of music. (Subotnik 1996, 157)

One of the problems with such a notion arises from the way that it inevitably favors only a narrow range of possibilities among various musics—those are specifically the panromanogermanic canon of the eighteenth and nineteenth centuries, with a few stragglers in the twentieth century.[2] Most music has never aspired to the autonomy demanded in the model of structural listening, and so it must be consigned to a lesser position.

Second, although the kind of music elevated by structural listening must demonstrate its rationality by subordinating itself to some unifying principle (in practice the principle of motivic development), this kind of subordination is characteristic of only a limited range of works within the panromanogermanic canon itself. Furthermore, this rationality, while a powerful criterion for success as determined by structural listening, seems to require balance by the musical establishment of a complex sonic-intentional domain that can be interpreted as signs of individuality, but it is exactly such individuality that can be spoken of within models of structural listening only with the greatest difficulty. This leads us as scholars into poor and misleading arguments. (Simply consider our notorious failure to provide convincing analytical accounts of the music of Ockeghem.) All in all, such difficulties seem in Subotnik's understanding to limit unacceptably our abilities as scholars and listeners to engage with a wide variety of musics, a wide variety of interpretive possibilities.

Breaching the Subject

Subotnik generously demonstrates that structural listening is appropriate for only a small selection of musical works and styles, and that it requires a larger economy of models of listening (and analysis) in order to be appropriately effective. It is better, in other words, to imagine structural listening as part of a larger system of mutually incommensurable and incompatible strategies, to be employed as the occasion warrants. This is an eminently practical proposal, and one that certainly deserves to be established within the various subdisciplines of music. But structural listening should be subjected to some further pressing critique for the sake of productive thought about music and ethics. We must find ways to breach the subject, in every sense of the phrase.

Note that structural listening aspires to a freedom from everything that might be thought contingent: social function and genre, references to ceremony, dogma, all kinds of historical context ought not to be considered when thinking about music in terms of its quiddity. Although Joseph Kerman famously derided analyses of Schumann's *Dichterliebe* for neglecting lyrics, surely those analysts would be correct to maintain that the demands of musical autonomy—certainly the notion of autonomy they wish to elevate—*require* the discarding of the words. Along with such an austere approach to musical works, commitment to structural listening would mandate a focus on the internal developments of works, particularly motivic development, as the sure guarantee of rationality and therefore of significance. Since some measure of individuality seems to be crucial to our nomination of particular works (and therefore composers) as exemplary, however, it follows that structural listening is always already supplemented by ad hoc references to originality, expressivity, and other such individuating notions.[3] These kinds of values, promulgated in specific examinations of pieces, are also reflected in our notions of large-scale music history. What is the history of music, commonly understood, if it is not the history of successive refinements in musical technique?[4] Adorno's greatest difference from Grout in this case may lie in his belief that individuality and rationality had gone increasingly out of balance after Beethoven, and that this presented an insoluble moral problem.

The problems and some possible ways out of them arise when we juxtapose this account of music with a recent discussion of modernist notions of selfhood, and the moral claims they seem to embody. In his influential study *Sources of the Self: The Making of Modern Identity* (1989), the philosopher Charles Taylor argues that three of the central components of our modern understanding of what it is to be a self are: atomistic individualism, the centrality of "disengaged instrumental reason," and romantic notions of expressivity as the result of an internal "deep" self. I will take up a short discussion of Taylor's first two components as the most relevant for my purposes.

Atomistic individualism may be taken to be some variety of the claim that persons are to be understood in an important sense as independent of the social worlds within which they move, and that this independence should be thought of as trumping in most respects the social embeddedness of persons. That is, although we are born into and educated through specific social worlds, the crucial part of ourselves can be, and indeed ought to be, independent of those worlds. In a sense, then, individuals are best thought of as prior to the social worlds within which they find themselves. There is no need to demonstrate the omnipresence of this idea, since it ramifies in uncounted ways within contemporary cultures. There is unquestionable power in such an idea, and it is attached to a distinctive conception of the dignity of individual persons. And arguably, this fundamental moral vision is

centrally responsible for such widespread allegiance to the notions of atomistic individualism that seem to serve it so well.

By "disengaged instrumental reason," Taylor describes the kind of reason
defined primarily by matters of procedure, and conceived of as necessarily
separate from contingencies. The best model for this is found in mathematics: a binomial equation is a universal. The American legal system, with its
strong focus on correct procedure as the best way of securing a minimum of
injustice, can be taken to provide a framework for the attempted exercise of
disengaged instrumental reason as well, and its frequent failures and bad
decisions only make more poignant the untenability of its ideal disengage-
ment. Surely the best way of grounding all kinds of reason within an individual would be to seek to apply this kind of reason as extensively as possible.
In terms of moral thought and action, for instance, this would require that
we make ethically sound decisions by means of principles that could be
understood as universal and accessible to all rational human beings; this
would also, however, require the removal of any contingencies that could be
shown to be merely historically or geographically bounded. The results
would matter as well only to the extent that they were gained by rigorous
observance of the procedural logic.

These principles not only make sense in the context of reflections on selfhood and morality, but also can be seen to operate within the concept of
structural listening. Pieces instantiate atomistic individualism to the extent
that they can be regarded as essentially separate from specific social contexts, whether we seek justification in structures, transcendentalisms, or
some other sources of autonomy. Again, following Subotnik, rationality in
such an abstracted interpretive frame tends to be connected to particular
uses of the term "logic," as if musical procedures contained the kinds of truth
content that allowed them to function within chains of procedural logic.
This situation should suggest that we take structural listening to embody a
strong claim not only about what is good in music, but also about what kind
of moral activity we may imagine a piece of music to contain, evoke, or perhaps summon. That is, music that is proved adequate through structural listening may be presented to us as music that contains precisely those features
that are adequate to us in terms of our moral sense. Music occupies itself
with moral thought and action in ways that strongly resemble the ways in
which human beings occupy themselves with moral thought and action. Our
problem arises from the fact that this system of morality can then be demonstrated to be incoherent and possibly unsustainable. The philosopher Alasdair MacIntyre, whose widely noticed critique of modern morality will
occupy much of my attention here, argues that the two best modern solutions to the problem of manufacturing morality (understood in this context
as a question of rules) are those proposed by Kant and by the utilitarian

philosophers. But MacIntyre goes to great lengths to point out that not only are these two solutions vulnerable on many logical grounds, they also have no historical record of effectiveness at all. He dramatically proposes that for such reasons, they be discarded in favor of ethical thinking that employs the older concept of "virtue." But such a concept can only be understood through historical accounts.

Selves and Others

MacIntyre has noted that in classical Latin and Greek there is no equivalent to "the moral" as we understand it. The Latin "moralis, like its intellectual predecessor 'êthikos' . . . means 'pertaining to character' where a man's character is nothing other than his set dispositions to behave systematically in one way rather than another, to lead a particular kind of life" (MacIntyre 1984, 38). There is an important history behind this. The Greek word *aretê*, usually translated as "virtue," means something closer to "excellence" in the *Iliad* and *Odyssey*.[5] This means that the term can apply to things we do not nowadays usually consider especially virtuous: uncommon physical grace or beauty, for example, or special skill in performing a particular social role. Such a definition assumes the unity of morality and social structure in the specific configuration of a heroic society. MacIntyre sees this as the historical background to the account of virtue developed most comprehensively in Classical Athens, where various parties, including the sophists, Plato, the tragic playwrights, and Aristotle, all attempted to resolve the incompatibilities between Homeric virtue and the society of the *polis* by offering new accounts of virtue that would remedy the defects of their predecessors. The most adequate Classical formulation, for MacIntyre, is that of Aristotle. In MacIntyre's understanding of Aristotelian virtue, it is crucial to note that anything that might be considered a virtue is defined with respect to a (good) *telos*. If the Good for a human being is *eudaimonia*—happiness, well-being, flourishing—then virtues are those qualities that aid the achievement of *eudaimonia*. Thus, any argument about a particular virtue will presuppose a particular conception of human flourishing, or at least it will be open to a further argument about that conception's definition. Furthermore, it will also follow that virtue cannot be exclusively about action, but must also include feeling and attitude. Character—especially as it relates to our picture of a particular type of person we consider the model of human flourishing—will matter more than rules. The teleological character of Aristotelian virtue finds a parallel in that of Christianity, in that Christian notions of the Good also presuppose an ultimate form of human flourishing. Nevertheless, the degree of emphasis the two models place on the role of the supernatural, the function of law, and the roster of virtues differs strikingly, and MacIntyre holds that it was not until Aquinas, for a variety of historical reasons, that a comprehensive synthesis of the two models took place. The specifics of this synthesis matter less for MacIntyre's overall narrative than his idea that, however briefly, a coherent picture of moral reasoning was established. It is this synthesis that was rejected during the Reformation and the Enlightenment, resulting in the confused moral landscape within which MacIntyre's enquiry begins.[6]

If we accept MacIntyre's argument that the models of moral reasoning that took hold in the Enlightenment were in the end internally incoherent, and that our most plausible hope of making sense requires the restoration of the notion of virtue in its Classical sense, how are we to do so without recourse to clearly superseded ideological accompaniments? (I am thinking here of Aristotle's "metaphysical biology," and his damaging unhistorical assumptions that the *polis*, as the highest political organization established by natural law, demands the exclusion of numerous human beings, notably women, slaves, and anyone at all who works.) MacIntyre proposes that we substitute highly specific forms of social *telos* for the biological *telos* characteristic of Aristotle's account. The substitution requires definitions of the terms "practice" and "tradition" so that virtue can be understood to operate within them, as well as an emphasis on the notion of the self as narratively constituted.

A practice is

> any coherent and complex form of socially established cooperative human activity through which goods internal to that form of activity are realized in the course of trying to achieve those standards of excellence which are appropriate to, and partially definitive of, that form of activity, with the result that human powers to achieve excellence, and human conceptions of the ends and goods involved, are systematically extended. (MacIntyre 1984, 187)

The circularity of this definition is crucial: in our attempts not only to hold to the standards of a practice but also to surpass them, we interrogate and gain space to improve those very standards. The grounding of this definition in MacIntyre's description of virtue from Homer to Aquinas is apparent. The account in *After Virtue* goes on to outline the difference between the general concept of a practice and more specific activities that we could call "technique," and to make clear that the range of practices is wide enough to encompass music and farming, teaching and some understandings of politics. To be engaged in the practice of music—any of a number of practices of music—requires skill in producing the appropriately "organized sounds," but producing sounds does not encompass the whole of what we mean by the practice of music. I take it that we acknowledge this when we praise or blame specific performances on grounds larger than those of particular errors of execution, including those difficult to articulate sensations and intuitions we group under the rubric of "expression" or "interpretation." And the discourse in which we evaluate specific performances is itself a part of the practice of music writ large, shaped by and shaping those performances.

But it is also necessary to unpack the definition further. By making an implicit distinction between external and internal goods MacIntyre means to separate those rewards such as status, money, and security from those that can be apprehended only by engaging in the practice. The practice of music is not the only way to acquire such things as status and money—certainly not the best way to acquire them!—hence these goods are external. Those things that we discuss by reference to the various evaluative words at our disposal are internal, in that they can be got by no other means. A good performance is good in its various ways whether or not it is paid for. This distinction furthermore suggests that external goods tend to be limited, acquired in competition, and by extension held individually, while internal goods, though acquired in competition as well, are held in such a way that they benefit all those who engage in the given practice. Consider the qualities of grace or subtlety or power as exemplified in one or another performance by a particularly skilled musician and you consider internal goods; consider salaries and photo shoots and you consider external goods.[7]

Such internal goods are dependent on our entry into the particular social configuration within which standards of excellence are subject to some kind of authority. This authority, to be sure, is always subject to historical revision and development—in fact, for the maintenance of a practice, development would seem to be a requirement—but its dependence on the social never absolves us from giving our allegiance to some extent to the formation within which it is constituted. As MacIntyre, noting that practices entail specific kinds of relationships, insists, "the virtues are those goods by reference to which, whether we like it or not, we define our relationship to those other people with whom we share the kind of purposes and standards which inform practices" (MacIntyre 1984, 191). This is precisely the point that can be expected to trouble many who have always given their allegiance to modernist notions of the self. Authority? Whose authority, and by what right? MacIntyre answers, "To enter into a practice is to enter into a relationship not only with its contemporary practitioners, but also with those who have preceded us in the practice, particularly those whose achievements extended the reach to its present point. It is thus the achievement, and *a fortiori* the authority, of a tradition which I then confront and from which I have to learn" (MacIntyre 1984, 194). It is important to be clear that MacIntyre's position need not reduce to a pallid, dishonest, vulgarized Arnoldism of "the best that has been said and thought," with no reference to historical particularities. Indeed, he distinguishes practices carefully from the institutions that at once sustain them by their attention to external goods, and corrupt them by that same attention. The developing and sustaining of institutions demands certain virtues just as much as the practices the institutions support, though the configuration of virtues is not necessarily the same. To think at once of practices and institutions as necessarily historical therefore requires a careful if limited form of relativism that must always beware of hubristic universalist claims.

To return to a practical example, to examine the virtues that might be contained in Lully's *Armide,* we must disentangle various kinds of musical virtues and vices from the virtues and vices that sustained the institutions through which the music could be realized; though we are likely to understand the moral qualities in each case as deeply intertwined, they are nevertheless *not* necessarily identical.

So far MacIntyre's account is devoted to defining virtue in a way that removes many of the problems in Aristotle's account. Let me emphasize once again the irreducibly social nature of virtues as they arise within practices and the institutions that house them. But of course virtues cannot be restricted only to practices and institutions, though they may find their most durable home there; a primary goal of virtue theory should consist in locating the Good (admittedly, an extraordinarily complex and possibly irreducible object) within human life as a whole. An entire human life can easily be wracked with conflicts between virtues, or what appear to be virtues. Not all goods may be compatible. This would seem to install the autonomous individual firmly at the point of moral origination from which s/he seemed to have been dislodged. Furthermore, if virtue is defined in such a way that it requires some kind of end, it would seem that virtue must be restricted to aspects of a given human life and thus have little or no way to speak to that life as a whole. If we wish to preserve some kind of social *telos* here as well, we must ask ourselves what form it might take.

In modern life, subject to the complicated effects of our incoherent distinctions between public and private as well as our central allegiance to atomistic individualism and its concomitants, it is our understanding of what makes a self that can be seen to produce much of the problem. MacIntyre's solution to this begins with the argument that human actions, to be intelligible, always require description under a certain frame of intentions, which themselves may be ordered:

> We identify a particular action only by invoking two kinds of context, implicitly if not explicitly. We place the agent's intentions, I have suggested, in causal and temporal order with reference to their role in his or her history; and we also place them with reference to their role in the history of the setting or settings to which they belong. In doing this, in determining what kind of causal efficacy that agent's intentions had in one or more directions, and how his

short-term intentions succeeded or failed to be constitutive of long-term intentions, we ourselves write a further part of these histories. Narrative history of a
certain kind turns out to be the basic and essential genre for the characterization of human actions. (MacIntyre 1984, 208)

Crucial to MacIntyre's understanding of such narrative is the notion of intelligibility. That is, we must be able to place human action such that it links the
action to a context of "intentions, motives, passions and purposes."[8] Only
such a context allows us to explain and respond. Borrowing a term from
Bakhtin, we might say that intelligible narrative is what makes it possible for
meaning to be dialogic.

Of course, the self constituted dialogically is not thereby bereft of all personal identity. On the contrary, MacIntyre points out that, although selves
enter the world already implicated in a number of different narratives, subject to fortune and aspects of their continually developing histories, their dialogic nature means that not only are selves answerable in various ways to
other selves, they also have the power to question those other selves. In moral
terms, we are able to ask not only about the Good for ourselves, but about
the Good for other selves particularly and generally. Put this way, "The unity
of a human life is the unity of a narrative quest. Quests sometimes fail, are
frustrated, abandoned or dissipated into distractions; and human lives may
in all these ways also fail. But the only criteria for success or failure in a
human life as a whole are the criteria of success or failure in a narrated or
to-be-narrated quest" (MacIntyre 1984, 219).

If that quest is a quest for the Good, a quest that in seeking the Good continually learns more adequate ways of understanding what it seeks, then the
virtues are not only those things that prove necessary to practices, but also
those that enable this larger narrative quest. Furthermore, since such a Good
may be sought narratively only within the contexts of the social identities we
have received or claimed and incorporated, revised, or rejected, that Good
can never be comprehended from the standpoint of a disembodied, isolated
individual. That is to say, the Good, to be apprehended at all through the
virtues, must be apprehended with respect to particular traditions or combination of traditions.

The term "tradition," in line with the self-reflexive definition of "practice," denotes not only a particular array of goods as articulated through
practice(s), but also the arguments about how that array of goods or their
constitution through practice is to be understood. There is once again a crucial historical dimension to the term:

Within a tradition the pursuit of goods extends through generations, sometimes through many generations. Hence the individual's search for his or her

good is generally and characteristically conducted within a context defined by those traditions of which the individual's life is a part, and this is true both of those goods which are internal to practices and of the goods of a single life. Once again the narrative phenomenon of embedding is crucial: the history of a practice in our time is generally and characteristically embedded in and made intelligible in terms of a larger and longer history of the tradition through which the practice in its present form was conveyed to us; the history of each of our own lives is generally and characteristically embedded in and made intelligible in terms of the larger and longer histories of a number of traditions. (MacIntyre 1984, 222)

Traditions, as arguments about goods, provide another way in which the virtues are shaped and become visible; they also find themselves sustained by the virtues they help form. The same criteria of rationality that apply to practices also apply to traditions, so that to be rational, traditions must demonstrate the highest degree of internal coherence historically possible. Complex internal disagreements and debates are to be expected, because it is through argument that coherence is tested. Between traditions also there may be areas of agreement as well as areas of incompatibility and incommensurability.[9]

We can at this point begin to see how structural listening may be understood as a tradition within which a particular set of practices (in composition, performance, listening, and commentary) have developed over the course of the last two hundred years or so. Structural listening necessarily refuses some virtues and requires others (obviously, since all kinds of listening do), and does so in the service of specific (and specifically elevated) notions of musical goods. The difficulty lies in some aspects of the goods to which structural listening aspires.

These goods may entail the following claims: that music's relation to human life is one whereby the work can be treated as an abstract person—the classical meaning of *persona* thus renovated in sound; that to some extent (nearly always left unspecified) music can act upon individual human beings through a kind of sympathetic magic, such that the music's "harmony" can shape the soul's "harmony" in fairly direct ways; that a salutary difference between music and life is that in music, contingency can be reduced and perhaps even eliminated; that music's value adheres precisely in its consequent freedom from the vulnerabilities of accident and circumstance, which freedom can then be translated into individual terms; that the best way to capture this picture of the Good requires a severely chastened language of discussion, not only to diminish any interference with the transfer of freedom from music to listener, but also to exemplify the uncontextualized being that is sought; that this Good is also only adequately available to those able to establish a kind of contemplative life for themselves; and that allegiance to this Good also requires that it present itself as universal and not open for debate. This complex sequence of assumptions establishes an image that has as much potential imaginative power, it seems to me, as Plato's myth of the cave: call it the myth of the sounding noumenon, maybe. But I fear that few of these assumptions may be true. The power of the image may chiefly come from a poignant sense that it cannot be sustained.

"e voi nasceste con diverso ingegno"

So what is to be done? Perhaps we should begin to think where we begin to listen, in *medias res:* first principles are not what we reason *from,* but what we reason *to,* and thinking about musical virtues is difficult and various enough that it seems likely that any first principles will in this domain remain an abstract *telos* in human life.[10] And it seems best to avoid the single most characteristic mistake of writers who speculate on music as an activity of moral reflection or music as a source of moral effects: that is, the error of assuming a direct and unproblematic correspondence or sequence of transmission from musics to persons.[11] Instead, our considerations of musical virtues— what they are, how they are to be located, the extent of their relevance in particular situations—can most profitably begin, as Eve Kosofsky Sedgwick has suggested in another context, by risking the obvious: people are different.[12] In this case, we may note that people are musically different, in such ways that we as yet have only the most inadequate means of approaching their musical differences.

The great benefit of the dialogic, tradition-minded approach I have been outlining here arises from its requirement that any sense of ethics be based in some specific social structure(s) instead of an abstract collection of propositions. In this case, our understanding of the ethical import of listening (specific acts of listening by specific people, directed toward specific music) cannot be separated from the careful specification of our place, and from an equally careful sense of those to whom we are speaking. And yet the kinds of projects that grow from just this specification attempt to accommodate such variance that any statement will necessarily be incomplete.

It is to make concrete these interpretive *desiderata* that I will end with three short musical discussions. In each case, I have tried to frame some potential lines of ethical inquiry that resonate with ethical moments within the pieces. These accounts do nothing to exhaust the number of moments from which ethical inquiry can begin, and they do not pretend to treat fully any of the issues raised. As commentary, my discussions will be of moral use only to the extent that they engage the ears of others in a consideration of what additional virtues or vices may be heard in these specific pieces, in what

circumstances, and by whom. I speak, as I listen, in the service of the potential virtue of difference.

II

Johannes Brahms, Intermezzo, op. 118, no. 2

It is most true, stylus virum arguit, —*our style betrays us.*
ROBERT BURTON, *Anatomy of Melancholy*

Although writers and listeners note the pervasive tone of melancholy in
much of Brahms's late music, its presence has seemed less important in the
critical literature on Brahms than many other musical qualities. Observations about the music's formal structures—ambiguous tonalities, subtle harmonic and motivic relationships, delicate reinterpretations of traditional formal schemes—have typically provided the foci for discussion, and attention
paid to such questions has often been demonstrably worthwhile.[13] But even
so, we are entitled to ask what we can hear in Brahms's late music in light of
its variegated sadnesses, and in what ways we can think about the ethical trajectories of our discernment. Let me take up this question briefly with
respect to the well-known *Intermezzo* op. 118, no. 2.

The pleasures of melancholy in Brahms are inevitably bound up with
questions about what it means to be a *gebildet* listener in an epoch of self-conscious lateness. The lineaments of such a *Bildung* are relatively easy to trace:
Brahms's elaborate indebtedness to other composers, as it is instantiated in
allusiveness and adherence to lapsed idioms, is among other things a multi-
valent way of soliciting certain kinds of listener cultivation at the same time
that it also describes that cultivation and enacts some of the processes by
which it is acquired.[14] Its seeming obviousness masks great interpretive
depths, chiefly those concerned with stance and tone. The rich presence of
other music in Brahms's work gains additional reinforcement from the powerful learnedness of his style, and these features together crucially reinforce
a notion of lateness as *Bildung*. These terms—melancholy, allusiveness,
learning, lateness—are so much a commonplace of the critical literature,
however unexamined they often are in practice, that it becomes easy to forget that the very notion of lateness possesses an intense ethical charge. On
the one hand, retrospectivity as a mode of feeling can be condemned as
effete, crabbed and conservative, life-hating, cowardly, academic, Alexan-
drian, and so on.[15] On the other, it is important for us as listeners to be aware
of how this retrospectivity exists in a larger ecology of feeling through which
we can reimagine the emotions that inform such concepts as inheritance,
memory and nostalgia, alienation, limitation, and self-revelation.

I want to consider two small but specific moments of listening, together with several more general musical features, from which we might begin a consideration of the ethics of lateness in this *Intermezzo*. Listening to the opening gesture of the piece, I am always struck by how close it is to ending by the second measure, and yet how reluctant it is to close. The affective tension at the beginning is mostly the result of the extended D-major triad in second inversion, which is audibly "unreal": the ear (well, my ear) pulls vainly at the upper-hand D♮ and F♯ at the beginning of measure 1 in the hopes that they will follow the lead of the initial right-hand notes and fall to C♯ and E♮, and when Brahms intensifies this desire by pushing on to the expansive tenth of A♮ and F♯ at the downbeat of measure 2, the push to ending seems intensified. And yet the music carries on. If we must think in structural terms, we can note that the tonic triad of A major is only genuinely resolved at the very ends of the A sections, and thus we are able to hear the need for resolution in the opening two bars as partially satisfied by the music's fall to the dominant in measure 4, by changing inversions and assisting the tonicization of the dominant in the following phrase.[16] Was this chord a functional but strangely placed subdominant, or was it a temporarily unresolved melodic shape? Both, of course, and movingly unsatisfactory either way.

It's no great art to begin a piece in the German canonical tradition with a gesture of farewell, and its quality of commonplaceness is part of the point. The emotions that ought to accompany a phrase such as "there is nothing new under the sun" will most clearly appear when even the threat of newness seems to be excluded. It follows as well that we are summoned to assume stock emotional responses at the very beginning of this piece, but as the music continues, we might realize: (1) that the very ordinariness of stock emotional responses, though usually regarded as the source of their unsatisfactoriness, can be understood as on the contrary part of what makes them worthy of as much attention as those rare and thrilling "original" responses—the omnipresence in life of stock emotions, treated here artistically, might begin to suggest something of their intrinsic value within the frames of human lives; (2) that, in any case, stock emotional responses can be understood as much more nuanced than we are ordinarily inclined to think, such that their typological nature ought not to preclude them from being taken seriously. The music of this *Intermezzo* in this way begins to be reminiscent of the poetry of someone like Thomas Hardy, in which verse after verse reveals how conventional poetic emotions turn out to be immensely rewarding and subtle.

Pessimism and its attendant emotions are multifarious, perhaps always more so than simple happiness, and this is again apparent in the *Intermezzo* in places such as the lovely sad melody that opens the B section of the piece. One of the most affecting points in the melody occurs at measure 54; this is the second measure of a phrase that acts as both a very weak consequent and also amplification of the initial phrase in the B section. The affective weight is for me concentrated in the right-hand minor sixth, G♯/E♮, an appoggiatura that clearly means to sink down by step to F♯/D♮, but never does so. There are several larger reasons to care about this unresolved appoggiatura. First, the unresolved G♯ sits a tritone away from the root of the chord, and this sonority often tends to appear in situations of longing (cf. the famous first resolution in the Prelude to *Tristan* as an obvious example), and tritone appoggiaturas appear in a number of places in this *Intermezzo*. Moreover, the antecedent phrase of the B section is importantly out of kilter metrically, and measure 54 is ironically the moment when the metrical planes seem to be coming back into alignment. The hanging appoggiatura can begin to stand in for numerous other moments in the *Intermezzo* where what is implicitly promised, what is so nearly immediate that longing begins to be replaced by satisfaction, in the end falls away into lack. Even the deliberately weakened final cadence—a resolution oddly "inauthentic" in its voicing—sounds hollow. It begins to seem as if lack is the normal state of affairs in this piece, as indeed it is in human life, and we can push this line of thought further in connection with the piece by coming to interpret it as a way of teaching us what it means to live with reduced expectations, to learn to reveal this poverty as partially (though only partially) compensated for by art, and thus to find a way of showing that regret, like death, is the mother of beauty.

III

Steve Reich, Come Out

We flinch and grin,
Our flesh oozing towards its last outrage.
That which is taken from me is not mine.
GEOFFREY HILL, *"I Had Hope When*
Violence Was Ceas't"

Steve Reich's 1966 piece *Come Out* begins with a real voice. To quote Reich's own program notes:

> it was originally part of a benefit presented at Town Hall in New York City for the re-trial, with lawyers of their own choosing, of the six boys arrested for murder during the Harlem riots of 1964. The voice is that of Daniel Hamm, now acquitted and then 19, describing a beating he took in Harlem's 28th precinct station. The police were about to take the boys out to be "cleaned up" and were only taking those that were visibly bleeding. Since Hamm had no actual open bleeding he proceeded to squeeze open a bruise on his leg so that he would be taken to the hospital. "I had to like open the bruise up and let some of the bruise blood come out to show them." (Reich 1987)

Reich deserves credit, certainly, for his desire to account for the social and personal particulars of his piece, but such specificity is also clearly necessary to the aesthetic or ethical trajectory of *Come Out*. It matters a lot that we are listening to Hamm's voice in all its grainy individuality, with its accent and idiosyncrasies of pace and pronunciation intact, and that his voice is describing a specific assault not only on his bodily integrity but also and more importantly on his claims to dignity. There's no question of us understanding the text, because it's repeated in full three times before Reich's musical processes begin their work (this takes up the first 20 seconds of the piece).

When the music launches into its sequence of repetitions of the final phrase, "come out to show them," however, interpretation must take multiple but probably incompatible directions. By approximately thirty repetitions of the phrase (up to around 1'8") we can hear that some slow transformation is taking place: Hamm's speech acquires more and more reverberation, and after the first minute of the piece gradually dissociates into first two vocal layers, then more and more fragments of sound, panning between speakers. Within three minutes the pitch centers of each syllable (approximately between D♮/B♮/C♯ and E♭/C♮/D♮ according to my piano) become more distinct, and the specific syllables fade increasingly into the background, sibilants, dentals, then finally guttural. That is, the words "come out" stay in the texture until around 8'40" in part because *C*, the only guttural consonant and the first consonant of the phrase, can retain its individuality under the pressure of Reich's tape manipulations far longer than the nasal *M* or the sibilants *S* and *TH*, and even longer than the dental *T*.

To return to the relentless progress of the music, by minute 4 Daniel Hamm's words are increasingly submerged in musical process, and even the residual presence of the words "come out," which begin to seem like a bass part, fades by about 8'40". The remaining approximately four minutes of the piece are a ferocious continuation of abstract procedures.

Critics who have written on *Come Out* have mostly concentrated on the way it was made—the kind of account most likely to persuade readers who are committed to the tenets of structural listening.[17] But Reich's own words on the technique of composition are much more relevant for a consideration of ethics: "By using recorded speech as a source of electronic or tape music, speech-melody and meaning are presented as they naturally occur. By not altering its pitch or timbre, one keeps the original emotional power that speech has while intensifying its melody *and* its meaning through repetition and rhythm" (Reich 1987). Reich furthermore mentions his interest in the poetry of William Carlos Williams, Charles Olson, and Robert Creely as a way of connecting *Come Out* to his other work, presenting the piece as a problem in the setting of American speech as well as invoking the poets' interest in the connection between art and distinctively American ways of world-making. But the central point to be taken up in an ethical hearing of *Come Out* might best begin from Reich's claims that the locus of meaning in speech comes from its connotative dimensions, so that emotion is the province of speech as music. Note that his comments suggest a model in which music and speech shade into one another, and speech itself is internally divided such that meaning is to "speech-melody" as thought is to emotion, or perhaps idea is to body. We might conclude, then, that Reich would wish us to hear the development of sound in *Come Out* as retaining the emotional content of Hamm's narrative all of the way through the piece.

The problem is, content matters, and its gradual attenuation in *Come Out* is difficult to interpret. But it is not that hard to provide exegetical possibilities, and here is a short list:

1. The disappearance of speech can be taken as a metaphor for the crushing of individuality under one or another Ideological State Apparatus. When we hear Hamm's words fade into procedure we hear an actual human being ground up in an infernal machine that resembles bureaucracy, administration, or any other incarnation of the principle of disengaged instrumental reason in the way it so easily disarticulates meaning from the bodies bearing it. The very susceptibility of the piece to be taken as a kind of "Absolute Music," moreover, can establish an uncomfortable resonance between what we are usually taught to hear as abstract musical process and the mechanisms of modern state management. Reich's rigor thus contains its own critique of the very system that creates it.

2. The disappearance of speech signals Reich's triumphant ability to absorb the materials of someone else's voice and someone else's pain into his own serene compositional processes. Real violence is transmuted into a representation of violence in a way that renders it unaccountable and ultimately inconsequential. When the axiom "It must be abstract" is taken so seriously, what happens to real people in real pain? Granted, the piece was performed on a benefit concert, and raised money for legal defense. Is the sentimentality risked in this process so potentially harmful that the piece ought not to be heard in any other contexts? And who gets the royalties, anyway?

3. The disappearance of speech comes as a result of Reich's articulating something quite profound about violence, time, and repetition. Many people who have experienced serious violence, whether as the result of human action or as the result of an accident, report significant temporal distortions. Time speeds up, slows down, or seems to recur. Slowing and repetition are the essence of this piece, as the moment of trauma cycles through ever distilled versions of its moment of occurrence. With each reiteration of the self-inflicted violence implicitly coerced by the police, the account pales in comparison with the literal re-presentation of that violence. Words disappear into action. By the end of the piece, are we hearing an audible representation of the bruise blood itself?

4. The disappearance of speech signifies an act of mourning. Mourning and melancholy come, according to Freud, from a refusal to relinquish the

object lost. What has been lost is not only the dignity of Daniel Hamm as a human being, but also the dignity of his oppressors and the dignity of all bystanders, and in fact this is an object that cannot be released without devastating moral consequences. Reich's obsessive repetitions take the structure of mourning and allow it to shape the piece in such a way that *Come Out* acts as a reliquary for pain and an attempt to offer it as recompense for what is lost. That it can only fail makes the offer more moving.

The point to be drawn from all of these possible interpretations is that they can all be heard in the piece; and it seems to me not only impossible but also completely undesirable to choose among them. As I write this essay, the city of Los Angeles faces a massive scandal involving the Ramparts division of the LAPD, where perjury and violence toward innocent people has made a mockery of justice. It is crucial to remember how various and complicated the issues surrounding the scandal are, however, even as we begin to try to measure the kinds of damage inflicted. Reich's piece, in all its ambivalent tensions, seems to embody just such crucial issues in a pattern of continuing beauty, pain, and relevance.

IV

Trent Reznor/Nine Inch Nails, "Reptile"

> *If thou were to see in liknesse of fleisch and blood that blessed sacrament, thou schuldest lothen and abhorren it to resseyve it into thy mouth.*
> JOHN WYCLIFFE, *Elucidarium*

In 1994, Trent Reznor, the author of the group Nine Inch Nails, released *The Downward Spiral,* a remarkably grim work that nevertheless achieved notable critical and commercial success; the song "Reptile" appears as track 12. Even for an album permeated by revolting verbal and musical metaphors as well as horrific violence, this song retains a striking ability to disgust. The opening verse, for instance, combines repellent imagery that evokes contamination, hybridity, decay, and putrescence, all in the service of vicious misogyny directed toward an ex-lover:

> she spreads herself wide open to let the insects in
> she leaves a trail of honey to show me where she's been
> she had the blood of reptile just underneath her skin
> seeds from a thousand others drip down from within

These lyrics are framed musically by an instrumental introduction composed of sounds of unspecified assembly-line equipment overlaid with slightly irregular chains of pizzicato string patterns (mostly a chain of alternating major seconds and perfect fourths); when this introduction gives way, it is to an extremely harsh ambience in which a strong percussion battery establishes a dialogue with a distinctive sound like a piston/carriage return, over a rumbling, obscure bass D♮. (Significantly, the piston noise retains a slightly vocal quality because of its relatively high pitch content as well as its characteristic glissando.) After a vamp of eight bars, Reznor's vocal line enters. In the context of the song's lyrics that piston sound, in particular, acquires an especially distasteful resonance: listeners familiar with virtually any of Reznor's music videos will find it difficult not to think of the characteristic and wholly nauseating spectacle of animal parts (specifically, carrion) attached to machinery. Other sounds later in the song that combine mechanical and vocal qualities reinforce this notion. That is, taken as a whole the song *sounds* at once obscenely mechanical *and* obscenely fleshly. This complex combination of dark affects, however, exists in an odd tension with several exquisite musical gestures, notably a lyrical whole-tone ascent from D♮ to A♭ during a brief quiet interlude about three-quarters of the way through the track.

The extreme difficulty for listeners established by Reznor's tropes of the disgusting is the point of the entire song, not to mention the entire album. Any ethical inquiry into the nature and aims of a song like this must consider what is meant by the representation of things that, were they to appear in an actual human situation, many of us might agree to characterize as depraved or at least insalubrious. One way of addressing this is the Aristotelian notion of catharsis: we argue that the hatred and disgust presented in the song acts to purge listeners of those same feelings in a kind of homeopathic cure. A more resonant answer, however, might be found in the interpretive contexts out of which Reznor's composition grows.

Soon after the album's release Reznor described his goals in constructing the whole in terms that self-consciously open a space for considerations of ethics and music: "the big overview was of somebody who systematically throws away every aspect of his life and what's around him—from personal relationships to religion, this person is giving up to a certain degree but also finding some peace by getting rid of things that were bogging him down. The record also looks at certain vices as being ways of trying to dull the pain of what this person is hiding."[18] In other words, the album documents an ambivalent asceticism so exigent that even the grounds upon which self-denial is built must themselves be sacrificed. This sacrifice marks a *kenosis* so extreme that good must be emptied out along with evil in an attempt to reach some transcendent term. Listeners unfamiliar with Reznor's work may not expect to find such a potentially religious framework behind an album containing such horrific verbal and musical imagery, but this combination is absolutely normal in terms of the traditions with which Reznor is engaged.

Reznor's musical poetics derive most strongly from the specialized pop genre of Industrial music. Growing out of various rock avant-gardes in the later 1970s, and particularly developed in the work of experimental groups such as Throbbing Gristle and Cabaret Voltaire, Industrial found its most prominent exponents in '80s groups such as Ministry, Skinny Puppy, or Einstürzende Neubauten. Most Industrial music depends upon a fusion of various dance styles, notably disco and New Wave dance techno-pop, with noise and found sonic materials such as machinery sounds, all of which are considered especially appropriate to post-industrial cultural products. For all its emphasis on technology, however, Industrial music is anything but giddily technophile. Instead, the music in its settings and lyrics pays enormous amounts of attention to categories of the obscene and the abject, and it may be important to the resonance with youth cultures in the 1980s and 1990s that the Industrial genre seemed to offer an aesthetic shape to house many of the adolescent sentiments that developed in the strikingly punitive, child-hating culture of late twentieth-century America.[19]

The poetics underlying Industrial music certainly can be traced back to late Romanticism in its most gothic manifestations. Particularly with respect to French literature, a line running from Nerval and Baudelaire through Rimbaud and Lautréamont, and into the twentieth century with the revival of interest in Sade seen among writers such as Georges Bataille, makes perfect sense of Industrial's thematics of obscenity and damnation as holy activities.[20] Another line of historical tradition might be seen as coming from the poetics of German Expressionism. In both cases, the notion of violation as a form of the sublime seems central to understanding the projects as a whole.[21] It should follow, then, that underlying Reznor's work is the attempt to reach an Absolute through the darkest of paths. What this means for listening is complex, but it seems to require that when we listen to "Reptile," we hear it to some extent as the record of a left-hand *askesis.* St. Catherine of Siena drank pus: is *The Downward Spiral* so far away from her?

V

It is also true, *lectio virum arguit:* the examples I have chosen to discuss clearly bespeak a particular set of moral interests and encourage reflection on various sets of virtues. These do not reduce to the overly simple kinds of fables compiled by would-be Aesops such as William Bennett, because there are multiple sets of potential virtues (and vices) in each piece I have offered up. Nevertheless, it would be disingenuous not to acknowledge that I have favored minor-mode affects and dispositions in my interpretations. In Brahms's *Intermezzo,* I tend to hear musical evocations of qualities such as modesty and restraint, I contemplate the connection of these qualities to feelings of reduced expectation and belatedness, and I remain impressed that so much beauty can be wrung out of sadness. Reich's *Come Out* also works nearby with grief and violence, but in my hearing its interpretive trajectory moves toward a more abstract intersubjectivity rather than the construction of individualized, exemplary interiority. With Reznor's song "Reptile," the hatred of self and other that drives the disgust at the heart of the ascetic process offers, among other things, a location in which I note how the difference between virtue and vice becomes a little harder to see.

In each case, my account is extremely partial, and were discussion to stop there, the possibility of listening to and for virtue and vice would be stymied. MacIntyre observes that it is only within the context of human relationships that we can speak of morality; abstract principles of universal application make a poor place from which to view the moral life precisely because they are insufficiently attentive to the contingencies that make up human conditions. I have suggested that structural listening is subject to similar criticisms. If music—writing it, playing it, listening to it, talking about it—is to recover its capacity to be recognized as a kind of moral activity with an important role in shaping our understandings of what is good, then we must be able to speak with one another about just those qualities, contentious, partial, and difficult of definition, which are at present the ground of our disagreements. If we listen to the virtues of our music, perhaps we can listen to the virtues of the music and speech of others. In some sense, music becomes like our Torah: we are not required to complete the work; neither are we allowed to abandon it.

NOTES

1. Subotnik 1996, 150. See the introduction to this volume for further discussion of Subotnik's characterization of "structural listening".

2. The term is of course Richard Taruskin's. See the discussions in Taruskin 1997.

3. This supplementation can also lead to power relations that are (perhaps by accident) morally suspect. Consider, for instance, the pedagogical problems posed by I. A. Richards's notorious New Critical primer *Practical Criticism* (1964). Assuming that his task is to promulgate a quasi-Kantian view of poems, Richards in fact systematically withholds crucial contextual information from his test subjects, then mean-spiritedly chides them for not being able to deduce the information from the poems themselves. By a sleight of hand, the critic's authority is thus placed beyond question, hence beyond dialogue.

4. On this point see Williams 1993.

5. MacIntyre 1984, 122. The following summary depends on MacIntyre 1984, chapters 10–13.

6. There is an interestingly ironic resonance between MacIntyre's Aquinas and Adorno's Beethoven with respect to their crucial but poignantly brief synthesis of moral worlds.

7. On this point see McMylor 1994, 151–53.

8. MacIntyre 1984, 209. See also in support of this the discussion in McMylor 1994, 153–60.

9. On these points see especially MacIntyre 1984, chapters 18 ("The Rationality of Traditions," 349–69) and 19 ("Tradition and Translation," 370–88).

10. Cf. MacIntyre: "Such inquiry does not begin from Cartesian first principles, but from some contingent historical starting point, some occasion that astonishes sufficiently to raise questions, to elicit rival answers and hence, to lead on to contending argument. Such arguments, when developed systematically through time, become a salient feature of the social relationships they inform and to which they give expression" (MacIntyre 1994, 147).

11. At times it seems as if this mistake is near universal. It may be that our predisposition as human beings to imagine music's power as manifesting through contagion says important things about how we listen; but it is death to listening as bound up with moral discourse. For a recent critique of this problematic, see Goehr 1999.

12. Sedgwick 1990 seems to me to be one of the best models for the kind of ethical and aesthetic engagement I have in mind. And some recent work on gay and lesbian studies in musicology, of course, suggests that Sedgwick's model resonates more strongly with musical preoccupations than may seem intuitively obvious. See, among others, Morris 1992, Brett 1994, and Cusick 1994.

13. Though to cite one protest: "it is ironic . . . that [Brahms's] compositional method has so often inspired a formalistic critical reaction—one celebrating architecture rather than process" (Rink 1999, 80).

14. Usefully nuanced discussions of Brahms's citational habits include Hull 1989 and Knapp 1997 and forthcoming.

15. Certainly this rhetoric of condemnation attaches to any number of composers, particularly those whose music depends upon effects that summon emotional states of sentimentality, vicariousness, obliquity, and extended irony: all of these terms entail complicated forms of listener relations, which achieve their greatest potency through their aptness to move even more easily toward ill than toward good. But it is exactly this rhetorical and ethical charge that can be gained no other way. On these issues, see Morris 1995 and 1999.

16. David Epstein (1979, 175) notes the weakness of the tonic as a formal property. In general, as he notes elsewhere (1990, 198–99), the paucity of structural downbeats can be understood as a general feature of Brahms's music, and specifically connects the weak cadences of this *Intermezzo* with its air of melancholy.

17. The central examples are Nyman 1999, 155–57 and Strickland 1993, 189–92.

18. Alan di Perna, "Machine Head," *Guitar World* (April 1994); transcribed by Mile Katzenborg in *Painful Convictions: words and so much skin* [Online]. Available: http://www.9inchnails.com/articles.cgi? [2000, February 10].

19. Moreover, it is possible to suggest that one of the most vital strands of popular music during the '80s and '90s develops its most characteristic stances from a crucial cluster of notions associating abjection, marginal positions with respect to gender and sexuality, and youth. Industrial music thus joins British techno-pop (notably the Pet Shop Boys), less classifiable groups such as the Smiths and R. E. M., and some post-Punk in defining the kinds of abject identities stylized in films such as *The River's Edge* or *Heathers,* not to mention fantasies like *The Lost Boys* or *The Basketball Diaries.*

20. Of particular importance here is Rimbaud's concern with the artist as *voyant*, plainly including all that term's religious connotations. Also resonant are works such as Bataille 1986. And Mario Praz's classic work, *The Romantic Agony* (1970), could be considered a basic guide to this tradition.

21. I have examined some aspects of the nineteenth-century sublime in Morris 1998. An especially interesting discussion of the affect of disgust is found in Miller 1997. A set of concerns closely related to the French and German traditions mentioned informs the work of writers such as Kathy Acker, J. G. Ballard, or Dennis Cooper, all of whom have been cited in the contexts of Industrial music. And to return to grotesqueries such as the marriage of corpses and machines, this kind of fusion is a widespread thematic interest in much Industrial culture, and may be thought of as another way of approaching the kinds of issues discussed in academic contexts under the rubric of the Post-Human or the Cyborg.

THREE

The Chosen One's Choice

TAMARA LEVITZ

In her critique of what she calls structural listening, Rose Subotnik departs from the premise that music can be defined in terms of a binary opposition between rational, abstract structures and sound or style, which in her account includes aspects of music as diverse as medium, history, and corporeality.[1] She argues that structural listeners have focused too adamantly on the structuralist pole of this key binarism, thereby neglecting crucial aspects of musical experience. With the expression "structural listeners" she is referring in particular to Arnold Schoenberg, Igor Stravinsky, and Theodor Adorno, whose extensive theoretical writings she does not aim to analyze in detail (especially in terms of contradictions, modifications over time, and nuances), but rather to summarize conceptually, explicating them in terms of broad common denominators. This focus leads her to define Schoenberg's and Adorno's differentiated approaches to listening "for present purposes" "as one," and to summarize Adorno's contribution as that of "locat[ing] musical value wholly within some formal sort of parameter, to which it is the listener's business to attend," even though one of his central Marxist arguments concerned the immanent historicity of musical material (Subotnik 1996, 150 and 152–53). Her discussion of Stravinsky is similarly focused: rather than investigate the practical considerations involved in Stravinsky's work as a ballet and theater composer, she defines his approach to listening on the basis of his ghostwritten *Poetics of Music* of 1936, concluding that Stravinsky "celebrated the activity of musical construction and would confine musical meaning within the boundaries of the individual composition, exclusive of contextual relationships and (at least in theory) of intent" (152–53). Thus distilled to their essence, the principles of structural listening can function ideally as one pole of Subotnik's primary conceptual binarism of form versus content/style.

In my essay, I suggest an approach to listening in which structure is not opposed to history, meaning, or style, as Subotnik proposes, but rather itself understood as immanently historically meaningful. In other words, I reject Subotnik's notion that one must choose between binary opposites, and propose instead mediation between the two. I realize this shift by considering structural elements as gestures, which do not *represent* meanings within abstracted two-dimensional spatial graphs, or communicate them through association or reasoning by analogy, but rather constitute part of the meaning of the original work as a performance event.[2] Eduard Hanslick (1982, 74) interpreted musical form in such visual terms in his discussion of music as arabesque—an analogy that enabled him to think of structure in other than abstracted architectural or mathematical, measuring terms. As a living line that weaved itself into a visual arabesque, structure was immanently visually expressive. My model of musical structure builds on this idea, yet departs from Hanslick through its use of the notion of gesture, which unlike the arabesque is associated with communication of meaning and the construction of subjectivity. I emphasize this aspect in my essay by linking structure to gesture through the actions of the human body.

I have chosen as the subject of my study one of the first twentieth-century ballets whose musical structure critics understood as immanently gestural, Stravinsky's *Le Sacre du printemps*.[3] The premiere of this modern-day *Gesamtkunstwerk* on 29 May 1913 offers a particularly fruitful point of departure for a study of musical structure as gesture, especially because of the role played therein by the choreography of Stravinsky's collaborator, Vaslav Nijinsky. Inspired by Jaques-Dalcroze's *plastique animée*, Nijinsky revolutionized dance by realizing every detail of Stravinsky's musical structure as a gesture or physical movement in space. Nevertheless, musicologists and theorists have continued to ignore his contribution to *Le Sacre,* largely because they consider his gestures to be ontologically distinct from Stravinsky's music, and therefore of secondary importance to any study of the latter. I overcome this distinction by considering *Le Sacre* not as a musical object, but rather as a historical event that took place within a performative context in which musical meaning was constituted in part through the visual impact of dance. Inviting the dancing body back into music allows me to broaden Subotnik's definition of vision, which she associates solely with reading the score. In contrast, "vision" in my text includes the experience of watching music realized spatially through dance, and of perceiving the meanings communicated by gesturing dancing bodies.[4]

I study *Le Sacre* from the perspective of musical gesture and dance not only as a means of overcoming Subotnik's dualistic approach, but also because I feel that the neglect of this aspect of the work has led to misinterpretations of its meaning. Operating within the same dualistic parameters as Subotnik, well-known interpreters of *Le Sacre* like Theodor Adorno, Pierre Boulez, Allen Forte, Pieter van den Toorn, and to a far lesser extent Richard Taruskin, have characteristically confined its musical meaning to the score, relegating the choreography and even staging to the realm of the "extra-musical." Their approaches, which Subotnik might call structural, become problematic only when they use their analytical insights about the music to attribute to *Le Sacre* moral qualities, values, or historical meanings. By critiquing them, I am not rejecting analysis of a certain structural kind, but rather simply suggesting that it may have limited value in speaking about historical performance events of music and dance, and that it thus may not be the best means to the end of conducting an ideological critique of music.

In the first part of my essay, I respond to Subotnik's call for a closer examination of the premises of structural listening by critiquing the two authors who have provided the best-known and most influential examples of ideological or philosophical critiques of *Le Sacre* based on musical analysis: Theodor Wiesengrund Adorno and Richard Taruskin. I question in particular how these authors define human subjectivity based on immanent musical form, and how they use their conclusions to determine the humane value of *Le Sacre*. In disputing their work, I support some of Subotnik's main arguments against structural listening, and provide them with differentiation and further support in the form of close readings of specific texts.

In the second part of my essay, I counter Adorno's and Taruskin's structuralist analyses of *Le Sacre* by offering an alternative reading that recognizes the importance of bodily gesture in danced works of music. I focus on the figure of the Chosen One, the young virgin whose sacrifice to the Sun God Yarilo is portrayed at the end of the work. Although both Adorno and Taruskin recognize the Chosen One's ability to choose as central to understanding the morality of *Le Sacre*, they examine neither the person who created her choreography (Nijinsky) nor the gestures of her "Danse sacrale." By interpreting this dance, I am able to argue that the Chosen One may not have been a passive victim who succumbed to her community without conflict, as Adorno and Taruskin claim, but rather a subject who experienced deep animosity toward her peers. Viewed in this manner, the "Danse sacrale" becomes less an essay in inhumane musical form than a physical expression of a critical spirit of opposition. Moral values cease to be fixed in structure, as Adorno and Taruskin want them to be, and become determined by historical context and the changing events of performance. I explain the sociological and cultural reasons for our long denial of the Chosen One's bodies, and give a plausible reason why I think her presence could enrich our understanding of Stravinsky's musical work.

THE CHOSEN ONE'S LACK OF CHOICE:
THEODOR ADORNO AND RICHARD TARUSKIN

Immanent Musical Analysis

Theodor Adorno and Richard Taruskin base their arguments about the humanity of *Le Sacre* and the role of the Chosen One on the fundamental premise that the cultural meaning of music is revealed in the musical material itself. In his *Philosophie der neuen Musik* of 1949, Adorno argued that musical material was in itself "sedimented spirit—something preformed that was social and had gone through people's consciousness."[5] As is well known, he placed the key to musical progress in the hands of the composer—the only subject who had resisted the standardizing impact of technological civilization and who could thus reflect the most contemporary states of consciousness in his compositional material.[6] Adorno's composer did not express ideas about society or his own subjectivity in his music, but rather forgot himself in the process of obeying the musical material's progress, thereby allowing subjectivity to regain a universality that went beyond himself.[7] The resulting artworks "record [ed] the history of mankind more accurately than documents [did]," and thus became "forms of knowledge" ("Gestalten der Erkenntnis"); the truth they contained was immanently historical, reflecting the most recent developments in human society (Adorno 1978, 47).

Much twentieth-century music criticism revolved around Adorno's choice of Schoenberg's atonal music as a positive model of how a critical and conscious music could reflect the objectified subject. Adorno praised Schoenberg for having rejected the lost collective subjectivity of tonality, and for having remained truthful to history and the historical subject by creating structures in which an autonomous or alienated subject took control of the musical material through thematic or motivic development, or "developing variation."[8] Such organic development of a central idea enabled the music to move forward in time, thus achieving transcendence.[9] Yet Schoenberg had also used dissonance and musical shocks that disrupted the necessary organic unity of the composition, thereby questioning the very possibility of a healthy oneness between the subject and society. The thus revealed alienation of modern society revealed the most recent stage of social and human development and constituted "the content of the art work itself" (Adorno 1978, 126).

By identifying objective human subjectivity with organic, motivic, teleological musical processes, Adorno abstracted it from the body, imbuing it instead with a deeply deceiving metaphorical corporeality. This practice allowed him to find objective subjectivity in absolute music, while denying its presence in danced works of music—a philosophical stance that had devastating consequences for his analysis of Stravinsky's *Le Sacre* and for the twentieth-century practice of ideologically critiquing music.

As is well known, Adorno countered the positive example of Schoenberg with the negative model of Stravinsky. As Schoenberg's dialectical opposite, Adorno's Stravinsky necessarily rejected organic musical development. In works like *Le Sacre*, he renounced any attempt to "redeem or fulfill that which had appeared in the immanent dynamic of the musical material as an expectation or demand" (Adorno 1978, 138, note), and reduced his melodies to "rudimentary successions of notes" or "cut off, primitivist patterns" that did not develop and thus lacked the unfolding of a subjective being (139 and note). Diatonic, folkloristic, and chromatic melodic particles bled together, as if they had been randomly inserted, creating a contradiction between the "restrained horizontal" and the "daring vertical" that resulted in chords becoming coloristic rather than constructive (140). In many spots, pedal points replaced "genuine" harmonic unfolding and harmonic development. Yet *Le Sacre* most egregiously rejected the subject by ignoring "the dialectical confrontation with the musical course of time . . . which has constituted the essence of all great music since Bach" (171).[10]

Adorno's perspective on musical subjectivity had little influence in North America until Subotnik's courageous critiques of the 1980s. They resurfaced indirectly in Richard Taruskin's work, however, especially as he attempted to reintegrate ideological critique into the traditional discourse of music theory throughout the 1990s.[11] Chastising North American theorists for blindly embracing music's aesthetic autonomy, Taruskin campaigned for new interpretive approaches that would take into account social, historical, and political context. By asserting that what he called Stravinsky's "fascism and anti-Semitism" were an immanent aspect of his musical compositions, he hoped to prove false the claim of his opponents that political attitudes and social circumstances existed parallel to, yet independent of, the music.[12] In so doing, he hoped to give *Le Sacre* back its history and to demand for it a moral reckoning.

Although Taruskin distanced himself from North American practices of music theory, his interpretation of *Le Sacre* remained firmly grounded in a "structural" theoretical approach. Frustrated by what he called the North American obsession with composers' lives, experiences, and intentions, and by the "poietic fallacy," the popular belief that the meaning of music was exhausted in the story of its making, Taruskin based his work on what he called "immanent criticism," the study of musical structures as embodiments of their maker's political and social allegiances.[13] Such analysis departed from the premise that the "artistic qualities of the music, however narrowly they may be defined or evaluated, are decisively—indeed *internally*—connected with its conceptual metaphors" (Taruskin 1997, 461). Taruskin's "immanent criticism" of the music revealed a surprising intellectual turn: in his attempt to escape theoretical abstraction, he returned to the conceptual practices of the father of immanent criticism, Theodor Adorno. Unlike North American music theorists, Adorno had never denied the moral and social value of art or the historicity of the musical material. And like Taruskin, he had attempted to prevent the return of fascist thought by exploring "the cultural roots of some of the most terrifying anti-cultural phenomena of our time" (Adorno 1986, 416), and by examining musical structure as a key to revealing false consciousness or ideology.[14] Perhaps for these reasons, Taruskin interpreted *Le Sacre* in a manner that echoed Adorno's conclusions in *Die Philosophie der neuen Musik*.[15] His writings displayed an affinity not only for Adorno's criteria of structural listening, but also for his moral and critical stance.

Taruskin's immanent criticism of *Le Sacre* is based on a notion of musical subjectivity that on the surface resembles that of Adorno. For example, Taruskin also thinks that such subjectivity is realized only as music organically develops through time. He comments that "ego identification with musical process" depends on "functionally directed harmony"; and that the "autonomy of 'das Individuum' " is mirrored and protected in the "structural complexity and profusion of highly differentiated detail" of "panromanogermanic" music with its tonal harmonic function (and its ability to represent desire, and hence subjectivity).[16] These premises lead Taruskin to conclude that the ego is transcended in works that meander around symmetrical chord structures, and dissolved in works like *Le Sacre* that show no continuous development.[17] Like Adorno, he believes that dynamic form is replaced in *Le Sacre* with "extension through repetition, alternation, and—above all—sheer inertial accumulation" (Taruskin 1996, 1:954). The "static, vamping harmonies," "ego-annihilating ostinatos," and "long stretches of arrested root motion and pulsing rhythm" indicate the "annihilation of the subject and the denial of psychology" (Taruskin 1995, 18–19). The work's "highly individualized static blocks in striking juxtapositions" (1996, 1:954) likewise create an infamous discontinuity that can be associated with "the absence of recall and forecast" or "the absence of memory" that characterizes the subhuman or animal kingdom" (1995, 18–20).

Adorno's and Taruskin's Chosen One

Both Adorno and Taruskin define musical subjectivity as constructed through developmental musical processes. Consequently, both can define Stravinsky's *Le Sacre* as lacking subjectivity, based on the analytical fact that its score contains no such processes. Significantly, however, they do not limit their analyses to the score alone. Rather, they strengthen their arguments about *Le Sacre*'s lack of subjectivity by appealing to the ballet's synopsis, and,

more specifically, to the story of the Chosen One. She remains the most disturbing figure for both of them, and so it is to her that I now turn.

The cultural image of the Chosen One as a helpless victim without individuality, corporeality, or choice is so persistent in the secondary literature,
that one is compelled to ask where it came from. The best source seems to
be Stravinsky himself, who described how he understood the Chosen One in
a revealing dream that he claimed inspired *Le Sacre* and that is quoted rev-
erently in all accounts of its history: "One day, when I was finishing the last
pages of *L'Oiseau de feu* in St. Petersburg, I had a fleeting vision which came
to me as a complete surprise, my mind at the moment being full of other
things. I saw in imagination a solemn pagan rite: sage elders, seated in a circle, watched a young girl dance herself to death. They were sacrificing her to
propitiate spring."[18] Stravinsky made sure everybody knew that the ballet was
about this sacrifice of a chosen victim by originally calling his work *Velikaya
zhertva* [The Great Victim].[19] His envisioned choreography suggested that
the Chosen One would not show any resistance to her fate: he planned "a
series of rhythmic mass movements of the greatest simplicity which would
have an instantaneous effect on the audience, with no superfluous details or
complications such as would suggest effort."[20]

Taruskin often lamented the fact that so many scholars gave Stravinsky's
comments ultimate authority in defining the meaning of his works. Given
Taruskin's worries, it is surprising that both he and Adorno chose to adopt
wholesale Stravinsky's vision of the Chosen One, without considering or
comparing it to Roerich's or Nijinsky's interpretations of that role. They both
defined the Chosen One, to a certain extent with Stravinsky, as lacking individual choice, dancing vacuously, and ready to sacrifice herself without the
slightest hint of conflict with her community.

Adorno understood the Chosen One's death, like Petruschka's, as an
"antihumanistic sacrifice to the collectivity: a sacrifice without tragedy,
offered not to the image that was gradually arising of mankind, but rather
the blind confirmation of a condition that was recognized by the sacrificed
one herself, whether through self-ridicule or through self-effacement"
(Adorno 1978, 135–36). Solely on the basis of the synopsis of the ballet,
Adorno assumed that the Chosen One agreed to the collective will imposed
on her without showing resistance, opposition, subjective will, or tragic
incongruity. He concluded that "there is no aesthetic antithesis between the
sacrificed one and her tribe, rather, her dance carries out the unopposed,
direct identification with the latter. The subject exposes as little conflict as
the musical structure delivers" (147). Even the musical shocks in *Le Sacre*,
which Adorno understood as essential to avant-garde music (because of the
way in which they made the individual aware of his "futility against the gigan-
tic machine of the whole system"; 144), have been reduced to mere effects,
and thus create no sense of antagonism or conflict: "In Stravinsky there is

neither a readiness for fear nor an opposing ego; rather, it is accepted that the shocks cannot be adopted by the musical subject, which gives up trying to maintain itself and thus remains content with participating in the thrusts (shocks) as reflexes" (145).

Adorno's interpretation of the Chosen One was shaped by his understanding of dance, which he defined as "the static art of time, of turning itself in circles, of movement without progress" (179). In his opinion, the music of *Le Sacre* allowed only purely physical, almost ecstatic movement, separated from emotional and intellectual thought:

> [The body] is treated by the music as a means, as a thing that reacts exactly to it; it obliges the body to perform at its maximum, as is drastically displayed on stage in the "Jeu de Rapt" and the "Jeux de Cités Rivales." The severity of *Le Sacre,* which makes itself as insensitive to any stirring of subjectivity as the ritual does to the pain of its initiates and sacrificial victims, is at the same time the supreme command that forbids the body from expressing pain by permanently threatening it, and which trains it to do the impossible as in the ballet, which is the most important traditional element of Stravinsky's work. Such severity and ritual driving out of the soul contributes to the impression that *Le Sacre* as a product has not been subjectively brought forth and is not reflective of human beings. Rather it exists as a thing in and of itself. (Adorno 1978, 159)

Adorno concluded that the subject had been alienated from bodily sensation in *Le Sacre,* resulting in a ballet that centered on a dancing body foreign to itself (161). Haunted by the fear of communal and round dancing that dominated in Germany in the post-Nazi years, Adorno condemned the Chosen One's dance as primitive, and based on a notion of collectivity that denied the individual subject:

> The Chosen One dances herself to death, in the same manner as anthropologists report that savages who have unknowingly broken a taboo actually die thereafter. Nothing of her as an individual being is reflected in her dance than the unconscious and coincidental reflex of pain: according to its inner organization, her solo dance is, like all others, a collective dance. It is a round dance void of any dialectic of the general and the particular. Authenticity is obtained through the denial of a subjective pole. This occupation of the collective standpoint in the manner of a surprise attack causes the following to occur: at the moment when an agreeable conformity to an individualistic society is dismissed, a conformity of a secondary and indeed highly disagreeable kind, namely with a blind integral society, the same as one of castrated or headless people, takes its place. (Adorno 1978, 147)

Stravinsky's music showed little concern either for its own fate or for that of the Chosen One: "The abomination is watched with some pleasure, and shown not in a transfigured, but rather unalleviated fashion" (136). The subject ceased to exist musically: "The choreographic idea of the sacrifice shapes the musical treatment of the subject itself. In the music, and not on the stage, everything is eradicated that distinguishes itself as individuated from the collective" (145). The composition of *Le Sacre* thus equals a "deletion of the self, unconscious skillfulness, fitting in to the blind totality" (156).[21] Dance "from the start forces the composition into a subservient position and into renouncing its autonomy," turning *Le Sacre* into a "parasite" (179).[22]

This is a remarkable conclusion from someone who had probably never seen Nijinsky's original choreography of *Le Sacre,* and gave no indication of having studied or seen any of the subsequent choreographies of the work either.[23] With striking confidence Adorno defined as objective truth the visual fantasy he had dreamed up.[24] Having never examined in any detail the dynamics of the dancing body, he was probably not entirely aware that he had reduced the Chosen One to a mechanized, abstract vision of human corporeality.[25] In his world, the body lacked the concrete presence of the musical score he so cherished; it was an abstract idea without physicality and subjectivity, whose movements necessarily remained meaningless.

Like Adorno before him, Taruskin defined *Le Sacre*'s politics on the basis of the fact that "the 'petty I' [was given up] in the interests of . . . the absorption of the individual consciousness in the collective" (Taruskin 1995, 17). His Chosen One became the individual (or non-individual) who had to subjugate herself to the masses or collective subjectivity *(das Volk)* for the fascist politics of *Le Sacre* to work. By adopting a subjectivity of the masses, or collective ego, she allowed herself to be controlled from the outside by a leader or *Führer,* who Taruskin hinted was Stravinsky or the conductor. Stravinsky just has to put pen to manuscript paper in order to transform sensible human beings into jerking, kicking automata.

Rather than explore the philosophical consequences of an imagined dancing Chosen One, as Adorno did, Taruskin supported his claims about her lack of choice by returning to immanent musical meaning. His study of the score led him to conclude that Stravinsky, and not some false collectivity, had killed the Chosen One. The "terrible dynamism" of his "crashing orchestra" in the "Danse sacrale" embodied the "opaque, constraining" force of society, which inhumanely killed her, and coerced the audience into sharing its point of view (Taruskin 1995, 20). Stravinsky had organized his "cells" or "motivic tesserae" in her dance to heighten the antihuman effect of "hypostatization—[or] extreme fixity of musical 'objects'," that represented the Chosen One's lack of subjectivity (Taruskin 1996, 1:962–64). By including a facsimile sketch for the music of this scene, he offered visual proof for the authority of his interpretation. The reproduction emphasized the physical presence and thus historical truth of the document. Taruskin invited the reader to notice the age of the paper, the personal feel of the writing, and the impatience of Stravinsky's scrawl, which could easily convince him or her that the Chosen One's death had resulted from an arbitrary and somehow viciously unsympathetic compositional game on Stravinsky's part.

Although dance is hardly central to Taruskin's analysis, he does refer to it when arguing about the Chosen One's lack of choice and conflict. Instead of analyzing existing choreographies of the work, however, he followed Adorno in describing the Chosen One as dancing an ecstatic "whirling dance" (Taruskin 1996, 1:886–87), inspired by a music that elicits "a primitive, kinesthetic response."[26] He supported his argument by referring to anthropological research on the whirling dances in Slavic ritual, which interested Roerich and Stravinsky, and which he could associate with *Le Sacre*, in spite of the fact that it was not danced that way.[27] Taruskin found the ritualistic dance he uncovered foreign to his sensibilities, and viewed its emotional ecstasy, primitivism, and lack of rationality with suspicion.[28] He lamented that the choreography envisioned for the Chosen One was "devoid of plot in the conventional sense," and that it *was* a ritual with primitive immediacy, rather than a represented narrative (1996, 1:865). In Adorno's spirit he concluded that "the maiden herself does not perform a culminating dance [at all]; rather, one is done around her—in the presence of the Elders, as all versions of the *Rite* scenario specify" (1996, 1:886).

The image of a spinning female body was useful to Adorno and Taruskin, because it allowed them to understand the Chosen One as lacking subjective choice and corporeality. Their vision, so contrary to most actual danced versions of *Le Sacre*, says much more about them than about her. Like many others before and after them, they have donned the bearskins and joined the elders, to sit in the circle with Stravinsky and watch the Chosen One dance herself to death. Using the authority of structural listening and the brilliant wit of their lucid pens, they erase the Chosen One's individuality from the *Le Sacre* with dashing final strokes. She is not a subject, but rather a twirling image, a silent victim, an empty canvas, a wispy curl of smoke, a spinning arabesque, thin air.

In spite of their shared ideas about spinning female bodies, Adorno and Taruskin came to different conclusions about Stravinsky's *Le Sacre*. Adorno accused Stravinsky of having tried to achieve an authenticity that was no longer possible in his time. He glorified the negation of the individual subject, thereby neglecting the critical role of art and betraying his mission as an avant-garde artist. His regressive music entertained, lulled, and mollified its audiences, preventing them from developing their critical potential. Yet what was most pitiful was that Stravinsky had pretended that this "retrogression of musical language and of the state of consciousness appropriate to it was *up to date*" (Adorno 1978, 137).

In contrast to Adorno, Taruskin is neither a Marxist nor a historical materialist, and has no allegiance to either the Hegelian objective spirit or *Geschichtsphilosophie*. Instead of backing up his claims about *Le Sacre* with a

theory of musical material as Adorno does, he turned for evidence to Stravinsky's sketchbooks and to comments from established composers like Elliot
Carter—a methodology that revealed his indebtedness not to European critical thought, but rather to North American music theory. He likewise linked
stylistic features in Stravinsky's music to social and political meanings not
through a Marxist theory of musical material, but rather by associating them
with the cultural and philosophical concepts surrounding them, that is, with
the words written about them. Thus *Le Sacre* became for Taruskin a deliberate exercise in what Alexander Blok described around the turn of the century
as *stikhiya,* or "primitive immediacy" as opposed to the *kul'tura* associated
with European intellectuals.[29] Taruskin's reader is led to believe that Stravinsky consciously promoted features of Russian neo-nationalist art as they were
discussed by Blok and others. In that Blok's theories were associated in his
time with neo-nationalist politics in Russia, and in that the opposition
between *kul'tura* and *stikhiya* resembles the German debates on *Kultur* and
Zivilisation that preceded the rise of fascism, Taruskin could assume that the
"primitive immediacy" of *Le Sacre* was proto-fascist. He argued that Stravinsky was not the victim of false consciousness, but rather an artist who believed
in antihumanism and fascism, and expressed it through his art, afterwards
hiding what he had done. By allowing his knowledge of political systems to
determine how he analyzed Stravinsky's work, Taruskin went against
Adorno's philosophical principles. His critique of "structural listening" from
the viewpoint of a structural listener shifted attention from scores to cultural
context, yet retained a structural interpretation of the Chosen One.

THE CHOSEN ONE'S CHOICE
Le Sacre as Art plastique

Adorno and Taruskin situate social meaning, subjectivity, and bodily movement within the music itself. Their fictional Chosen One is thereby arbitrarily detached from her body and denied her place in an extremely illustrious,
long tradition of dance that includes the most significant dancers and choreographers of this century, from Nijinsky through Massine and Pina Bausch
to Martha Graham.[30] All these leading dancers were attracted to the role of
the Chosen One, whom they treated as a vehicle for their most intense personal expressions. They did not think she was a spinning rag doll, and they
rarely interpreted her as having no choice. Their powerful dancing bodies
gave her an individuality Stravinsky could deny her. The Chosen One's
potential for choice was nowhere more evident than in the choreography of
the man who invented her and gave her physical life, and who participated
with Stravinsky in establishing her individuality during the very genesis of the
work: Vaslav Nijinsky.

The tradition of excluding Nijinsky from histories of *Le Sacre* goes back over seventy years and may have begun with Stravinsky himself. Although the composer at first admired Nijinsky's choreography,[31] by 1921 he had rejected it as too bound to the "tyranny of the barline."[32] Stravinsky's reasons for condemning Nijinsky may have been partly financial (in that he may have been trying to get Nijinsky's share of one-quarter of *Le Sacre*'s royalties), and partly aesthetic (in that by 1921 he had adopted what was to become his neoclassical aesthetic). Whatever the case, the damage he did to Nijinsky, and the degree to which he distorted the original *Sacre,* was considerable. This legacy of violent refusal is still felt in Pieter van den Toorn's *Stravinsky and "The Rite of Spring": The Beginnings of a Musical Language* (1987). Van den Toorn investigates the origins of *Le Sacre* in dance in the introduction to his book. But rather than enrich his analysis with the information he finds, he proceeds to reject the very interpretive path he has dared to open up: "the scenario itself, the choreography, and, above all, the close 'interdisciplinary' conditions of coordination under which the music is now known to have been composed—these are matters which, after the 1913 premiere, quickly passed from consciousness," van den Toorn writes, "like pieces of scaffolding, they were abandoned in favor of the edifice itself and relegated to the 'extra-musical.' They became history, as opposed to living art" (van den Toorn 1987, 2). He implies through his use of passive voice that unseen and unknown forces rather than developments in contemporary music, philosophy, and the discipline of music theory stripped *Le Sacre* of its history. He feels confident in reducing *Le Sacre* to "the music itself" because he had the support of Stravinsky himself, whose process of rejecting *Le Sacre*'s original staging and choreography he describes in careful historical detail. His well-researched and informative history of the reception of the *Le Sacre* leads him to the disturbing conclusion that the new sources linking the work to its original choreography were "enlightening as commentary, [but] in no way undermine the integrity of *The Rite* as 'musical construction'" (21). Stravinsky may have remembered the original choreography fondly in his late years and desired a revival, but van den Toorn considers this a slip in judgment (16–17).[33]

There are several reasons why van den Toorn and many others have rejected Nijinsky's contribution to *Le Sacre.* First of all he was a dancer, and thus the creator of an ephemeral art that could not be captured in rational analysis or linked ontologically to music. Second, he was also mentally ill, suffering from what Peter Ostwald later clinically categorized as both manic-depressive psychosis and schizoaffective disorder in a narcissistic personality, which caused him to be hospitalized in 1919 (Ostwald 1991, 349–50). This illness, from which he never recovered and which kept him in and out of institutions until his death in 1950, lead many commentators from the 1920s on to assume tacitly that he had always been "crazy" and that his choreographic work was thus somehow invalid.[34] Finally, Nijinsky was a bisexual whose sexuality frightened and confused many people, during his time and long afterwards. One need only read Acocella, Garafola, and Greene's vivid description of who caused the sexual violence in *Le Sacre:*

> Female sacrifice is an obsession of 19th century . . . But this is sacrifice with a difference. Here there is no pretext: no poisoned scarf, no madness. The girl is forthrightly sent to her death in order to benefit the community. The situation could hardly be more horrible. . . . In addition to sacrifice, there is scandal. Nijinsky's life was dogged not just by sorrow, but by scandal, and particularly sexual scandal . . . [and by] the extraordinary role played by libido and aggression. . . . There is also the sexual obsession that marked his unfinished ballets, and that filled his diary, in the period immediately preceding his institutionalization. . . . *[Le Sacre]* is not just a biological ballet, but a ballet about sex, and the violence with which that force can erupt into life, just as Nijinsky's audience erupted at the premiere. (Acocella, Garafola, and Greene 1992, 69–70)

This description remarkably avoids the question of power in the ballet by defining its rape in abstract terms (violence simply erupts all on its own). The narrative implicates Nijinsky as the perpetrator, his lifestyle having made him the most likely suspect. Acocella, Garafola, and Greene, however, find the person who created the first Chosen One, and who can thus most feasibly be associated with her victimization, guilty of the crime perpetrated against her. Such a quotation is not characteristic of Acocella's and Garafola's extraordinary work on the Ballets russes.

Stravinsky's self-propaganda and the widespread fear of Nijinsky's mental illness and bisexuality should not allow us to forget that Stravinsky, Roerich, and Nijinsky originally collaborated on *Le Sacre,* and that they intended its meaning to be communicated simultaneously through dance, the staging, music, and costumes.[35] Even Stravinsky admitted that visual images of moving bodies had inspired the music of *Le Sacre.* Early on in the collaborative process, he confided to Roerich, for example, that "the picture of the old woman in a squirrel fur sticks in my mind. She is constantly before my eyes as I compose the 'Divination with Twigs': I see her running in front of the group, stopping them sometimes, and interrupting the rhythmic flow. I am convinced that the action must be danced and not pantomimed."[36] At the time Stravinsky conceived of *Le Sacre* in terms of what critics were calling "art plastique"—or music realized visually in space through dance. The dancer expressed meaning through movement itself, rather than by miming recognizable narratives. Therefore, the music had to embody bodily movement that could express the message of the ballet directly to listeners. In *Le Sacre,* Stravinsky felt, for example, "that I have penetrated the secret of the rhythm of Spring and that musicians will feel it."[37]

The notion of an "art plastique" that would combine drama, music, and dance into a new form of artistic communication was very much on the minds of French critics at the time of *Le Sacre*'s premiere, and found its intellectual and visual formulation six months later in a special issue of the journal *Montjoie*.[38] Ricciotto Canudo, Auguste Rodin, André Biguet, and others described a new type of dance that they associated with the Futurist dancer Valentine de Saint-Point, and with a composer who wrote for her, Erik Satie.[39] "Metachorie" (as Saint-Point called her invention) originated in the spirituality of ancient myth and yet was realized in the modern forms of geometry.[40] It required "equivocal bodies," which had neither the female nor male attributes, and which acted in space according to "the relation of body mass."[41] Although Isadora Duncan had initiated this dance revolution by recreating "plastic Greek myths," she had made the drastic mistake of trying to dance to sentimental and expressive nineteenth-century music. In contrast, the promoters of "metachorie" envisioned a music that would itself embody the idea of the dance, and found such an art form first realized in *Le Sacre:*

> Expressive music needs conventional, banal, and even anti-artistic mime. Dance does not succeed in translating artistic emotions with facial expressions. What is really deep is the spirit, the gesture, the line that unrolls simultaneously in depth and breadth. It is the dynamism of the two dimensions that creates the marvelous beauty of dance and that nostalgically haunts the minds of painters. Choreographic music must also develop in spatial depth. It must be constructed architecturally and rhythmically, in broad values and plans, like the groups of Rodin, in order to mix with the geometric schemes of the choreography and to penetrate it. This music was born with *Le Sacre du Printemps*. Before that, there was dramatic music, descriptive music, and even so-called pure music: since then there is choreographic music, fashioned in a certain sense plastically according to the rhythm of the idea, in order to form with the dance a new synthetic communion . . . For this to happen the essential idea must encrust itself simultaneously in the being of the musician as musical rhythms, and in the being of the choreographer as plastic rhythms. There has to be an absolutely intimate penetration. (Chennevière 1914)

Although the contributors to the journal did not seem to think that Nijinsky had been as successful as Saint-Point at realizing such music in dance, they comment frequently on the importance of his choreography as "art plastique." The editor of *Montjoie*, Ricciardo Canudo, accompanied the reprint of his manifesto on "art cérébriste," as well as other articles in the issue, with Valentine Gross-Hugo's illustrations of the choreography of *Le Sacre*. In their minds, Stravinsky's *Sacre* was inextricably intertwined with Nijinsky's choreography as *plastique animée*.[42]

By January 1914, Stravinsky no longer agreed with the authors writing for *Montjoie*. In 1912, however, he had been delighted to work with Nijinsky, to whom he referred as "the ideal *plastique* collaborator."[43] From March to

November 1912 they had met on more than five occasions (including a trip to Venice), to work on *Le Sacre.*[44] For a short time, their opinions on how dance should express meaning corresponded.

Nijinsky's Tragic Expression

In contrast to Adorno and other structural listeners, Nijinsky did not find meaning in the language of musical structure, but rather in direct bodily expressions. Throughout his life, "it had always been primarily by moving his body or holding it still, by gesturing and posturing, by expressing himself nonverbally, that he had been able to show what it meant to 'be in the world' " (Ostwald 1991, 223). In the diary he wrote on the verge of his mental breakdown, Nijinsky circled obsessively around this topic: "I think little and therefore understand everything I feel. I am feeling in the flesh and not intellect in the flesh. I am the flesh. I am feeling. I am God in the flesh and in feeling. I am man and not God. I am simple. People must not think me. They must feel me and understand me through feeling."[45] In *Le Sacre,* Nijinsky wanted to create a "visceral understanding" of the story of the ballet through metakinetic choreography (Hargrave 1985, 92). In simpler terms, he spoke of the audience understanding the work in their gut; his *Sacre* would be "a jolting impression and emotional experience."[46]

Nijinsky's belief in the communicative potential of bodily movement led him to depart from the norms of classical ballet, in which, traditionally, a narrative had been mimed. Now, movement told its own story, with the result that the ballet lost its basis in narrative and focus on a main protagonist or hero. *Le Sacre* abandoned the very notion of dance as mimesis. For this reason, many reviewers defined it as abstract. Jean Marnold commented, for example, that, " dance here is the action itself, stylized in its rhythm in order to express the action of the legend, which is human and quasi-liturgical at the same time. This dance replaces the *ronds de bras* and the *chasses-croisés des quadrilles* with gestures and a figuration that are expressly symbolic, realizing a stylization in the manner of Gauguin."[47] Jacques Rivières believed Nijinsky's greatest achievement was in the "doing away with dynamic artificiality, in the return to the body, in the effort to adhere more closely to its natural movements, in lending an ear only to its most immediate, most radical, most etymological expressions."[48] By breaking up movement and bringing it back to the simple gesture, Nijinsky allowed it to become more expressive. "One doesn't explain *Le Sacre,*" Émile Vieillermoz concluded, "one submits to it with horror or pleasure according to one's temperament."[49]

The theory of bodily expressivity developed by Nijinsky for *Le Sacre* was strongly inspired by his visit to Jaques-Dalcroze's school of eurythmics in Hellerau, Germany in 1912.[50] During that visit, Diaghilev, Nijinsky, and his sister Nijinska had watched a group of girls walk in 2/4, gesticulating with one arm in 3/4 and the other in 4/4. Diaghilev had been so inspired that he had hired Jaques-Dalcroze's student Marie Rambert to supervise the rehearsals of *Le Sacre* in Monte Carlo in winter 1913.[51] According to Nijinska, Nijinsky himself performed such rhythmic counterpoints with ease. She reported that he was so precise in translating rhythm into movement that he could perform a 5/4 bar in midair. He first leapt into the air. "On beat 1 he bent one leg at the knee and stretched his right arm above his head, on count 2 he bent his body towards the left, on count 3 he bent his body towards the right, then on count 1, still high in the air, he stretched his body upwards again and then finally came down lowering his arm on count 2, graphically rendering each note of the uneven measure."[52] Nijinsky understood such an approach to dance, in the spirit of Jaques-Dalcroze's followers, as "plastique animée," and as a means of linking movement to feeling and training the spirit through the body.[53] He drew on these lessons when designing the "Danse sacrale," in which he gave the Chosen One an individual movement for every event in Stravinsky's music, translating it note for note into dance. The "Danse sacrale" thus offers the rare example of a choreography in which musical cells or motives are directly, literally associated with the specific gestures of a dancing body. By using Dalcroze's approach (which also appealed to Stravinsky) Nijinsky gave each of the Chosen One's gestures expressive power and symbolic significance.[54] Together, these gestures constituted her identity as she danced through time. Through such detailed movement she expressed her opposition to the people who had chosen her to die. Her movements were immediate, yet not primitively void of subjective will and choice, as Adorno and Taruskin imagined.

How does one begin to recover the lost movements Nijinsky felt communicated so much about how he understood *Le Sacre* and the choices of its Chosen One? Perhaps the answer lies in the very real, twisting, tense, springing, angry body of Nijinsky, as it moved in a humid practice room in Vienna or London in winter 1913. Nijinsky, intense and concentrated, is teaching his sister Nijinska the movements of the Chosen One's "Danse sacrale." Frustrated, he asks the rehearsal pianist, Steiman, to play over and over again individual passages of the handwritten score that Stravinsky had sent him.[55] Mesmerized by the tragedy of Nijinsky's movements as he performs the dance for her, Nijinska tries to visualize the dark clouds gathering in Roerich's painting *The Call of the Sun,* and to imagine what he has described to her as the "awakening of the spirit of primeval man" (Nijinska 1992, 449–50). The room is filled with physical tension and conflict—the tightening of muscles that we will have to learn to remember if we are going to do justice to the Chosen One.

What was Nijinsky expressing through the movements he created in that forgotten practice room over eighty years ago? The dominant emotion, from all accounts, seems to have been exactly what Adorno and Taruskin find missing in *Le Sacre:* fear and a deep antagonism between the Chosen One and her surroundings.[56] Nijinsky experienced Stravinsky's music in Taruskin's spirit as "some kind of monster, breathing evenly as it got nearer and nearer, a monster with many hands, many legs, many eyes" (Krasovskaya 1979, 234). He wanted the Chosen One to react to this horror with terror and outrage— over her tragic fate and her helplessness in face of it. She would express her anger through body tension, which Nijinsky created by choosing positions and movements that contained the energy of the moving body, such as turning the feet inwards or holding the elbows close to the torso.[57] No matter how jagged and distorted Nijinsky's movements became, he would never lose the sense of rooting them in his "extraordinarily profound sense of his own center," creating a tornado of contained energy.[58] This movement would not be casual or light, but rather "conscious right down to its last detail" (Krasovskaya 1979, 244). In order to communicate to his sister how to express the emotion he associated with such an intense exaggeration of body tension, he told her that her body had to "draw into itself . . . and absorb the fury of the hurricane" (Garafola 1989, 71; Nijinska 1992, 470). His performance of the Chosen One's dance expressed this tragic confrontation with fate: "With clenched fist across his face, he threw himself into the air in paroxysms of fear and grief. His movements were stylized and controlled, yet he gave out a tremendous power of tragedy."[59]

Nijinsky expressed the Chosen One's painful confrontation with her community in *Le Sacre* by creating physical tension within her very body. This choreographic practice contrasted starkly with "academic ballet [that] emphasized effortless surface tension to obliterate any hint of energy expended" (Kirstein 1976, 145). Through her knotted, tense body, the Chosen One expressed all the conflict missing in Adorno and Taruskin—a confrontation between her own subjective will and the crushing threat of her community and her fate.

One can speculate widely on the sources of Nijinsky's angry passion for the Chosen One. If Lynn Garafola is correct in arguing that she is a "creation of twentieth-century male sexual anxiety," and that she "takes the place of the feminized artist," than it would not be entirely misguided to interpret her as representing Nijinsky himself, in which case his investment in her would be self-explanatory.[60] By the time of *Le Sacre,* audiences in France had marked Nijinsky as a feminized artist or androgynous, exotic, foreign and mysterious Other—an image Diaghilev had promoted, perhaps at Nijinsky's expense, by casting him in roles such as the Golden Slave in *Schéhérezade* or in the *Spectre de la rose.* With Nijinsky, ballet had also become overnight a "privileged arena for homosexuals as performers, choreographers, and spectators"—a gay revolution that forced the women who had traditionally dominated the ballet into the back seat.[61] Nijinsky later struggled with this sexuality, especially in his diary of 1919. It is possible that the community's threat in *Le Sacre* reminded him of the hostility toward his sexuality that he experienced in his own life and subsequently internalized. He also created *Le Sacre* in a hostile atmosphere, albeit of a very different kind, in which most of the dancers rejected what he was doing (Nijinska 1992, 462). By not dancing the role himself, but rather forcing his sister and then, when she got pregnant, Maria Piltz, to dance it exactly as he wished, Nijinsky may have been experimenting with expressing his own desires through a female body.[62] This may explain why he was so passionate about the role, and why he did not want the Chosen One to submit to the violence perpetrated on her. He expressed his feeling of victimization by depicting the Chosen One in one of the episodes of her dance as a maimed bird, as Nijinska remembered:

> Suddenly, spontaneously, Nijinsky jumped. It was an awkward jump, as if he were a wounded bird, one leg folded beneath him. He raised a clenched fist to the sky and held the other to his body. Then he squatted down, touched the ground with one hand, and began to stamp, beating his hands against his bent knees. Now he resembled a bird busily building its nest. Still in his squatting position, he took long paces off to the side and then covered his head with his arm. As if in a low arabesque, he stretched out his leg, stuck out his arms and banged them against the floor—as if they were wings.[63]

In his diary, Nijinsky links this bird symbolization to Diaghilev and himself:

> Diaghilev is a terrible man. I do not like terrible men. I will not harm them. I do not want them to be killed. They are eagles. They prevent small birds from living, and therefore one must guard against them. . . . Eagles must not prevent small birds from carrying on with their lives, and therefore they must be given things to eat that will destroy their predatory intentions.[64]

Nijinsky felt intensely angry and increasingly violent during rehearsals for *Le Sacre*. Perhaps this rage inspired him to give the Chosen One a subjectivity and presence that distinguished her from traditional prima ballerinas. In contrast to the latter, the Chosen One did not float gracefully about the ground in beautiful revealing attire, but rather moved in a fashion that accentuated her ugliness, lack of grace, and attachment to the earth. Even her leaps upward were drawn downwards and reflected the pull of gravity. Nijinsky used this emphasis on weight and falling to make audiences aware of the Chosen One's corporeal presence as an expression of her subjective individuality.[65] Such a heavy, ugly being was not easily forgotten, construed as fiction, or confused with anyone else in the ballet.[66] Her tense and unfamiliar movements constituted a "crime against [the] grace" that had traditionally transformed dancing ballerinas from individual bodies into stereotypical representations of abstract fantasy. Here was a female haunted by the male body of its creator, Nijinsky (Garafola 1999, 255).

The Gestures of the "Danse sacrale"

The Chosen One's conflict is vividly expressed in the gestures of her "Danse sacrale." In this section I compare Pierre Boulez's, Allen Forte's, and Pieter van den Toorn's analyses with an interpretation based on gesture, in order to demonstrate how theoretical means of representing musical structure have distorted and misconstrued the spatial dimensions of danced music, leading interpreters like Adorno and Taruskin to false conclusions about the work's humanity.

Pierre Boulez wrote his influential analysis of Stravinsky's "Danse sacrale" just as he was rejecting the teachings of his mentor René Leibowitz, the music of Schoenberg, and Adorno's interpretation of the second Viennese School. By explaining Stravinsky's compositional strategy of creating musical form out of small, malleable, primarily rhythmic cells, Boulez hoped not only to prove the progressiveness of Stravinsky's compositional approach, but also to justify his own desire to organize rhythm independently of pitch and dynamics in his totally serial compositions (Boulez 1966, 75–146).[67] In contrast to Adorno, who understood *Le Sacre* as a ballet, and who based his analysis to a large extent on the brief synopsis of the story that accompanied that ballet's original performance, Boulez understood the piece as a score, as orchestral music, and nothing more.[68] His approach had its advantages in that, unlike Adorno, he provided exact detail about the score before him.

Boulez's discussion of the Chosen One's "Danse sacrale" omits her entirely. He erases any memory of her bodily imprint on the music by reducing the latter to neatly laid out, largely symmetrical, two-dimensional graphs and musical examples excerpted from their original context.[69] His desire to negate the choreographic foundation of the piece is reflected in his definition of the "Danse sacrale" as a rondo (with two refrains, two couplets, and a coda on the refrain; Boulez 1966, 126). He is most interested, however, in the relationship between the three musical cells that make up the basic material of the refrain (see ex. 3.1).

Boulez labels these three cells A, B, and C. A is the equivalent of measure 2, while B represents measures 3 and 4 of the 1929 score. C appears in measure 9, or at rehearsal no. 144, and is defined by Boulez as a means of "balancing" A and B in an overall scheme in which all three cells (A, B, and C) fit neatly into a fixed phrase structure (Boulez 1966, 127–28). He does not define these cells according to measure or meter, however, but rather by the number of beats they include, using the basic beat of a sixteenth note. He describes how Stravinsky manipulates the lengths of these basic cells, creating a rhythmic structure that is not necessarily evident to the ear. Measures 1–8 become in his chart a symmetrical structure, in which A_3 first precedes and then follows A_5 and B_7. Cell C is inserted at the start of the second period, which runs until rehearsal no. 146. In this period the A_5 cell of A_5 and B_7 is

Example 3.1   Pierre Boulez, graph of the opening of the "Danse sacrale" (Boulez 1966, 128). © From *Relevés d'apprenti*, Éditions du Seuil.

Exemple XVII.

$$I \begin{cases} 1. - \underbrace{A_3 \ A_5 \ B_7}, \ \underbrace{A_5 \ B_7 \ A_3}, \ \text{ce qui donne:} \\ \qquad \Gamma_{15} \quad \Gamma'_{15} \\ 2. - C_8, \underbrace{A_4 B_7}, C_5, \underbrace{A'_5 \ A_4 \ B_7 \ A_3} : C_8 \ \Gamma_{11} \ C_5 \ \Gamma'_{19} \end{cases}$$

$$II \quad . - \underbrace{A_5 \ B_4}, \underbrace{A_2 \ B_4}, \ \underbrace{A_3 \ A_5 \ B_4}, C_5, C_7 : \\ \qquad \Gamma_9 \ \Gamma_6 \ \Gamma_{12} \ C_5 \ C_7$$

contracted to A_4 (four beats), while cell B_7 remains the same. C_5 and A_5 are inserted before the repeat of A_4 and B_7, giving a clear example of Stravinsky's additive practice. The third period again involves the manipulation of all three cells.

When the refrain returns after the first "couplet," it does not use cell C at all. In the coda on the refrain that appears at rehearsal no. 187, however, C is used extensively and even exclusively from rehearsal no. 196 forward. Boulez makes one nod to the choreography, by noting that the coda ends with "an obvious movement dialectically tied to an implied immobility."[70] Otherwise, his approach flattens and detemporalizes the piece in a visual representation that emphasizes subtraction and addition rather than the continuous flow of time and movement. His geometrical representation suppresses the bodily action that could disrupt the static architectural construction of the piece.[71] His repeated rhythmic units cannot suggest forward dynamic movement, and seem alienated from any sense of a bodily rhythm. The analytical methodology, for all that it purports to focus on the rhythmic dimension, actually abstracts this rhythm from the danced bodily continuity that gave the piece its rhythmic life.

Boulez's legacy left its mark on Allen Forte's *The Harmonic Organization of "The Rite of Spring"* (1978). Whereas Boulez concentrated on rhythm, Forte focuses exclusively harmony, with the now familiar aim of securing Stravinsky a place in the musical canon next to Schoenberg by proving his newness (Forte 1978, 19). His lack of interest in the historical, social, and cultural context of *Le Sacre* is reflected in his inability to create a narrative for his book. He replaces the richness of literary prose with a list-like description of the pitch-class sets used throughout the piece, which drains the piece of all its rhythmic vitality. The Chosen One is no longer mentioned, her fate deemed as secondary as the timbres, rhythms, musical gestures, and melodies that surround her. His sanitized structural approach retains at least one historical trace, however, that of Stravinsky's sketches, which help Forte to prove that Stravinsky intended to use the pitch-class sets found in the score.[72]

In *Stravinsky and "The Rite of Spring": The Beginnings of a Musical Language*, Pieter van den Toorn, like Forte, brackets out in his interpretation of the "Danse sacrale" all "extra-musical" elements except the sketchbook, which he also accepts as part of the musical score.[73] He divides his analysis between different chapters of his book, on issues ranging from re-barring Stravinsky's music and rhythmic structure to and pitch structure. In this manner, the reader loses all sense of the dance as a unified piece; the Chosen One likewise disappears behind an analysis that emphasizes systematic regularity. Van den Toorn criticizes Boulez for having "taken the irregular or shifting meters [in *Le Sacre*] at face value" and for having ignored "the role of steady metric periodicity" (van den Toorn 1987, 67). He argues that "if the shifting accents or stresses are to have meaning, then this can come only to the extent that the resultant patterns are tied to regularity . . . [or] hidden implications of steady periodicity" (71). In his graph (which strongly resembles Boulez's in configuration, even in his choice of the 1929 score), van den Toorn cleverly demonstrates that Boulez's A and B cells be better understood if placed within the feasible context of a fixed meter of 2/8, which makes the shifting accents evident (see ex. 3.2).

Van den Toorn notes that such a graph can not explain "the impact of the disruption" in the passage. This does not prevent him, however, from letting it stand as it is, in spite of the fact that it omits important sections of the music (96). Note, in particular, how he omits Boulez's A_3 cell at the end of the second system, for example, and how he jumps to the repetition of the combination of A_4 and B_7, omitting everything that happens between. Visually, he presents his analysis in a static chart, resembling a carefully stacked tower of building blocks, whose vertical alignment is indicated with neat dotted lines. In a separate chapter of his book, he gives further background unity to Boulez's cells (which he calls blocks) in terms of their pitch-class set and octatonic content. Cell C becomes neutralized as the "continuation of the [pitch] collectional implications of cell A" (203).

The neutralized graphs and lists of Boulez's, Forte's, and van den Toorn's analyses contrast sharply with the dynamic, conflicted images of the "Danse sacrale" as live dance. The antagonism between the Chosen One and her community there becomes immediately evident, even in the dance movements used for the first seventeen bars of the "Danse sacrale."[74] Nijinsky's choreography for this section begins with the Chosen One standing in place: "her folded hand under her right cheek, her feet turned in" (Rambert 1972, 64). She has been standing this way for a very long time, and Stravinsky indicates in his four-hand piano score that she will remain fixed to this spot for another while.[75] Her excruciating period of immobility is important to the psychology of the work, because it provides a stark contrast to the dynamism of the dance solo that follows.[76] The Chosen One's potential victimization is emphasized by the circle of dancers around her, which reflect the circles of Roerich's geometrically ornamented costume designs.[77] This human circle blocks the Chosen One from the audience's view. Nijinsky understood such a circle as the "center which generated feeling," and dramatically built tension to a point of release. By positioning the body within such a closed geometric space, Nijinsky perfected his idea of containing bodily tension.[78]

The ancestors in bearskins encircle the Chosen One in a hostile fashion that hardly indicates the expression of an undifferentiated community. Stravinsky also gives no indication that these ancestors have made the Chosen One feel at one with them. He initially labeled the section preceding this one "Wild Dance—Amazons" *[Dikaya Plyaska (Amazoni)]* and emphasized that the women surrounding the Chosen One at that point should dance a

Example 3.2   Pieter van den Toorn, example from the opening of the "Danse sacrale" (van den Toorn 1987, 95).

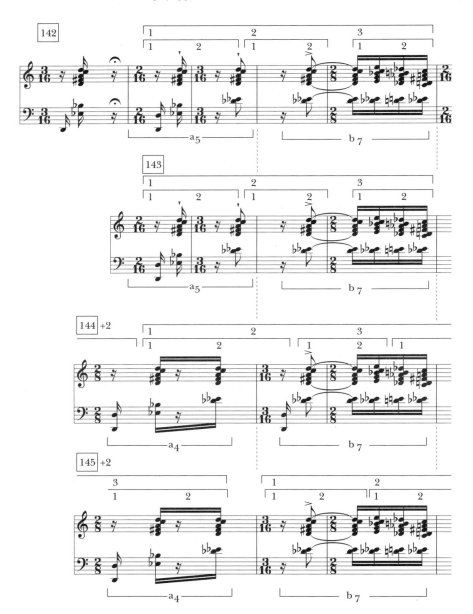

"wild martial" dance.[79] She was not glorified, but rather ostracized, cruelly chosen for her sacrifice because of the simple fact that she trips just before rehearsal no. 101. Marie Rambert indicated the violent reaction of the women around her: they stomp their feet at rehearsal no. 103, and rush at the Chosen One with fists "as though they want to hack her" at rehearsal no. 107.[80]

The community's hateful response in Nijinsky's choreography is more clearly put in perspective if compared with Mary Wigman's feminist production of *Le Sacre* in 1957. Wigman choreographed the very same music and yet allowed the Chosen One to be part of a caring and respectful community led by a group of older priestesses. At the moment when she would have tripped in Nijinsky's choreography, Wigman's Chosen One is just about to meet a young man—an event that will emphasize her humanity. She is thwarted in this attempt by the three older priestesses, who know she must be saved for the sacrifice. When Nijinsky's amazons would have stomped in anger, Wigman allows men to come on stage with rope, in order to tie the Chosen One as the maidens around her sway in devotion. Finally, at rehearsal no. 107, where Nijinsky's women rush at the Chosen One with their fists, Wigman allows them to sway and vibrate while she prepares to receive her crown—surrounded by the three old priestesses who accompany and guide her to her death.[81] The Chosen One's ritual sacrifice in Wigman's *Le Sacre* takes place within a (albeit ideologically problematic) community with venerated traditions and a sense of its own future. In Nijinsky's choreography, on the other hand, it is an act of sheer terror and panic.

Suddenly, at rehearsal no. 142, Nijinsky's Chosen One leaps vigorously into the air, timing her movements to occur on each off-beat sixteenth-note chord of cell A. The light attack Stravinsky required on these offbeat chords facilitates her leap toward the sky, as an expression of her desire to live and to escape her fate and the clutches of the ancestors who surround her. Stravinsky further underscored her physical move away from the earth by having these chords played pizzicato.[82] This movement is in extreme contrast to the rest of the ballet, which has been primarily about the body's attachment to the earth. The astonishing optical allusion of these leaps is that they are not actually at regular intervals, as they at first seem to be. Rather, the Chosen One respects the addition of the sixteenth-note to the sixteenth-note off-beat chord in measure 3, and thus delays her leap so that it coincides with the next off-beat eighth-note chord in measure 4. In measure 10, when Stravinsky omits part of cell A, the Chosen One omits her leap; when he allows cell A to return in measure 13 with a sixteenth-note missing, the Chosen One shifts her leaps so she lands on the ground on the downbeat of measure 14.

Nijinsky follows the cell structure of Stravinsky's music, by having the Chosen One perform a new, distinct gesture for cell B. According to Millicent Hodson, the Chosen One bends painfully backwards from the waist here, ending her phrases in a twisted turn in which something coming from above appears to crush her. This movement symbolizes vividly the weight of the oppressive forces she has upon her, and her inability to free herself from them. This expression of weakness is followed immediately, however, by the surprise interruption of cell C at rehearsal no. 144. Here, a startling new symbol of resistance is inserted into the choreography: the Chosen One "makes a convulsive jump on one leg, having crossed and raised the other in front of her; squeezing one hand into a fist, she threatens the heavens while the other hand is held close to her body" (see fig. 3.1).[83] This moment marks a surprising break and hardly has the neutral character of an "insertion" sought in both Boulez's and van den Toorn's analyses: it pierces the musical fabric, disrupting any notion of a unified voice in the work.[84]

As the sacrificial dance proceeds, the opposing gestures associated with cells B and C become more prominent. The refrain returns four times, accompanied by the same movements to cells A, B, and C, yet varied to reflect the Chosen One's exhaustion and dejection over the inevitability of her fate. The fact that she dances this refrain each time to the same fast tempo, which is otherwise not maintained throughout, and especially not in her final episode, emphasizes how important this section of the music is to the Chosen One's assertion of her will.[85] Between the refrains, during her episodes, the Chosen One succumbs more to her community, by acting like a maimed bird, spinning ever so briefly like a top, and banging her straightened leg on the ground.[86] She repeatedly emerges from these moments, however, to return to her initial phrase, most strikingly at rehearsal no. 180, when all the ancestors gather to watch her. This refrain is an abrupt interruption of five measures, containing only cells A and B. After this startling interruption, the Chosen One gathers the strength to return to this position of defiance one last time, from rehearsal no. 186 onward, when the refrain returns as a coda. Stravinsky originally scored this section lightly to emphasize the Chosen One's leaps into the air.[87] The conflict she feels between defiance and oppression is best expressed after rehearsal no. 192, when the music is reduced to the alternating gestures of cells B and C. Stravinsky was dismayed at how most interpreters missed this moment, which he called a "dialectical structure of phrases."[88] At rehearsal no. 197, cell B is suddenly left out, in what Stravinsky called a turning point in the music (Vera Stravinsky and Robert Craft 1978, 514). The Chosen One is left to end her dance with an incessant hammering out of her most powerful physical motive of defiance (on cell C; see fig. 3.1). Her driving music successfully destroys the static background of the ancestors. She will die, but not without making her final defiant gesture. Cell C will prevail.

Figure 3.1 Valentine Gross-Hugo, drawing reprinted in Hodson 1996, 166.

Perceiving the Chosen One's Choice

The first audience to witness *Le Sacre* was so baffled by the "Danse sacrale," and especially by Nijinsky's decision to adopt Jaques-Dalcroze's method, which many critics frequently interpreted at that time, especially in Germany and France, as a mechanical and inartistic means of visualizing music.[89] The critics perceived Nijinsky's choreography as inanimate, machine-like, and inartistic, and were blind to its symbolic meanings. Often, they understood it as primitive, without realizing, as Nicholas Roerich noted, that their romanticized primitivism "had nothing to do with the refined primitivism of our ancestors, for whom rhythm, symbols and refinement of gesture were essential and sacred concepts."[90] Their impressions of Nijinsky's choreography were distorted by the performance of Maria Piltz, who had been called in to dance the Chosen One at the premiere after Nijinska discovered that she was pregnant. According to Prince Volonsky, Piltz had mechanically acted out what Nijinsky told her to do, replacing his conscious moves with limp empty gestures.[91] Marie Rambert also recalled that Piltz's "reproduction was very pale by comparison with [Nijinsky's] ecstatic performance, which was the greatest tragic dance I have ever seen" (Rambert 1972, 64). Her frightened movements unfortunately formed the basis for over seventy years of critical interpretation of the work.

The audience who experienced the first *Sacre* expected a narrative, familiar gestures, overwhelming sensual impressions, and beauty, and had little training in how to concentrate on the meaning communicated by the pure movement of desexualized bodies. Nijinsky's practice of sacrificing himself totally to a dramatic role became alienating when transferred over to the entire ballet troupe, whose lack of sentimental involvement in the narrative struck critics as terrifyingly inhuman. Nijinsky's choreographic approach was so unfamiliar that most critics wondered how to interpret it.[92]

The exception was Jacques Rivières, who wrote a remarkably insightful review for the *Nouvelle revue française*. Rivières spoke at length about Nijinsky's aesthetic experiment, which he understood intuitively. Stravinsky's music had choreographic properties that had led Nijinsky to create a dance stripped of what Rivières called "le sauce," or any extra, superficial elements. "The newness of the *Sacre du printemps* was in the renunciation of this dynamic sauce, in a return to the body, in the effort to grasp more closely its natural steps, in listening only to its most immediate, radical, etymological indications. The movement here is reduced to obeying. It is brought back unceasingly to the body, fastened to it, recaptured, pulled backwards by it, like someone whose elbows we are holding so that they don't get away" (Rivières 1947, 86). This movement does not render and make visible emotion, but rather uses the latter only as its point of departure, from which it quickly departs through its involvement in its own development (89). The ultimate goal of such an approach is to "arrive at a material, full, and somehow opaque imitation of the emotions" or "physical image of the passions of the soul." "Each gesture of the dancer is like a word that resembles it," Rivières concluded, ending his essay with a brief contemplation on how uncomfortable and sad all this made him feel.[93]

The Chosen One's capacity for defiant expression was not lost on all the spectators who crowded into the Théâtre du Champs Elysée on that spring day in May 1913. Valentine Gross-Hugo perceived her in this manner, and expressed her interpretation in a series of sketches of the "Danse sacrale," which were published in the dance issue of the journal *Montjoie* discussed above.[94] Gross-Hugo reproduced very brief excerpts of the score, associating with each a drawing of one of the dancer's individual gestures. She depicted six excerpts of Stravinsky's piano score:

No. 1: presents rehearsal no. 142, measure 2, the beginning of cell A. Gross-Hugo has depicted the Chosen One's first leap into the air.

No. 2: presents rehearsal no. 149, during which the Chosen One stands "trembling on the spot cheek trembling on folded hands" (Marie Rambert). The ancestors proceed back on stage, entrapping her as she tries to flee.[95]

No. 3: reflects rehearsal no. 165, the Chosen One spinning as the ancestors begin to exit. Gross-Hugo later noted that the dancer "turns in a vertiginous way like a top, so long and so fast that her long hair flows from her in a horizontal line" (Hodson 1996, 179).

No. 4: depicts rehearsal no. 174. Gross-Hugo comments that "the chosen one moved her limbs more freely in this section, into ever larger movements, all leading toward the final entreaty, all rendered desperate and ecstatic at the same time. A call, a repeated strident cry, amplified itself and raised itself to the level of a terrifying threat in the ultimate paroxysm."[96]

No. 5: offers rehearsal no. 181. "The dancer executes a sort of *pas de chat* landing on the right leg and then on the left, assisted by the arms . . . the body following the exact rhythm of the measure in a sort of continual *pas de chat,* but the position of the arms is as unusual as that of the feet in the landing" (Gross-Hugo, quoted in Hodson 1996, 190).

No. 6: illustrates rehearsal no. 195. The Chosen One's "final paroxysm" (Gross-Hugo, quoted in Hodson 1996, 197).

Gross-Hugo's narrative for the sacrificial dance depicts it in three-dimensional images and gives it an optimistic turn. She visualizes the music, giving it back its original sense as *plastique animée.* Understanding the importance of the leap upward in Stravinsky's and Nijinsky's work, she sketches the Chosen One almost exclusively in flight, in a state of dynamic, energetic movement. Although the Chosen One was dancing to her death, Gross-Hugo represents only her acts of defiance and choice. Thus a variation of cell C, the gesture of defiance, receives important emphasis in the center of the page. Gross-Hugo even exaggerates the Chosen One's freedom by depicting her more in the style of Isadora Duncan, leaping gracefully into the air, instead of being bound by Nijinsky's choreography to the earth. In interpreting the score in this way, she allows her readers to recognize that the Chosen One has the potential to take control of her own life, rather than remain a victim. Perhaps the Chosen One "chose" to die, to dissolve into her own movement and energy, as Nijinsky himself later decided to do.

Performed only five times in Paris, and three times in London, Nijinsky's *Sacre* did not survive as part of the repertoire of twentieth-century ballet. Yet his sister, Nijinska, the first Chosen One, went on to become one of the most important choreographers of the 1920s, while his assistant Marie Rambert founded the Ballets Rambert in England. All the dancers in *Le Sacre* remembered the movements Nijinsky had taught them, and passed them on. Most spectators did not quickly forget Nijinsky either, or the statement he had made in his *Sacre*. In this manner an unwritten tradition was created, which developed momentum as the century moved on. Social codes of behavior changed, allowing Mary Wigman by 1957 to create the first "feminist" *Sacre*. And by 1976, Pina Bausch would use the role of the Chosen One to define "women [a]s the subject rather than the object, experiencing her feelings from the inside, intent on her own events," as Christy Adair has eloquently commented.[97] The Chosen Ones they created had vibrancy, social meaning, and cultural relevance and created a tradition for the piece that was distinct from, but hardly inferior to, its tradition as a concert piece. Frequently, the soloist dancing the Chosen One argued and disagreed with the choreographer, thus replicating the spirit of dissension that characterized the collaboration between Stravinsky, Nijinsky, and Piltz.[98] Their historically contingent work demonstrated the limitations of any project that tried to define *Le Sacre* as an expression of an objective spirit, essentialist politics, or of pure reason based on structural listening. With his *Sacre*, Nijinsky stood up to Stravinsky, and held strong. The tension of their physical and creative struggle, transformed into the passionate, contained but defiant gestures of the Chosen One, strains against all totalizing readings of the music. At that infamous premiere in Paris over eighty years ago, Nijinsky opened a door, not to inhumanity and fascism, but rather to a new form of dance for the twentieth century. As Nijinska (1992, 470) concluded: "An awareness of the need for fearless self-expression—of the original, of the individual, of the unknown in art—awakened that night."

NOTES

I am grateful to the Social Sciences and Humanities Research Council of Canada for a three-year research grant that enabled me to begin work on this project in archives in Germany and Switzerland. I would like to thank in particular Werner Grünzweig at the Akademie der Künste in Berlin, and Ulrich Mosch and Felix Mayer at the Paul Sacher Stiftung in Basel for their kindness and permission to view materials in their archives. Finally, I want to extend my deepest gratitude to the Stanford Humanities Center, a remarkable institution where I had the good fortune to complete my work on this topic as a fellow in fall 1999.

1. Subotnik 1996, 149; 162–63; 168. See the introduction to this volume for some of my further remarks on Subotnik's argument.

2. In recent years, Nicholas Cook has published some of the most illuminating arguments on why and how musicologists are moving toward performance studies. See Cook 1998 and 2001.

3. I have chosen to use the French titles of the piece, because they accompanied its first publication in a four-hand piano version in 1913, and are well established. The

English titles were only added to the published score in 1967. See van den Toorn 1987, 25–27 and Taruskin 1996, 1:861.

4. Subotnik mentions the dancing body only briefly, in note 75 of her chapter. Characteristically she quotes a source that describes modern ballet as "abstract." In other words, she evokes an image of modern ballet that negates or tries to transcend the dancing body, revealing in this way her own tendency to view dancing bodies as distinct from the visuality of the musical experience. See Subotnik 1996, 251.

5. Adorno 1978, 39. All translations from German and French to English in this essay are my own.

6. See Witkin 1998, 144; and Adorno 1978, 40.

7. See Witkin 1998, 129; 130.

8. Dennis 1998, 53–56. See also Paddison 1993, 48.

9. See Adorno, "Stravinsky: Ein dialektisches Bild," *Forum* (June/July/August 1962); republished in Adorno 1997, 208.

10. This argument remains an important part of Adorno's later "Stravinsky: Ein dialektisches Bild" (Adorno 1963).

11. See Taruskin 1995, 6–7. This article was republished, in a modified version, in Taruskin 1997, 360–88.

12. Taruskin 1995, 3. In the late 1990s, Taruskin's main opponents were Kofi Agawu and Pieter van den Toorn. In *Music, Politics, and the Academy*, the latter questioned the "musical significance" of Taruskin's historical and analytical studies of Stravinsky's Russian roots (van den Toorn 1995, 196). Van den Toorn claimed that "once individual works begin to prevail for what they are in and of themselves and not for what they represent, then context itself, as a reflection of this transcendence, becomes less dependent on matters of historical placement." Van den Toorn confused the notion of music as a form of communication necessarily invested with societal and historical meaning with the idea of music as representation of something outside itself (van den Toorn 1995, 144). Kofi Agawu likewise judged Taruskin's historical work on the octatonic scale to be of "dubious" significance, consisting of nothing more than "a corroborative evidence for patterns observed in Stravinsky's scores" (Agawu 1993, 92). The fact that Agawu demands that historians provide a "technical demonstration" of how context relates to music shows how unwilling he likewise is to accept a hermeneutical approach in the cultural sciences as a viable alternative to scientific inquiry.

13. Taruskin 1992, 197; and 1993, 288–89. See also Taruskin 1995, 2–3.

14. Adorno differed from Taruskin in offering an alternative to music that was ideologically tainted, namely music that mirrored the most progressive state of consciousness and thus contained philosophical truth. Taruskin offered no such model to counter the negative image provided by Stravinsky, leading us to the conclusion that the affirmative music he envisioned may be utopic in Paul Ricoeur's sense, although I think Taruskin would adamantly deny such a proposition. (See Ricoeur 1986.)

15. Taruskin confirms his sympathy for Adorno's conclusions about Stravinsky on occasion, and links his own interpretation to Adorno's theory of permanent regression. See Taruskin 1995, 20; 1993, 287; and 1997, 385–86; 424.

16. Taruskin 1997, 344; 424. See also 1995, 17. I am not sure why Taruskin uses the German word "Individuum" here, which is quite distinct from Adorno's "Subjekt."

17. Taruskin describes such a transcendence of the individual ego in Scriabin's use of the six-tone, symmetrical mystic chord. See Taruskin 1997, 344.

18. Igor Stravinsky, *Chroniques de ma vie*, vol. 1 (Paris: Les Éditions Denoël et Steele, 1935), 69; translated into English in Stravinsky 1962, 31. Taruskin (1996, 1:849–66) gives a remarkable history of Stravinsky's fabrication of this dream. According to his account, Stravinsky originally reported this dream to his first biographer, who described it as "a young maiden dancing to the point of exhaustion before a group of old men of fabulous age, dried out practically to the point of petrifaction" (André Schaeffer, quoted in Taruskin 1996, 1:862). Note how the issue of a pagan rite is not included in the original dream, which emphasizes rather the opposition between the sexual potency of the young girl and the impotent older spectators surrounding her. Note also that Roerich did not envision such a sacrifice in his original version of *Le Sacre* (see Taruskin 1996, 1:861).

19. The term "zhertva" means simultaneously sacrifice and victim in Russian. Nevertheless, this title is most often translated as "The Great Sacrifice." See the libretto for *Le Sacre* in Stravinsky's hand reprinted in Vera Stravinsky and Robert Craft 1978, 78; and Stravinsky's letter to Alexander Benois from 16 November 1910, ibid., 82. See also Taruskin 1996, 1:871.

20. Stravinsky 1935, 1:105; 1962, 48. Stravinsky described the adolescents in *Le Sacre* as "not fully formed: their sex is unique and double, like that of a tree" in "Ce que j'ai voulu exprimer dans *Le Sacre du Printemps*," *Montjoie,* 29 May 1913; reprinted in Lesure 1980, 14.

21. In spite of Adorno's suspicions that *Le Sacre* was neither a critical nor an enlightened work, he shied away from identifying its absence of subjectivity with fascism. Rather, he believed that the work could never have been performed in the Third Reich, because the National Socialists would not have stood such an expression of their own barbarism. Adorno saw the roots of Stravinsky's inhumanity not in fascism, but in liberalism. See Adorno 1978, 137.

22. Adorno uses the word "parasite" on p. 178.

23. In spite of the intensive critical attention that has been focused on Adorno's *Philosophie der neuen Musik,* I have not been able to find a single account that takes into consideration his definition of dance. In that it is highly unlikely that Adorno saw Nijinsky's original performance of 1912 (when he was nine years old), or Massine's in Paris in 1920, one can assume he probably saw Marion Hermann's choreography in Frankfurt am Main in January 1931 (or, less likely, Lasar Galpen's choreography in Cologne in May 1930). He did not arrive in Hollywood early enough to have witnessed Lester Horton's Americanized version of the ballet. There is all but no information on Marion Hermann's choreography and performance of the work. See Manning 1991, 129–58. See also Berg 1988. For a list of choreographies of *Le Sacre* to 1991 see Acocella, Garafola, and Green 1992, 68–100.

24. In focusing on Adorno's subjective experience and imagination, I am not ignoring the fact that he defined his *Philosophie der neuen Musik* specifically as an objective *Geschichtsphilosophie* of modern music that did not reflect his own subjective opinions, but rather his insight into the Hegelian objective spirit *(objektiver Geist)* of

the musical works he analyzed. (See Adorno, "Missverständnisse," *Melos* 17, no. 3 [1950]; republished in Adorno 1975, 203–6.) In contrast to Dahlhaus and other critics, however, I do not think Adorno's claims for his philosophy should stop us from examining its roots in his own experience. I believe looking for objective spirit in a dancing body is a highly problematic enterprise. See Dahlhaus 1987a, 9–15.

25. Dominique Dupuy notes that the body can frequently turn into a body-machine in the minds of those who have forgotten it. He urges his readers to think of the living body in other terms than as an object made to express something. See his comments, quoted in Launay 1993. See also Dupuy 1995, 165–66.

26. Taruskin 1995, 19. Taruskin admitted at one point that he thought audiences created "tremendous" stagings in their imaginations of how *Le Sacre* would be danced, and that their actual visual exposure to the work thereafter was "often disappointing." See ibid., 8.

27. It is interesting that Taruskin did not find it relevant to examine Nijinsky's choreography for Stravinsky's work, especially in view of the fact that he completed such a thorough investigation of the work's genesis. In no fewer than 117 pages on the composition of *Le Sacre,* Taruskin mentions Nijinsky only once, in passing (Taruskin 1996, 1:875). In *Defining Russia Musically,* Taruskin dismisses Nijinsky's work as playing a "negligible role in the ballet's history" (Taruskin 1997, 380). See also Taruskin 1995, 16.

28. Milan Kundera has lamented the fact that so many critics have been frightened by the ecstasy expressed in *Le Sacre,* rather than enjoying and reveling in it. See Kundera 1991.

29. Taruskin 1996, 1:865; for Blok's involvement, see 849–51.

30. A survey conducted by *Dance Magazine* in 1998 concluded that Nijinsky was the most loved dancer of all time, although the vast majority of people have never seen him dance (in that no film documentation exists). How powerfully Nijinsky must have danced himself into our historical consciousness and creative imaginations, to have achieved such a status over seventy years after he last danced on stage! And what a strong will it must have taken to have barred him from the history and analysis of his most famous work, *Le Sacre.*

31. Stravinsky, letter to Max Steinberg, 5 June 1913, reprinted in translation in Vera Stravinsky and Robert Craft 1978, 102. In this letter, Stravinsky writes that "Nijinsky's choreography was incomparable. With the exception of a few places, everything is as I wanted it." See also Lesure 1990, 16; and van den Toorn 1987, 16. Charles M. Joseph concludes that Stravinsky was worried about Nijinsky's well-being at the time of preparing *Le Sacre,* and arranged diversions for him. See Joseph 1999, 194–96.

32. Stravinsky, "Interview with Stravinsky," *The Observer,* 8 July 1921; reprinted in Lesure 1990, 76–77. Some of the most devastating criticism of Nijinsky is included in Stravinsky 1935, 80–106 (Stravinsky 1962, 36–48). Stravinsky complained most often about Nijinsky's lack of musical knowledge and skill. Although this has proven to be an unfair judgment, Pieter van den Toorn continues to promote it (see van den Toorn 1987, 8). For more positive assessments of Nijinsky's musical abilities, see Nijinska 1992, 458; and Denby 1977, 18.

33. I am not sure why van den Toorn and others feel they have to choose between *Le Sacre* as music and *Le Sacre* as a ballet. Why were they not able to let the two tradi-

tions of *Le Sacre* peacefully coexist, as they surely have historically throughout the twentieth century?

34. When Stravinsky was completing *Memories and Commentaries,* he planned to undermine Nijinsky further by remarking that "Everyone who knew Nijinsky expected he would relapse into insanity; he had a mad brother, a blind uncle, a deaf cousin, Diaghilev said that the family was syphilitic." Nijinska asked him to omit this passage, and he subsequently did. These documents are held in the Stravinsky Archive at the Paul Sacher Stiftung. I am curious why Stravinsky felt compelled to lash out at Nijinsky in this manner.

35. Stravinsky called the work a "choreodrama" in a letter to N. F. Findeizen, translated into English by Robert Craft in appendix II to Stravinsky 1969, 32. See also "*Le Sacre du Printemps,*" in Vera Stravinsky and Robert Craft 1978, 512.

36. Stravinsky to Nicholas Roerich, 13 (26) November 1911; translated into English by Robert Craft in appendix II to Stravinsky 1969, 30.

37. Stravinsky to Nicholas Roerich, 6 March 1912, translated into English by Robert Craft in appendix II to Stravinsky 1969, 30.

38. *Montjoie* 1–2, Numéro consacré à la Danse Contemporaine (January–February 1914). There has been so much focus on Stravinsky's article for *Montjoie* on 29 May 1913 that this later issue has been overlooked.

39. For information on Saint-Point, see Berghaus 1993 and Satin 1990. See also Brandstetter 1995, 366–85; and Franko 1995, 21–24.

40. Saint-Point 1914. There are several articles in this issue about ritual dances of peoples outside Europe, which the writers associate with a spirituality required for the new art of dance. See, for example, Kharis, "La danse d'orient"; Jean-Paul d'Aile, "Les danses sud-américaines"; and Henri Siégler-Pascal, "La religion de la danse."

41. Postel du Mas 1914. Stravinsky's vision of using adolescents for *Le Sacre* whose "sex was not fully formed" can be related to attempts at blurring gender identity in modern dance in this period.

42. There are several sources that are helpful in gaining a preliminary insight into the nature of the "art plastique" and abstract dance Canudo and other were proposing. I would mention: Copeland and Cohen 1983; Franko 1995; and even Acocella and Garafola 1991.

43. Stravinsky, "Ce que j'ai voulu exprimer dans *Le Sacre du Printemps,*" in Lesure 1980, 14.

44. The best chronology of the genesis of *Le Sacre* is still provided in Vera Stravinsky and Robert Craft 1978, 84–92. See also Hodson 1987, 53–66.

45. Nijinsky 1995, 24. In this passage Nijinsky continues: "Scholars will ponder over me, and they will rack their brains needlessly, because thinking will produce no results for them. They are stupid. They are beasts. They are meat. They are death."

46. Nijinsky, letter to Stravinsky from 25 January 1913, quoted in English in Garafola 1989, 68.

47. Jacques Marnod in *Mercure de France,* 1 October 1913; quoted in Lesure 1990, 21–22; rpt. in Lesure 1980, 35–38.

48. Jacques Rivières, "*Le Sacre du printemps,*" *Nouvelle revue française,* November 1913; rpt. in Rivières 1947, 90.

49. Émile Vieillermoz, quoted in Jameux 1990, 25.

50. Odom 1997, 29–39. See also Nijinska 1992, 451; and Rambert 1972, 53–54.

51. Marie Rambert thus began her work with Nijinsky on *Le Sacre* after the first rehearsals had begun in late fall 1912. It is likely that Nijinsky's choreography changed under her guidance. See Nijinska 1992, 457–58.

52. Nijinska 1992, 460. Hodson assumes that these moves would have been danced by the Chosen One, and yet gives no evidence to support this claim. See Hodson 1996, 168.

53. On Dalcroze's method as "plastique animée" see Giertz 1975, 59 and Levitz 2001. Concerning Jaques-Dalcroze's teachings at this time, see Jaques-Dalcroze 1912/1913; Jaques-Dalcroze 1912 and 1965.

54. Stravinsky's correspondence with Dalcroze is documented in Stravinsky 1984, 77–83.

55. Bronislava Nijinska remembers practicing the "Danse sacrale" before November 1912, using a "score" sent by Stravinsky (Nijinska 1992, 448–49). This seems to contradict other evidence that exists about the work. First, Stravinsky only finished the work on 17 November 1912. He commented in a letter to Roerich on 14 December 1912 that Nijinsky had only begun the staging on 13 December 1912. On 18 December, Serge Grigoriev wrote that Nijinsky had still not started the rehearsals, and was waiting for Roerich's costumes. By the end of January, Nijinsky had still only had five rehearsals of the ballet (since Stravinsky left Vienna that month), and made no mention of having done the "Danse sacrale." Most remarkably, Nijinsky wrote Stravinsky on 24 March 1913, requesting the music for the "Danse sacrale" (see Vera Stravinsky and Robert Craft 1978, 92–95). I trust van den Toorn's argument that Nijinsky would have used a four-hand arrangement of the piece that did not include the "Danse sacrale" for almost all or all of these early rehearsals, because the full score was only finished on 8 March 1913. (See van den Toorn 1987, 35–36.) Robert Craft claims, however, that Nijinsky used a "sketch-score" of the "Danse sacrale" as early as November 1912 (Craft 1988, 173). In view of the fact that his article consists of so many erroneous facts and misplaced quotes, I can only take it as a complete fabrication on his part. (See also Taruskin 1988b, 385.) Concerning the extant manuscript copies of *Le Sacre*, see Cyr 1982, 98–114. If Nijinsky started the "Danse sacrale" in winter 1913, rather than in November 1912, then Millicent Hodson errs in assuming that it was choreographed first, and that it formed the basis for the movement vocabulary of the rest of the ballet. Hodson also claims that Irina Nijinska reported that Nijinska rehearsed the part of the Chosen One with her brother by hearing the synopsis of the ballet read aloud over and over again, and not by hearing the music. (See Hodson 1980, 43 and 1996, 167.) It is clear from many accounts that Roerich's libretto had a deep influence on how Nijinsky designed his ballet (see, for example, Nijinska 1992, 457–61). Nevertheless, I remain convinced that Nijinsky was not listening to a synopsis, but rather to the music played by the rehearsal pianist when he created the dance. See Rambert 1972, 56–57. For an accurate chronology, see Hill 2000, 26–34.

56. Taruskin comments (in reference to Whittall 1982) that it is "sentimental" to identify with the Chosen One, or to find conflict or tragedy in her role. I am not sure why he finds this sentimental. See Taruskin 1995, 20.

57. Hodson 1986, 67. She notes the similarity between this posture and the figures on Russian totems, which Nijinsky probably became familiar with through Nicolas

Roerich. Nijinsky wanted the dancers to achieve the concentrated focus of such carved figures. This again shows his affinity for the "art plastique" being promoted by his French contemporaries.

58. Acocella 1987, 65. Denby (1977, 18) commented in detail on Nijinsky's emphasis on the center of weight in his body, which allowed him to perform particularly meticulous movements. See also Kirstein 1976.

59. Description provided in Hargrave 1985, 93. It is important to note that Nijinsky expected the emotion of the dance to be communicated through movement, and not through facial expressions. Dancers who showed emotion in their face infuriated him (see Rambert 1972, 62). Edwin Denby (1977, 19–21) has called him a "classical" dancer for this reason.

60. Garafola 1989, 72. Nijinsky's sister believed that the Chosen One's dance was "his [Nijinsky's] own dance, inspired by the music." Nijinska 1992, 450.

61. Garafola 1999, 247. Burt Ramsey has offered valuable insight into Nijinsky's public role around 1912, and his homosexuality, in Ramsey 1995, 74–100.

62. Kopelson 1997, 190. This would partly explain Nijinsky's violent reaction to and intense anger over his sister's news that she was pregnant and could not dance the part. Nijinsky afterwards feared that he had been on the verge of killing his sister's husband at that moment. See Rambert 1972, 58; and Nijinska 1992, 461–63.

63. Krasovskaya 1979, 238–39. She describes Nijinsky's "sacrificial dance" based on a letter from Bronislava Nijinska of 11 December 1967, and on a conversation with Maria Piltz on 28 March 1968. Hodson has attempted to match Nijinska's general description to specific points in Stravinsky's music in *Nijinsky's Crime against Grace*. I find this problematic for three reasons: (1) Nijinska's account was given over fifty years after the fact; (2) Nijinska did not dance the final part of the Chosen One; and (3) her account is general and not accompanied with indications of how the movements coordinated with the music.

64. Nijinsky 1995, 37. It is important to remember, however, that these comments were written after Diaghilev and Nijinsky had broken contact, and thus do not reflect the state of their relationship in 1912–13. Nevertheless, I believe they demonstrate how remarkably Nijinsky and Stravinsky differed in their degree of empathy for the victims of violence. Whereas Stravinsky loved bullfights, for example, they terrified Nijinsky, who felt sorry for the tortured animals. See Nijinsky 1995, 43–44.

65. On the notion of representing corporeality through the fall, see Varilio 1994, 35–60, esp. 43–44.

66. In an earlier interview in the *Pall Mall Gazette* on 15 February 1913, Nijinsky claimed that the dance had no human beings in it. This comment is frequently cited in studies of the ballet. Note, however, that this remark was made before he completed work on the Chosen One's dance. I believe that he probably started training Nijinska as the Chosen One only around February 1913, in spite of reports that he began the dance in November 1912. Nijinska gave birth in October 1913, which means she would only have found out she was pregnant around March 1913. Surely she had not been working on the dance for five months before finding out she was pregnant. It is also not clear that Nijinsky even had the music for the "Danse sacrale" before this time. See note 55.

67. Boulez shares Adorno's opinion that *Le Sacre* failed in its form, development, and harmony. See Boulez 1966, 142–45.

68. Boulez mocks the only visual realization of *Le Sacre* that he considers, namely Walt Disney's *Fantasia*. He remarks sarcastically that whereas *Le Sacre* was once the object of scandal, it was now used for animated cartoons (Boulez 1966, 75). It is culturally interesting to note that Boulez even saw *Fantasia*, let alone felt it worthy of commentary.

69. Boulez does not indicate which score he used, thereby bypassing the thorny issue of Stravinsky's revisions of *Le Sacre*. This is not surprising, in that the idea of a score being revised would not have fit into his notion of what constituted the musical work. The rhythmic examples he uses in his article indicate that he was using the 1929 score or a copy thereof. On the issue of editions and revisions of *Le Sacre*, see Cyr 1982, 89–148; Cyr 1986, 157–73; van den Toorn, "Sketches, Editions, Revisions," in van den Toorn 1987, 22–56; and Fink 1999b, 299–362.

70. Boulez 1966, 136.

71. Concerning the philosophical consequences of music theory's use of two-dimensional graphic representation in the twentieth century, see Gilmore 1995 and Koozin 1999. Koozin makes the mistake of proposing three-dimensional representations that fail to depart from two-dimensional thinking.

72. As sketch studies became popular, the sketch emerges as a significant form of visual representation in musical analysis. The sight of etchings, sketches, or scribbles evoked the palpable presence of a real composer with tired fingers, broken pencils, spilling ink, and the very real presence of pens, lead, paper, and other materials required in order to compose. It is interesting that the body found its way back into music studies in this way, even in a period that wanted nothing to do with it, and which favored heightened intellectual rationality.

73. Van den Toorn 1987, 19 and all of chapter 2.

74. I am referring to this dance as it was reconstructed by Millicent Hodson for the Joffrey Ballet in 1987. I refer only to gestures for which we have historical documentation, and thus avoid the issue of the validity of her reconstruction. She used the following sources for her reconstruction: (1) Marie Rambert, *Le Sacre du Printemps*, Piano Score for Four Hands, choreographic notes (1913), introduction (1967) (London: Ballet Rambert Archives); (2) Nijinska's letter about this solo to Vera Krasovskaya in December 1967; published summary in Krasovskaya 1971, 440–42; (3) Valentine Gross-Hugo's drawings; (4) the reconstruction of the dance by Olga Stens in France and by Nicholas Zverev (see Stanciu-Reiss 1957); (5) Stravinsky 1969. The appendix consists of the notes. For a review of these sources, see Hodson 1987.

75. See Stravinsky 1969, appendix, 42. Stravinsky indicated that the Chosen One should stay in this spot from rehearsal numbers 142 to 149.

76. Jann Pasler (1981) develops this thought in convincing detail. The scenery for scene 2, which depicted a vast Slavic sky, enchanted rocks, and the magic mountain of sacrifice, also contrasted sharply with the dance. See Garafola 1989, 67–68.

77. Nijinska 1992, 448–49; see also Stravinsky's letter to Nicholas Roerich, 1(14) December 1912, translated into English by Robert Craft in Stravinsky 1969, appendix, 31.

78. Gabriele Brandstetter (1998, 48–49) argues that the circle structure in *Le Sacre*

has the multiple function of shutting out the audience while also shutting it in, and of acting as an index for the representation of ritual.

79. Taruskin (1996, 1:890) traces the roots of this dance to Herodotus's *The Persian Wars*. Stravinsky labels the dance this way in his sketchbook. He calls it a "wild martial dance" in his letter to N. F. Findeizen, 2(15) December 1912, translated into English by Robert Craft in Stravinsky 1969, appendix, 33.

80. Marie Rambert's notes are given in Hodson 1996, 135–40.

81. Mary Wigman's extensive drawings and notes for her choreography of *Le Sacre* are kept in her archive at the Akademie der Künste, Berlin. These documents include the 1926 piano reduction of Stravinsky's work with her meticulous comments, as well as extensive drawings. Wigman fought with Dore Hoyer over the Chosen One's dance, however, and left no indication in writing or images of how she envisioned that part of the piece. See also Steinbeck 1987.

82. Stravinsky only later removed that indication because he thought string players would be too incompetent to play it that way. See van den Toorn 1987, 42–44. A weightless, precise performance of these chords best embodies the motion of leaping into the air, which both Nijinsky and Stravinsky envisioned. In spite of this, Stravinsky was one of the few conductors ever to perform these chords that way. Most conductors perform these chords with enough crashing intensity to stifle anybody's attempt at escape.

83. Nijinska, quoted in Hodson 1996, 166. Hodson associates this gesture with cell A, but I believe she is mistaken, especially in view of Valentine Gross-Hugo's drawings. I find there are many errors in Hodson's reconstruction, and in this book. (For a highly insightful critique of Hodson's reconstruction, see Acocella 1991.) Jacques Rivières described this gesture as an "arm raised to heaven and waved straight above her head in a gesture of appeal, threat, and protection" (Rivières 1947, 93). The Chosen One learned this gesture from her tribe, who demonstrate it for her in the "Evocation des ancêtres." This fact lends support to Nijinska's thesis that in her "Danse sacrale," the Chosen One is protecting the earth against the heavens, and that the ancestors had taught her the gesture she needed to win that battle. Such an interpretation makes the ancestors less hostile than they otherwise appear to be.

84. I am keenly aware of the dangers inherent in trying to analyze dance by creating a narrative out of individual gestures. Nicholas Cook warns against such approaches, which can be equated with constructing the body as text. Cook prefers to understand the body as "sound," as a "site of resistance to text": "Instead of seeing the relationship between work and performance in terms of a transparent revelation of underlying structure, as epitomized by the Schenkerian concept of performing from the middleground, a variety of terms come into play which thematize the opacity of the relationship: quotation, commentary, critique, parody, irony, or travesty, for example" (Cook 2001). I, nevertheless, analyze the dancing body of the Chosen One in this way, because I believe this is how Nijinsky, following Jaques-Dalcroze, understood and conceived of it. I would not support such an analytical approach for all choreographed works of music.

85. See Fink 1999b.

86. Nijinsky never allows the Chosen One to spin freely as Adorno and Taruskin want her to do. When she spins from rehearsal numbers 164 to 173, her movement

is "desperate and ecstatic at the same time," and when she spins again after rehearsal no. 181, she spins with "feet almost on the points striking the ground like daggers," according to Valentine Gross-Hugo (Hodson 1996, 177; 191). Her spinning is also always stopped or interrupted by the return of her refrain.

87. On the original scoring of this moment, see Fink 1999b.

88. Stravinsky to Ansermet, 30 January 1926, reprinted in Vera Stravinsky and Robert Craft 1978, 513. Boris Asaf'yev (1982, 53–54) discusses the tension between cells B and C. Remember that Boulez intuitively understood this moment (see note 70).

89. There was much opposition to Jaques-Dalcroze's approach to dance before World War I. See Giertz 1975, 47–59. Opponents of Jaques-Dalcroze included Claude Debussy, Rudolf Bode, and Hans Brandenburg. Adorno's later interpretation of the dance movement of *Le Sacre* as mechanical may have resulted from his knowledge of this body of criticism. This debate on mechanical versus conscious dance also finds an analogy in the controversy over vitalist versus geometric interpretations of the music of *Le Sacre*—a topic analyzed in Fink 1999b and, initially, in Taruskin 1988a.

90. Nicholas Roerich, *The Realm of Light* (New York: New Era Library, 1931), 185–91; quoted in French in Hodson 1980, 41.

91. Krasovskaya 1979, 243–44. A large number of critics commented on the fact that Piltz looked like she was being tortured in the "Danse sacrale." This was not necessarily Nijinsky's original intention. See Bullard 1971 and Lesure 1980.

92. Brandstetter speaks of *Le Sacre* as "not only . . . an attack on the representative code of the body in classical dance, but also . . . an affront against the norms of the reigning body aesthetic in general" (Brandstetter 1988, 46).

93. Rivières 1947, 91. I think historians in general have tended to focus too exclusively on the last few pages of Rivières' extensive analysis (pp. 95–97).

94. Hodson erroneously indicates that these drawings were published in June 1913, at the time of the ballet's premiere. She also uses drawings that were not actually ever published in *Montjoie* (Hodson 1996, 170). Many reprints of Gross-Hugo's actual drawing for *Montjoie* are included in Stravinsky's archive, Paul Sacher Stiftung. Gross-Hugo completed about twenty sketches of the Chosen One's solo, and twenty-five refined pictures of Piltz in the part. These drawings are kept in the Theatre Collection at the Victoria and Albert Museum in London. The collection also includes a diary in which Gross-Hugo talks about her drawings. The pages of her sketchbooks are detached and the original sequence is not intact. Marie Rambert found Gross-Hugo's drawings too Duncanesque and refined, and not as prehistoric as they should be. (See Hodson 1980, 45 and 1987, 57). A large selection of these drawings is published in Hugo 1971.

95. Hodson 1996, 171. This example is only one of many showing that Gross-Hugo is not accurately depicting the movement as Marie Rambert described it in her piano reduction of the piece.

96. Ibid., 183. In the better-known version of these drawings used by Millicent Hodson, Gross-Hugo uses a different movement for this measure! See Hodson 1996, 170.

97. Adair 1992, 210. See also Goldberg 1989 and Cody 1998.

98. It would be interesting to study why this dance in particular has led to such violent disagreements between dancers and choreographers—perhaps because dancers seem to embrace it as an intense vehicle for their own, personal forms of expression. Concerning Nijinsky's original arguments with Stravinsky over *Le Sacre,* see Marie Rambert 1972, 59.

FOUR

Beethoven Antihero

Sex, Violence, and the Aesthetics of Failure,
or Listening to the Ninth Symphony
as Postmodern Sublime

ROBERT FINK

. . . the carefully prepared cadence is frustrated, damming up energy which finally explodes in the throttling, murderous rage of a rapist incapable of attaining release.
SUSAN MCCLARY, *"Getting Down Off the Beanstalk"*

The postmodern would be that which, in the modern, puts forward the unpresentable in presentation itself; that which denies itself the solace of good forms . . .
JEAN-FRANÇOIS LYOTARD, *The Postmodern Condition*

A man in terror of impotence
or infertility, not knowing the difference
a man trying to tell something
howling from the climacteric
music of the entirely
isolated soul . . .
ADRIENNE RICH, *"The Ninth
Symphony of Beethoven Understood
at Last as a Sexual Message"*

ONE OF THE MOST MISQUOTED MUSICOLOGISTS IN HISTORY

"She must surely be one of the most misquoted musicologists in history." The lament is Suzanne Cusick's, on behalf of her feminist colleague Susan McClary. The sobriquet appeared in a recently published essay assessing the growth and prospects of a feminist musicology, in a section entitled "The Use and Misuse of *Feminine Endings*" (Cusick 1999, 488, n. 30). By "misquoted" Cusick meant that the passage of Beethoven criticism most often attributed to the author of *Feminine Endings* (McClary 1991), the passage reproduced above as the first of this chapter's epigraphs, does not actually appear in that book at all. The fact that a single book—worse, a single decontextualized,

sensationalized, and inaccurately cited remark standing in for that book—
had come to stand for the entire complex project of feminist musicology
seemed to Cusick a singularly unfortunate, if not actively malevolent, state
of intellectual affairs.

And who would not agree, faced with this (sadly typical) kind of tabloid
slop?

> Musicology has finally latched on to the post-modern marketing tool to beat
> all others: reinterpretation. After all, it worked for literature, so why not for
> classical music? . . . That's right, music is merely an extension of gender and
> politics . . . So what is that loud noise in the first movement of Beethoven's
> Ninth? Over to McClary, author of *Feminine Endings:* "The carefully prepared
> cadence is frustrated, damming up energy which finally explodes in the throt-
> tling, murderous rage of a rapist incapable of attaining release."[1]

Yada, yada, yada. After the drubbings in the *New York Times,* the slashing
attacks from neo-conservative dinosaurs like Robert Bork and Roger Kim-
ball, the brutal caricatures of "postmodern radical feminist" musicology that
graced the pages of journals as divergent as *U.S. News and World Report* and
Lingua Franca—one might well ask: Wouldn't it have been better for all of us
if Susan McClary's gloss on the moment of recapitulation in the first movement of Beethoven's Ninth Symphony had simply never been written? I
think this is Cusick's wish—her discussion of *Feminine Endings* never mentions the *Minnesota Composer's Forum Newsletter,* the 1987 source where
McClary actually did deploy her infamous metaphor. What thoughtful musicologist (old or new) would not want to erase the thuggish reception those
few words unleashed—even at the cost of erasing the words themselves?

But Susan McClary did in fact consciously compare the effect of one of
Beethoven's most famous passages to a failed rape; and I for one would hes-
itate before consigning her audacious image to critical oblivion. For it was
this stark passage, and no other, that reached out and slapped a young, somewhat disillusioned doctoral candidate upside the disciplinary head and set
him on the path that would eventually lead to a vocation in the "new" musicology, and the writing of this determinedly celebratory essay. When, in
1988, I first heard McClary quoted on the Ninth, I had no feminist context
within which to appreciate her sexual politics. I had no context at all, having read none of her work, when a renowned male musicologist dropped
that one fateful sentence into his subtly disparaging talk—and waited for the
inevitable snickering to begin.[2]

It did not occur to me then that McClary's quote was an attack on
Beethoven himself, nor did I understand her words as the opening salvo in
a musicological gender war. I just thought she was reporting her own experience of listening to Beethoven. I want to recapture and argue strenuously
for this "beginner's" reading of McClary in the argument to come.[3] It now

seems to me that McClary had, in the course of formulating a feminist critique of Western tonality of which at the time I was totally unaware, hit upon a singularly vivid image that concretized the pleasure and pain that await when one moves beyond modernist structural hearing. In a flash, I intuited that Susan McClary heard in Beethoven's Ninth what I did: not the abstract comforts of Hanslick's "musically beautiful," but an audible trace of what I later came to recognize as Jean-François Lyotard's *postmodern sublime:*

> Modern aesthetics is an aesthetic of the sublime, though a nostalgic one. It allows the unpresentable to be put forward only as the missing contents; but the form, because of its recognizable consistency, continues to offer to the reader or viewer matter for solace and pleasure . . . The postmodern [sublime] would be that which, in the modern, puts forward the unpresentable in presentation itself; that which denies itself the solace of good forms, the consensus of a taste which would make it possible to share collectively the nostalgia for the unattainable; that which searches for new presentations, not in order to enjoy them but in order to impart a stronger sense of the unpresentable. (Lyotard 1992, 148)

Deploying Lyotard's trope of the postmodern as "sublime" will help me justify the following extended discussion of McClary's Beethoven criticism as an investigation into postmodern listening; it will also motivate the structuring of what follows into two dialectical parts, corresponding to the two dialectically opposed moments of the sublime that Lyotard counterpoises in the quote above.

To anticipate the overall trajectory of my argument: the first modernist moment begins with the reaction to McClary's rape image as an uncovering, and a recovery, of painful (and previously unspeakable) *content* trapped within a severely abstract form reified as "organic" and inevitable; we thus rewrite Beethoven's Ninth as an instance of the modern sublime. As Lyotard himself notes, the roots of this modern sublime can be traced back into the early Romantic era, as far back as Immanuel Kant's justification of empty abstraction—"negative presentation" of content—as the ultimate in sublimity (1992, 146). The reception history of Beethoven's Ninth shows that McClary's take on the first-movement recapitulation is quite typical of a hermeneutic strategy I will dub with the quasi-neologism *sublimating.* An entire line of male critics have grasped at metaphors of (often sexualized) violence to situate this passage as a liminal case of the modern sublime, as the painful-pleasurable moment where the discomfort of unspeakable content is held in check—just barely—by the comfort of comprehending a great composer's formal genius.

Thus my opening gambit will be to recontextualize McClary by linking her to a hermeneutic tradition of sublimating description that predates high-modernist formalism. But her rape image—if read with full attention to its kinesthetic specificity—encodes with aphoristic brutality the complex and postmodern relation to *form* that is characteristic of Lyotard's second, postmodern moment of the sublime. The rape McClary describes is a failure, her antihero "unable to attain release." In the second part of my essay, I will argue this as a key formal insight into Beethoven's "aesthetics of failure." Identifying the moment of recapitulation as a failed rape will turn out to be not a distraction from form, a deviation away from the "music itself" into dodgy politics, but a powerful analytical key to just those formal questions it was thought to displace. McClary's infamous remark adumbrates not the "recognizably consistent," reassuring formal logic of the modern sublime, but the shattered illogic that "puts forward the unpresentable in [the form of the] presentation itself": the postmodern sublime. To listen to it with her—to hear Beethoven's failure as both sublime and postmodern—is my goal.

MOMENT ONE: THE UNSPEAKABLE CONTENT (ROMANTIC AND MODERN SUBLIMITY)

Violence, Failure, and "Beethoven's demonic intentions"

It is remarkable how often the adjective *erhabene,* "sublime," appears in nineteenth-century German descriptions of the first movement of Beethoven's Ninth. In fact, this moment of recapitulation could (and did) serve as a paradigmatic example of the Romantic musical sublime. Friedrich Michaelis, synthesizing Kant and Burke, gave an influential definition of the musical sublime in an 1805 article for the Berlin *Allgemeine musikalische Zeitung.* As summarized by Peter le Huray, Michaelis's description of sublimity in music could double as a description of the Ninth:

> The music may well achieve sublime intensity . . . when notes are sustained for unusually long periods of time and when the sheer volume of sound is shatteringly intense, when the music's progress is frequently interrupted, or when the textures are so complex that the imagination is stretched to its limits in an effort to follow what is going on. When we feel that we are poised over a bottomless chasm, when the imagination encounters the limitless and the immeasurable, then the experience may be described as sublime. (le Huray 1979, 98)

We cannot credibly assert that Romantic critics did not appreciate confusing, overpowering musical experiences like this one; abjection before the sublime is one of the things they valued most about listening to Beethoven's music. Yet the rhetorical violence of his Ninth Symphony is extreme even within the sublime, the built-in masochism of the aesthetic category harder to ignore. We would do well to remember the physical bluntness of Edmund Burke's famous epigram: the beautiful is founded on pleasure, but the sub-

lime is founded on *pain.* Such pain may well underpin the increasingly negative metaphors, extending to war, catastrophe, and violent rape, that the
more *erhabene* moments of the Ninth have accumulated over time.

Though the Ninth is now *the* canonical masterwork of abstract instrumental music, a nagging hermeneutic anxiety quickly crystallized around
measures 301–15 of its first movement. The *ff* D major of the recapitulation
and its immediate aftermath have fascinated and troubled almost every
commentator since the middle of the nineteenth century. This was not
always so; early descriptions of the symphony concentrated on the famous
opening, the thematic content of the first movement's exposition, and of
course discussed the propriety and success of the choral finale.[4] Yet the passage has loomed increasingly large in criticism, interpretation, and analysis
of the Ninth, so that for many twentieth-century scholars it is the pivot of the
movement, if not the entire work. There is clearly something intrinsic to this
spot that has attracted increasing aesthetic attention, perhaps because it
combines to an extraordinary degree the "violence and signification" that,
in Joseph Kerman's view, singled out Beethoven's Fifth as the "paradigmatic
'work of musical art' for the nineteenth century" (1988, 484). That signifying violence, whether acknowledged openly or not, seems to have drawn to
itself scholarly prose, both analytic and impressionistic.[5]

For the most part, hermeneutic approaches to this unexpected blast of
tonic major followed by tonal chaos define two (dialectically opposed)
strategies. The *sublimating* strategy, which attempts to focus on and interpret
its extremity, gives rise, dialectically, to the *beautifying,* which attempts to
deny or minimize any disturbing aspects, usually by exalting technical
description over exegesis. Beautifiers want to convince us that there is no
hermeneutic problem; they explain to us that the passage makes perfect formal sense. Sublimators revel in the problem, and are often delighted to hint
through tone and imagery that the passage *is* problematic: that it is extreme,
overpowering, at the limits of musical discourse. Sometimes, they move
beyond the modern sublime—and anticipate postmodern hearing—as they
intimate that the Ninth does *not* make formal sense.

The distinction is neatly thematized in the first extended description of the
recapitulation, a remarkable passage in Robert Griepenkerl's 1838 novel *The
Music Festival, or the Beethovenians (Die Musikfest, oder die Beethovener).* Years before
analysts and critics homed in on it, Griepenkerl described the exact moment
of recapitulation in impressive technical detail, as a moment of high drama:

> "*Crescendo! Sforzato!* Every man for himself!" cried Vicarius, loudly slamming shut
> the score he had been keenly following up until that point. And then began the
> most sublime passage in the entire first movement. Pfeiffer saw in it the battle
> between Old and New, the crucial gigantic and titanic battles of our times.
> . . .

> Everyone attacked the open fifths in *fortissimo*, except the bassoons and double basses, who once having achieved F# refused to let it go; they held it out in thirty-seconds against the mass of the orchestra hastening back into Chaos— thus turning the entire passage, if you like, into a single first-inversion triad. The previously-heard fifth-motives of the violins wandered *fortissimo* like angry ghosts in and around the thunder of the drums, the blasts of the trumpets, and the firmly anchored F# of the basses. (Griepenkerl 1838)

The author's voice already shows a beautifying-sublimating split. Griepenkerl uses the precise musical language of the professional, and even ventures on a reductive theoretical explanation: the whole passage is to be understood as a prolongation of "a single first-inversion triad." But his description is tellingly interspersed with more outlandish phraseology— bursts of supernatural metaphor that betray a perception of the uncanny ("wandered like angry ghosts") and the unintelligible ("the orchestra hastening back into Chaos").

Next we hear the excited reactions of onlookers, as Griepenkerl surveys representative aesthetic responses to this "most sublime passage in the entire first movement":

> "This is no street brawl," said Vicarius; "they are tearing off the granite tops of mountain ranges and throwing them at each other, they're scourging the boiling sea into the bridal bed of the earth. And suns and moons are their shields, fiery bolts of lightning their spears; out of their battle the dust of stars whirls heavenward!"
>
> "The theme, listen for the theme!" cried Adalbert.
>
> "It's stale, worn out," mocked Vicarius. "Away with you, deciphered Beauties! Your budding innocence is *passé*. Another Messiah for our century, say I! —" (Griepenkerl 1838)

In the persons of Vicarius and Adalbert, sublimating and beautifying criticism clash directly. Vicarius, overwhelmed, abandons himself to the experience. The sheer violent energy of the music seems to require a commensurate hermeneutic excess, and he responds with a sublimely blasphemous outpouring of eschatological imagery. What Vicarius is emphatically *not* interested in purveying is theoretical explanation—he disdains "deciphered Beauties" ("enträtselte Schöne"). He was the one who greeted this passage not by diving into his score, but by slamming it shut with a gleeful, "Every man for himself!"

Adalbert, the beautifier, attempts to reign Vicarius in; he wants to bring the discussion back around to "the music itself," to substitute analysis of formal structure for rhapsodic *Schwärmerei*. Variations on Adalbert's impassioned cry for the purely musical ("The theme, listen for the theme!") echo down through the critical discourse on the Ninth; it was the battle cry of Heinrich Schenker, and, in our day, Pieter C. van den Toorn. There will always be a beautifier, someone who has kept his control, kept his score firmly open, to tap the wild-eyed sublimator on the shoulder and point out a thematic or formal connection. And if in 1838 it was Vicarius who ultimately dominated the discussion, in the twentieth century it has been beautifying criticism that has, until recently, had the last word.

Of course, there has always been a small and not particularly influential minority who make an *overt* denial of any hermeneutic problem: they take the D-major tutti at its "triumphant" face value. The most famous was probably Sir George Grove: "[the first theme] is now given with the fullest force of the orchestra and the loudest clamour of the drum, and ending unmistakably in D *major*. Its purpose is accomplished, its mission fulfilled, its triumph assured; no need now for concealment or hesitation!" (Grove 1884). Grove's bluff good humor was followed by the authors of many English-language concert guides before Tovey (see below).

Another, vastly more influential group uses Adalbert's more subtle beautifying tactic—they look for the theme. This involves "hard" analysis: carefully avoiding emotional display, one presents the passage as a set of purely technical-compositional conundrums to be unraveled. One of the first to do this sort of thing was Hugo Riemann, in his *Grundriß der Kompositionslehre* (Riemann 1889), but at the same time he allowed himself wild flights of sublimating description in less formal venues, such as program notes (see below). Probably the first to undertake severely technical analysis of the Ninth as an explicitly polemical act was Heinrich Schenker in his book-length study of 1912—and it would not be unfair to say that ignoring all questions of meaning in Beethoven's Ninth has remained a polemical act to this day.

Schenker's 300-page study, undertaken years before the transcendental concept of the *Ursatz* heated up his prose, is so matter-of-fact and detailed as to be almost unreadable at length. He approaches measures 301–15 as a traditional *Stufentheorist*, providing a careful linear rationalization of its root succession. An "ideal" $I^{\#}3-^{\#}IV-V$ bass progression in D minor explicitly disciplines Schenker's hearing of the passage (see Example 1b, below). He uses it to dismiss any implication of D major other than as a chromatically-altered tonic (V/iv), and to give "organic necessity" *(organische Notwendigkeit)* to the sudden and apparently arbitrary appearance of the chord B♭–D–F–A♭. In general, Schenker prefers this complex chromatic root progression to the looser concept of "mode mixture" between D major and D minor, a dialectic all too susceptible to promiscuous interpretation in terms of joy-pain, triumph-defeat and so on. As he points out, "[in the context of this functional progression] the fundamental color change gains a sort of causality that mode mixture totally fails to give" ("enthält doch das chroma prinzipiell eben eine Art von Kausalität, wie sie der Mischung durchaus fehlt"; p. 123).

Schenker's rigidly neutral tone, and his overt use of analysis to control and rationalize this unruly passage was, of course, a reaction against previous excesses by sublimating critics, who gave themselves up to its extremity and found themselves driven to wild extravagances of emotive description.[6] A large and perhaps justifiable part of his impatience with these "analyses" was the paucity of actual formal analysis—their general failure to explain the music on its own terms. But if one rereads these accounts on their own terms, it becomes clear that Schenker was reacting against a presence, and not just an absence. His completely dispassionate analytical treatment of the recapitulation was an attempt to counter the tales of violence and confusion that his predecessors and colleagues had been spinning about this passage all along.

Most of the patterns of imagery that dominate evocative description of measures 301–15 are already present in the most influential nineteenth-century account, that of A. B. Marx *(Beethoven Leben und Schaffen,* 1859). Marx breathlessly describes the entire passage in one sweeping sentence; he points out the physical extremity of the orchestral setting, establishing the storm metaphor that will be copied by almost every later commentator: the "shriek of the full winds"; the "unbearable thunder-crashes of the timpani" ("aushallenden Schrei aller Bläser"; "unaufhörlichen Donnerpochen der Pauken").[7] But Marx did not just find this passage loud; he also found it irrational, strange, even uncanny—images he condensed into a characteristically Romantic evocation of the supernatural, from *Faust.* Here is Marx's take on the troublesome three chords (D^6–B$^{\flat}$7–d^6) that Schenker tried so valiantly to endow with root progression and "organic necessity":

> Now the sovereignty of this idea is fully established . . . it stands on F$\sharp$–A–D . . . for twelve long measures (immovable like a terrifying specter, like the gloomily flaming Earth-Spirit that stood before Faust, which he conjured up but could not withstand)—until in the twelfth measure—again at the last moment, the last eighth-note—it turns first to E-flat and three bars later to the tonic, to D minor, to conclude the opening period. Conclude?—that is not within the power of this troubled Giant-Spirit.[8]

Wallowing in the syntactic disruption that theorists would later explain away, Marx foregrounds irrationality and incoherence—the "unnatural" persistence of frozen D major and the sudden, offbeat shift to a seemingly unrelated key. Note in particular the melodramatic reference to the apparition of the *Erdgeist* in Goethe's *Faust,* scene 1. (This is the kind of thing that drove Schenker crazy.) In the poem, Faust calls up a figure of raw and elemental power that overwhelms his intellect and disappears as abruptly and arbitrarily as it came.[9]

Marx's "terrifying specter" *(Schreckensphantom)* is a generational descendant of the "angry ghosts" *(zürnende Schatten)* that appeared in Griepenkerl's 1838 description, of which Marx may well have been aware. But the hermeneutic gambit of reading Beethoven's Ninth through Goethe's *Faust* is probably a direct steal from Richard Wagner and the now-famous program he used to prepare the Dresden audience for his 1846 benefit performance of the work. Wagner systematically appropriated lines from *Faust* to construct an emotional program for the entire symphony. Although he makes no direct reference to the recapitulation as such, he links the movement's main theme to a line from *Faust,* and depicts its "uncanny" first appearance in language strikingly similar to Marx's invocation of the *Erdgeist:*

> The great chief theme, which steps before us at one stride, naked and power-
> ful, as if from behind an uncanny and spectral shroud *[wie aus einem unheimlich*
> *bergenden Schleier nackt und mächtig heraustritt],* might perhaps be translated,
> without violence to the spirit of the whole tone poem, by *Goethe's* words: *Ent-*
> *behren sollst du! / Sollst entbehren!* | Go wanting, shalt thou! Shalt go wanting!
> (Wagner 1846, 247)

The interpretive link between Beethoven's Ninth and Goethe's *Faust* was to prove immensely attractive to the critical descendants of Vicarius. In traversing the discourse around this work, one quickly learns to read any mention of *Faust* as an overt or covert sublimating gesture. But the nineteenth-century predilection for Faustian metaphor at the moment of recapitulation also betrays a covert fear that the passage, exciting as it, may go a little too far. Or perhaps it is exciting just *because* it goes too far. After all, isn't the figure of Faust one of the archetypal human symbols of the pleasures and perils of overreaching genius? Did Beethoven transgress here?

Most significant in this context is Marx's last observation ("Conclude?—that is not within the power of this troubled Giant-Spirit"), which begins to hint that the passage is to be heard as a dramatic mimesis of formal and harmonic failure. The first theme, though it has achieved provisional "sovereignty" in D major, does not have the power to "conclude," that is, to *cadence,* in any convincing way. In direct opposition to Schenker, whose chromaticized root progression provides a way of hearing ("eine Art von Kausalität") that allows this chord sequence to succeed, Marx's account simply accepts the momentary sense of mystification and failed progression.[10]

Corroborative evidence can be adduced from Wagner's 1846 description of the emotional progression within the movement as a whole: "Thus force, revolt, defiance, yearning, hope, near-success, fresh loss, new quest, repeated struggle, make out the elements of ceaseless motion in this wondrous piece . . ." (p. 247). Map this progression of emotional states onto sonata form, and it appears that the moment of recapitulation and its aftermath correspond to "near-success" (*Fast-Erreichen*) and "fresh loss" *(neues Verschwinden)* respectively. One might well ask why this passage only rates as a *near* success: could it be the failure to cadence—a purely formal failure—that Wagner is hearing?

Through the "hermeneutic analyses" in Kretzschmar's (1886) immensely popular *Führer durch den Konzertsaal,* an echo of Wagner's and Marx's impressions received the widest possible dissemination. Kretzschmar's discussion of the music itself is exhausted by mention of the thirty-eight-measure *ff* timpani roll on D and the violence of strings and winds that crash against each other ("heftig und wild gegeneinander angehen"; p. 244), but he ends with a fascinating variation on Marx's reference to Goethe. In this version it is explicitly the composer of the Ninth himself who plays the overreaching Faust: "the means of musical art hardly seem to suffice to carry out Beethoven's demonic intentions" ("die Mittel der musikalischen Kunst den dämonischen Intentionen Beethovens kaum zu genügen scheinen"; p. 244). Kretzschmar, like Marx, implies that the passage shows compositional strain—that it is flirting with unintelligibility, if not actual failure to make sense. Even more striking is how the violence and confusion of the music feed directly back into the image of the "demonic" composer: Beethoven Hero has already begun his transformation into violent Antihero.

A survey of later critical responses to measures 301–15 reveals a continuing redeployment of the same group of images and observations. Hugo Riemann, in an enthusiastic program note from the late 1880s, paraphrases Wagner, complete with extensive quotes from *Faust,* and then describes the moment of recapitulation in a single wild sentence that takes over Kretzschmar's demonic composer while upping the ante on Marx from tempest to apocalypse: "all the sections of the orchestra break loose in a wild battle amongst themselves, while the timpani pound out their D in a fearsome thirty-eight-measure-long crescendo as if the world itself was coming to an end—as if the strongest orchestral means would not suffice to depict the overwhelming, demonic fantasy of the Master's creative impulse!"[11]

Gustave Ernest describes the D-major *fortissimo* as "like a terrifying specter" ("wie ein Schreckgespenst"; Ernest 1920, 400). Karl Nef, in a popular book on the Beethoven symphonies, quotes A. B. Marx directly, makes the by-now obligatory storm metaphor, and calls the return a "catastrophe" (Nef 1927, 269–70). Olin Downes elaborated the storm image further ("over roaring drums, fragments of the great theme hurtle together and flash and splinter, as lightning might strike a mountain gorge"; Downes 1935, 83), while Romain Rolland, a second Vicarius, carried it again to the apocalyptic limit:

> This is the paroxysm of the tempest—the three apparitions of God on Sinai (as one might be allowed to characterize the great motive of falling fifths) totally surrounded by lightning and thunder. But for the first time the All-Mighty speaks in the *major,* over the rumbling of the timpani, so like a cannonade. Then brusquely, by means of one of those chromatic "lighting changes," over B-flat and by way of A-flat and then A natural, it returns to its original D minor, which the triplet eighths of the timpani never cease to reaffirm. We are at the

heart of the hurricane. Masses of sound collide violently. The winds set themselves up in contrapuntal opposition to the strings; and the lightning bolts
intertwine, both from the heights and depths.[12]

It was Donald Tovey who brought this predominantly Continental critical
matrix into the mainstream of Anglo-American analytic criticism. (See Cook
1993, 65–67 for a short tracing of English reactions to this spot.) Like Nef,
Tovey calls the recapitulation "catastrophic" and finds Grove's triumphant
major tonic "very terrible." Tovey provides his own extremely influential,
twentieth-century twist on the prevailing storm imagery, turning it into a
tempest in outer space: "instead of a distant nebula, we see the heavens on
fire" (Tovey 1935, 18). This incandescent image might well remind one of
the "darkly-flaming" Earth-Spirit; as Nicholas Cook points out, Tovey is
largely responsible in the English-speaking world for turning the imperialist
triumph of Grove's account into something "threatening, destructive, inhuman" (Cook 1993, 66).[13]

As German-language criticism approaches the present day, the critical
tone becomes more abstract; Riezler, much influenced by Schenker, seems
to take a theoretically detached attitude toward the fateful chord progression
(though he gives us little analytic detail). He sees it as not a catastrophe, but
a clever piece of compositional craft: "the reprise begins . . . over a first-inversion D-major chord . . . from which the following D minor is derived with the
greatest subtlety" ("die Reprise beginnt . . . über dem . . . Dur-Sextakkord,
von dem aus mit höchster Kunst . . . das erforderliche d-moll gewonnen
wird."; Riezler 1936, 218). Adorno's description of the formal struggles of the
musical subject in late Beethoven appear to influence the terms in which
later German critics transcendentalize the violent struggle of this spot; in the
view of Wilhelm Sauer, for whom this moment is the "flashpoint" (*Bren-
npunkt*) and the "heart" (*Herzstuck*) of the entire movement, what is at stake
is nothing less than man's existential predicament: "What is achieved here is
an amalgamation of the struggles of all men, all peoples, all mankind from
the point of view of the eternal law, the heavenly order-of-things. The *basic
idea of the first movement* is the universal wrestling of the divisiveness and multiplicity of Life toward heavenly harmony."[14]

The physical battle described by earlier auditors has been raised—sublimated?—to the more rarified level of "World-Tragedy," but it rages in "mon-
strous earnest" (*ungeheuren Ernst*) nonetheless.[15]

Sex, Violence, and the "murderous rage of a rapist incapable of attaining release"

It was left for Susan McClary to reacquaint the late twentieth century with
just how dangerously sublime, how physically threatening, this music once

sounded, before the total ascendancy of beautifying criticism. The present survey of the Ninth's rather disreputable reception history should mute the theatrical howls of astonishment that have dogged McClary's "outrageous" interpretation of the Ninth. Once aware of its parallels in tone, impression, and even imagery with an entire line of sublimating male critics, it is much harder to dismiss her narrative of desire, frustration, and violence as the product of a hysterical (not historical) imagination.[16]

But for a professional musicologist to hear Beethoven as transgressively violent in 1987 was to swim against an overwhelming discursive tide. Beautifying—the use of formalist analysis and the ideology of absolute music to neaten things up, to construct a *cordon sanitaire* around cherished works of music—has become the default interpretive strategy for canonic music.[17] Few respectable music scholars today would dare implicate themselves in the hermeneutic promiscuity, the enthusiastic rooting around for extra-musical imagery to communicate their subjective response to musical events, that solid nineteenth-century citizens like Marx and Riemann allowed themselves as a matter of course. Sublimating criticism survives only in sublimated form, where nothing is at stake but the clash of abstract nouns; or as a detached attempt to reconstruct the hermeneutics of earlier, more analytically innocent times (Treitler 1989, 30–33).

Swimming against the formalist tide is a familiar position for McClary; she has consistently been impatient with academic musicology's attempts to normalize disturbing musical constructions through grim adherence to structural hearing: "The combination of intense attraction and fear of the irrational or of the sensual creates a strange set of priorities: to seize the objects that are most profoundly disturbing and to try to explain away—through extensive verbalizing and theorizing—that which caused the disturbance" (McClary and Walser 1990, 286).

McClary's original take on the first-movement recapitulation of the Ninth was actually an aside within this more general critique of formalist analysis: "For most of the history of post-Renaissance Western music and in virtually all of its critical literature, the sexual dimensions of its mechanisms have been shamelessly exploited and yet consistently denied . . . the climax-principle has been transcendentalized to the status of a value-free universal of form" (McClary 1987, 12). Beethoven is the perfect counterexample, the composer who realizes these climax mechanisms with such blatant violence (McClary's infamous "pelvic pounding") that the "ongoing academic struggle to control music objectively" becomes absurd: "the musicologist must silence music, deny that it has meaning, and impose theoretical closure on this discourse that often provokes far more than it can contain" (23).

McClary was not alone in using Beethovenian extremity to uncover academic defense mechanisms: the very next year Joseph Kerman argued that Schenkerian organicism was a uniquely attractive alternative for those who couldn't take the physical violence of the Fifth (Kerman 1988); a year after that, Richard Taruskin lambasted pseudo-historical theses about performance practice that allowed performers to resist the unfashionably "cosmic" idealism of the Ninth (Taruskin 1989).

But—perhaps inevitably—McClary's Beethoven-based feminist criticism was read as a feminist criticism of Beethoven, and it struck a painful nerve. That first tangential aside in the *Minnesota Composer's Forum Newsletter* caused such furor that when the essay was reprinted in book form (McClary 1991) she evidently felt it necessary to expand her discussion and explain some of the structural assumptions that gave rise to her earlier impressionistic account. The general tone of this second description is quite controlled. McClary situates the passage as the climactic, "horrifyingly violent" moment in an Adorno-esque conflict between the musical subject (the first theme) and the pressures of a tonal narrative that relentlessly threatens its individuality:

> But for the subject of the Ninth, to return to the beginning is to actually regress to a point further back than its own conscious beginnings: it is to be dissolved back into the undifferentiated state from which it originally emerged. And if its hard-won identity means anything, the subject cannot accept such dissolution, even if it is toward that conventional moment of re-entry that the whole background structure of the movement has inexorably driven. (1991, 128)

There is a clear—and perhaps unexpected, given McClary's reputation—resonance here with the sternly philosophic, patriarchal view represented by German critics like Adorno and Sauer, in which this moment represents the tragic, doomed struggle of individual subjectivity with Society, Fate, or the principles of Eternal Law.

The 1991 description also echoes significant details of many earlier accounts. McClary, like Wagner, Marx, and Riemann, even invokes Goethe's *Faust* ("Verweile nur, du bist so schön," in reference to the slow movement). Marx's electrical storm and Tovey's supernova/air raid now appear in late twentieth-century guise, as a grim science-fiction battle in space: "the subject . . . finds itself in the throes of the initial void while refusing to relent: the entire first key area in the recapitulation is pockmarked with explosions" (1991, 129).

Yet there is something that does appear to be quite new in McClary's critical response; as a woman, she is much more sensitive to the repressed libidinal implications of this violent struggle. In 1991 she speaks of the "juxtaposition of desire and unspeakable violence"; in 1987 this juxtaposition was at the center of her description:

> The point of recapitulation in the first movement of the Ninth is one of the most horrifying moments in music, *as the carefully prepared cadence is frustrated,*

> *damming up energy which finally explodes in the throttling, murderous rage of a rapist incapable of attaining release.* The 'triumphal' end of the symphony—in which promised cadences repeatedly are withheld at the last moment—finally simply forces closure by bludgeoning the cadence and the piece to death. (McClary 1987, 12–13—emphasis mine, following that of posterity)

This image of "Beethoven the rapist" is, of course, painful in the extreme—and scandalizing to many readers. But if we examine the rape image in light of the descriptions of earlier sublimating critics, we can see its origin: McClary makes exactly the same imaginative cathexis as Marx, Kretzschmar, et al.—but she reinterprets the violent, confusing, overpowering physicality of the experience from her female subject position.

The inherent sadomasochism of the sublime now takes on a new, threatening aspect. When Beethoven's "demonic intentions" (Kretzschmar) and his "overwhelming demonic fantasies" (Riemann) are redirected, when the relation between the masculine composer and the masculine critic is replaced by that between a masculine composer and a *feminine* critic—what other gendered image carries as much force as rape?

> The pain suffered by the imagination in judgments upon the sublime has lead some critics of Kant to denounce the tyranny of reason, to which the imagination submits itself in judgments upon the sublime. Undoubtedly, Kant's references in this context to subjection *(Unterwerfung)*, violence *(Gewalt)*, deprivation *(Emphasis Beraubung)*, and sacrifice *(Aufopferung)*, encourage such an interpretation. The notion of *Beraubung Emphasis*is particularly significant here, since in addition to its usual meaning of "being robbed," it can also suggest rape.[18]

Push just a little bit on Marx's 1859 description and sexual violence is exactly what you will get. As we have seen, it was Marx who first linked Beethoven's recapitulation to a specific moment in Goethe's *Faust,* the apparition of the *Erdgeist.* For fin-de-siècle playwright Frank Wedekind, this "Earth-Spirit" was a frankly sexual being, a fact so self-evident that he could appropriate it as just another name for Lulu, his avatar of sexual destruction. (The first published part of Wedekind's "Lulu-play" was called simply *Erdgeist.*[19]) The scene Marx recalls reads easily as a barely-disguised episode of homosexual rape, as Faust evokes the (at that point male) Earth-Spirit in a flood of feminized, sexualized longing:

> Reveal yourself!
> Ha! How my heart is gored
> By never felt urges,
> And my whole body surges—
> My heart is yours; yours, too am I.
> You must. You must. Though I should have to die.

The swooning language is that of the bodice-ripping romance novel—or of Sacher-Masoch's *Venus in Furs*. The imperious Earth-Spirit is quite ready to play along, too: "Could it be you who at my breath's slight shiver / Are to the depths of life aquiver, / A miserably writhing worm?"[20] As Faust grovels on the floor in masochistic ecstasy, one might ask—at what peril does a woman enter into that kind of scene?

A specific concordance of detail may cement the point. In 1846, Wagner—who gave us that image of the first theme striding onstage, "naked [!] and powerful"—reported that he thought he saw two powerful wrestlers in a clinch right around this spot ("wir zwei mächtige Ringer zu erblicken glauben"; p. 247). McClary in 1991 echoes the image, postulating that we consider composers like Beethoven, who "push mechanisms of frustration to the limit" as "more serious, more virile"—"they don't pull punches, *they go all the way to the mat*" (p. 127). Take those two (male) wrestlers on the mat, and simply replace one of them with a woman, and ask yourself honestly what it is *you* think you see.

Let me stop here to draw the obvious conclusion: those who attack McClary for unacceptably stretching the limits of interpretation around the Ninth Symphony must rely on a biased, historically unsupportable reading of Beethoven reception that ignores reams of nineteenth-century sublimating description. Accepting her rape metaphor does not drop one into a bad postmodern episteme where "anything goes." Nor must one assume, as does Pieter C. van den Toorn, that only "unrelated personal animosity . . . fanned by an aversion for male sexuality" (van den Toorn 1995, 40) could lead her to invoke sexual violence when confronted with this music. Determinedly unaware of a coherent tradition of glossing this moment with a narrow range of highly-charged images, van den Toorn finds any metaphorical interpretation of its physical extremity as good (or as bad) as any other: "[there is] no reason to suppose 'pelvic pounding' rather than drunkenness, boisterousness, laughter, athletic exercise, aerobic dancing, or the like" (41). In response, I can only report that I have found no accounts in the literature analogizing this particular recapitulation as cheerful and healthy aerobic exercise; on the other hand, there are numerous accounts that evoke frustration, irrationality, physical violence, and pain. Further, one of the most popular interpretive gambits—the claim that Beethoven had conjured an uncontrollable musical *Erdgeist* out of his "demonic" Faustian fantasies—had already brought a strong undertone of transgressive sexual desire to the discourse as early as 1859.

Schenker pugnaciously claimed that his beautifying explanations had for the first time deciphered the Ninth in terms of its "true content"—by which he meant, paradoxically, the organic necessity of its *form* —a modernist triumph that would, in time, make all other hermeneutic strategies obsolete. And it did, for a while. Academic musicologists forgot what Schenker himself was painfully aware of: that other possessors of the Y chromosome, respected critics like Marx, Riemann, and Kretschmar, had previously experienced Beethoven's Ninth not only as prolongations and scale steps, but as "the overwhelming, demonic fantasy of the Master's creative impulse." Out of that collective fantasy they constructed not only Beethoven Hero, the man who freed music, but Beethoven Antihero, the Faustian purveyor of sublime eroticized violence. In the discourse around the Ninth, McClary is hardly outside the pale, and to dismiss her as a man-hating feminist (see below) is to repress large swaths of reception history. When it comes to sublimating criticism, she is just one of the guys.

And yet, for all its continuities in tone and imagery with a long line of male accounts, the value judgment implied by McClary's feminist critique (yet *not* overtly levied within it, I hasten to add) does appear to open up a radically new and negative hermeneutic, at least within high art music criticism. Where male critics felt only masochistic pleasure, McClary allows for the possibility of dread.

(Not Listening to the) Sex, Violence, and Failure:
"The theme, look for the theme!"

Lyotard asserts, paradoxically, that the postmodern actually *precedes* the modern: "Postmodernism . . . is not modernism at its end but in the nascent state, and this state is constant" (1992, 146). The reception history of the Ninth validates this seeming oxymoron quite precisely. The proto-postmodernist hermeneutic excess of old-fashioned Romanticism, "modernism in the nascent state," gives rise dialectically to full-blown modernist criticism; sublimating criticism begets beautifying. But the postmodern moment within the modern is constant; it does not disappear, and whenever it reappears, as in the work of McClary, it precipitates a violent high-modernist reaction. Schenker was quite brutal in his dismissal of Riemann and Kretschmar ("their complete unproductivity in all directions—that is, toward both interpretation and performance—must be affirmed"; Schenker 1992, 20), but his rhetoric pales in comparison with what Susan McClary has had to take from Pieter van den Toorn: "Fanned by an aversion for male sexuality, which is depicted as something brutal and contemptible, irrelevancies are being read into the music" (1991, 293).

That's just plain nasty. (To van den Toorn's credit, the above sentence does not reappear in his 1995 book.) But behind the personal animosity is a familiar beautifying strategy: like Schenker, van den Toorn wants to refocus attention away from "irrelevancies" and onto the formal specificity of the music itself. He is confident that the two can have no intersection, that musical detail and sexual politics cannot mix:

Drawn into greater and more explicit detail, the one side could only disappoint the other, become the distraction of the other. It would be diminished, reduced to a form of silliness. This happens with McClary's analysis of the Ninth . . . additional detail undermines the alleged relationship between music and sex or sexual politics; the two sides are pulled further apart. (van den Toorn 1995, 36)

If all that was at stake was the acknowledgment within the Ninth of the romantic-modern sublime, of unpresentable content mediated by the power of formal presentation, we might attempt to make a separate peace with van den Toorn. Lyotard's conception of the modern sublime does allow for a kind of appreciation that, moving away from a sense of powerlessness and pain, identifies with the intelligence that empowers a composer like Beethoven to present the unpresentable through formal abstraction: "the emphasis can be placed on the increase of being and the jubilation which results from the invention of new rules of the game" (1992, 147). In other words: one can beautify the sublime, one can "look for the theme."

But what if one reads McClary's failed rapist as an avatar of the presence within Beethoven's Ninth of the *postmodern* sublime, of the traumatic moment where the unpresentable breaks through into presentation itself? In that case beautifying criticism's defensive focus on formal innovation ("new rules of the game") would provide little protection, since the collapse of the masterwork's "organic" form would be precisely the issue. But to grasp the totality of that collapse, we must take up van den Toorn's challenge to work the rape metaphor deeply into the detail of Beethoven's music, the detail he so confidently assumes will make a mockery of it, that he assumes is unproblematically on "his" side.

How then to unravel the confusing welter of details at measures 301–15 of the first movement of the Ninth?

Most critics look to the bass of this passage: they are trying to come to terms with an essential failure of functional root progression at a pivotal moment in the harmonic drama. The dynamics of sonata form demand a major harmonic arrival on the home tonic at this point: if not a perfect V–I closure, at least some easily recognizable transformation. The general consensus is that measures 295–301 do not provide that closure: the dominant is too weak and abrupt, and the first-inversion major tonic too unstable for such an important formal juncture. Indeed, the F♯ in the bass of the tonic triad at measure 301 introduces another, conflicting harmonic imperative, for it sounds very much like a leading tone to G minor. Thus as we wait for the immobile D major to move in measures 301–12, expectation builds for the basic cadential progression that will neatly resolve both local and global harmonic needs: I^6–iv–V–i, as in example 4.1a. This tonic–predominant–dominant–tonic is the

Example 4.1   "Underlying" root progression for Beethoven, Ninth Symphony I, mm. 315–30.

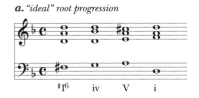

a. *"ideal" root progression*

b. *"raised IV"—Riemann, Schenker*

c. *"German 6th"—Treitler, van den Toorn*

"ideal-type" background progression from which most analysts have tried to derive what actually goes on at measures 312–15. The older, scale-step theorists (Riemann 1889, Schenker 1912) thus explain B♭–D–F–A♭ as a subdominant with a raised root, in first inversion (♯iv⁶₄), which leads to an elided root-position dominant and thence back to the tonic (ex. 4.1b). More recent analysts (Treitler 1980, 1982; van den Toorn 1991) do not feel obligated to ascribe root function to every triad; they account for B♭–D–F–A♭ as a linear chord—specifically a German augmented-sixth (G⁶) that functions as an exotic predominant replacement for iv. As in the earlier analyses, the root position V is elided—as well as the V⁶₄ that would normally precede it (ex. 4.1c).

The problem with these explanations is that when one actually listens to the passage, *neither* really makes sense of Beethoven's realization. Explaining B♭–D–F–A♭ as a linear-generated German sixth may seem more plausible than sophistically claiming a chord built on the sharp fourth scale degree is a functional "subdominant"; but it raises another, equally intractable problem. If the functionality of "♯iv⁶" is destroyed by its chromatic adulteration, the intelligibility of the "German sixth" is equally damaged by Beethoven's refusal to carry out its linear implications. It is not so much that neither the G$\sharp$ (= A$\flat$) nor the B$\flat$ of the G^6 are approached by step (G^6 usually provides a chromatic transition between iv and V, not a complete replacement of iv), but that the augmented-sixth interval is not allowed to resolve to an octave: G$\sharp$ moves to A, but the bass B$\flat$ does not progress to A, leaping instead down to F.[21] The distinguishing sound of a "functional" G^6, the chromatic approach to the dominant, as represented by the octave on scale degree 5, is totally lost.

This is the point at which a critic with sublimating tendencies throws up his hands and begins talking about "Beethoven's demonic intentions." But it is possible to go much further in the attempt to beautify this progression; one of the most extensive clean-up efforts was undertaken by van den Toorn to rebut McClary's reading. Van den Toorn admits that the G^6 in measure 312 is "from the standpoint of the voice-leading in the bass, approached and resolved in a highly unorthodox manner." But he immediately moves to minimize the problem: "Yet it should be noted that omissions of this kind occur elsewhere in Beethoven's music. . . . Indeed, shortchanging the counterpoint of this cadential cliché, circumventing its stylistic redundancy with inflections of a more immediately individual or contextual character, is fairly common in nineteenth-century music." The beautifying rhetorical strategy is clear: the traditional G^6–V$^6_4$–V–I is a "cadential cliché," worn out, used up—it should be so familiar to us ("stylistically redundant") that Beethoven can disrupt it freely without any danger of our failing to comprehend. The shift in perspective removes any sense of danger from the passage: instead of a dramatic gesture distorted into menacing opacity, we are asked to consider a boring platitude livened up by a bit of compositional play.

To buttress his analysis, van den Toorn points out two spots later in the Ninth, as well as famous passages in Brahms and Schubert, where a G^6–I cadence is presented with the root-position V either delayed or elided altogether. But all these examples postdate the passage in question, so their retroactive explanatory relevance to this particular spot seems somewhat diminished.

More crucially, not one of van den Toorn's analogous passages is actually as fundamental a linear "shortchanging" of the G^6 cadence as Beethoven's mangled progression at measures 312–13. The difference is small, but profound: it is true that neither Beethoven or his contemporaries felt that there was anything wrong with going directly from a G^6 to a tonic triad—as long as the tonic was in $^6_4$ position, so that the $^\flat$6 in the bass could progress correctly, falling a half-step to the dominant of the local key. This "tonic $^6_4$" at the cadence functions as a dominant. If the composer then chooses not to resolve the $^6_4$, the chord will eventually progress (or perhaps just metamorphose) directly into a root-position tonic; the resulting "V–I" bass progression is strong enough to make good the omission in the upper voices. This is in fact the case in every one of van den Toorn's counterexamples. But, as I pointed out above, the single most disruptive fact about measures 312–13 is that the G^6 "resolves" not to a common dominant substitute, but to an extremely uncommon first-inversion tonic, forcing the B♭ in the bass not to A, but to F. That is why Beethoven can keep the tonic D pedal sounding in the timpani underneath this G^6 *and its resolution,* underscoring the fact that there is actually no dominant functionality in the passage at all. This is, to my mind, the difference between "shortchanging a cadential cliché" and a much more radical compositional gesture: destroying any sense of comprehensible cadential syntax. Van den Toorn's comparisons covertly beautify: they put back in the structural dominant that Beethoven so disruptively left out.

But identifying the "deviation" (however extreme) is merely the first step; as van den Toorn quite rightly points out, the focus of analysis should be the *significance* of the deviation, how it functions in a particular context. In fact, of course, analysis creates that context, and this van den Toorn now proceeds to do. He rationalizes the irregular resolution of B♭ by pointing out that it is part of a local motivic relationship: the F–B♭–F in the bass is to be heard as an imitation of the preceding D–A–D in the strings, and thus, we assume, a thematic echo of the basic material of the movement (ex. 4.2). ("The theme, listen for the theme!") A more global context explains the "dramatic F♯–F slip" as an echo of another prominent half-step slip in the movement, the beginning of the development at measure 160. The loud F♯ itself echoes measure 186, cementing a symmetrical formal relationship between the beginning and the end of the development section.

One might quibble with some of the details of this context. The relationship between D–A–D (4th + 5th) and F–B♭–F (5th + 4th) is more complex than simple imitation, and surely the passage most echoed by measures 312–15 is not the opening of the development but the counterstatement of the first theme at measures 48–50, with its own sudden drop from D–A–D to F–B♭–F. But it is not my aim to "tyrannize" van den Toorn by forbidding him contextual hearing and the power of his analytical insights. It is certainly possible to hear this moment of recapitulation van den Toorn's way if one desires; the issue is not one of right or wrong. Rather, the questions that need to be asked are: What do we gain by hearing measures 301–15 only this way? Conversely, what must we give up?

Van den Toorn is forthright in describing the benefits he gains by hearing within the context he has constructed: "[the F♯–F slip] projects a large-scale formal association that tends to dampen, at least for this observer, its potential for alarm, the effect of 'horror' or 'murderous rage' felt by McClary" (1995, 34). Here is the clearest possible statement of the defensive, distancing aim of beautifying analysis. Over 150 years after Griepenkerl's novel, van den Toorn is still playing Adalbert to Susan McClary's Vicarius, using purely musical intuitions to call her back from dangerous hermeneu-

Example 4.2   Thematic "echo" in Beethoven, Ninth Symphony I, mm. 311–16; after van den Toorn 1995.

tic excess, his analytical counterargument not much more than a more sophisticated and extended version of . . .

"The *theme*, listen for the theme!"

MOMENT TWO: THE UNSALVAGEABLE FORM (POSTMODERN SUBLIMITY)

Recent critical musicology has foresworn beautifying projects on canonic masterpieces; faced with an entrenched post-Schenkerian tradition of using analytical rigor as the most effective way to repress the sublime, the "new" musicology has also tended to forswear rigorous technical analysis. Even now, we still inscribe a piece like Beethoven's Ninth under the sign of the modern sublime, the perfect form that rescues us from impossible or transgressive content. Formal analysis would then *by definition* be beautification, a subtle or not-so-subtle relaxation toward the reassuring certainties and away from the challenging confusions of this (or any) modern artwork.

But who is to say that the form of Beethoven's Ninth actually holds any reassuring certainties? In the second part of this essay, I intend to use the first-movement recapitulation as the touchstone in a wide-ranging analytical discussion that incorporates all the richness of musical detail I can muster. The burden of the argument will be that, far from offering us salvation from the symphony's unpresentable content, the form of Beethoven's Ninth is itself not salvageable, shattered at its critical structural turning points by the irruption of the unpresentable into the act of presentation. I believe, *pace* van den Toorn, that the deeper we delve into the specific musical and formal tensions this work enacts, the more "potential for alarm" we will find.

Let us begin by taking McClary's infamous evocation of the postmodern sublime not as a simplistic statement about content, but as a complex intuition about form. It might be schematically unpacked as follows. The thrusting drive of tonal music, the intertwining of harmonic and formal necessity, is physical, and gives rise to a physical desire—analogous to sexual desire. In measures 301–15, Beethoven focuses all the potential desire of a large-scale symphonic form onto a single cadential moment (McClary: "damming up energy"), and then proceeds to botch it unforgettably in a passage of terrifyingly violent orchestral kineticism (McClary: "which finally explodes in the throttling, murderous rage of a rapist") that is thereby frustrated, which is to say reconverted into potential (McClary: "unable to attain release").

It is worth pointing out how far this is from a man-hating condemnation of "Beethoven the Pornographer" (van den Toorn 1991, 291). We the listeners are both raped and rapists. It is both *our* desire that is frustrated by the botched progression, and *our* bodies and minds that are overwhelmed by the "noise" of the orchestra and the irrationality of the passage. McClary does not just "cry rape": she evokes the complex mimetic image of *a rapist who is unable to attain release.* And in this she provides a precise echo of previous male critics like A. B. Marx ("To conclude?—no, that is *not* within the power of this troubled Giant-Spirit"). She introduces them to Adrienne Rich, whose poem on the Ninth begins: "A man in terror of *impotence* . . ."

Thus the first step toward understanding the larger structural implications of this traumatic passage is to hear it as a violent acting out covering up a more fundamental formal impotence; this reading of the musical surface becomes increasingly insistent as we survey critical responses from Marx to McClary. To go any further, we must break new ground, and investigate in a more detailed and unconventional way just what it is that this passage was trying—and so conspicuously failing—to do.

The "Lydian" Ascent

First we can abandon the attempt to salvage the enigmatic bass progression at measure 318. Let it stand unrationalized as a mimesis of failure, a pure *negation* of some other musical process. We need to concentrate not on the

Example 4.3   Beethoven, *Missa Solemnis*, Gloria, mm. 176–90.

bass, but on what the bass denies: the soprano line, which it flatly refuses to support, specifically the A♭(G♯)→ A in the first flute. Physical extremity and rhythmic surprise mark this G♯–A as a significant melodic climax; the non-progression of the bass marks it (*makes* it) unequivocally a failure. In this case, Beethoven has annihilated his climax so thoroughly that little more than the indecipherable fragments from some kind of rising line are left behind. To reconstruct this ascent, and ascertain its place within some larger formal mechanism, we can attempt to read it through another failed ascent, analogous in structure, but less extreme and thus less distorted. Example 4.3 reproduces what I feel is a functionally identical spot in the *Missa Solemnis:* measures 176–90 of the Gloria ("Domine Deus, Rex coelestis, Deus pater omnipotens"). This passage displays a striking identity of surface detail, local harmonic progression, and large-scale formal function with measures 301–15. Once we determine how this earlier failed climax works, we can use that knowledge to comprehend the later and significantly more disrupted passage.

Simple enumeration will document a telling repetition of compositional detail: both climaxes are built around the same loud, off-balance anticipation of the B♭–D–F–A♭ sonority (*ff* in the Ninth, *fff* in the Gloria). Both surprise chords support a long A♭ in the flutes that progresses directly and enharmonically to A. Both passages are sonically extreme: the prolonged orchestral battering of the Ninth is matched in sheer violence by the Gloria's overwhelming and isolated blast (*fff* tutti with chorus, trombones) on the crucial B♭7 —a truly awesome depiction of the "pater omnipotens." Even the drumroll on a non-fundamental D is the same.

The convergence of sound is the visceral clue to an identity of function. Both of these passages attempt a piece of modulatory trickery very characteristic of Beethoven: they reinterpret a dominant-seventh chord (B♭–D–F–A♭) as a German sixth (B♭–D–F–G♯) to force an enharmonic shortcut out of a long flat-side excursion and back home to D major. The harmonic functions map quite neatly from one piece to the other (see ex. 4.4). Both passages come from the flat side of D—the Gloria from E♭ (locally IV/B♭; m. 174), the Ninth from F (measures 287 ff.). In both cases the sudden intrusion of an F♯ instead of the expected F creates a D-major triad, which functions locally as V/gm (Gloria, mm. 182–84; Ninth, mm. 301–11). At this point, the Gloria, composing out van den Toorn's "cadential cliché," gives us fully and explicitly what the Ninth elides and distorts beyond recognition. V/gm actually resolves to G minor in measure 185 of the Gloria, followed immediately by the pivotal B♭–D–F–A♭, whose enharmonic resolution to a unison A (= V/D, resolving in the next measure) this time makes perfect voice-leading sense.

Yet this modulatory progression, though more syntactically correct than its counterpart in the Ninth, is no less a failure to establish D major as tonic. Beethoven immediately undermines his seemingly "omnipotent" climax. Measures 192–95 provide an exceptionally vivid piece of mime in which the *fff* tutti falls apart before our eyes: fading shards of the movement's opening motive disintegrate into aimless woodwind chattering while the energy of rushing unison scales in the strings audibly droops and dissipates, section by section. And, just as in the Ninth, we realize retroactively that the big D-major chord at this climax was not a tonic, but a dominant. By allowing B♭ and E♭ to reassert themselves, Beethoven turns the omnipotent D into a somewhat querulous V9/gm—and we fall back to the flat side again. The final clue, though inaudible, is unequivocal in its symbolic import. The written key signature after the climax is the same as it was before: two flats. In terms of *real* modulatory activity, nothing has happened—just as in measures 301–15 of the Ninth, where the implied key signature both coming in (F major) and going out (D minor) is one flat.[22]

So it appears that no amount of physical (or rhetorical) force will convert this enharmonic trick into a true modulation; in retrospect, the brutal excess of both these G6 chords only betrays a foreknowledge of failure, the awareness that the rules are being broken, that this shortcut between third-related triads ultimately won't work. Indeed, the significance of this particular and complicated mimetic gesture (stressed G6 leads to instantaneous modulation up by third; premature arrival on major tonic; immediate disintegration) was being established by Beethoven as early as 1807. In mea-

Example 4.4   Linear-harmonic comparison of Beethoven, Ninth Symphony I, mm. 287–315 with *Missa Solemnis,* Gloria, mm. 174–200.

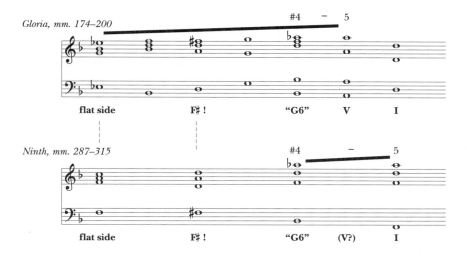

sures 73–91 of the slow movement of the Fifth Symphony, there is an abrupt "modulation" from the flat side (A♭) to the tonic major of the entire work (C major) accomplished by an unexpected and assaultive G6; this highly unstable tonic then fades away, evaporating back into the flat side through an amorphous chromatic passage.

The "G6 cadence" in this mimetic context becomes a signifier of harmonic failure; its similar appearance provides a convincing link between measures 185–89 of the Gloria and measures 312–15 of the first movement of the Ninth. As we know from tonal theory, G6 is primarily a linear chord, and it is as a signifier of *linear* failure that I ultimately want to consider it. It is in terms of long-range dramatic voice leading that reading the Ninth through the Gloria begins to pay off most spectacularly. These passages both use local harmonic failures to undermine the large-scale linear structures that aim to climax above them. But the linear ascent that was shattered beyond reconstruction in the Ninth is merely negated, after the fact, in the Gloria. In fact, the *Lydian ascent* that is momentarily achieved in measures 174–89 of the Gloria, together with the bass line that ultimately undermines it, gives us the basic outline of a complex linear-harmonic template that functions on a large scale in both the Ninth and the *Missa Solemnis.*

One can see the melodic significance of the G♯–A that is common to both failed climaxes more clearly in the more coherent linear context of the Gloria: there it functions as the powerfully stressed last step in a chromatic ascent from D to A that spans measures 173–89 (see the soprano line of ex.

4.3). This ascent to scale degree 5 (in the high soprano register) by way of a dramatically highlighted sharp fourth scale degree is the basic prototype of successful linear motion in the Ninth and the D-major sections of the *Missa* —thus the descriptive term "Lydian."

The Lydian Ascent, the Missing Dominant, and the Subdominant Collapse

A cursory look at the D-centered movements in the *Missa Solemnis* and the Ninth Symphony will uncover plentiful attempts at this climactic Lydian march up to the fifth scale degree (Gloria, measures 38–42, 303–12; 335–45, 509–25, 530–42; Dona nobis pacem, measures 350–74; Ninth I, measures 31–35, 55–63, 301–15, 531–39; Ninth IV, measures 325–29, 832–41; see Fink 1994). But what does it mean to argue that this melodic mannerism encodes some kind of possible formal success—and, conversely, that diatonic climactic progressions more firmly "in D" are to be heard as "failures"? How is it that the diatonic scale steps of D major are somehow *not good enough* for the Ninth?

I have discussed what Leo Treitler once called "the phenomenology of key relations" in the *Missa Solemnis* and the Ninth Symphony at length elsewhere (Fink 1994, 167–71). I will simply recall here what Treitler and others have noted: that large-scale tonal relationships in the Ninth Symphony are plagued by a pull toward the flat side, "down" toward "darker" keys like B-flat and E-flat, a pull that has the effect of derailing, time and again, the move "up" and sharpwards to the dominant (Treitler 1989, 57–63).[23] This seductive pull, if indulged, threatens to usurp the tonic–dominant polarity that is an absolute necessity if a traditional sonata form (which the Ninth still emphatically tries to be) is to make sense.

The battle against this flat-side pull lies behind two of the most commented-upon narrative threads in the Ninth's symphonic plot: the drive to move from D minor to D major; and the equally compelling need to exorcise B-flat so that it can no longer compete as a tonal center with D. The dramatic coups de théâtre are familiar to anyone who has studied the piece: sudden unmotivated drops by third to F, B♭, and even E♭ triads at critical moments in the form; systematic displacement of secondary key areas in the dominant or relative major with moves to the flat submediant; increasingly violent attempts to banish E♭s and B♭s from crucial cadential gestures; the final achievement of a hushed and radiant B major, followed by the heedless rush of a (seemingly) unsullied D-major corroboree.

Thus for most commentators, the story of the Ninth is about getting rid of the tonal intrusions that undermine the stability of the D-major tonic. But simply banishing "wrong notes" and "wrong keys," sharping all the F♮s and naturalizing all the B♭s, does not actually solve the fundamental tonal aporia of the work: the fatal absence, especially in the D-centered outer movements, of a firmly articulated structural dominant. Beethoven's attempted solution, unremarked by previous analytical commentary, seems to have been to change the actual character of his D tonic so that it could take over at least some of the function of this missing dominant—in effect, to "Lydianize" the tonic areas of the Ninth, to tilt them sharpwards, so that they *always already* carry the tonic–dominant polarity with them.

This sharpward tilt makes itself felt primarily as a melodic tendency toward the fifth scale degree. Consider the first tonic sonority of the Ninth, at measures 15–16: it is a "D chord," but only eight players are on D (the two bassoons and the two B♭ horns, doubled), while all of the sixty-odd other instrumentalists who are playing have the pitch A (there is no F).[24] To a remarkable degree the melodic goal of significant "tonic" climaxes in the D-centered sections of the Ninth is the dominant A, not the fundamental D— thus the famous opening of the Ninth, where A enters, grows, and ascends to the highest orchestral register *before* D appears, and is even allowed to generate its own upper fifth, E.

This is the crucial formal function of the Ninth's repeated attempts at dramatic "Lydian" approaches to scale degree 5: a melodic emphasis on G♯–A progressions at significant cadences attempts to provide the necessary sharpening force to establish D major as a tonic *without a dominant,* and in spite of the disruptive gravitational pull of the lowered mediant and submediant.

It is a risky tonal strategy, to say the least—and there are two distinctive ways ascending melodic gestures toward the dominant scale degree can fail to do the job. (Here, as promised, is at least the sketch of an aesthetics of failure. For a more extensive discussion, see Fink 1994.) If the Lydian inflection is absent, if the fourth scale degree is blandly natural, we risk "subdominant collapse": rising melodic lines may stall on G, precipitating modulatory cascades in the subdominant direction. Subdominant collapse is usually the first step in a structural modulation far into the flat side—to keys like F and B♭ (see Ninth I, measures 24, 50, 70–80; IV, measures 329, 594, 643). But the Lydian ascent can also be derailed by exactly that persistent flat tendency: as the soprano ascends through G♯ to A, it may be undermined by B♭ in the bass, producing the familiar augmented sixth. Though a melodic line may briefly touch the dominant, the G[6] progression underneath inevitably succumbs to submediant pressure, and collapses even more chaotically toward the flat side.

Failure upon Failure: The Moment of Recapitulation Revisited

Both of these failures concatenate at the fateful moment of recapitulation. The "G[6] cadence" is, of course, the brusque harmonic shortcut we have already identified at measure 312 as a sign of modulatory failure. In this context it is a gesture of complete formal disintegration, coming as it does directly on the heels of a *previous* failed attempt to avoid flat-side collapse and stabilize D major as tonic.

I consider the linear-dramatic significance of the famously "darkly blazing" D-major chord itself, voiced with a prominent A on top, to be the desperate attempt to avoid an incipient subdominant collapse, to progress directly from an unsharped fourth to a stable fifth scale degree. The first horn's seventh at measures 293–300 does not fall to the third; it *rises to the fifth* in direct and visceral contravention of voice-leading rules—in effect, against tonal "gravity." (Contrary to his received image as a brutal and heedless orchestrator, Beethoven could be exquisitely considerate of instrumental needs when it suited his dramatic purpose. So the hornists are the only players given rests on the last beat before D major crashes in; they alone have time to breathe and prepare a true *ff* attack. We *need* that high A.)

This to me is what is so terrible about the "terrible" D major: the sheer violence channeled into supporting the doomed D–A fifth—an interval whose imminent collapse will call into question a basic axiom of Beethoven's tonal harmony. The perceptual precision of A. B. Marx's Faustian fustian now becomes impressively clear: he is exactly right to focus on the way that Beethoven makes F♯–A–D sound as if unnaturally (and precariously) frozen in place: "er . . . steht . . . zwölf Takte lang, unbeweglich wie ein Schreckensphantom, auf Fis-A-D . . ." And Faust's cry of horror in the face of this "terrifying phantom" could double as Beethoven's cry of despair when the horns collapse down to low [D] in measure 312: "Weh! Ich ertrag dich nicht!" (The English equivalent that best captures the linear double meaning is "I cannot *bear* you"—both "I cannot *endure* you" and "I cannot *hold* you *up*"; the root of *ertragen* is *tragen* = "carry.") The open fifth, so cosmically weightless in the Ninth's opening bars, now carries all the weight of tonic–dominant polarity, and is literally insupportable without some dramatic reinforcement.

The crucial fifth scale degree is *so* unstable that Beethoven immediately resorts to a brutal G^6 cadence in hopes of generating a dramatic Lydian progression to shore it up. When that cadence collapses in a welter of voice-leading mistakes, the double failure extinguishes all hope for the strong push through sharp 4 to 5 that would buttress tonic–dominant polarity and in so doing, at least partially compensate for the movement's lack of a structural dominant. Beethoven's "inability to attain release" at this pivotal formal moment—he tries to get it up (to A), and fails *twice!*—threatens the global collapse of tonal logic. The unspeakable content ("A man in terror of impotence . . .") leaves its trace on the music itself: a failed recapitulation; a linear collapse; a shattered tonic–dominant polarity; ultimately, an unsalvageable form.

Example 4.5   Beethoven, Ninth Symphony I, Coda, mm. 531–38: Lydian ascent returns.

Aftermath

Flutes and horns grasp desperately for the dominant A while the bass line that spiked their G^6 cadence continues to wreak havoc: metrically out of step with both winds and strings, it gnaws away at the tonic pedal, gradually forcing it flatwards with grinding C♮s and F♯s. By measure 325 we have arrived, not at the hoped-for dominant, but at a root-position *subdominant* that quickly plunges to a Neapolitan E♭.

We must wait over 200 measures for a partial retrieval of the recapitulation's titanic collapse onto the subdominant; this is the function of the very last harmonic progression of the first movement (mm. 531–38; ex. 4.5). The Lydian ascent F♯–G♯–A blared out by the *ff* woodwind (the second time in brutal unison) is clear enough; it should also be pointed out that the harmonic progression taking place over the tonic pedal is an implicit recomposition of the failed G^6 cadence of measures 312–15. D major as possible V/iv is now followed by a "corrected" predominant sonority: B♮–D–F–G♯ as °V/V, instead of B♭–D–F–A♭ as G^6/V (see the reductions in ex. 4.6).[25] With the (momentary) purging of B♭, Beethoven can finish the ascent, progressing directly to the missing root-position V and thence to the tonic.

There are no more B♭s in the first movement, but that is only because Beethoven deploys the ascending melodic version of the D-minor scale to

Example 4.6 Beethoven, Ninth Symphony I: F♯–G♯–A as scale steps; long-range connections implied by Schenker (1912).

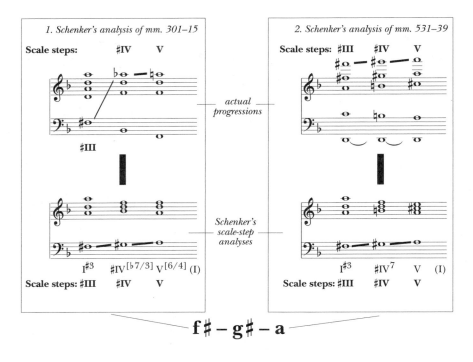

close. The first movement's final cadence, martial as it is, cannot "fix" the failure of the recapitulation by establishing D major as tonic. The second movement tries to further a Lydian agenda, moving immediately from D minor to C major (the dominant of the relative major, a "sharper" key than we might expect); it also, as van den Toorn points out, re-stages the crucial G⁶ cadence of the first movement at its own moment of recapitulation (mm. 248–83) with slightly better local results. But the ultimate outcome is yet another collapse onto B-flat as submediant (m. 304). This scherzo has a bad habit of spinning ever flatter through cycles of falling thirds (mm. 144–71); these disorienting descents prepare us for the topsy-turvy world of the slow movement, where D major is made to serve as secondary key to the submediant-as-tonic, B-flat.

That same B-flat is jammed like a dissonant splinter into the opening D-minor sonority of the last movement. This submediant-infected minor tonic is in first inversion, and "progresses" through a German-sixth chord to the dominant: with horror (nineteenth-century German critics dubbed this the

Schreckensfanfare, the "fanfare of terror") we recognize a garbled attempt at the failed progression of the first movement recapitulation. F–A–D–B♭ is an intensified version of the catastrophic i⁶, F–A–D, that closed the door on D major—and on the Lydian ascent—in the first movement; here it *precedes* the G⁶ in a sublime moment of formal and harmonic torment. (The second terror-fanfare is truly gruesome, jamming pitches from *both* submediant and dominant scale steps into F–A–D to create the proto-expressionistic hexachord F–A–D–B♭–C♯–E; see Fink 1994, 196–99.) The stage is set for the resumption of the Ninth's fundamental tonal tragedy, with the hubris of Lydian moves to impossible dominants (mm. 207, 325, 715) followed inevitably by nemesis, in the form of ever-more-vertiginous subdominant collapses (mm. 208, 329, 728).

But Beethoven allows us one visionary gleam of escape from the insoluble formal contradictions that derail the Ninth's every attempt at tonal resolution. He abandons (momentarily) his frenzied attempts to pound home a Lydianized tonic. In fact, he abandons the tonic altogether.

As the solo quartet launches into a final Lydian ascent, "poco adagio" and notably free of pelvic pounding, the soprano reaches high G, and then G♯; now, miraculously (and in context, it really does sound like a miracle), E major, the "double dominant" of D, does not fall away to the subdominant; it *becomes* the subdominant, leading to a prolonged bass pedal on F♯ as the dominant of B major. This is the same F♯ that froze in the bass as the third of an unstable first-inversion D-major triad "for twelve long bars, immovable like a terrifying specter, like the gloomily flaming *Erdgeist.*" Now—if I may be permitted my own overheated Faustian metaphor—the *ewig Weibliche* opens her gentle wings over its quiet persistence. The pervasive undertow of B-flat is effortlessly banished by a single ecstatic moment in B-natural.

What if Beethoven had ended the whole symphony right here, with this hushed and unhurried meditation in B—and *not* with the noisy machismo in D we know is coming? (I think he wanted to, at least subconsciously. Why else would he write out the five sharps, and dignify a seven-measure harmonic excursion with two double bars and a notated change of key signature?) In that case, the Ninth Symphony would become Modern: ending in a key other than the one in which it began, it would anticipate developments in symphonic logic not actualized until the early twentieth century. (Gustav Mahler's Second Symphony begins in C minor and ends in D-flat major; his Fifth moves from C-sharp minor to D major; his own Ninth begins in D major, but ends in D-flat major.) And I would yield to no one in my admiration for Beethoven's daring essay into the fully modern sublime, for his "increase of being and the jubilation which results from the invention of new rules of the game" (Lyotard). After all, the absence of the home dominant scarcely matters if one has the freedom to transcend the home tonic!

But Beethoven, tragically, lacks this transcendent freedom; the Ninth is inexorably pulled back to D major, and a last attempt to banish all the moments of impotent falling away from it. No matter that his manic striving after potency will shatter the formal logic of the work and usher it into the realm of the postmodern sublime: Beethoven wants his orgasm—and he wants it on his "own" (D-major) terms.

And of course, so do we, his equally non-transcendent audience. The final *Prestissimo* provides the orgiastic release we demand, no more decorously than the Rossinian stretta-finales whose shrill sound world (bass drum, cymbals, triangle, piccolo) it so brazenly appropriates. Ironically or not, Beethoven appears to be acknowledging that if there was in fact a musician who could give a kiss to the whole world, ca. 1825, it would be the composer of *Il barbiere*—and not that of *Fidelio*. (Nicholas Cook [1993, 103] seems to agree with me here.)

But it is a serious oversimplification to see the noisy finish of the Ninth as nothing but a calculated drop into the demotic, a sacrifice of decorum in the name of *liberté, egalité, fraternité*. The analogous final *Presto* of the *Missa Solemnis*'s Gloria is loud and exciting, but it also exhibits a carefully controlled linear structure: a complex final ascent that, even as it grabs for the gut, deftly recapitulates and exorcises all the linear-harmonic tensions of the movement. (Opus 123 is more formally "correct"—and thus less sublime—than op. 125.) Beethoven has no time for such niceties in the Ninth: I have searched in vain for a final symbolic ascent that wraps up the melodic desires of the work in a neat and intellectually satisfying way. Nor do the conflicting tonalities receive any kind of epigrammatic final resolution. The *Prestissimo* does begin with a paradigmatic Lydian ascent to scale degree 5, strikingly similar to a passage of similar function at the end of the Gloria. And there is, at "Tochter aus Elysium," one last symbolic collapse of momentum linked to the natural fourth scale degree. But Beethoven throws away this opportunity to reactivate his linear mechanism and drive it home.

The last bars of the *Maestoso* (mm. 918–19) clearly represent the final transcendental climax of Beethoven's drama—and they ascend through scale degrees 3, 4, and 5. There is, however, no trace of Lydian inflection. Why the bald I–IV–V–I cadence—why not a significant correction of scale degree 4, or at least a final engagement with the flat side? In this last rush to climax, Beethoven seems satisfied to forgo linear and harmonic subtlety for brute force. He hammers home the dominant scale degree and the Lydian tonic with what even a sympathetic critic might term "strenuous affirmation"—and a feminist might call "bludgeoning the cadence to death."

She would have a point: the level of orchestral violence needed to maintain the celebration of brotherhood cannot easily be glossed over. Aside from the constant assault of brass and percussion, the massed woodwinds are topped by a truly egregious piccolo part. This stratospheric obbligato is only playable at an unremitting *fortissimo*. When attempted by two early nineteenth-century piccolos at the extreme limit of their compass it cuts right through the texture, just on the border between a succession of musical pitches and an out-of-tune shriek.[26] One might excuse Beethoven on purely physiological grounds: it seems likely that by 1825 this high-pitched whistle was the only musical sound that had any chance of surmounting his hearing loss.

But how much of this sound's impact is in fact "musical"? The end of the Ninth feels so extreme because the energy it embodies constantly threatens to leave the realm of the musical altogether; in these final seconds, pure energy takes over and emancipates itself as *pure noise*. Consider the wild passage that begins thirteen bars from the end: it is a prolongation of the D-major tonic, as well as the melodic pitch A. But scale degree five is not stabilized by harmonic or linear logic, by some performative use (or abuse) of musical syntax; it is held up by sheer dynamic force. This is the ultimate Rossini crescendo, one that *starts* from double-forte: nothing but a blazing tonic chord, repeated sixteen times in a row. The ululating piccolos and horns, savagely scrubbing strings, and pounding drums pump energy into the D-major triad until it incandesces.[27]

To return to the language of sublimating criticism: it was Beethoven's demonic genius to know that this symphony—which emerged so hesitantly into music from amorphous noise—must end by rocketing right out of music and back into ecstatic noise. There is no formal resolution. Kretzschmar was right: even the most extreme means of musical art would not have sufficed to bring the Ninth to a close. The only thing that can drown out the noise of failure in this symphony is *not music*, but the even more violent noise of form-annihilating "success."[28]

EPILOGUE

> . . . *yelling at Joy from the tunnel of the ego*
> *music without the ghost*
> *of another person in it, music*
> *trying to tell something the man*
> *does not want out, would keep if he could*
> *gagged and bound and flogged with chords of Joy*
> *where everything is silence and the*
> *beating of a bloody fist upon*
> *a splintered table.*
>
> ADRIENNE RICH, *"The Ninth Symphony*
> *of Beethoven Understood at Last as*
> *a Sexual Message"*

Beethoven Antihero

Noise is the trace the unpresentable leaves in a musical presentation, the high-decibel, high-distortion edge of the postmodern sonic sublime. And it seems in the late twentieth century it has mostly been women listening to Beethoven's Ninth as noise. They are the only ones who are willing to talk about it, at any rate; and their reaction has been uniformly troubled. After all: the sixteen-fold trochaic repetition of a *fortissimo* D-major triad I just finished celebrating—wasn't that the exact passage in the Ninth that inspired Adrienne Rich to the brutal trochaic pentameter of "*Gagged* and *bound* and *flogged* with *chords* of *Joy*" (Rich 1973, 205–6)? There are sixteen trochees from "gagged" to the end of her poem; you could sing her words to Beethoven's music. *(Go on—I dare you.)*

It was Susan McClary who introduced most of us to Rich's poem, and McClary is well aware of the insoluble dilemma that this *Prestissimo* represents:

> The "triumphal" end of the symphony is likewise problematic, for how could any configuration of pitches satisfactorily ground the contradictions set forth over the course of this gargantuan composition? As the conclusion is approached, the promised (though by definition, inadequate) cadences repeatedly are withheld at the last moment; and finally Beethoven simply forces closure by bludgeoning the cadence and the piece to death. (1991, 129)

What could be a clearer intuition of the formal collapse inherent in Lyotard's postmodern sublime? McClary points out the "much higher level of violence" at the end of the work, and sees this attempt to "force closure" as a failed correction of the violent failed closures ("unable to achieve release") in the first movement recapitulation and the opening of the finale. She cuts to the heart of the argument that I have made here at much greater length: that there is not any musical gesture ("any configuration of pitches") that could possibly resolve the tensions of the Ninth—that the resort to sublime, form-destroying noise is inevitable (1991, 129–30).

But there is a profound unease in her description of the closing bars; in both Rich's and McClary's accounts, imagery and tone again conjure up the specter of rape. The logic is hard to dismiss: If we accept that the noise of the first movement recapitulation is the rage of impotence, of violent desire unable to achieve release—and my entire analysis is based on this observation—then doesn't the last movement end with the terrifying elation of *potency*—with that violent D-major desire now satisfied, through the all-too-masculine expedient of increasing the level of violence until someone gets (raped and) killed? There is indeed something sinister about the moment when the tonal phallus is no longer clothed in formal dialectics, when

Beethoven's overwhelming desire for the tonic major strides forth, "naked and powerful."

"Seid umschlungen"? Maybe not.

The title of Rich's poem is "The Ninth Symphony of Beethoven Understood at Last as a Sexual Message." Understood that way, as we have understood it here, the message really is profoundly dystopic and disturbing, a message totally at odds with the work's utopian Enlightenment surface. But it would be a serious mistake to think that the feminist demurral in the face of the Ninth's triumphal ending is merely an artifact of their sexual reading, and can be erased by refusing to hear the piece "their way." The doubts they raise resonate with other radical critiques of music and society—even those untainted by sexual hermeneutics. For example, it's easy to link this musical violence to actual social and political structures. There could hardly be any simple, unambivalent approach to "alle Menschen werden Brüder" in Metternich's Austria, after the Napoleonic Wars and the Congress of Vienna. (Nicholas Cook puts it well: "can Beethoven really have been so unthinking, so *dumb*, as to remain unaffected by the history of his own time, holding true to the beliefs of the 1780s in the Vienna of the 1820s, with its censorship, secret police, and network of informers?" [1993, 102]) One could point out that by 1825, Beethoven himself had experienced (if vicariously) the dialectical relation between Enlightenment reason, violence and totalitarian control. The canceled dedication of the Eroica is a famous example of Beethoven's sensitivity to the failure of revolutionary politics. Is the Ninth his *Sinfonia anti-eroica*? Did he, twenty years later, compose a little bit of the Terror and the Restoration into his belated paean to the ideals of the French Revolution? (The Ninth, by the way, is dedicated to one of the founding members of the counterrevolutionary Holy Alliance, King Friedrich Wilhelm III of Prussia, "in tiefster Ehrfurcht.")

Explicit political metaphors for musical violence—anarchy, class war, civil insurrection—already appear in Greipenkerl's 1838 account of the first-movement recapitulation. "Old Hitzig," the principal bassist, is under no illusions that, in the midst of music like this, "all men are brothers":

> Through the entire passage the double basses held on to D, once again in thirty-seconds. Old Hitzig, who completely understood the gigantic pedal point of which he was the Atlas, leaned into his instrument and counterbalanced the storm breaking over his head with all his God-given strength of arm. He pulled notes out of his old Luizi that cut through the orchestral mass like the pedal tones of an organ.
> "Stand firm," he encouraged the other double-bassists. "The rabble above us is really going crazy. *[Das Gesindel über uns treibt wahrhaftig zu toll.]* Don't let go, and it will all pass right over us. The scoundrels have a good mind to toss us bass players in the pan and make pancakes of us. Damn, those triplet-sixteenths in the flutes and violins whistle like bullets through dry grass, I'll soon take one

in my hide."—"The colors are saved, Music Director," he loudly cried, as he arrived on C♯. "The basses've held out, I think!—"

A bystander like Vicarius (thus his name?) can afford to indulge in sublime affirmations of this welter of sound ("this is no street brawl"). Hitzig is in the thick of it. Trying, like any good bass player, to preserve the remnants of orderly root progression, he hears above him only the threat of a mob rioting dangerously out of control ("Das Gesindel über uns treibt wahrhaftig zu toll"). History tells us that we unleash this revolutionary force at our peril; there is only a short step from brotherhood to blood-brotherhood. When D major returns at the end of the piece, is it because all men are brothers—or just that they all, finally, love Big Brother?

For a dialectician like Adorno, the choice is moot. Rose Subotnik introduced many of us to Adorno's "diagnosis" of Beethoven's late style, a style that for Adorno was inconceivable in isolation from the successive political disillusionments of the years 1789–1824. Confrontation with the fundamental truth of modern society—that individual freedom and social order are not reconcilable—rendered the affirmative critique inherent in Beethoven's "heroic" second-period style impossible to sustain. Earlier, Beethoven had created optimistic musical narratives in which individual subjects (themes) enacted struggle and synthesis with society (form). But by 1824 this utopian synthesis was no longer a believable prospect:

> if Beethoven's style had maintained its affirmative character in the third period, giving no sign of the irreconcilable dichotomies now perceptible as fundamental to reality, his music would have become what Adorno calls "ideology": . . . it would have contributed to the preservation of a "false consciousness," which served not human integrity and freedom but an oppressive world. His music would have lost its status as authentic art . . . (Subotnik 1991, 24)

Thus Adorno finds "authenticity" in the late style's refusal of the heroic manner, its denial of synthesis. Musical works now act out the impossibility of synthesis: the battle between the individuality embodied in themes and the necessity inherent in forms shatters the musical discourse. Form either fragments into anarchy, or becomes overtly conventional and oppressive; subjectivity flees behind equally fragmented or conventional musical material.

From this point of view, the embattled first movement of the Ninth is brilliantly negative, and the "sublime" moment of recapitulation is actually its most tragic and authentic denial of synthesis (this Adorno-esque subtext is particularly strong in McClary 1991). But the heavy-handed utopianism of the *Ode to Joy* is out of touch, dangerously close to "false consciousness." Indeed, Adorno had problems with the Ninth as ideology: choosing between the late choral works, he spurned the Ninth in favor of the *Missa Solemnis,* a piece he read as a hieratic retreat from subjectivity, and which he anointed as Beethoven's "alienated Masterwork" *("verfremdetes Hauptwerk")*—a masterwork, one presumes, precisely *because* of its unassimilable alienation. Perhaps this is why it was the Ninth, particularly, that Adorno demanded Western civilization retract in Thomas Mann's 1948 novel *Dr. Faustus.* (*Faust,* once again!)

Subotnik suggests that if we accept Adorno's valuation of late Beethoven, the affirmation of the Ninth is impossible to accept: "[this] suggests that Beethoven not only failed to communicate the content of his last symphony, but actually came very near to violating that content in the attempt to communicate it" (1991, 34). One assumes that Adorno would not be at all surprised if we felt that violation, if the end of the Ninth actually *felt* oppressive; it would then stand as a perfect example of what he called the "dialectic of Enlightenment." Trapped in a falsely absolute affirmation of Enlightenment ideals ("the stars above us, and the moral law within"), Beethoven makes the inevitable slip from Kant and Rousseau to their successor in the negative dialectic, the equally "enlightened" Marquis de Sade:

> When utopia, which provided the French Revolution with its content of hope, entered German music and philosophy (effectively and ineffectively), the established civil order wholly functionalized reason, which became a purposeless purposiveness which might thus be attached to all ends. In this sense, reason is planning considered solely as planning. The totalitarian State manipulates the people. Or as [the Marquis de] Sade's [police chief,] Francavilla puts it: "The government must control the population, and must possess all the means necessary to exterminate them." (Horkheimer and Adorno 1991, 88–89)

From utopia to the death camp. And if Furtwängler could conduct the *Ode to Joy* and then reach down to shake Goebbels's hand, how can Adorno or any of us exonerate Beethoven's Ninth from its portion of guilt?

But we can, if we choose, leave the National Socialists out of it; there are even more fundamental critiques available if we draw back from orgiastic celebrations of *(Strength through)* Joy. Consider Jacques Attali, for whom the concept of "noise" is the foundation of a unique and brilliantly post-structural "political economy of music." Revisit the end of Beethoven's Ninth with Attali's basic premise in mind:

> Noise is a weapon and music, primordially, is the formation, domestication, and ritualization of that weapon as a simulacrum of ritual murder. . . . it symbolically signifies the channeling of violence and the imaginary, the ritualization of a murder substituted for the general violence, the affirmation that a society is possible if the imaginary of individuals is sublimated (Attali 1985, 24–26).

Both the feminist and the post-structuralist deal in basic instincts: for McClary music constructs and disciplines sexuality, for Attali music constructs and disciplines aggression. And Attali, like McClary, is well aware of how far this combination of sublimated sex and violence is from our idealized picture of musical appreciation:

> The hypotheses of noise as murder and music as sacrifice are not easy to accept. They imply that music *functions* like sacrifice; that listening to noise is a little like being killed; that listening to music is to attend a ritual murder, with all the danger, guilt, but also reassurance that goes along with that; that applauding is a confirmation, after the channelization of the violence, that the spectators of the sacrifice could potentially resume practicing the essential violence (Attali 1985, 28).

Perhaps we should be more hesitant about applauding after the Ninth, since Beethoven has effectively forestalled us by composing this resumption of the "essential violence" directly into the final bars of the piece! In Attali's formulation, the reversion to noise at the end of the Ninth is threatening for the same reasons that Lyotard would laud it as postmodern and sublime. Insofar as the celebration of an ideal society actually *sounds like* a murder to us as listeners ("bludgeoning the piece to death"), it flirts with the collapse of societal order, as it flirts with the collapse of the musical form through which that order is embodied in sound.

ENVOI: WHO SPEAKS FOR THE NINTH?

I want to finish by taking issue, once again, with Pieter van den Toorn, Susan McClary's most vehement and persistent scholarly interlocutor. Van den Toorn expanded his original article-length response to her reading of Beethoven's Ninth into an omnibus attack on New Musicology *tout court* in his 1995 book, *Music, Politics, and the Academy*. Both the article and the book open with what is perhaps the least edifying moment in the entire discourse around McClary's Beethoven criticism. Van den Toorn begins his discussion of "Feminism, Politics, and the Ninth" with an insidious rhetorical question: "Is music inviolate?" One realizes with mounting incredulity as his argument progresses that he is actually attempting to turn the rape metaphor back on McClary herself. Hermeneutic criticism as practiced by the New Musicology is a "violation" of music; McClary, not Beethoven, is the rapist; the coerced victims are the Ninth itself, and sympathetic listeners like van den Toorn, for whom "it is no longer permitted . . . to allow oneself to be enticed spontaneously, to allow for an immediate, intuitive response" (van den Toorn 1995, 11; 41–42). Music theory assumes the right to defend the music—and prosecute the musicologist.

This attempt by a male music theorist to cry rape on behalf of a symphony shows a confused grasp of sexual politics, to say the least; but it is worth revisiting the question of just who is raping what *in re* Beethoven's Ninth one last time. As we have seen, the identity of Beethoven with "the rapist" is not as clear-cut as simplifying accounts of McClary might imply, since the tonal desires frustrated are as much ours as the composer's. But—to go a final step further—Beethoven does bear some individual responsibility. Our most canonic composer is in fact a musical rapist, *but it is his own composition that he violates.* Beethoven sets up an immense and complex formal dialectic, uses it to channel huge amounts of musico-libidinal energy—and then finally, impatiently, violates his own form by forcing it to enact his crude, solipsistic tonal desires. ("music without the ghost / of another person in it . . .")

Adrienne Rich was right—the music of Beethoven's Ninth *is* "trying to tell something the man does not want out." He was formally impotent, and smashed his own Ode to Joy into pieces (pieces whose postmodern sublimity can still terrify and inspire) to hide his shame. Who is it who covers up for the man? And who speaks for—no, not the *woman, she can do that for herself . . .*

Who speaks for the music?

APPENDIX: ACCOUNTS OF BEETHOVEN, *NINTH SYMPHONY*, I, 301–399

[Note: the dates given in the margin are the earliest publication dates; the citations that follow are to the actual editions used in this essay.]

1838   Griepenkerl, Robert Wolfgang, *Das Musikfest oder die Beethovener.* [Quoted by Dieter Rexroth in *Ludwig van Beethoven Sinfonie Nr. 9*, ed. Rexroth (pocket score; Mainz: B. Schott's Söhne, 1979), 386–87.]

1846   Wagner, Richard, "Bericht über die Aufführung der neunten Symphonie von Beethoven im Jahre 1846, nebst Programm dazu," in *Richard Wagners Gesammelte Schriften und Dichtungen*, Vol. 2, 2d ed. (Leipzig, 1887), 56–58. (English translation is based on "The Choral Symphony at Dresden: Programme," in *Richard Wagner's Prose Works*, vol. 7, trans. Ellis (London, 1898), 247–48.

1853?   Elterlein, Ernst v. (pseud. Ernst Gottschald), *Beethoven's Symphonien nach ihrem idealen Behalt*, 3d ed. (Dresden, 1870).

1859   Marx, Adolph Bernhard, *Beethoven Leben und Schaffen* (Berlin, 1859).

1873   Wagner, Richard, "The Rendering of Beethoven's Ninth Symphony," in *Prose Works*, vol. 5, trans. Ellis (London, 1898), 231–53.

1886   Kretzschmar, Hermann, *Führer durch den Konzertsaal*, 4th ed. (Leipzig, 1913).

1884   Grove, George, *Beethoven's Nine Symphonies* (London, 1884).

1880s? Riemann, Hugo, *Concert Program w/Analysis*. Unpub.

1889   Riemann, Hugo, *Grundriß der Kompositionslehre (Musikalische Formenlehre)*, Vol. 1 (Berlin: Hesse, 1920).

1896   Grove, George, *Beethoven and His Nine Symphonies,* 3d ed. (London: Novello, 1898).

1912   Schenker, Heinrich, *Beethoven Neunte Sinfonie* (Leipzig, 1912).

1920   Ernest, Gustave, *Beethoven* (Berlin: G. Bondi, 1920).

1927   Nef, Karl, *Die Neun Sinfonien Beethovens* (Leipzig, 1928).

1935   Downes, Olin, *Symphonic Masterpieces* (New York, 1935).
       Tovey, D. F., *Essays in Musical Analysis II* (London: Oxford University, 1935).

1936   Riezler, Walter, *Beethoven* (Berlin: Atlantis, 1936).

1941   Rolland, Romain, *Beethoven: Les Grandes Époques Créatrices,* vol. 4 (La Cathedrale Interrompue), 1 (La Neuvieme Symphonie) (Paris: Sahler, 1943).

1958   Sauer, Wilhelm, *Beethoven und das Wesen in der Musik* (Berlin: Hesse, 1958).

1980   Treitler, Leo, "History, Criticism, and Beethoven's Ninth Symphony," in *Music and the Historical Imagination* (Cambridge, Mass.: Harvard University Press, 1989).

1981   Hopkins, Antony, *The Nine Symphonies of Beethoven* (London: Scolar Press, 1981).

1982   Treitler, Leo, " 'To Worship that Celestial Sound': Motives for Analysis," *Journal of Musicology* 1 (1982): 524–58.

1987   McClary, Susan, "Getting Down Off the Beanstalk," *Minnesota Composer's Forum Newsletter* (February 1987).

1989   Taruskin, Richard, "Resisting the Ninth," *19th-Century Music* 12/3 (spring 1989): 241–56.

1991–95 Van den Toorn, Pieter. "Politics, Feminism, and Contemporary Music Theory," *Journal of Musicology* 9/3 (summer 1991): 1–37. Revised and reprinted in van den Toorn, *Music, Politics, and the Academy* (Berkeley and Los Angeles: University of California Press, 1995).

1991   McClary, Susan, "Getting Down Off the Beanstalk," in *Feminine Endings: Music, Gender, and Sexuality* (Minneapolis: University of Minnesota Press, 1991).

NOTES

This essay is—obviously—inspired by and dedicated to Susan McClary. In the nearly ten years it has been in gestation, it has benefited immensely from the direct input and the indirect example of Joseph Kerman, Richard Taruskin, Mitchell Morris, Judith Peraino, Gretchen Wheelock, Ralph Locke, Rose Subotnik, David Levy, Fred Maus, Suzanne Cusick, Marion Guck, Cecilia Sun, Elisabeth Le Guin, Raymond Knapp, Robert Walser, and Andrew Dell'Antonio.

1. "Artyfacts," *Guardian,* 1 December 1995, p. T9. The anonymous sarcasm of the *Guardian* reviewer is all the more depressing in that it repackages seminal misinformation from that most "respectable" of sources, Edward Rothstein of the *New York Times.* It was Rothstein who, a few days before, in discussing (among other "new musicological" publications) *Feminine Endings,* had allowed himself to reuse *as if it came*

from the book the infamous quote he had attacked several times before ("Musicologists Roll Over Beethoven," *New York Times,* 26 November 1995). The most charitable explanation is that he had not yet actually read McClary's work, a full four years after its publication.

2. The talk in question, "The Feminist Critical Perspective on Musicology," was later published by Leo Treitler as "Gender and Other Dualities of Music History" (Treitler 1993). To give Treitler credit, he seemed genuinely troubled by the effect his decontextualized use of McClary's words had on audiences in 1988, and made significant and salutary changes in the way he framed her in his 1993 argument.

3. Suzanne Cusick might see this "effortless" moment of trans-gender intersubjectivity as rather less than innocent: "It is easy to understand why McClary's work would have seemed, at first, comprehensible to traditional musicologists in a way that more explicitly women-centered musicology had not. . . . Because such an enterprise can be immediately understood to rescue both women and men from disciplinary practices that rigidly channel our relationships to sensual and bodily pleasures, McClary's feminist scholarship promises a kind of liberation for all of us. Thus it promises a space for feminist men with a clarity that some other feminist musicologies do not have" (Cusick 1999, 487). As a once-traditional male musicologist radicalized by McClary's writing, I would not deny that Cusick (whose work is no less admirable than McClary's) has my number. My only disclaimer is that I am just as conscious of the equivocal position of "men in (musicological) feminism" as I intuit her to be. I have tried to make some of my post-McClaryite gender allegiances clear in the opening and closing pages of Fink 1998.

4. The critical reception of this recapitulation is treated at greater length, with extensive selections from primary sources, in Fink 1994, 132–60. For a compendious collection of early critical references to the Ninth, see Solie 1988. Contemporary references to the Ninth in German musical periodicals are reproduced in Wallace 1986; and a more general survey, covering some of the same ground as this study, is in the Cambridge Handbook on the Ninth by Nicholas Cook (1993).

5. A short list of the accounts of the recapitulation passage (Beethoven, *Ninth Symphony,* I, 301–99) on which the following discussion is based is provided in the appendix at the end of this essay. The full text of these descriptions, in the original languages, can be found in Fink 1994, appendix A; all translations in the following section are my own, except where otherwise noted.

6. Virtually all the emotion in Schenker's study comes in the appendices to each analytic section, where he brutally chastises the "Schwärmerei" of earlier critics. He carries both Hugo Riemann and Hermann Kretschmar along with him to be ritually beaten up at the end of each analytical section. Riemann he often dignifies by disputing the earlier critic's harmonic readings; he quotes Kretschmar's descriptions merely to ridicule what seemed to him a total lack of content.

7. By contrast, Schenker only mentions the timpani as an afterthought—because their rhythm intermittently reinforces that of the theme ("In kompositorischer Hinsicht beachte man endlich noch den Rhythmus der Pauken in den Takten 304, 308, 310, die thematisch mitwirken").

8. "Jetzt ist die Herrschermacht des Gedankens entschieden; er . . . steht . . . zwölf Takte lang, unbeweglich wie ein Schreckensphantom, wie der trübflammendes Erdgeist vor Faust stand, der ihn heraufbeschworen und nicht ertragen konnte, auf

Fis–A–D, um sich im zwölften Takte—wieder auf dem Nebenmoment des vierten Achtels—nach Es-dur und drei Takte weiter endlich nach dem Hauptton, nach D-moll zu wenden und da als Hauptsatz zu vollenden. Vollenden?—das gewährt der trübe Riesengeist nicht."

9. "Im Lebensfluten, im Tatensturm / Wall ich auf und ab / Webe hin und her. / Geburt und Grab, / Ein ewiges Meer, / Ein wechselnd Weben, / Ein glühend Leben" (Goethe, *Faust,* ll. 501–8 [ed. and trans. Walter Kaufmann, New York: Doubleday, 1961]).

10. As it turns out, he agrees with Schenker that the ultimate function of the D major is as V/iv in D minor; the crucial difference is his vivid sense of the confusion that the chord's initial non-resolution creates.

11. "alle Theile des Orchesters in wildem Kampfe aufeinander losstürzen, während die Pauke 38 Takte lang zu furchtbarer Stärke anschwellend ihr d wirbelt, da ist's, als Thäte sich die Erde auf, Alles zu verschlingen, da ist's als reichten selbst die stärksten instrumentalen Mittel nicht aus, die übermächtige, dämonische Phantasie des Meisters erschöpfend darzustellen!" Riemann 1880s.

12. "C'est le paroxysme de la tempête,—des trois apparitions du Dieu sur le Sinaï, (comme il nous plait d'appeler le grand motif de quinte descendante) la plus environée de foudres et d'éclairs. Mais pour la première fois, c'est en *majeur* que parle le Tout-Puissant, sur les roulements répétés des timbales, comme un tonnerre; puis brusquement, par une de ces variations de lumière chromatique, sur *si bémol,* par *la bémol* et *la naturel,* il rentre dans son *ré mineur* originel, que n'ont cessé d'affirmer les battements en triple croches des timbales. On est au coeur de l'ouragan. Les masses sonores se heurtent avec fracas. En contrepoint, les bois s'opposent aux cordes; et les éclairs s'entrecroissent, d'en haut, d'en bas." Rolland 1941, 59–60.

13. Antony Hopkins' book on the symphonies converts Tovey's imagery back into a passage redolent of Greipenkerl and Marx: "[the D major] is awe-inspiring in the same way that a vision of the avenging angel would be; one's eyes would be dazzled by his radiance though one's heart would quake with terror" (Hopkins 1981, 251–52).

14. "Hier erfolgt die Vereinigung der Strebungen aller Menschen, aller Völker, der Menschheit unter dem Gesichtspunkt der ewigen Gesetze, der göttlichen Weltordnung; das ist die *Grundidee des ersten Satzes:* das Weltringen der Gespaltenheit und Vielfältigkeit des Lebens heraus zur göttlichen Harmonie." Sauer 1958, 161–63. On Adorno and late Beethoven see Subotnik 1991, 15–41.

15. It is this striving toward the eternal, the transcendental, that Richard Taruskin accuses Roger Norrington of "resisting" in his 1989 review of Norrington's recording. We can note his sublimating concentration on the sound of the timpani ("the horripilating tattoo") and chalk up another influential critic who hears the progression at mm. 301–15 as a failure: "the very progression the first movement never gets to consummate. It is the progression the timpani tries so hard to insist on at the recapitulation, but can never browbeat the bass instruments into vouchsafing: their unstable F-sharp falls inexorably to F-natural, and Elysium is lost" (Taruskin 1989, 251).

16. Some credit must be given to Leo Treitler here. In two groundbreaking essays from the early 1980s ("History, Criticism, and the Ninth" and "*To Worship That Celestial Sound:* Motives for Analysis," both in Treitler 1989), he used the Ninth Symphony as the ground upon which to construct his own critique of formalist analysis. He felt

the "historical imagination" was better served by a looser, more phenomenological, and more hermeneutically engaged analytical method. But his historical interest in more flexible (and often somewhat sublimating) analytical explanations stopped short of accepting the full-blown sublimating tendencies of McClary's sexual-political hermeneutic; the essay in which he attempts to come to terms with her reading still has some striking moments of ambivalence and bad faith (Treitler 1993, 23–45). See Fink 1994, 8–12; 148–50 for a fuller discussion of Treitler and the Ninth.

17. The term is Taruskin's. See his critique of formalism and his discussion of the twentieth century's paradigmatic exercise in violence and signification in Taruskin 1995.

18. Rodolphe Gasché, "Violence and the Feeling of the Sublime," *Basileus* 2, no. 2 (1999) [www.helsinki.fi/~rpol_bas/index.html].

19. Wedekind originally called his "Monster-Tragedy" of 1892–94 *Pandora's Box;* the play was split, partially to evade the censors, into *Erdgeist* (1895) and *Die Büchse der Pandora* (1904).

20. "Enthülle Dich! / Ha! Wie's in meinem Herzen reißt! / Zu neuen Gefühlen / Alle meine Sinnen sich erwühlen! / Ich fühle ganz mein Herz dir hingeben! / Du mußt! Du mußt! Und kostet' es mein Leben!"; "Bist du es, der, von meinem Hauch umwittert, / In allen Lebenstiefen zittert, / Ein furchtsam weggekrümmter Wurm?" Goethe, *Faust,* scene i, ll. 476–81, 496–99 (trans. Walter Kaufmann, New York: Doubleday, 1961).

21. I cannot agree with Treitler's assertion that the Ab/G♯ comes from the A♮ of the preceding chord ("the outer voices drop a half-step to F and Ab . . ." [Treitler 1980, 24]). Beethoven has deliberately blocked the possibility of hearing any A–Ab connection in m. 312: the A in the first flute and first oboe moves up to Bb on the second beat, just to make it perfectly clear that the actual voice leading is A–Bb–D. The tritone leap up in the first flute D–Ab, linearly improbable as it sounds, is unmistakably the "real" voice leading.

22. Beethoven is quite punctilious in the *Missa* about changing the key signature within a movement; if a major "modulation" other than the usual move to V occurs without a change in signature, that is a clear sign that the move is not to be considered structural. In relation to the Gloria, mm. 174–200, the "real" modulatory progression is not the third progression Bb to D (2b→2♯) at m. 190, but the simple rising fifth Bb to F (2b→1b) at m. 210, where the key signature *does* change.

23. It may be well to note that all "exotic" third-related secondary keys in Beethoven sonata forms do not function in this sharp-denying way. In many earlier cases, Beethoven's secondary key was a sort of "super-dominant" like the mediant major, much *farther* up the sharp side than V. The "Waldstein" sonata, which modulates up from C major to E major, is a familiar example. Even a third drop may introduce a sharping effect: thus the secondary key area of the "Hammerklavier" sonata (G major) is a third lower than the tonic (Bb), but creates a net climb up of three sharps.

24. This somewhat arbitrary player count is derived from the 1989 Hogwood recording (L'Oiseau-Lyre 425 517-2); cf. Treitler 1989, 21: "the role of the D root is dampened by the continued sounding of the A in the violins and cellos."

25. This local tension–release mechanism may mitigate the lack of any rigorous dramatic voice-leading linkage in the 200-odd measures that span the second theme

group in the recapitulation. One might quite reasonably doubt the experiential valid-ity of this long-range connection. For I am not only claiming that the $I^\sharp$–$^\circ$V/V–V–i progression of mm. 531–39 is a provisional correction of the gnomic $I^{\sharp 6}$–G^6–(V)–i^6 of mm. 312–15. I also need to assert that the actual melodic line F♯–G♯–A in those later measures is *heard* as a straightened-out and successful version of the failed F♯–G♯–A ascent in mm. 301–15—even though the earlier ascent's very existence depends on our perception of a highly abstract melodic link between F♯ in the bass and A♭–A♮ in the soprano.

But the skeptic need not rely on the evidence of my ears alone. We can call another witness, disinterested, and perhaps even hostile: the *Stufentheorist* Heinrich Schenker, as he is on record in his 1912 monograph. As example 4.6 attempts to show, his harmonic analysis of these two passages implies this linear connection, which he evidently at that time had no theoretical interest in pursuing.

Here is Schenker's harmonic explanation of mm. 301–15:

[The tonic's] major third F♯ does not arise, as it might at first glance seem, from mode mixture, but from a chromaticization leading to the soon to appear scale-step IV:

> D minor: $I^\sharp$–IV
> In effect: G minor: $V^\sharp$–I

This last (IV) then actually appears in m. 312, although it is itself—as before—immedi-ately chromaticized, as if scale-step V were actually what we were waiting for:

> D minor: $^\sharp$IV–(V)
> In effect: A maj/min: VII–(I)

. . . Therefore, what we actually have here is the progression, in D minor: $I^{\sharp 3}$–$^\sharp IV[^{\flat 7/3}]$–(V)–I .

Compare the above with Schenker's analogous discussion of mm. 531–39:

[The tonic] pedal is decorated with the progression $I^{\sharp 3}$–$^\sharp$IV–V in mm. 531–34—a pro-gression that achieves repetition in mm. 535–38. . . . The winds carry a melodic line that, considered by itself, seems strange, but in which we can easily discern the scale-step pro-gression given above: the third of scale step I, F♯; the root of the raised scale-step IV, G♯; and finally the root of scale-step V, A.

In both cases Schenker identifies the harmonic progression as $I^{\sharp 3}$–$^\sharp$IV–V, and the underlying bass motion as #$\hat{3}$–#$\hat{4}$–$\hat{5}$. In the later passage, he states explicitly that the "strange" F♯–G♯–A melodic line is the simple result of transposing this succession of chord roots into the soprano. It is hard to escape the conclusion that he heard the earlier passage the same way: that we are supposed to follow a #$\hat{3}$–#$\hat{4}$–$\hat{5}$ root pro-gression through the moment of recapitulation, whose strange melodic move from A♭ to A♮ is thus the result of a partial transfer of this conceptual bass line into the tre-ble.

26. This assumes, of course, doubled winds as in Christopher Hogwood's 1989 recording with the Academy of Ancient Music.

27. For one of the most impressive recorded reactions to this passage, listen to Wilhelm Furtwängler's 1951 Bayreuth recording. As Taruskin (1989) pointed out in "Resisting the Ninth," he whips the ensemble into a frenzy that surpasses anything on record in tempo, except perhaps his own 1942 recording in Berlin. By the end, as pitch, intonation, and ensemble disintegrate under Furtwängler's lash, the Dionysian frenzy simply transcends "the musical."

28. The original version of this sentence (Fink 1994, 206) lacked quotation marks around the word "success." At that time I was much more heavily invested in Beethoven's ability to create a viscerally exciting—and thus "successful"— form based around dramatic moments of harmonic-linear failure (as I freely admitted; see 1994, 213–16). The goals of that earlier study were somewhat different than the present one (I was more interested in Beethoven the Master of musical "Energy"); but the intervening years have also brought a greater degree of critical distance from the piece itself—and a more mature sense of what is culturally interesting about form in a postmodern musical episteme.

FIVE

Passion / Mirrors (A Passion for the Violent Ineffable: Modernist Music and the Angel / In the Hall of Mirrors)

PAUL ATTINELLO

This discussion is intentionally split in two: the first part is an essay about the subjective hearing of a particular body of music; the second is about the subjectivity of writing that essay, refracted through the personal and social contexts that led to its creation. I'm not sure anyone can fairly examine the first without examining the second: the subjectivity of listening always ought to remind us of the unavoidable subjectivity of musicology itself.

PART I. A PASSION FOR THE VIOLENT INEFFABLE: MODERNIST MUSIC AND THE ANGEL

The educated and 'proper' view of the more difficult musical products of modernism is that they represent experiments in organization, transformation, and sound. However, even the educated and sympathetic listener is frequently struck by an unavoidable impression of violence, chaos, and attempts to stretch human perception. The widespread denial of this sonic violence suggests that it can be seen as a cultural symptom and, in fact, as a distinguishing characteristic of modernist music at the point where it looks into the abyss of the future. In a context where subjectivity might be acceptable in a scholarly discussion, it is plausible to read this history for its feeling or affect.

A validation of this symptom is its tendency to aim beyond mundane understanding toward some ineffable quality, a kind of transcendence that recalls the terror and shattering vision of both Rilke's and Benjamin's angels—one annihilatingly beautiful, the other grappling with the detritus of history. These links suggest the essentially mystical underpinnings of modernism, often ignored in analysis of its surface characteristics. I seek here to identify metaphors of destruction, collapse, and transcendence in works by composers such as Barraqué, Boulez and Maxwell Davies, looking for the way in which impatience with the world as it is and a horror of the predictable result in shattered sounds that force the listener to imagine a world beyond the known. Such a world may be a common modernist trope: one that may be suggested in sound, but which can only be inhabited by terrifying angels.

The Angel of Terror

> *Who, if I cried out, would hear me among the angels'*
> *hierarchies? and even if one of them pressed me*
> *suddenly against his heart: I would be consumed*
> *in that overwhelming existence. For beauty is nothing*
> *but the beginning of terror, which we still are just able to endure,*
> *and we are so awed because it serenely disdains*
> *to annihilate us. Every angel is terrifying.*
> RILKE 1984, 151

This, the beginning of Rilke's *Duino Elegies,* is a poem that causes the earth to crack open. Historically, this first stanza of a set of extraordinary poetic experiments is the point where Rilke leaves behind the merely beautiful pictures of his Symbolist work to create an image that is both a summary of many aspects of nineteenth-century poetry and at the same time convincingly modern. It is thus tied, both chronologically and conceptually, to the first of his *Sonnets to Orpheus,* with its then shocking venture into proto-Surrealism. The historical move is, however, only a part of the important shift represented in the poem; Rilke, powerfully taking over a space of being that is only obliquely suggested in his earlier poems, creates a vision of possible existence that demands the demolition of everyday experience. The complex, allusive world established in this new approach to the sublime thus becomes an existential earthquake. The poetic earthquake is teased out into verbal explanation, as it must be; but in music we have a more succinct, more exact expression of such an earthquake: the explosive, apparently instantaneous accented chord that opens Boulez's *Pli selon pli.*

This earthquake is characteristic of both of the times when modernism shattered the existing landscape, first in the years before World War I and then again after World War II. Rilke's difficult language, hinting at realities that are not quite accessible in words but which nevertheless insist on being understood, opens up a future that will include both Pound and Wittgenstein, while the passionate demand for a new way of being invokes the subsequent Heidegger. Although we are accustomed to separating out the time spans of the figures and works involved, I need to breach period divisions in order to tease out a shared vision that, I suggest, spans most of the century: a vision of destroying the world to transcend it, of discovering a 'passionate ineffable' beyond any normal experience. In that context, Rilke's metaphors may seem historically distant from the work of Boulez, and not a part of the same cultural movement that produced the brittle explosion at the beginning of *Pli selon pli;* but I assert that, at an imaginative level, they represent the same relationship to reality. It should be clear that I am not terribly interested in tracing a chain of influences—either particular words or particular images—that result in a series of directly comparable artistic products. I am certainly not tracing images of angels that appear in the poetry of early modernism or the music of high modernism. I instead hope to define an important constellation of desires, those passionate wishes to crack open the sky and pass through to whatever may be on the other side.

The cluster of works that most clearly express such desires include some of the classic works of musical high modernism. I suggest that it would be useful for readers to go and hear the pieces I cite—even those they know well—in order to remind them of the sensual impact of their experience as sound, rather than as score, abstract memory, or theoretical construct. In choosing these works I am aiming at characterizing, not the composition degree zero aspect of works like Boulez's *Structures Ia,* but the development of a style of passionate violence that occurs on both sides of that zero point. Accustomed as we are to the homily that the music of the 1950s was intended to project an absence of meaning, I believe that we have ignored the evident expressive results that are composed into such works, especially when they are considered collectively. Indeed, so much avant-garde music of the 1950s and 1960s, which was said to be designed to leave behind the past (whether the past of music, the past of Europe, or the past of bourgeois stability), is more a constantly refashioned attempt to blow up that past. It is easy to speak of the fearsome or transcendent implications of specific staged or texted works by Berio, Barraqué, Nilsson, and many others; but it also seems important to acknowledge that many untexted musical works of high modernism share a remarkably specific common sensibility. Although the invocation of Rilke and Benjamin may seem historically inappropriate when speaking of Boulez or Maxwell Davies, I believe I am justified in using their language; not because they could be seen as specific influences on these composers, but simply because they said it best.

To paraphrase the Rilke quoted above: if I suffer and cry out, it is hard to believe that any infinite beings, caught up as they are in the structures of a radically different reality, would even notice me. What is worse, if one of them did notice, any intended help from such a being, symbolized in an embrace, would destroy rather than save me. This sensually personal image is used by Rilke to insist that what we call beauty—what, in fact, most of his earlier poems celebrate—is really the edge of the sublime, and that the sublime is the destructive but full-fledged form of beauty. So these terms, usually opposed, are shown to be identical—at least in this context. I suggest that this identification of the two terms becomes a background concept in much modernism, especially in music after 1945.

Rilke's first *Elegy* continues its rapid flight through various possible modes of being, but with frequent references to the awesome nature of existence and our painful inadequacy to recognize even a small part of it:

> whom can we ever turn to
> in our need? Not angels, not humans,
> and already the knowing animals are aware
> that we are not really at home in
> our interpreted world
> RILKE 1984, 151

Not only are we helpless against existence, but we are embarrassed even in facing the animals, who are, however humbly, part of a real, immanent kind of existence. Language, as well as the habit of speaking, art and representations of beauty, are merely attempts to stave off existence. This is also, of course, a demand that we aim for the zero point of existence; although Rilke does not try to express this by reaching a zero point of poetry (which could be said to have been reached in Surrealist and Dadaist texts before the war, and long before it was approached in music), he insists that endeavors outside that zero point are always essentially inadequate. Of course, one of the advantages of musical expression is its ability to bypass the verbal, which helps to distance us somewhat from our usual interpretations: although we may still be lost in our minds rather than aware in the world, musical expression can sometimes point, with somewhat more virtual "reality" than poetry, towards "real" experience.

Certain phrases in the next few stanzas present real understanding as just as unavoidable as it is impossible: "there is night, when a wind full of infinite space / gnaws at our faces," or the lines on being unable to preserve the image of the beloved because of "all the huge strange thoughts inside you / going and coming and often staying all night" (Rilke 1984, 151). The second elegy again flings terror into our faces, as it begins with the conclusion of the first stanza of the first elegy: "Every angel is terrifying." The end of the first stanza of the second elegy moves it all ruthlessly closer:

> But if the archangel now, perilous, from behind the stars
> took even one step down toward us: our own heart, beating
> higher and higher, would beat us to death. Who are you?
> RILKE 1984, 157

This is an earthquake again, or perhaps (it can be imagined) still the same earthquake in an infinitely extended moment: but, this time, the earthquake happens inside of us.

The immense crack in the world that begins *Pli selon pli* is repeated at the end of the piece, suggesting not so much any ABA structure as that the entire work happens in a single instant. Both the first and last such 'cracks in the sky' are associated with brief, aphoristic lines from Mallarmé, sung by the soprano solo. In both cases, its detachment from the original poem makes the action of each line—in the first case the gift of a poem, in the last the bitter, surreal chaos of death—almost incomprehensible, and more of a magical invocation than a meaningful statement of any kind. Once again, in historical terms, the linking of Boulez in 1957, Rilke in 1912, and Mallarmé in 1865 may seem unworkable; but I continue to claim that, in poetic and imaginative terms, it makes a kind of sense that is more important—and which explains more of our need for, and usage of, these pieces—than any historical sense.

The Angel of History

A Klee painting named 'Angelus Novus' shows an angel looking as though he is about to move away from something he is fixedly contemplating. His eyes are staring, his mouth is open, his wings are spread. This is how one pictures the angel of history. His face is turned toward the past. Where we perceive a chain of events, he sees one single catastrophe, which keeps piling wreckage upon wreckage and hurls it in front of his feet. The angel would like to stay, awaken the dead, and make whole what has been smashed. But a storm is blowing from Paradise; it has got caught in his wings with such violence that the angel can no longer close them. This storm irresistibly propels him into the future to which his back is turned, while the pile of debris before him grows skyward. This storm is what we call progress. (W. Benjamin 1969, 257–58)

This frequently cited paragraph is a sensual shock among the complex assertions of Benjamin's *Theses on the Philosophy of History*—which were written in 1940, in the midst of a storm that would make such feelings relatively familiar, especially in European artistic expression.

The painting itself, which was painted in 1920, purchased by Benjamin in 1921, and which hung in his various studies until he fled Paris in June 1940, does not really illustrate Benjamin's complex image in a definite or allusive way. Klee's angel floats in space, staring in a way that may be unsettling, but which does not suggest any detailed metaphor of catastrophe, storm, or debris. It is important to register the rhetorical shift in Benjamin's third sentence away from the description of the painting to a separate train of thought only inspired by it. On the other hand, art historian and Klee specialist Otto Werckmeister points out that the "angel of history" can be seen as a developed form of a meditation written twenty-five years earlier by Klee himself:

Today is the passage from yesterday to the present. In the great mine of forms lie ruins from which one still partly hangs. They offer material for abstraction.

A broken field of unreal elements, for the creation of impure crystals. So it is today. . . . I have long had this war in me. So, inwardly, it concerns me not at all. To work myself out of my ruins, I had to fly. And I flew. In that demolished world, I only spend my time in memory, as one thinks back occasionally. So I am "abstracted with memories."[1]

This suggests that Klee and Benjamin may have communicated with each other about these feelings and ideas. Werckmeister analyzes the same painting from a different point of view, pointing out the hand-like wings and apparent suspension in midair; but unexpectedly, after this physical description, he reaches a surprising conclusion: "with the Angelus Novus, the effort to fly succeeds. . . . It may be taken as an image of the artist's exaltation, by means of abstraction, into a spiritual counterworld" (Werckmeister 1989, 241–42). Certainly, some kind of "counterworld" is common to all of the texts and interpretations resonating out from this painting. Benjamin also referred to Klee's painting in writing at an earlier date, but despite the much calmer political circumstances of the time, he interpreted it as representing something that was terrifying without being evil. In his lengthy 1931 essay on Karl Kraus, Benjamin celebrates the destructive instinct as a valid, even a Promethean, foil to the creative instinct. This destructive instinct is at its most valuable when life has become habitual:

> And therefore the monster stands among us as the messenger of a more real humanism. . . . He feels solidarity not with the slender pine but with the plane that devours it, not with the precious ore but with the blast furnace that purifies it. . . . One must have followed Loos in his struggle with the dragon "ornament" . . ., or seen Klee's New Angel, who preferred to free men by taking from them, rather than make them happy by giving to them, to understand a humanity that proves itself by destruction. (Benjamin 1979, 289)

So where, or what, is Benjamin's angel? One of the fascinating things about these dense images is their peculiar and essential rightness, which is dependent on the fused resonance of the whole (as happens in good poetry) rather than in the precise linear relationships of ideas. This dense resonance also, of course, makes them tricky to parse. In any case, I would want to talk, not about revolutionary politics, but about the possibility for redemption that revolutionary politics can represent—which is, I think, not out of line when one is speaking through Benjamin, or being spoken through by him.

For Benjamin's angel, history is singular: it is the past as a whole, which endlessly spews wreckage at him—a wreckage I interpret as being simply itself, that is to say, tradition. At the same time, Paradise—which seems to come from the same direction, and possibly even to be the same thing, as the past—flings an unending storm at him, pushing him into a future that, Benjamin implies, is terrifying but inescapable. The laconic coldness of the final line, which bluntly identifies the storm (and implicitly the entire image) as "progress," makes the whole even more chilling, implying that we are always already caught in this situation as our (modern) temporal reality. The fractured, tangled mess of tradition and progress becomes an eschatological trap that prevents the angel from either controlling or slowing his movement into the future, or on the contrary returning to Paradise (where the past is perhaps not merely wreckage). He is always already moving forward in time, as are we.

The terrifying explosion that forces us forward in time, or at least a response to the feelings created by such an image, suggest the eschatological world of Barraqué with its resistance to movement and frozen, perpetual reaction to awaited death and failure. While completing his famous piano sonata in 1952, Barraqué wrote, angrily and satirically, of the trap he was thereby creating for himself:

> You see, in our time, what the "serial principle" actually means: a two-fold abstraction, which both constructs and destroys. The creative act in its aesthetic necessity remains incomprehensible, for one knows full well that it is not sufficient to employ rows and place *f* and *p* signs in order to produce a valid work; but in the moment when the spark ignites, one sets foot in a region which is just as absurd as that where a rock turns into a man, where a man takes leave of rationality against his will, and falls prey to irrationality and becomes insane. As I wrote to Boulez, all of the present experiments are not very satisfying, because all of these people are content when they have written a row and placed a *f* or *p* and (the pinnacle of on the other hand) an accent or portato on every note. Almost no one has RECOGNIZED the disturbing temperature of our times, our historic truth. They don't know that more than ever an understanding of the world in its totality is the only *Possibility*, and that outside of this everything is not just incomplete, but totally *Useless*.[2]

The best example of Barraqué's "historic truth" is the entire second movement of the Sonata wherein, as Hodeir says,

> Music cracks under the unhuman strain, disintegrates and is sucked into the void. Whole slabs of sound crumble and vanish beneath the all-engulfing ocean of silence, until only the twelve notes of the row remain, and even these are plucked off, one by one (Hodeir 1961, 195).

The first movement of the same piece generates a powerfully changing rhythmic field within serial bounds and, like many serial textures, creates an aural effect of a seemingly infinite field of elements separated from each other in extreme tension. I would assert, again, that this tension should not be seen as merely technical, that is, as a tension between musical elements: in "subjectively" listening to these sounds, it inevitably becomes the unbearable tension of time and of our awareness of the present, which is always slipping away.

*   *   *

Naturally, the question arises: am I merely attempting to redefine expressionism? Talking about expressionism is much simpler than talking about whatever it is that I am seeking here. Although it is a bit tricky to bring musical expressionism into focus, because it is entangled with the technical concepts of atonality and early twelve-tone theory, its more convenient incarnations in the literary and visual arts allow us to lean on extensive discourse from those fields to explain its psychological and spiritual aims. What I am looking for is admittedly comparable to expressionism—perhaps closely related to, but also distinct from it, since this different sensibility is not rooted in a fascination with the Freudian unconscious.

Susan Sontag, in separating out certain modernist sensibilities, remarks almost in passing:

> There is a kind of seriousness whose trademark is anguish, cruelty, derangement. . . . I am speaking, obviously, of a style of personal existence as well as of a style in art; but the examples had best come from art. Think of Bosch, Sade, Rimbaud, Jarry, Kafka, Artaud, think of most of the important works of art of the twentieth century, that is, art whose goal is not that of creating harmonies but of overstraining the medium and introducing more and more violent, and unresolvable, subject-matter. This sensibility also insists on the principle that an oeuvre in the old sense (again, in art, but also in life) is not possible. Only "fragments" are possible. . . . Clearly, different standards apply here than to traditional high culture. Something is good not because it is achieved, but because another kind of truth about the human situation, another experience of what it is to be human—in short, another valid sensibility—is being revealed. . . . The . . . sensibility . . . of high culture . . . is basically moralistic. The . . . sensibility . . . of extreme states of feeling, represented in much contemporary "avant-garde" art, gains power by a tension between moral and aesthetic passion (Sontag 1966, 287).

A musical image of such tension can be found in the ending of the last movement of Maxwell Davies' First Symphony. Although the work is "permeated by the presence of the sea and the landscape of this isolated place [Orkney] off the north coast of Scotland,"[3] the effect is not in any way pastoral, but is instead eerie and vastly transcendent. The texture of the symphony is fast, complex and—like that of the Barraqué Sonata—frequently on the edge of perceivable coherence; if this is indeed a natural world, it is one that is already too infinite and too dangerous for us to possess, or even fully to grasp. In such a context, the extraordinary drive of the final passage, which follows a long passage of slow but increasing movement, suggests to me an attempt to reach beyond the world toward something far beyond physical experience; the tangled line rising from the basses up through the orchestra explodes through the ceiling of audible sound to progress to some other inconceivable place, past the limits of time and mere understanding. Why might a discussion as subjective as this one be in any way meaningful—or even, perhaps, important?

The music of high modernism has become, over the decades, institutional, acceptable, safe. Boulez never did blow up any opera houses, and instead constructed the most elaborate and authoritative of modernist musical institutions. Archives of modern music manuscripts are built, and to some extent run, like bank vaults, the notation of elaborate bursts of imagination transformed into expensive fetishes. Barraqué is dead and largely forgotten; Maxwell Davies, increasingly a celebrity, calls himself "Max" and writes audience-pleasing concerti. Exhibitions of scores and letters, concerts dutifully attended as educational penance, and glossy, problem-free new recordings of modernist "classics" are a predictable part of our world. And, of course, all of the most bizarre and shocking works eventually appear in the final chapters of our history texts and anthologies.

However, despite all of this—and admittedly among various other meanings and intentions—a crucial aspect of this music remains its attempt to blow the world apart. The never fully comprehensible or manageable explosions of serialism, and the disturbing qualities of many of the works of high modernism, can never be completely plowed back into the museum of musical history; they can never, in fact, have all of their edges removed, not even by the powerful forces of theory, pedagogy, grants, or publicity. And I think we may be very lucky in that.

PART II. IN THE HALL OF MIRRORS

This—by which I mean both part 2 and the combined article made up of both parts—is, inevitably, a work in progress. That sounds like an apology, the kind we so often hear (and say): implicitly it suggests that the forthcoming discourse is not the perfected object that it intends to be. It implies that the flaws or seams of the piece haven't been covered over; sometimes the footnotes aren't complete or the ending is a bit fuzzy; in reading my own not-quite-finished work I may hear sour notes—sentences that don't quite work, ideas that no longer seem fully valid, or that I have disproved or diverged from since first writing them. This introduces reflexivity—a look in the mirror—appropriately because, of course, that's where the reality of writing, as well as its musical object, actually operates. No matter what I do, no matter what effort I put into the work, I remain unavoidably a human being creating a specific discourse in fragments of time between periods of sleep and activity, and among numerous other habits and projects, all of which distract me from intermittent epiphanies and change the meaning of the sentences, even if the words themselves do not change. As a former performer, I know that I can use the same words to tell slightly different stories, that each time I read a paper it is a different narrative: the vectors represented by the words can always operate at different angles to each other, and the resultant super-structure heads off in different, and sometimes unexpected, directions. And, just as every live performance of the paper is somewhat different, so is every reading of any "final" published version—all of the complex or unpre-dictable experiences that constitute reality contribute to the discussion of a particular body of music and my understanding of it.

Various such contributions led to the creation of part 1, which in part 2 becomes an object of study—the discussion is itself subject to discussion. My youthful fascination with the dark sensuality of high modernist music, which included such works as *Le marteau sans maître* and Blomdahl's *Aniara,* a fas-cination rediscovered after years of study, is the original foundation of the article "A Passion for the Violent Ineffable." Indeed, my desire to tease out that particular quality led to my dissertation on some of the more chaotic and bizarre works of the 1950s and 1960s. The original impulse should, ide-ally, be the pure source of part 1; but the source is muddied, unpredictably altered, not only over time but by peripheral circumstances such as the con-ditions of writing—a dorm room in Surrey, another in Turku, my expecta-tions of a British audience and a Scandinavian one, and the imagined or real reactions of various listeners or readers, who may or may not have been, at the time, thinking of something else entirely.

We are accustomed to discounting many of these circumstances but, in my imagination, which is of course where the writing occurs, these aspects remain acutely present. And we do work with our imaginations, there's no doubt about it: although I often explain the object of our subjectivities to my stu-dents as "cultural products," that is a disappointingly cold, and therefore inac-curate, phrase. What we are working on is an art form, and one that impels an inner world of feelings and dreams. I suggest that that is why we started working with music in the first place, way back before we entered graduate programs, got degrees, or dug ourselves into jobs. Indeed, as we are educated into academe, in a discipline that has been heavily influenced by the sci-ences—that is, by a discipline that still prefers to lean toward what is pejora-tively called "positivism"—we learn to control our various imaginings. We don't entirely ignore them, of course, except in very few cases—one might consider the graduate student forced to write a dissertation documenting music in which he or she has no interest as an extreme example. We sublimate our imaginative impulses and ideas, sneakily arranging topics and projects to allow ourselves to talk about things that fire us up, all the while pretending to be purely scholarly and coolly objective. More broadly, we become socialized into subgroups that encourage agreement on certain permitted infractions of the norm: thus the attachment to arcane mystery that one sees in many medieval scholars, the passionate and slightly guilty liberalism expressed by many ethnomusicologists, and—of course—the mathematical formalities affected by scholars of my own period, the period of high modernism.

Ultimately, this is a form of reader-response criticism, but one where I don't wish to try to create an image of the ideal reader of Boulez and Stockhausen, but instead to better understand how we read, reread, and ultimately reconstruct the objects of our own work. This is not about our possible subjectivity in relation to the music—which is, in a peculiar way, an objectified subjectivity; instead it is a more complex subjectivity in relation to our own subjectivity. This is like living in a hall of mirrors, to invoke the name of Blomdahl's cantata, and the cycle of poems by Lindegren for which it is named.[4] And when there are mirrors on all sides, they don't merely reflect the objects standing between them, but also each other, and the reflections of their own reflections . . .

The First Mirror

Part 1 was originally written in and for a conference held in England. Its structure and language were affected by that context: after all, an American academic in England is often conscious of jumping higher, "Oxbridge" hurdles, of being more careful than the locals perhaps need to be, of making sure that, beneath the structures of one's main argument, one includes a subliminal rebuttal of the expected prejudice that an American scholar will be naïve, uncultured, a bit sloppy—hopelessly, in a word, colonial.

These colonial fears and resentments are not entirely baseless. For instance, although many of the conference discussions were friendly and open to speculation, some were decidedly not. After one paper discussing Kurtág's analysis of a Bartók piece—an analysis that was clearly faulty in relation to Bartók, but also clearly of interest in understanding Kurtág's compositional intentions—there were no fewer than five responses that began with the phrase: "We must be very careful not to . . . " $f(x)$. Assertions were made about the apparent danger of this analysis that seemed to me quite absurd: what were we afraid of—that young girls and old ladies might get hold of this analysis and be "ruined" in some peculiar way? These warnings, although they may have become less common in musicological circles during the 1990s, both in Britain and America, can be extended to any discussion of interpretation, speculation, and subjectivity. Is not all such work dangerous? Another facet of this danger came up in a conversation with a senior colleague who cut short my enthusiastic story of meeting another musicologist, dismissing the absent one as a "phrase-maker." This worried me, because often I feel as though I am myself a phrase-maker: if I could not say it distinctively, gracefully, and in a way to convince the most recalcitrant reader, would my argument actually make any sense? Is there any "objective truth" behind the impact of the words themselves? How many ways are there to close down discussion, speculation, interpretation—and how many of those ways do some academics employ to keep their colleagues from discovering new ideas or unexpected approaches?

My anxiety over the British professional reception of part 1 was actually one important source of the passion of that paper: I was frankly nervous about putting over my argument in that context, and wrote accordingly. This was also true because, at that particular conference, a number of other speakers made presentations that (more carefully) circled around the idea of interpreting modernism. Most of them followed more traditional, more historically focused, courses than I did. I was in fact sharply intimidated the day before my paper by someone taking Boulez apart in terms of Lyotard: would my poetic, demented vision of high modernism be shot utterly to pieces by a surging crowd of critical, and of course quite British, senior academics?

But it wasn't. In fact, and for me quite unexpectedly, they liked it. Suddenly colleagues wanted to have breakfast with me, to ask elaborate and surprisingly expressive questions about exact points of the paper, even later to write me e-mails about it—evidently they thought I had said something interesting that they needed to hear. Much as I would love to flatter myself, I find it difficult to believe that they responded this way because of any innate genius in my work. Instead, is it possible that in musicology we are simply lacking expressions of imagination, of subjectivity, so much that we'd rather hear Benjamin and—out of all the more possible, citeable, "great" names—Rilke? That we'd rather hear poetry, instead of historical documentation? Has our discipline gotten, perhaps, a bit too dry for its subject matter, or even too dry for us to sustain interest, even in our own work?

The Second Mirror

An interesting, peripheral but surprisingly well-known, work of high modernism is Blomdahl's opera *Aniara*, based on Harry Martinson's poem cycle of the same name. The story is a science fiction tour de force about a spaceship that is thrown off course and ends up heading into emptiness with no hope of return. The opera, based on fairly schematic patterns that emphasize the mechanistic mathematics of serialism, is nevertheless deeply involving. Martinson's dramatic gestures symbolize a universe where we are lost, and terrified of being lost, where we are faced with emptiness and our inadequacy to respond to it. Martinson's eerie fourth poem, one of the most successful in the English translations, runs as follows:

> That was how the solar system closed
> its vaulted gateway of the purest crystal
> and severed spaceship Aniara's company
> from all the bonds and pledges of the sun. . . .
>
> Though space vibrations faithfully bore round
> our proud Aniara's last communiqué

on widening rings, in spheres and cupolas
it moved through empty spaces, thrown away.

In anguish sent by us in Aniara
our call sign faded till it failed: Aniara.
                                    MARTINSON 1999, 36

Although, when I was younger, I had no access to a recording of Blomdahl's opera, a suite from the work was released on the flip side of the popular American recording of music used for Kubrick's movie *2001*.[5] The suite has several impressive passages, including some rather spooky concrète and bizarrely satirical pseudo-jazz; but the most striking music is right at the beginning, which presents sounds that are freezingly cold and distant, schematically arranged notes of a Großmutterakkord that suggest the emotionless, intentionless passage of particles through empty space. I still turn to these musical images when life and other people seem too circumscribed or suffocatingly predictable—when our everyday world shows its triviality.

The Third Mirror

Who would write about such stuff, about the airless serialism of the fifties and sixties? Who, in another sense, would want to? That question is not necessarily sarcastic: it is a part of the intent of this discussion—a discussion that is personal, even uncomfortably so—to outline one kind of person who might care about "such stuff." The answer for me, an answer that became increasingly obvious over the years, is that I am fascinated with networks of masculinity, authority, and tradition—but only when they are in trouble, when they are exposed or collapsing or forced into change. In my case, this may have something to do with growing up gay in a 1970s "clone culture" where short hair and insistently masculine fashions were the norm. This sets me off from other colleagues in gender studies whose work focuses more on flamboyance or androgyny. It is important for me to understand why certain things fascinate me, why certain things demand study, while others are merely matters that can be considered by other musicologists, if they choose. I believe that most musicologists of any bent choose their topics of study and discussion through reference to some inner, sometimes secret world, some view of the universe that impels them toward certain questions and not others. The fiction that we stand on a level plain of discourse and rationally choose the topics that most need attention is merely that—a fiction.

The question of who would write about a given topic is linked to a broader question: who are we, writing and reading academic papers at the turn of the millennium? Are our activities pertinent to anyone, in any generalizable way? It is evident that this particular discussion is useful to me, because I can work through my own relationship to myself and my work. That was, ultimately, one of the functions of the article "Performance and/or Shame" (Attinello 1995), which unexpectedly turned into an exploration of things I'd known but had almost forgotten about my personal history. It may be of interest to know that this exploration was remarkably useful for me: I can state, with psychoanalytic certainty, that my relationship to my own past, and thus of course my future, changed quite a bit over the process of writing that paper. But the question of How Useful Is Our Work—which may be rooted in old 'relevance' arguments from the 1970s—continues to bother me: espe-cially in the past few years, after finally getting a job, etc., following a long and messy indenture, it often appears that I have become a part of a machine that mass-produces presentations and publications as though in a factory. I was amazed this spring when a paper that had been rejected for a conference was requested for the published proceedings of that conference; the editors refused, then accepted, the article on the basis of the same one-paragraph abstract. I couldn't help thinking: they need to fill out the book, don't they? They need to make a commercial product with the correct number of pages, and don't much care what is on those pages. It is as though the strug-gle to make a piece of work worthwhile, or at least good enough to justify the time and energy to read it, is actually superfluous to the needs of academic publishing.

So: of what use to you is the discussion of my background experiences, of my reasons for writing? One critical concern comes from a comment I heard in a writing workshop, after someone expressed enthusiasm for a young nov-elist's story of his childhood: "Well, it's fascinating to read about anybody's childhood." Are my experiences in writing part 1 of (some) interest merely because they are experiences, and thereby offer a frisson of drama in a con-text that usually lacks such thrills? Or are experiences actually transferable, and are our own lessons somehow learnable by other readers—such as your-self?

I believe that each of us operates within a particular window of under-standing, whose borders are the limits of our backgrounds and predilections. There are things—musics, methods, interpretations—that we find innately difficult to understand because their implications are inconsistent with deci-sions we have made about ourselves and (our version of) the universe. There are other things we simply cannot grasp because our experience, and what we have learned from it, cannot stretch far enough; and finally there are things, too many I think, that we would prefer not to understand (or would prefer to pretend not to understand) because any expressed comprehension of them might be inconsistent with things we have said or implied, which then might make us seem foolish. Even when faced with an exciting or sim-ply plausible new idea, we too often try to avoid any appearance that we might ever have changed our minds—a common concern for the writer and scholar, as others might be examining our work for consistency. So, as a group of scholars engaged in an ongoing discourse: what is the window of understanding that we might possibly see in musicology, or in any kind of aesthetics, analysis, or interpretation? Is it plausible to enlarge that window, as on a computer screen, or at least to acknowledge the differences between our individual limitations, such that a given group (or discipline) could reach a larger understanding than any single member of it? (Of course, the discipline of ethnomusicology managed these questions rather well during the methodological discussions of the 1980s. But it remains a challenge always waiting to be re-met by any group or individual scholar.)

Part of my experience of teaching various genres of twentieth-century Western music in Hong Kong was the realization that my students do not have the cultural expectations that would make the stresses and fractures of that music self-evident to them. Even if I am imposing a particularly violent interpretation on high modernism in part 1, it is not, I think, very controversial to claim that much of the music of our century expresses some kind of rage, rebellion, or at least doubt, aligned against tradition, predictability or grand narratives. Since my students don't have any instinctive sense of this rage—their own culture is constituted entirely differently—none of it quite makes sense to them, not Boulez, and not Nirvana.[6] Their response to dissonance at all levels seems to be more of a "culinary" interest in interesting sounds, rather than a sense of cultural disruption. In fact, when I use tunes like "Smells Like Teen Spirit" in my Music Appreciation class, or joke about music that "sucks," I am making references that mean little to them—and whose cynicism and brutality leaves them wondering why anyone would want to play or study this "stuff."

The Fourth Mirror

This essay, and the music that impels it, inevitably bring up questions of rigor. At least, they inevitably bring it up if you care about arguing fairly: if one is willing to polemicize or sway opinion without concern as to whether arguments are conscientious, then rigor is no problem. But that suggests irresponsibility: rigor is the way that we make our actions correct in line with some authoritative (or authoritarian?) expectation. As for the music of high modernism, most of its most important disagreements were over the place and constitution of rigor, creating a bizarre context where a piece of music could be dismissed on logical grounds alone.

Questions for and against rigor bring up the problem of precision, the concept of embedding one's statements in a larger and hopefully more secure armature of thought, as opposed to exploring the anecdotal, the local. But that is to replace real experience, actual data, with concepts, thereby reifying the universe into something that might be, or might seem, consistent. This is also affected by our view of the linearity of a given argument. In reading and listening, we repeatedly ask ourselves: what's missing in this paper, or in that paper? When has too much that is important been excluded, or too many tangents been included? Chances are that we will judge rigor more exactingly than any other parameter of value—such as interest, involvement, contribution to the culture (or merely to the existing literature). Sometimes this judgment is unfair, as when scientific parameters are imposed on contexts where they are inappropriate (such as, frequently enough, in music).

Rigor, and its implied correlate consistency, is of course not only a method of controlling ideas and arguments. It is also a means of avoiding boredom on the part of the reader or listener: after all, how many people have disconnected or inconsistent ideas that are actually interesting? Not many, that's certain. But is this merely human nature, a common aspect of the human condition, or is it our modernist education hampering us in our work? Has our training made it impossible for us to think freely—has it reduced us to two alternatives, the rigorous and the lazy (with a bow to Deleuze and Guattari, as these can be reinterpreted as the paranoid and the schizoid), with the latter always inadequate? Certainly, we allow composers a certain leeway that isn't allowed to scholars, the idea seeming to be that the creative mind can't be bothered with consistency. Why, then, should the scholarly mind be so concerned about it? And, to bring the argument back to part 1: what is our relationship to rigor, and what can it be, if we are reflecting on an era where avant-garde scientism is the fashion, such as the 1950s? Do we pretend not to notice the short haircuts and dark suits in all the group photographs from Darmstadt?

The Fifth Mirror

When mirrors face each other, the objects reflected in them become smaller and less distinct until the mirrors seem merely to reflect themselves. And strangely enough, in the processes of living and writing, subjective relationships to things that seem to be entirely separate—different parts of one's life, different personae, different masks—reflect each other in unanticipated ways.

Over the past few years, cropping up intermittently in notes I take in interviews, in archives, even at conferences, the music of high modernism—Darmstadt, Donaueschingen, serialism, the avant-garde—and the concepts of gay and lesbian studies keep intersecting in unexpected ways. It is a badly-kept secret that many of the figures of the post-war avant-garde were gay—Boulez, Bussotti, Cage, Henze, and Metzger, just for example. Discussions with some of these and their colleagues show clearly that a network of sexual relationships and identities, together with the gleeful, shocked, or disgusted reactions to them by others, impacted upon many of the crucial aesthetic decisions and schisms of the 1950s and 1960s.[7]

This conflates several uncomfortable problems in subjectivity: how much am I allowed to talk about this? It's a dangerous topic, after all, and some of the wealthier composers have lawyers. And can I manage to remain cool and unattached, and manage to seem cool and unattached, in relation to this subject matter? Can I avoid the impulse to play "IMRU"—the game of claiming about almost any famous figure, "Oh, you know he's gay"? Is everything infected by possible motives and agendas, such that any statement on a topic that matters to the speaker is always suspect?

The Sixth Mirror

We're not supposed to psychologize: psychologizing is forbidden, psychologizing is bad; because we are not professional therapists we're not allowed to comment on, for instance, the emotional reason that a given piece of music goes a certain way. But clearly psychology is the science of this century, that new view of everything that was so largely missing before the period of early modernism. Clearly, our understanding of daily life is contingent on our assumption that people's patterns, feelings, and unconscious forces drive practically all of their behavior—including, of course, composition, interpretation, and even musicological writing.

In this context, I find the ideas of Deleuze and Guattari (and, of course, part of their scholarly validation is the fact that Guattari is a 'real' psychologist) extremely useful. One of their basic ideas is that our everyday patterns of thinking are not entirely different from those that occur in extreme states of paranoia and schizophrenia. Certainly, in studying something that arouses such deep passions as music, a sensitivity to the mindset implied by a given creative product would be very useful, even if that mindset seems a bit strange or extreme. Sass, another 'real' psychologist, has written about modernist literature and art in terms that suggest at least one interpretation of Rilke's angels, and also suggest the entire problem of transcendent difficulties in modern music:

> Many schizophrenic patients "delightedly believe that they have grasped the profoundest of meanings; concepts such as timelessness, world, god and death become enormous revelations which when the state has subsided cannot be reproduced or described in any way—they were after all nothing but feelings." It is understandable that such concerns might often reduce a person either to silence or to oblique and vague attempts at description. . . . At least some of the statements that strike observers as woolly or empty philosophizing . . . may thus be attempts—sometimes inept but sometimes not—to express concerns that are just too all-encompassing or too abstract to be stated in clear and specific terms, even by the most clear-minded of speakers. (Sass 1992, 191)

It is of course important to remember, in any psychological discussion related to an art form, that one is not analyzing a person so much as an image of a persona—that is, if one reaches conclusions about a particular cultural product, those conclusions may not apply to other aspects of the person who created it. Virginia Woolf said that we are all a thousand different people inside; in our everyday lives, it is the people around us who demand consistency in our behavior, which we supply in the form of a predictable persona. But it would be a mistake to infer, as many do, that our personalities are consistent . . . as it would be to assume that a given composer should project an image of the same persona in different works.

In the interpretation of a certain sensibility via Rilke and Benjamin in part 1, my context is perhaps more spiritual and transcendent than psychological. However, a useful psychological counterpart would be Jung's thesis of the power of the unconscious—the claim that imagination, art, and spiritual change have real rather than illusory power, that art is not merely the sublimation of something else, that the battles, losses, and victories we experience in dreams are not mere fantasy, but have real effect.

The Seventh (and Last) Mirror

To what extent does this become intellectual masturbation?

Who, after all, cares if I am interested in my own subjectivity? How can we discuss our own imaginative backgrounds—our feelings, our various levels of reasons for doing what we do—in a way that doesn't make a reader drop the book in boredom? One useful aspect of this is that people who have not talked much about their imaginations, about their subjectivities, about their selves, tend to do a much clumsier job of it than those with more experience. This was frequently clear in discussions among members of the Gay & Lesbian Study Group of the American Musicological Society in its early days: people who evidently hadn't thought much about their own sexuality sometimes stood up to present the meeting with the most astonishing statements. This must be accepted in a group context, of course, because there must be room to speak, to develop a group dynamic. But the less experienced seem to have difficulty in distinguishing what is interesting to themselves from what might be interesting to others: they have become accustomed to the academic distinction of objective and subjective (despite its somewhat illusory nature), but still have trouble distinguishing the generalizable or the communicable from the private or the contingent, from their more personal or accidental memories and wishes.

This is perhaps the most useful thing to consider at every point in a discussion of subjectivity: who cares? Does anyone care about what you want to say, or is it something that has only private resonance? And of course, some things which are utterly private can nevertheless be communicated if they are situated within a larger discussion . . .

Most importantly, a discussion of subjectivity should always, at least eventually, end. You can't live in a permanently self-conscious state—you can't dance if you're always looking at your feet. It is useful to think about subjectivity frequently enough to remind yourself of its reality: but ultimately it is always necessary to stop analyzing oneself, to break the mirrors, and act.

NOTES

Versions of part 1 were read in July 1999 at the Third Triennial British Musicological Societies 1999 Conference in Surrey; in October 1999 at the Skagerak Network seminar Självreflexivitet i musikforskningen (Self-reflexivity and Musicology) in Turku, Finland; and in April 2000 at the annual national conferences of the Musicological Society of Australia and New Zealand Musicological Society in Sydney. A version of part 2 was given as a continuation of part 1 at the Skagerak Network seminar; I am grateful for their invitation to write it.

1. Quoted in Werckmeister 1981, 98; my translation. "Heute ist der gestrige-heutige Übergang. In der großen Formgrube liegen Trümmer, an denen man noch teilweise hängt. Sie liefern den Stoff zur Abstraktion. Ein Bruchfeld von unechten Elementen, zur Bildung unreiner Kristalle. So ist es heute. . . . Ich habe diesen Krieg in mir längst gehabt. Daher geht er mich innerlich nichts an. Um mich aus meinen Trümmern herauszuarbeiten, mußte ich fliegen. Und ich flog. In jener zertrümmerten Welt weile ich nur noch in der Erinnerung, wie man zuweilen zurückdenkt. Somit bin ich 'abstrakt mit Erinnerungen.' "

2. Quoted by Heribert Henrich, translated by Mark Bruce, in booklet for *Boulez: Troisième Sonate / Douze Notations / Barraqué: Sonate pour Piano / Pi-Hsien Chen* (Telos Records TLS 006), 7.

3. [N.a.], booklet, *Maxwell Davies: Symphony no. 1* (Collins 14352), 1995.

4. Karl Birger Blomdahl and Erik Lindegren, *I speglarnas sal/In the Hall of Mirrors* (Caprice [LP]), 1972.

5. *Music from 2001: A Space Odyssey/Suite from Aniara* (Columbia MS 7176), 1968. This album was apparently taken off the market as a result of Ligeti's lawsuit against Columbia for using his music without permission; a Deutsche Grammophon recording, for which Ligeti did receive royalties, replaced it on the American market. The DGG recording had no Blomdahl on it.

6. Nirvana, "Smells Like Teen Spirit," *Nevermind* (DGC), 1991.

7. These ideas are greatly expanded in an essay I have co-written with David Osmond-Smith, "Gay Darmstadt: Flamboyance and Rigor at the Summer Courses for New Music," which will appear in the *Proceedings of the Second Biennial International Conference on 20th-Century* Music, ed. Keith Potter, Arnold Whittall, and Christopher Mark, published by Ashgate in 2004.

SIX

Uncertainty, Disorientation, and Loss as Responses to Musical Structure

JOSEPH DUBIEL

What I like best about the problematic notion of musical "structure" is the attention it can direct to the *constructedness* of musical identities. By the identity of a musical thing, I mean principally *how it sounds;* by saying that such an identity is constructed, I mean that how a musical thing sounds is engendered by relationships in which we understand that thing to partici-pate. And by relationship I mean any kind of juxtaposition, contrast, or affin-ity—that is, my idea of musical relationship is not constrained by connota-tions of orderly or logical progression. An unprepared departure from what a passage has been doing is every bit as relational as the fulfillment of an implication; so, for that matter, is an event that resists characterization in the terms that have previously been in play, and invites reconceptualization of everything heard so far.

With a notion of "structure" as inclusive as this, it is not clear that any par-ticular kind of listening experience can usefully be picked out as the hearing of "structure." Anything we hear might be—must be—significantly the result of "structure" in the inclusive sense. If such a thing as "structural" listening is to be reified at all, then perhaps it is not to be defined by any characteris-tic of the *listening;* perhaps it could better be identified as a certain way of *thinking about* listening. It might be a kind of listening that involves wanting to make the way in which one's experience is elicited an object of apprecia-tion in itself. The distinctive feature of such listening might be a certain kind of self-monitoring, motivated by a certain kind of wonder—wonder that sounds can do *that.* As a composer, I always have a specific interest in notic-ing how it's done, alongside noticing it done; but even when I'm off duty I like having room in my listening mindset to marvel at the fact that such mul-tifarious experience can be elicited by arrangements of noises. To prevent misunderstanding, I should specify that I do not want to set up a dichotomy between imperceptible (or anyway unperceived) "structure" and perceived effect; the relevant sort of contrast is between different kinds of perceptibility, different terms of conceptualization for what is sensed. Wonder is at the different kinds of conceptualization that the same phenomena can sustain.

Almost certainly, "structure" is not a good word to use for an idea as inclusive as I favor. The word is a magnet for needlessly restrictive connotations, which I have had to fight off practically from my first mention of it here: "structure" as pattern, as logical consecution, as the satisfaction of a requirement (otherwise the music falls to pieces), as validation (nothing is done "merely for its own sake"). My complaint is not only that this is an oddly narrow range of musical possibilities to pick out; it is more specifically that such picking out leaves room for—in fact, appears *designed* to leave room for—the notion that some significant part of what happens in music might be *other* than "structural": "ornamental" or "coloristic" or "expressive." The idea is suppressed that ornament and color and expression are, among other things, *aspects* of "structure" in the inclusive sense, the sense of identities engendered by relationships. And insofar as the various supposed opposites of "structure" may be taken as shallow or frivolous, as opposed to deep and serious, the more restricted understanding of "structure" also tempts us—particularly those of us who have made it our business to seem (and, if possible, to be) intelligent in our interaction with music—to bend our experience of music (at least our representation of it, but therefore probably also our experience) in the deep and serious direction; so that listening well to music can be presented as more like alertly following a train of thought than like appreciating the qualities of something.

The idea of "structural" listening easily goes wrong, then, through a compounding of a limited idea of "relationship," as similarity and regulation, with the expectation that the experiences engendered by these relationships will share the character of the relationships themselves: listening then becomes the seeking of experiences that have that limited "relational" character. "Structure" is expected to inhabit musical experience as a sort of *tone* of rationality—paradoxically (as Marlon Feld put it) a kind of affect. I see no reason to make this a privileged kind of musical experience, or even to accept it as an adequately defined kind. The invitation to make such a mistake is what I like least about the notion of "structure."

I hope in this essay to expose and disarm this booby trap. I want to describe a few musical experiences that have something to do with "structure" in the sense that I like (that I can *show* to be "structural" in that sense) but that don't have the character of "structure" about which I have just expressed reservations. They are not experiences like following a line of reasoning, understanding implications fulfilled and conclusions drawn—in some cases, they are not even much like knowing what's going on. And more: they don't necessarily have the character of the *specific* "structural" attributions that I set up to support them. That is, the experiential reports do not necessarily have the qualities, or the dynamics, or concern themselves with the same entities, as the technical reports that I develop alongside them. So even if you're already with me in being over the idea of "structure" as order, there is something this essay can offer you, namely a particular look at the possible discrepancy between an attribution of "structure" and the experience, presumably *of* this "structure," that the attribution is meant to account for. In a way, what this essay offers you is a problem: Why build into your theoretical account of a passage a distinct character that is different from that of the experience you want to capture? Why tolerate such a difference, or why bother? How should we expect a theoretical model to resemble the experience it is set up to account for?

I am not going to try to answer those questions, especially not in any principled or general way. I state them here in an effort to define the contexts in which my examples might matter. Probably the most I can offer in the way of generality will not be any general proposition at all, but a demonstration of the workability of a few attitudes. One is an attitude of unprincipled pragmatism about the relationship between analytical constructions and the experiences to which they respond: unprincipled in that I am willing to accept almost any kind of incongruity between the terms of an analysis and the experiences that go with it; pragmatic in the sense that I am tolerant of almost any kind of suggestiveness or resonance, but completely inflexible in the expectation that there be some articulable relationship between analysis and hearing. Even though my overt point is going to be that we cannot insist on any *particular* parallelism between a theoretical formulation and its experiential correlate, the last thing I want to do is offer comfort to the kind of analysis that just identifies a pattern (any pattern) and then helps itself to the assurance that this pattern (because it is such a *lovely* pattern) must be working on us somehow—"unconsciously," as people often say. If the pattern matters to the music, then there must be some way we *hear* the mattering, and what we hear, we're conscious of! (We might at the same time *not* be conscious of *how* the configuration of sounds is provoking this experience; we may well not be conscious of some concepts that would help us to report and explain this. But those are different issues.)[1]

This is why I am not completely at ease with the (in many ways useful) image of unperceived "structure" being responsible for perceived "effect." I would rather think of music being perceptible in a variety of different ways, and of the coordination of different kinds of observation as being a useful topic of inquiry—and of the *effort* to coordinate different kinds of observation as itself a useful *mode* of inquiry. My procedure, in most of the musical analyses that follow, will be to begin with some "structural" fact that I know by some means other than hearing, which I am for some reason unsure how to hear (to put it less crudely, whose relation to experience, actual or possible, I do not yet know), and to try to find out what it might mean to hear it. In all of these cases, I find myself developing an account that does not much resemble my initial account of the fact; part of what I would claim to have learned in each case is what might count as hearing this fact, that I would not have expected.

With not very many presuppositions about what kinds of musical experiences to discuss, and especially not the presupposition that these experiences are going to resemble theoretical discourses, the main thing that I am ever going to be able to say in favor of an analysis is that it can stimulate a great deal of specific observation—or, to put it another way, it allows a lot of the particulars of a musical passage to matter, and even creates kinds of particulars and kinds of relevance for them. It follows that I'm going to be presenting a lot of analytical detail. What I hope to demonstrate is not an all-on-top-of-it mastery, so much as the potential for responsiveness along unforeseen lines.

It was a quite unforeseen lapse in mastery that got me thinking along the lines of this essay. In a work that I thought I knew well—the *Tristan* prelude—I one day came across a structural fact that I didn't think I'd ever been hearing and that, at the same time, I couldn't imagine not hearing, so that I had to do some work to figure out what would count as hearing it.

What I realized is that the big tune that enters at the deceptive cadence, after the introductory fragments, doesn't maintain a consistent relationship to its bass line when it recurs. (See ex. 6.1.) The first time (m. 17), the tune's upbeat comes in over F in the bass, and on the downbeat the bass starts an ascent, F♯–G–A. The next time (m. 32), the bass gets underway first, with F already rising to F♯ at the first upbeat. The tune even changes to adapt to this difference: its big downward swoop, occurring over G in the bass instead of F♯, is C–E instead of C–D. Eventually the difference between these two settings fades: the bass of the second version includes a chromatic passing tone that the first one doesn't, G♯ between G and A, and so the bass line's high point A coincides with the same point in the tune both times, and its subsequent descent to C♯ fits the tune the same way. (The descending step from A to G is also filled chromatically the second time, but in such a way that the overall alignment of bass and tune is unchanged.)

The difference fades: but still—what a thing not to have noticed! I don't know many tonal melodies that can be displaced by half a measure against their bass lines without at least some effect of powerful transformation being wrought upon them. (Or maybe I do, and just don't realize it.) And it isn't only that I *hadn't* noticed; it is also that, once I was aware of this, I *still* had a hard time noticing, even with the evidence right before my eyes, and under my fingers. To this day, I have a hard time noticing, in a sense: the theme

Example 6.1   Wagner, *Tristan und Isolde*, Act I, Einleitung: two occurrences of the theme, with the melody in different relations to the bass.

doesn't *sound* that different to me, one way and the other, certainly not as different as I think I should expect. (Try it—even if you know the passages well, and are in the habit of glossing over the examples when you read about music. Play the melody with one bass line, then with the other.)

Or perhaps—the point I have been preparing—I am not listening for the relevant sort of difference. Perhaps I do hear some difference, have been all along, only it is not the kind of difference I have thought to listen for, or thought to connect to the contrapuntal rearrangement of the theme. In any event, here is something to investigate. I have a contrast that I can reasonably call structural, even in a very conventional sense: it's a matter of how the notes are arranged. In this instance, I recognize its structural status in the very uneasiness I feel about not clearly noticing it. A lot of facts that might be veraciously pointed out in a score, I wouldn't be at all surprised to find inaudible; and in the right context I would be prepared to question whether such facts should be considered music-structural at all. But this one can't *not* be significant, somehow. So there it is, and I need to do some work to say what it means for my hearing. Even for something as macroscopic—as blatant—as a melody and its bass going out of phase for a while, it is not obvious what sort of experience ought to count as "hearing it."

Now I can be more specific about what I am not hearing that I might have expected to: in the second (and later) occurrences of the theme, I am not getting any very strong sense of departure from a norm or prototype presented by the first occurrence. I suppose that the first version must be, in some sense, the normal one, if any one is. It is the version that recurs later in the opera—for instance, when Isolde narrates her first meeting with Tristan, and when the two of them have their drink together later in the first act—and it and Tristan eventually expire simultaneously in the third act. It probably is the way I vaguely and inaccurately thought all the thematic statements went, when I thought they all went the same way.

Statistics aren't exactly to the point, but as a matter of fact this first contrapuntal arrangement is the exception in the prelude. The second arrangement is the one reproduced at the next occurrence of the theme (m. 55), and at another occurrence shortly after that (m. 58). (The first recurrence is transposed up a major third and moved to the opposite metrical position, but the relation between melody and bass is the same.) That these statements match the second one may not be so remarkable, since their textural surroundings are essentially the same as those of the second statement. More interesting is what happens at the next occurrence of the theme, when a return to the first version seems explicitly called for by another approach to the deceptive cadence (m. 74), proceeding from a reconstitution of the prelude's opening. (See ex. 6.2.) Here the original counterpoint does recur, but also does not. It does, in that the melody does begin over F♮ in the bass, and the bass has (and needs) no passing G♯ between G and A. It does not, in that the melody is out of its normal metrical position, and the interval of its first big descent is again altered (this time to C–D♯)—this even though the leap still occurs over F♯. The metric repositioning is easy to notice, because the melodic entrance overlaps, instead of waits for, the resolution of the appoggiatura in the deceptive cadence. Because the entrance is thus vividly "too early," the restoration of the original contrapuntal alignment sounds not quite like a restoration—sounds more like a new realignment on top of the old realignment. And these accumulated changes make this fifth statement seem, of all the statements, the most obvious departure from some inferred norm, despite the return of the original counterpoint.

Without overestimating the relevance of such a survey to the hearing of events locally, I can acknowledge the difficulty of identifying any "normal" version of the theme. Accordingly, it might be best to characterize the "original" version of the theme as (simply) the particular version that follows the deceptive cadence (not only in the prelude, but in its later occurrences as well).[2] It might be thought of as the version *adjusted to* the deceptive cadence, and the second version, similarly, as the one *adjusted to* the contrasting circumstances of its entry, and the idea of norm and departure might be dispensed with. Taking this point completely to heart, the way to respond to the difference between the versions might after all be not to hear the theme as different on these various occasions, but to hear (as if) the *same* theme, embedded in various contexts, and to assimilate the differences, insofar as they are noticeable, to this embedding. It may even be a good interpretive

Example 6.2   Wagner, *Tristan und Isolde,* Act I, Einleitung: another occurrence of the theme, with another relation between melody and bass.

strategy actively to *minimize* the difference between one occurrence and another—to assume that some aspects of their surrounding contexts have dictated the differences, and that the remarkable compositional feat is precisely to have concealed these differences as much as Wagner has. On account of some other considerations, things are "already" going to be different in the vicinity of these two entrances, and now compositional finesse consists precisely in directing a listener's attention *away from* the difference. What would we expect of delirious phantasmagoric music, if not something like this?

The obvious candidate for a contextual feature that can be the matrix of this embedding is the degree of continuity: sheer continuity of sound, and, beyond this, continuity of motion. The opening of the prelude is conspicuously (and famously) a concatenation of fragments, everything about which—their restricted but colorful orchestration, their abstruse and incomplete harmonic progression, their sequential succession—points to the possibility of a sound that is bigger, more complete, better able to sustain itself. The deceptive cadence is the moment when these conditions are alleviated, or at least most of them are: the sound is from this moment full and unbroken. A moment later this sound is shaped and directed into continuous *motion* by the theme. The sequence of events is nicely worked out: first, a moment to bask in the chord that the deceptive cadence has produced; then, the upbeat of the new melody—with the forthcoming pace of the bass line just insinuated by the rescoring of the chord; and then, coming along with the melody, the steady movement of the bass.

When the theme occurs the second time, the establishment of continuity, of sound or of motion, is no longer an issue (at most the maintenance of it may be, insofar as a return to fragments is soon to follow); therefore the theme will not be able to contribute, let alone lead, but will instead fit in. At most there is a change in the *kind* of motion, a change that is best understood by reference to the bass. While the bass moves steadily by step, by passing motion, during the theme, its motion lapses during contrasting passages (in the first instance, between the two statements, mm. 25 ff.) into something less "linear," more "harmonic" (as well as generally descending, and somewhat slower). Accordingly the bass of the second thematic statement, though no longer the first stirring of bass motion, still does represent revival after a kind of lull. Compared to this, the entrance of the melody is a less decisive event, for which the bass does not wait: the bass moves from F to F♯ at once in the first measure, and the melody comes along after. Soon enough, the extra chromatic passing tone will allow the original alignment to be restored, and the theme will run its course.

Actually the story is subtler than this. The theme's bass does not simply *initiate* rising motion; rather it makes more vivid, by accelerating it, a rising motion that, at least in retrospect, takes in the preceding E (m. 31)—the E–F succession even vaguely recalling the environment in which the theme first arose, after the E–F of the deceptive cadence. For that matter, this ascent reaches back still further, to D♯ (m. 29). (See ex. 6.3.) While the ascent from D♯ to E does not seem to be *driving* the music in which it occurs (for a variety of reasons, notably a certain obscurity in the harmonic rhythm and progression), this ascending step is nonetheless available for eventual assimilation into an ascent gradually accumulating toward the rising bass of the theme. There are two measures from D♯ to E, one from E to F; and one-half measure per step thereafter. Unless the bass moved from F to F♯ within the measure, no acceleration would occur; and so it moves.

The interpretive strategy that has now emerged is to portray the bass, in each of the theme's occurrences, as moving when and how it does for reasons of its own—essentially reasons of textural pacing, independent of the theme—and then to hear the melody fitted in to each of these contexts as smoothly and neatly as it can be. This might be how it makes sense for me not to be struck by the change of contrapuntal alignment as a phenomenon in itself.

From one point of view, there is nothing especially original in this. I've worked myself around to a conclusion that I might have started with, that smoothly worked transitions—concealment of the seams—might be an important aspect of Wagner's technique. Why have I had to work myself around to it? It is not normal for an analysis to take the elusiveness of a perception as a topic, and to try to order some observations around, and in support of, the difficulty of making a particular expected observation. The admission of difficulty—in both senses of admission: owning up to it, and letting it into the discussion—is an unusual analytical maneuver, if not indeed the opposite of the work analysis tries to do. I end up having elaborated a sense in which *not* hearing the difference between the two contrapuntal arrangements might be counted as *gaining* access to the prelude's structure—as much as anything might.

That said, I think it is possible to give a more characterful account of how the difference between versions can be noticed (while not being noticed).

Example 6.3   Wagner, *Tristan und Isolde,* Act I, Einleitung: the slow bass ascent preceding the second occurrence of the theme.

It manifests itself as a difference in the theme's power to dominate the scene—a difference whose magic is greatest if we do not notice any feature of the theme itself as *causing* the change in its power.

The first time, the tune steps into a scene that has been abundantly prepared for it—that we come to recognize as having been prepared for it—as it initiates a new line of action. The deceptive cadence is the time for a good heroic entrance, after all that longing, and here comes a big memorable tune streaming forth in an impressive section of the orchestra, an active individuated agent.

The second time, the tune emerges from within something else ongoing. It *becomes* noticeable as *having been* active already, though not in the foreground (this despite the not inconsiderable number of wind instruments that enter to play it). In a fairly literal sense, the tune *has* to emerge, from a context that includes not only its bass line, with all its backward connections to the immediately preceding context, but from a welter of other counterpoint. This counterpoint is hard to characterize: its lines rise and fall, mostly by small intervals, in a very flexible relation to the meter, tending not to be "motivic," the way the melody is, or even the way the steady stepping of the bass manages to be. (Their figures may have just enough identity, in the smallness of their intervals, to allow the theme's upbeat to be inconspicuous among them.) The counterpoint also clouds the harmony to a considerable degree, and continues to do so after the theme begins; which is to say that it takes away the theme's original characteristic of being in a clearer harmonic idiom than what surrounds it—one more of the traits by which the theme originally made everything before it sound like an introduction to *it*.

In the linear and harmonic murk, one moment that stands out is the clearing to a six-four chord on G, on the tune's first downbeat (m. 33; see ex. 6.4). This chord stands out, first of all, simply by being an intelligible chord, suddenly lighting up the obscure pitches of the inner voices with a harmonic interpretation. In particular the E of the inner voice C#–D–D#–E (which must

Example 6.4   Wagner, *Tristan und Isolde,* Act I, Einleitung: the counterpoint from which a six-four chord emerges over G.

be regarded as at least a *little* motivic), hard to grasp when it arrives over F♯ (a passing tone? to what?), is clarified as an anticipation, along with the rhythmically more conventional anticipation of C in the melody. More than this, a six-four chord, in this piece, is about as strong a tonality marker as we're ever allowed to hear: no less clear in its key implications than a dominant, *and* a representation of its tonic triad, which we otherwise probably won't hear at all. The key marked by this particular six-four is (locally) a new one: C major, standing out against the A major of the preceding theme (all the more as the pitch class C♯ has just survived a serious brush with C♮ in the harmonies of measures 28–32). C major thus emerges, suddenly and unexpectedly, after the tune does—and apparently through the tune's agency. This harmonic and tonal turn is what the theme brings (while the resumption of bass motion is agentless, part of the general fluctuation of intensity).[3]

This is another point of significant contrast with the first version of the theme. Like the second version, the first is in C, and its bass G likewise carries a six-four. But in the first version the six-four occurs on an upbeat (that feels like one), and does not seem to be a point of arrival in relation to the preceding chord over F♯. Although not inconceivable as the next harmony in the theme's progression IV, V/V, the six-four is reabsorbed, as a passing chord, into the continuing elaboration of V/V, with a more effective resolution to follow (ex. 6.5):

Example 6.5   Wagner, *Tristan und Isolde,* Act I, Einleitung: voice-leading interpretations of the first occurrence's bass, on different temporal scales.

but then also

and even

So the six-four here lacks the news value of the one in the second version—a difference completely compatible with what I have already proposed about the character of the theme's first entrance. The news value of the first entrance is concentrated right at the beginning.

The first time, the theme is presented to us on a silver platter; the second time it sneaks up on us, but is then no less decisive in its effect (in fact, it is perhaps even more so, at least tonally). Put another way: the first time seems like the well-prepared entry of an agent, the second more a glimpse or recollection of it, now in the coils of something powerful but impersonal. And I don't see anything "unstructural" about these attributions: I can't imagine what the Tristan prelude is built to do, if not something like this. So I have come around to a sense of "the same thing, somehow striking me differently" that I can believe is (in part) the perceptible effect of the contrapuntal realignment *and* that is compatible with, and even to some degree may depend on, my not noticing the realignment as a feat of "convertible counterpoint."

And *that* is how I wasn't being just dumb, or inattentive, all those years when I didn't catch on to this. Perhaps I was responding wonderfully to it all along. Truth be told, I can't say: I never really tried to articulate this until I was provoked by my confusion over the counterpoint. I am convinced that the beginning of wisdom here, in this case, was my learning to live with, and then learning to celebrate, a state of affairs that might seem to epitomize theoretical failure. I refer not only to my initial sense that a difference clear in the score was difficult to recover, but also to a residual sense that the contrast of character I have ended up with still may not as *definite* as the placement of F or F♯ in the bass under the theme's upbeat. This doesn't bother me any more.

One reason is that the definiteness of any report of hearing such as I have just given is bound to be spurious, beyond a certain point. Obviously I cannot just now have been reporting any single real occasion of my hearing.

What I am doing is using the narration of a possible hearing—a staged hearing, perhaps—as a device to communicate a possibility of experience that has caught my imagination. At least I am trying to tell you something you can do with the easily identified facts, that might not have been easy to infer from the theory that produced those facts. The theory in which there are such things as six-four chords might not, in itself, suggest to you what I've lately asked you to do with the different placement of the six-four chord in the theme, the one time and the other. In any event, the guidance I am offering for what to do with such facts is meant not only, perhaps not even primarily, to direct your hearing; in this context, it is also meant to show how far the terms of experience might sometimes be from the terms of report, and so to illustrate how big and difficult a problem it can be to determine what it means to hear a certain fact.

My next example takes a further step along this line. If, in the Tristan prelude, it ends up being debatable whether noticing various differences in character between instances of the theme should count as hearing changes in the counterpoint or not, Morton Feldman's *Triadic Memories* presents a case where I'm happy to concede that I don't hear the thing that Feldman has notated, at least in the terms in which he (appears to have) notated it.

At the beginning of the piece, the rhythmic notation is quite remarkable: a division of each 3/8 measure into four parts, against which are set syncopated figures that entail further subdivision of those four parts. (See ex. 6.6.) What is not notated, that is, is the simple 8/16 measure that would suffice to specify the durations, or even, assuming that an underlying triple meter matters somehow, the subdivision of the 3/8 measure into, in effect, a 24/64 measure, that would allow those rhythms to be written directly in relation to the beat. In fact, the ostensible triple meter is not expressed in any way for more than twenty pages of score, lasting many minutes.

Is triple meter a "structural" feature of the passage, then? Is four against three? Syncopation against four against three? Should we admit as "structural" a feature that we do not hear and do not know how to hear, just because it is notated? Do we have any use for a concept of structure like that? (There is, I suppose, a tradition of retreating from perceptual questions in situations like this and aligning "analysis" with some kind of reconstruction of the composer's decisions; but, aside from the general evasiveness of this strategy, it is specifically useless in this case: precisely the perceptual obscurity of the notation makes it hard to understand as a compositional choice.)

On the other hand: is there *no* way to hear the notated rhythm? That is, is there nothing to hear that is plausibly a consequence of the peculiar notation? Suppose that the result of the passage being written the way it is, is— though not any sense of these rhythms laid against a triple pulse—a sense of

Example 6.6   Feldman, *Triadic Memories,* Opening.

the rhythms *wobbling*. They are likely to be pretty wobbly as a matter of chronometric fact, if we play by Feldman's rules and seriously try to produce them by setting quadruplets against a triple beat. The effort to do this will keep us (performers *and* listeners) intensely involved in shaping events *within* the measure; will inhibit us from taking the measures as the units of a larger "flow," as we might if they were internally simple. Add that these rhythmic patterns, played as accurately as we like, include several that hardly differ from "one, two, three" anyway: the rhythm of the first measure, for instance, if counted out in the meter, places its first attack one sixty-fourth note after the second beat and its second attack one thirty-second note after the third beat.[4] What we're likely to hear, then, are a lot of measures that are sort of, but not *quite,* one-two-three, and that almost match one another, but not well enough for us to gain any clarity—and, now and then among them, one measure, like the fourth one, that is obviously enough different to leave the other ones sounding even more strongly but indistinctly alike. And this means that the question of whether the measures all are alike as instances of *some* rhythm will remain fresh for us, will keep being renewed.

The effect is a little like hearing something just once and then turning it over in memory: replaying it with slightly different attention each time, the way one does, and noticing its changing aspects; and eventually no longer retaining an exact sense of how it originally was, except insofar as this sense survives in the aggregate of its slightly differing remembered versions. Only this doesn't happen really in memory: it is "composed out" in the sounds, the progress of the music being like such a succession of versions. (Well, more dogged and exact; but what do we expect of a composing-out?) The thing being turned over in memory is not exactly the single measure, of course: the pitch pattern *extends* the figures into pairs of measures, and, even more significantly, *complicates* them, by making them composites. (Eventually, further articulations are created by the changes of register, but I won't pursue these.)

So: whether we think of this experience as hearing the rhythmic notation or not (a question driven away by more interesting ones), it is part of the sense of this music that something extremely delicate and fussy is going on, giving each event a kind of "hand-made" individuality that we're to notice but not to go too far in *construing*. This isn't the kind of experience that first comes to mind in the name of hearing "structure." But what's missing (that matters)? It is a determinate, vivid characteristic that I can hear in the music—that, as a bonus, I enjoy hearing and find distinctive. It is in significant part a consequence of the way the rhythms are written, even to some extent a plausible motivation for them to have been written that way. I can't argue that the notation is a uniquely determinate way to have produced this effect (though in fact I don't have a counterproposal)—but it is not a project of mine to make the composer look efficient. At most, I suppose I could be said to be assuming, for the sake of argument, that the notation is efficient for doing *something*, and then trying to work out what it could be. Part of what I find interesting in this account of this music, actually, is the degree of overkill in the notation relative to what I say I'm getting out of it; or, to put this in a more encouraging way, the degree to which what I'm proposing as a hearing *does not* involve recovering every bit of detail that I can see (or think I see) in the notation. The perceived outcome of this oddly specific notation, I'm claiming, is a particular kind of *vagueness* about a particular kind of thing. And in all my examples I have to admit a similar underdetermination of experience by "structure." The disparity may be more disturbing, in the other cases, because it will be more familiarly "analytical"-looking information that will be left underutilized.

This example from Feldman is in a sense peripheral, because it is about a notational feature, difficult to realize in performance, not about the kind of referential or developmental relationships between things that analysis usually treats; and much of the question about it is whether any sonic consequences of the notation reach our ears *at all*—never mind what the character of the experience is like. The justification is that, as I have suggested, "what the composer did" is at least an ingredient of the notion of structure: the notion of something done, apart from us (listeners) that will (or will not) have consequences for us (listeners). Even if we don't identify what's "structural" with what was done by the composer (perhaps even done "intention-ally," if we have an idea of what that means), we may think of it as something that we can intelligibly *imagine* someone doing for the sake of the effect it (perhaps) produces. Our analysis may say, in effect: it is as though the piece were contrived to do such-and-such; we may conceive of it as so contrived, whether this is a biographical fact about the composer or not.

And—more important—what the "such-and-such" is may take some imag-ination to figure out. As a corollary, "do you hear that?", asked with reference to a structural feature, may be a bad question, at least without sufficient attention given to the necessarily prior question "what would it be to hear that?" And the answer to this question cannot be counted on to sound like a report of the seizing of some information. Who knows what kind of sensation it might be? Actually, a good reason to carry on music-analytic investigations is that they may help us to recognize sensations that we didn't realize we were having. The effort to figure out what the effect could possibly be of some fea-ture of the sonic configuration may lead to a raising of consciousness.

Think of this untypical example as chosen to illustrate these two points in a relatively uncomplicated context. What it is to hear something may take some imagination to figure out (enough to disconcert a yes-or-no approach to the question of whether you hear something). Hearing something—responding to it intensely and relevantly—may not involve mastering it, being (or becoming) able to give it back in the terms in which it was set up; may involve specific sorts of confusion or loss of information.

From the first of these points it may follow that a music-structural propo-sition may not have (have to have) a one-to-one audible correlate to be audi-bly relevant. (This is a lax position; behind it is a strict interest in holding the-oretical propositions to a standard of audible relevance, but the ways of meeting this standard are meant to be multiple, even beyond anticipation.) From the second it follows that some of the connotations of "structure"—those of logic, pertinence, comprehensiveness—may limit our imaginations for the first point; may even actively lead us away from good possibilities. Let us say at least that the thing we hear, the thing we put together in experience, in reaction to, in consequence of, our encounter with a musical "structure" need not be expected to have those connoted characteristics. And in that case, why should we even take the trouble to expect the thing encountered to have those characteristics?

My next example takes its departure from a piece of theoretical writing, by David Lewin (1982–83), about the sixth of Schoenberg's *Six Little Piano Pieces* op. 19. In this case, the sonic facts are more or less incontrovertible, but their construal is intensely under construction. Lewin notes that the two chords chiming through most of the piece resemble one another intervallically in a number of ways, none of them comprehensive. The two perfect fourths of the lower chord, G_3–C_4 and C_4–F_4, resonate with the perfect fourth on top of the upper chord, $F\sharp_5$–B_5; and, more abstractly, the minor seventh G_3–F_4 resonates, as an instance of pitch-class interval 2, with the major ninth A_4–B_5. Thus every interval of the lower, later chord reflects an interval of the upper, earlier one, although the chords are not equivalent in any familiar sense.

Rather than label the chords as instances of set-type X and set-type Y and attribute to them a high degree of similarity in interval-class content, Lewin interprets the intervallic resemblances specifically as so many *incomplete* relationships of transposition or inversion "in the air" between the chords, describing the sound of their juxtaposition as "fairly T_6-ish" and at the same time "fairly T_1-ish" and "fairly inversion-about-A-ish," and so on (338). And each of these incomplete transformations has *dynamic* potential: the potential to be completed by the emergence of the note that transforms the last note of one chord the way its other two notes have notionally been transformed. There are six of these incomplete transformations (because each of the three intervallic matches can be construed as transposition or as inversion), and there are twelve notes that would complete them (because each transpositional or inversional match could be made exact by an alteration to either one of the two chords), though not twelve different ones. A little fancifully, Lewin speaks of "generative lusts" for these notes—of "musical tensions and/or potentialities which later events of the piece will resolve and/or realize to greater or lesser extents" (341).

The appealing thing about this account of the piece is the dynamic aspect that Lewin conjures up for what enter the discussion as static *resemblances* between the chords, with the possibility for the interaction of these dynamics to motivate the events of the piece. How these various potentials might be addressed is a complex matter, since the note that fulfills one transformation may be irrelevant for another (and not all the notes come in at once!). Lewin presents a chart of the various notes' appearances, but does not narrate the piece in these terms, beyond the general gloss that the transformational potentials "jockey one with another for priority" (341).[5]

It is hard to see how the sequence of events in the piece relates to one of the most interesting facts that the theoretical apparatus extrudes, namely that some notes are more lusted for than others—at least more multifariously, whether or not this means more intensely. Four transformations lust for E, two each for B♭, C♯, and D, one for D♯; and even one for A, which is already present. (Poor G♯ isn't lusted for at all.) This differentiation cannot readily be seen to motivate the order of events in the piece; and indeed Lewin's "jockey one with another" implies that the order of events does not result from a single cumulation of all these forces. For example, consider the first figure added to the chords: D♯, as little lusted for as any note, ornamented by E, the most lusted for: how do the relative strengths of the lusts account for that? So perhaps the transformational reading of the piece should not be called on to predict or explain what happens in the piece. Perhaps its role is to elaborate the meaning of things that do happen, along the lines of "*should* C♯ come along, it may do so with an air of filling out F♯–B into a complete transposition or inversion of G–C–F."

Which probably is as it should be. After all (as Martin Scherzinger once pointed out in a discussion of Lewin's article), this is about the least lustful-sounding piece anyone has ever heard. The sense of earlier events driving later ones to happen, which Lewin has so productively synthesized in this atonal context, may not carry over directly from the realm of abstract transposition and inversion to the temporal flow of this composition.

Here is another way to read the technical information. The fact that D♯ is compatible with only one of the many possible transformational relations between the two chords, means that D♯ does as much as any note could to *differentiate* one relationship from the others, thus at least momentarily to disambiguate the cloud produced by the chords' combination. In this sense, D♯ is the most *eloquent* note that could have been chosen to come first—as it does, alone, and scored to pierce the haze—the single note that can do most to define the relationship between the chords. And then E, the note that ornaments D♯ (in one of the two registers in which D♯ occurs), is the most *neutral* note that could be chosen for this role—the one that, in itself, does least to diminish the ambiguity of the original combination, and therefore does least to counter the clarifying effect of D♯.[6]

To appreciate this alteration of imagery, it helps to direct your auditory attention away from the two chords as they are attacked, toward the sound of all six notes (and fifteen intervals) ringing together, a state that persists for quite a long time. Elaine Barkin encourages this move in her writing about this piece: most concisely in Barkin 1979b, with the word "INTERACT" written out vertically, interlaced with the ties that sustain the two chords, and later (even after D♯) with the ties (rearranged as they are in the score) followed by a vertical "intermit", but also throughout Barkin 1979a, which makes a theme of "not . . . 'letting go' " (21) when it would be tempting to say that nothing is happening. What happens, while the chords fade away together, is that an initial unclear configuration—unclear in that it is full of suggestions—*remains* unclarified, and even blurs further; and then is recreated, before anything else is added. This is not the dynamic that Lewin's unfulfilled transpositions and inversions might immediately suggest; but it is one to which his technical information can productively be harnessed. We simply have to notice that attacks of notes are not the only kind of event in the piece.

Theorists may be interested to note that this interpretation of Lewin's material, though on the face of it less "deterministic"—that is, less concerned with describing the course of events as a process of the realization of implications—paradoxically succeeds in recuperating the way in which theorists often claim to be *explaining* the events of a piece: it defines a field of alternatives from which the actual events can be considered to have been chosen, and it defines some respect in which the actual events offer the *most* of something, or do the *best* job of something, that would be possible in that field. Theorists concerned with hearing will of course agree that there is rarely any such thing as *hearing* that some event is the possible choice that would maximize some quality; what we can hear is that the event does have this quality, strongly, perhaps, and we can somehow believe that this is a quality worth having. But it is routine that an analytical explanation framed along these lines will include this sort of "excess" information.

I say this partly by way of admitting that I have no story to tell about how to *hear* that D♯ is the most eloquent note (in the sense I have defined) that could have occurred; I wouldn't know how to begin listening for mostness. The analytical construction helps me by sensitizing me to the possibility of this sort of eloquence—by enabling me to conceive of this sort of eloquence in the first place. Until I can conceive of it, I have no way to inquire whether any auditory experience (actual or possible) exhibits that quality to any degree.

Like any analytical predicate, this word "eloquence" that I am beating to death should not be expected to hold up very well under the treatment. No matter how well I have defined it (and I can imagine doing better), I don't ever expect it to do very much for me, in its capacity as a theoretical *term*. What I expect it to do (as I have said elsewhere) is "be rendered generic by comparison with the specific experience it engenders" (Dubiel 1999, 273, emphasis removed): that is, to open up to further description. And so it does—even in the rather limited intervallic terms that I have been using for most of my description so far.

Going back to Lewin's construction, we note that the relationship articulated by D♯ would be that of tritone transposition between the two chords. To state it a bit mechanically, if the lower register's C and F had come with a D♯ (rather than with a G), then this chord would have been a complete tritone transposition of the upper register's B, F♯, and A. (See ex. 6.7.) Given this account, we might wonder what D♯ is doing in the *upper* register; or, conversely, given the register, we might wonder what to make of a theoretical description of an upper-register D♯ as supplying something that would help the low register match the high one. In any event, a question about register would make us especially interested in the fact that this high D♯ occurs in *two* registers: D♯5 and D♯6. Those of us in a more intimate relation with the piece than just listening to it cannot fail to notice how peculiarly Schoenberg asks us to use our hands to produce this doubling, or how specific he has suddenly become about dynamics and articulation (especially after his blank *pp* for the

Example 6.7   Schoenberg, *Sechs kleine Klavierstücke*, op. 19 no. 6: D♯ added to the second chord completing T₆ of the first; then an extension of T₆ between two sonorities, both including D♯.

opening chords). At a minimum, we must feel encouraged to do something much more complicated in our listening than *either* simply assimilate D♯ to the lower chord, in completion of the T₆ relationship, *or* simply assimilate it to the upper register, where it is presented. And if we hear D♯ as belonging in some sense to *both* registers, then the transpositional relationship becomes more inclusive: that is, the B, F♯, A, *and* D♯ of the upper register are all tritone-transposed by the F, C, and D♯—*and* A—of the lower. The spacing of the two-chord sonority makes it easy for A's position to become equivocal: the largest gap anywhere is between A and the rest of the upper chord, the smallest between A and the top of the lower chord (smaller than any interval within a chord).

I can think of a few things to say in favor of this interpretation, all of which I hope will make it easier to understand what this interpretation might *sound* like. First, with the registral distinctions blurred, the atmosphere of T₆ishness is thickened by D♯ to an even greater degree than our initial construction suggested; in this sense, D♯ even more does what we said it did. One way to listen to this point is to try and hear what intervals D♯ seems to be involved in when it enters. I am suggesting this as a sort of ear-training exercise—and I don't promise that your perceptions will be the same as mine, but no one I have ever tried this with has said that D♯ sounds decisively like a major sixth above F♯. To me, the sense of D♯'s participation in a tritone is particularly strong, as is the sense of its participation in a "minor seventh" above F—suggesting to me that both the clarification of T₆ in the sonority and the subliminal realignment of A and D♯ with both of the chords are indeed factors in what I hear.[7]

Second, the continuation of the piece after these first chords includes a process of qualifying—and, eventually, surprisingly undermining—the simple high–low distinction that the chords establish. Moving on after D♯ and the ensuing interruption in the sound of the chords: the chords sound again, and then the *upper* chord is slurred to a much lower chord that is an exact transposition of the original lower chord, by the interval that dominates the original lower chord, and that shares two pitches with the original lower chord—so what has become of "upper" and "lower"? And then what becomes of the pair of chords when something new comes in below all of this? At the very end, the same registral configuration—the original high and low chords, and then something below them—occurs in a more extreme form, with the new low thing lower, and therefore with both of the original chords recharacterized as high, the distinction between them not sounding as it once did. My suggestion is that the ambiguous registral situation of D♯ is the first step in this process.

I find it encouraging that a percept as macroscopic and (relatively) untheoretical as a gradual reconfiguration of our sense of registral location should turn out to be so thoroughly intertwined with a sense of intervallic differentiation and character developed in (and from) a context where none seems to be given a priori—a story of the tritones, to put it simply. I feel that, after some effort, I have really found something in the sound that I can believe is significantly a consequence of the transformational configuration constructed by Lewin.

It is interesting that I had to work away from an "implicative" account of the music (at least a little) to find this. It is as though a certain, not-altogether-thought-through image of what analytical-perceptual success would look like had to be to some degree overcome to reach this conception of the sound. The ambition to say why things happen—to represent events as *caused* within the piece—is in this case worth setting aside, in favor of the ambition only (only!) to say what things are when they do happen. And the analysis includes, as a central feature, a long passage of music that is hard to characterize in the terms of the analysis. For me, the key thing to find here (or to let myself accept) was the *unclarity* of the coexisting chords—the *constructed* unclarity. Here, I gained by allowing myself not to be on top of events.

All of my examples so far have involved pieces of "structural" information that I did not know how to hear, and therefore did not even know *whether* I was hearing, when I first confronted them; I have told stories of working out what it might mean to hear them, and made a point of the hearings that I eventually found being neither conventionally "structural" in character nor necessarily similar in character or in density of information to the structural descriptions with which they are associated. In my last example I proceed in the other direction, from a vivid perception that does not have the conventionally "structural" character to detailed further examination of the score to support and elaborate that perception. In this process I encounter a degree of tension with my developed skill as an analyst, which would direct me to a different kind of observation, and indeed almost direct me to make the perception go away.

The piece is the C-sharp minor Prelude in Book I of Bach's *Well-Tempered Clavier;* the perception is of an unrealized modulation to E major suggested by the beginning of a thematic statement in that key early in the piece (m. 8). This E major does not even last the full length of the figure, from one downbeat to the next: the B♮ that would complete the figure is supplanted by B♯, and C-sharp minor easily reabsorbs the whole thing. A hopeful event is swallowed up, and the music goes on remarkably as though it never happened. It's a sad moment.

It's the vanishing to which I want to do justice, analytically—including the sadness. I'd like to find something to say about how a composition isn't just going astray if it puts something behind it, but that does let a loss sound like a loss. In a way, this shouldn't be hard. Why can't a composition do that, if it wants to? But even if am I hyperconscientious on this point, still the weight of analytical tradition is against portraying the progress of a piece in this way. The most traditional thing to do about a passage like this is precisely to *deny* that a modulation takes place, to deny it precisely for the reason that it is not sustained. The view is obvious almost beyond discussion in our Schenker-influenced analytical world, but we hardly need Schenker to appreciate it; in fact, the most conventional and limited harmony book is likely to make precisely this sort of distinction, between "real" and merely "apparent" modulations, its topic of greatest intellectual intensity.

More specifically and interestingly, analytical culture places a high value on the identification of details that follow up, refer to, and in that sense sustain the sound of, unusual events, with a certain extra cachet given to events that do this unobviously. So the routinely "sophisticated" way to handle an unrealized modulation would be to acknowledge that lesser minds might ignore it and then counter that, if we do recognize it—recognize it *as* unrealized, that is—then we can find such-and-such interesting reflections of it later in the piece; and in that sense, the modulation turns out not to be lost at all, as nothing in a great piece is allowed to be lost. A prime candidate for such an unobvious reflection (just to show I know my business) would be the (deservedly) celebrated dissonant clash, late in the piece, between B♯ in a chord and B♮ in a descending scale—thus, between the diagnostic pitch classes of C-sharp minor and E major (at the end of m. 29—a favorite moment of Schoenberg's). But I rather like a hearing of this piece in which E major just goes lost after the early adumbration of it; in which the prelude's tone changes, as it proves to be in many ways a looser and more obscure composition than it initially seemed it was going to be. And no matter the merits of this hearing, I ought to have the capacity to construct it; maybe someone else would prefer a different story, but it ought not to be the theory that decides for us.

In retrospect, there will be plenty of reasons not to have trusted in E major, even as the thematic statement begins. The preceding sequence does not lead to a cadence in this key, only to the triad; the dominant preceding this triad is not even in root position; and this dominant represents essentially the first harmonic occurrence of B♮,[8] and not, as a fully elaborated modulation would require, the resituation in E major of a B♮ already introduced within C-sharp minor. And although there is a familiar Baroque pattern comprising a few statements of the motive in the tonic key (mm. 1–4), a modulating sequence (mm. 5–7), and an arrival at a new key, marked by the motive again, all the features of the prelude just cited are departures from the pattern's ideal form—to which familiarity with the form paradoxically sensitizes me.

In this sense, perceiving an E-major key, even at the prompting of a thematic entrance, is getting ahead of myself—*allowing* myself to get ahead of myself (or is that the way it always happens?). It's not making up a new key out of whole cloth; it's not even ignoring contradictory evidence, really (evidence doesn't seem like quite the right concept, although some music theory might talk of it this way); it's just going quite far on the strength of some understated suggestions. Is it or isn't it wishing a new key into existence?

The first thing I have to work with—even before the motive unfolds—is the harmonic clarity of the E-major triad, in contrast to the airy dissonance of the sequence. Over and above this clarity, the E-major measure is much richer harmonically than any measure of the opening: besides the gentle expression of the subdominant on the last quarter note (a precedented detail),[9] the transitory combination of D♯ and F♯ on the way to this quarter note even suggests the dominant; and in the piece so far, any major-triad sonority stands out, let alone a mutually reinforcing combination of them.[10] The exposure of the neighboring subdominant, intensified further by the ornament, prepares the particular cruelty of its capture by C-sharp minor in the place of its resolution: warmth and fineness of detail turn out to be vulnerability.

The music that comes with B♯ does not even act to erase E major, really, so much as carry on as though E major had never happened. Its most chilling aspect may be its reimposition of a pattern of strong and weak measures that seemed to have faded away. The metrical regularity of the opening measures (like their harmonic sobriety) is suspended during the sequence, or at least not reinforced: a series of parallel measures, as clearly articulated as these are by suspensions and resolutions, can easily be taken "one, one, one," with the strong–weak pattern promising to reemerge at the time of the new motivic statement. And with respect to the reemergent pattern, the B♯ chord that cuts off the statement makes a surprising accent—in effect a syncopated one; but it can also be heard as simply strong, as falling back into the *original* two-measure rhythm, which had been displaced only so briefly and inconclusively that its recovery is easy.

The psychology of the hypermeter is all of a piece with that of the tonality. Nothing in the sequence actively interferes with the original pairing of measures; and so the metric implications of the E-major measure, however optimistically I accept them, remain devastatingly open to erasure. If, as they recede, I want to reprimand myself for having accepted them, it is open to me to notice how specifically the E-major measure resembles, not the initial measure of the piece, but the *second* measure, with the motive in the tenor, and the same E4 and G♯4 in the upper voices.[11] Why shouldn't it be treated like a second measure?

A further irony is the degree to which hypermeter fades from the piece once it has helped to do in E major. During the next few measures, a degree of emphasis is placed on the downbeats of the ostensibly weak measures (mm. 10 and 12) by the development of complicated, many-voiced suspensions, resolving during those measures. And because the rhythms of the first two half-measures of the motive, ♫♫♫ and ♩♪♩, proliferate independently in both halves of the measure, the potential of the 6/4 measure itself to sound hypermetric is strengthened. By the time this passage reaches its goal, a cadence in G-sharp minor (m. 14), approached with a stretto of the complete rhythm ♫♫♫ ♩♪♩ in the outer voices (mm. 12–13), the measure has become my world and my sense of it as strong or weak has gone.

Need I point out that the process of modulation to G-sharp minor makes no use of the E-major triad? I'm not sure how to go about *hearing* the unrealized potential for it to have done so, but I definitely perceive the prompt reinflection of the C-sharp minor triad toward G-sharp minor, and more generally sense that all the functional commerce is among *minor* triads (and their dominants).

In this analysis, I've been proceeding from a hearing of the piece to some more technical observation that supports it. I won't say proceeding toward that hearing's "structural" substrate; I think there is no boundary to be drawn between more detailed elaboration of the hearing report and the identification of facts in the score that could be imagined to elicit the hearing (and as I said earlier, I am not very interested in there being such a boundary). If I were proceeding in the direction of my first three analyses, toward a definition of a hearing, I could imagine a number of different hearings being made of the information I have provided so far.

One would be a hearing that I mentioned, not very respectfully, as I was getting started: there is no modulation to E major—don't fall for it. You can hear going in that there's no cadence to E major, you can hear that the motive is deflected before it's completed, and you ought to be listening for the larger motion anyway. I can't stop anyone from taking this position, even if I don't find it very interesting or, more important, very attentive to the particulars of the passage. Arguing against it wouldn't seem like the right sort of response; but I might wonder where it is established that a larger motion, such as the modulation to the dominant, ought to be expected to be *direct*.

Another hearing would recognize the movement toward E major, and then hear the larger motion *uncovered* by E major's dissolution. Thus it is no mistake to hear the local E major; it's simply that something larger was going on as well, and a realization of this gradually takes over. If an event sounds like a modulation for a moment, then it is a modulation for a moment; if this modulation isn't borne out by the continuation, then it isn't. This is a view with which I'm reasonably comfortable. In this case, I like its emphasis on the change of timescale, from the localness and detail of the E major to the slowness and imperturbability of what supplants it (and proves to have been there all along). This hearing can even recognize a hint of indifference in the slower progression.

The hearing that I have been trying to articulate goes further. The sense of loss that I am trying to portray really does depend on acknowledging an element of misconstrual in my perception. In a sense, it *was* a mistake to invest in E major—in the sense that *lots* of factors turn out to have been arrayed against this perception, including ones that I allowed myself, indeed *tried,* to ignore, overlook, overcome, whatever I call it. After suggesting E major, this passage drops it in a way that leaves *me* feeling responsible for it, while *it* goes on as though the intimation of E major *never happened.* What defines my project, I can now say, is my effort to understand how the notes might interact with, specifically promote, my awareness of my own involvement in the forming of these perceptions. This is crucial to the specific sense of loss that I am trying to articulate.

I would like to continue this thought experiment by speculating about how to let this loss affect my hearing of the rest of the piece. As I suggested when beginning this analysis, I would especially like to find a way to do so that does not involve looking for the lost thing in every crevice.[12] The last thing I want to do is show that the piece is orderly after all, because E major isn't really lost.

The piece is permanently marked by its brush with E major in at least one way: the motive is never whole again. I have already pointed out the separation of the two halves of the motive's first measure, beginning immediately after the E-major triad: a continuous succession of versions of just the eighth-note figure, passing from voice to voice, coexisting with a scattering of the dotted figure. And the dotted figure is often isolated, generally not maintaining its original form of a step motion to the next downbeat. The complete original configuration is attempted or approximated at important triadic arrivals later in the piece, but never manages to recur. In the G#-minor triad (m. 14), the figure's mid-measure leap is diffused into a written arpeggiation, and the descent, with its usual rhythm lost, trails off without covering its normal distance. In the F#-minor triad (m. 20) the motive comes closer to its original form, but again deviates before completing its descent, this time by continuing in eighth notes, not pausing on the last quarter. So it is specifically the latter part of the motive that is never restored. After these two times, the complete motive is not really attempted again, even though the prelude has almost half its time yet to run; and for that matter none of these near attempts is in the upper voice.

What is it like to hear this? I'd have to be analytically on edge to notice the motive's not recurring, let alone its not recurring as a reaction to something that happens to E major early on. I would expect the fact to strike me, not at any particular point, but perhaps as something about the *tone* of the continuation, the way the prelude spends the rest of its time in flux, thematically and to some degree harmonically. Apart from the incipits of the principal motive, the thing that the prelude comes nearest to "recapitulating" is its modulating sequence; and it is remarkable how strangely placed and blurred this is. Its beginning overlaps the F♯-minor motivic statement (perhaps even takes over from it), half a measure out of its original metric position; only the upper voice is parallel to the earlier passage; and the newly composed lower voices are only intermittently sequential (the second half of m. 22 is approximately parallel to the second half of m. 21). Nowhere can the prelude work itself up to a decisive large-scale dominant: what seems to happen is that the dominant triad is laid over the root of the subdominant, as a big $^4_2$ chord (this happens in m. 29, after one more start on the motive in an F♯ triad, and it eventuates in the scale that produces the B♮ against B♯), and then the piece goes into its most extreme state of textural flux, in effect a written two-voice cadenza, reeling further and further from its motives until the cadence.

It is hard to describe hearing what the piece does not do. I suppose this must involve infusing my hearing of what the piece does do with a sense of "instead of" or "when it *might* have"; and it would be difficult to identify this sense with particular times (*when* does the piece not go to the dominant?). It would be difficult to make it part of my listening to tot them up as evidence that E major must have been really important, as I have (more or less) been doing analytically. Most of what there is to hear from them, I have been suggesting, is a change in the prelude's tone, a loss of clarity of articulation.

This is the attitude I would take, as well, toward the dissonant B♮ of measure 29, to which I referred earlier: insofar as I recognize the pitch as a reference to E major at all, I want to interpret the reference as an indication of *just how far we are* from a recovery of E major. Theorists often use the idea of reference very casually, often running it together with "resemblance" and leaving it at that. But a reference doesn't always have to be a positive one; an event can take its meaning in significant part from its relation to E major but not necessarily *sound like* E major. A particularly delicate instance of this occurs in the passage that revisits the modulating sequence (mm. 20–24). Supposing that a diatonic circle of fifths is a relevant model for the passage— certainly its last few steps (mm. 23–24) clearly express the roots G♯, C♯, F♯— then its first few roots, after the F♯ from which it begins, could well have been B, E, A. Of course they aren't allowed to be: the details of the (nonsequential) counterpoint, including elaborate on-the-beat passing motion delaying the B and a 7–6 resolution of D♯ to C♯ over E, prevent my hearing these major triads, and indeed superimpose the sound of the primary triads of C-sharp minor. To work these details back into my hearing would be in effect to start this essay over; and this is no time to do that.

I've been talking about some musical percepts that don't carry the connotations of intellectual mastery; now I'll end by rearticulating a few values and intentions, without particularly trying to clinch anything. I'd like the main value of my analyses to be something like responsiveness instead, so that what I'm demonstrating in presenting them is my ability to be led, nudged, and pushed by the music I'm discussing, whether or not this impetus corresponds to a prior model I hold of what I ought to allow to happen to me. A related value is frankness. You don't distinguish between two things that are different? Fine; say so in your analysis. You hear something in a way that the further progress of the music doesn't sustain? That's interesting to know about.

It is along these lines that a notion like "structure" might serve as a way to hold open the possibility of discovery, the possibility of responding aurally to something in a piece to which I was not antecedently attuned. And although I may derive a stimulus from some bit of musical analysis, it is important that I avoid any sense of obligation to listen to, or for, the particular facts the analysis manages to mention, in the terms in which it mentions them—obligation to push the experience back along the chain of its possible causes, one might say. A lot of the anxiety about "structural listening," I suspect, has to do with people's picking up this sense of obligation, and wishing not to fall short. By this discussion, I hope at least to some degree to deflect the fear and resentment that can attach to the idea of "structure."

I would like to retain the idea primarily as a source of wonder. I hope that thinking about musical structure as I am proposing might help us to acknowledge the power of musical sound to realize systems of resemblance and contrast, categorization and progression, that may not be given to us elsewhere—which is to say, its power to stimulate *us* to entertain these systems, forming and changing at various angles to the perceptions that they engender.

NOTES

I thank Christopher Bailey, Marlon Feld, Jason Freeman, Marion A. Guck, Richard Plotkin, Martin Scherzinger, and Melanie Schoenberg for valuable comments on various aspects of this essay.

1. I want to acknowledge my indebtedness, throughout this discussion, to several writers, and this may be the point when specific connections are easiest to draw. Mark

DeBellis, in *Music and Conceptualization* (1995), shows how the idea of perceiving something under one concept and another, or perhaps under none, more efficiently does much of the theoretical work that is usually attempted with the ideas of conscious and unconscious perception or, even more vaguely, with background and foreground. Kendall Walton (1993) and Marion A. Guck (1993) describe and illustrate the possibility of a cause of one's experience becoming, through analysis, another object of appreciation.

2. It is interesting to notice, incidentally, how, in the second act (less obviously characterized by unfulfilled longing), this theme pointedly and repeatedly does not enter to continue any of the very many references to the deceptive cadence.

3. By pointing out that the bass notes D♯ and E that precede the thematic entrance occur within inchoate versions of the theme—up a small interval, down a big one, B–C–D♯, C–C♯–E—Richard Plotkin suggested to me a still more complex story, in which the theme's agency cannot be discounted, even though its identity is still blurry.

4. There is no metronome mark; but if the speed of the measure were set at ♩ = 63–66—practically the default tempo of Feldman's late music, as Paul Nauert has pointed out to me—then a sixty-fourth note would last something like 1/26 or 1/25 of a second, only slightly longer than the period of the vibrations of the lowest A on the piano, which come twenty-seven and one-half to the second. It seems safe to say that this duration is not perceptible as a duration.

5. No one is more scrupulous than Lewin about the difference between an elaborated analysis and the assembly of technical material to inform such an analysis—even here, where he has done such a remarkable job of building qualities of movement and implication into the technical material. And therefore I wish to be very clear that my subsequent reflections on this material are not intended as criticism of Lewin's ingenious proposals; rather, they represent my continuation after the point where his article turns to other matters.

6. Of course, E itself represents another moment of incompletion under the transformation that D♯ reinforces, T_6; its counterpart under this transformation, B♭, is the next new pitch class to enter the piece.

7. For an extended discussion of listening to single notes in this way, and, more generally, of treating "structure" as a way to confer characteristics upon individual elements, see Hirata 1996. The influence of ideas developed by Hirata in her dissertation about Feldman (Hirata 2002) is too pervasive for me to identify (it is by no means limited to my discussion of Feldman, and indeed may be more prominent in all the other examples), and I gratefully acknowledge it throughout.

8. There is a B♮ on the downbeat of the second measure of the sequence, and it is good enough to make the bass F♯ dissonant; but either it is absent by the time the bass resolves to E or it is dissonant against C♯ in the tenor, which moves in parallel with the bass.

9. The last quarter note of the measure is a moment of subtle harmonic interest through the opening statements of the theme, expressing an ostensibly neighboring harmony that, a little more each time, shows the potential to do something more—prepare a dissonance (m. 2), displace the main harmony (m. 3)—and then recedes.

10. It is obvious how one would go about dismissing these consonances as *zufällig*, in Schenker's sense; but it is more interesting to recognize the relevance of their

triadic implications to the powerful conjuring of E major in a very brief time. I am inspired here by Schoenberg's discussion of some "passing harmonies" in a Bach chorale, in the " 'Non-Harmonic' Tones" chapter of Schoenberg 1978 (pp. 342–43).

11. It isn't impossible to hear a progression to the soprano G♯ across the downbeats of the preceding sequence, C♯–B–A–G♯, a slow rendering of the end of the original motive. This works two ways: it does that much more to establish the E-major triad as comparable to the opening C-sharp minor one, and by the same token, it places the E-major triad within the grasp of the C-sharp minor one.

12. I have done an analysis like that, finding ways to interpret the lack of any reference to an unresolved D♯ as a way of dealing with the unresolved D♯ in the Beethoven Violin Concerto; see Dubiel 1996.

SEVEN

Collective Listening

Postmodern Critical Processes and MTV

ANDREW DELL'ANTONIO

Structural listening strategies imply a model of one-to-one communication: the listener, in understanding the structural development of a musical text, is made privy to the composer's creative processes. Under this model, the composer's intentions are tied up with an individual's understanding of the unfolding of a musical work. This is the kind of authorial presence and individual interpretative engagement that modernist critics such as Adorno, Horkheimer, and Jameson have bemoaned as lacking in popular music.

Semiotician Umberto Eco has instead argued for an "intention of the text": the text itself, providing clues as to how it "wants" to be read, may present sufficient intentionality to create its own "Ideal Reader" (or perhaps, in the case of music, "Ideal Listener"). This model opens up the interpretative field and might provide a useful alternative to the search for a composer's original intentions. Eco's discussion still, however, works within the framework of individual communication: *a* text creates *an* ideal recipient.

Expanding on Eco's lead, this essay explores the idea of the "intention of a musical text" in the context of music videos and MTV. These are complex sources, comprising multiple layers of media and hence authorship. Music videos are also consumed in ways that differ from Eco's model of detached critical reading, and thus construct their "Ideal Viewer/Listener" (or Ideal Appraiser) through significantly different procedures. Most importantly for this essay, I will argue that the Ideal Appraiser for such texts is not individual but collective: music videos on MTV appear to be meant to be consumed not by an individual but by a group. Indeed, in those occasions in which MTV displays critical reactions to videos, such reactions are collective rather than individual: MTV portrays collectivity and group participation as crucial to the listening/viewing experience.

The idea of a collective listener/reader for a collective text is incompatible with Adorno and Horkheimer's formulations of artistic autonomy or Jameson's ideal of stable subjectivity, but it does seem to mesh with recent theories (such as those of Deleuze and Guattari) that characterize post-modern subject positions as multiple and shifting. Collective listening strategies may be not so much postmodern as non-modernist; their presence and premises certainly call into question an idealization of structural listening as normative practice.

Since the idea of a collective critical process seems to resonate with MTV's public, this raises the question whether MTV has fostered this tendency or responded to it (or possibly both): Gramsci's concept of "organic intellectual" activity will be brought to bear on this issue. MTV's portrayals of collective critical response to music video are undoubtedly shaped by the network's commercial considerations, but they also create spaces for active participation on the part of MTV's public. Collective critical processes may therefore well be a viable example of "organic intellectual" practices within late-capitalist culture. *[handwritten: ▷ articulate what the masses cannot say for themselves]*

1.1 Structural listening strategies imply a model of one-to-one communication: the listener, in understanding the structural development of a musical text, is made privy to the composer's creative processes. Under this model, the composer's intentions are tied up with an individual's understanding of the unfolding of a musical work.

This is the model that Rose Rosengard Subotnik outlines in her essay "Toward a Deconstruction of Structural Listening" from her recent collection *Deconstructive Variations:*

> The concept of structural listening, as Schoenberg and Adorno presented it, was intended to describe a process wherein the listener follows and comprehends the unfolding realization, with all of its detailed inner relationships, of a generating musical conception, or what Schoenberg calls an 'idea' . . . Such structural listening discourages kinds of understanding that require culturally specific knowledge of things external to the compositional structure, such as conventional associations or theoretical systems . . . Structural listening is an active mode that, when successful, gives the listener the sense of composing the piece as it actualizes itself in time. (Subotnik 1996, 150)

As Subotnik observes, this model (usually tempered by some degree of historical contextualization) has long been the prevalent model in the American academic musical curriculum. Having provided a preliminary "deconstruction" of structural listening strategies by revealing the historical contingency of such models, she goes on to speculate on alternative listening strategies, settling on an ideal of a more comprehensive "stylistic listening" process.[1]

It will not be my task in this essay to examine the implications of Subotnik's proposed "stylistic listening" paradigm; others in this collection have done so (see, for example, the essays by Tamara Levitz and Martin Scherzinger). Rather, I will explore another alternative to a "structural listening" model, one that appears to emerge from the appraisal of popular music videos, especially as reflected through programming on the Music Television network (MTV).[2] I will argue that this model rejects the assumptions that allow the critical listening paradigm to operate, and presents an alternative paradigm based on collective rather than individual critical processes, immersion rather than critical distance, and fluidity rather than stability of subject and object positions. I will further argue that this model is useful not only for "postmodern" repertories such as music videos, but for any "non-modernist" repertories, since through its prism we can see the historical assumptions and limitations of the structural listening model. But before describing the "collective appraisal" model, we should explore some of the assumptions of the structural listening process and their implications for the study of vernacular musics.

1.2 This is the kind of authorial presence and individual interpretative engagement that modernist critics such as Adorno, Horkheimer, and Jameson have bemoaned as lacking in popular music.

The idea of autonomy and irreproducibility as essential to a work of art (or any "authentic" cultural artifact) is linked in the modernist tradition to the ideals of autonomy, self-determination, and uniqueness as defining characteristics of the individual, whether as author/composer or as reader/listener. Fredric Jameson, for example, remarks that "the modernist aesthetic is in some way organically linked to the conception of a unique self and a private identity, a unique personality and individuality, which can be expected to generate its own unique vision of the world and to forge its own unique, unmistakable style" (Jameson 1983, 114). His rhetorical repetition of the word "unique" underlines the importance of autonomy and individuality to a modernist notion of the artwork.

Criticism of mass culture from the modernist perspective suggests that such "uniqueness" is invariably annihilated by the economic considerations implicit in mass-produced cultural items. According to Max Horkheimer, for example, "the economic necessity for rapid return of the considerable capital invested in each [motion] picture forbids the pursuit of the inherent logic of each work of art—of its own autonomous necessity" (Horkheimer 1972, 288). In other words, considerations of efficiency and profitability prevent the creator of the mass-culture work from taking the time—and the aesthetic risks—that Horkheimer considers inevitable for the organic development of a true artwork.

Horkheimer's assessment of the effect of the commercial culture industry

is aimed in this case at motion pictures, but such critiques are regularly
applied to other commercially-driven artifacts, including popular music.
Jameson explicitly draws a comparison between the "authenticity" of the
experience of "popular" versus "classical" music, to the clear detriment of
the former:

> I will argue that we never hear any [contemporary pop works] "for the first
> time"; instead, we live a constant exposure to them in all kinds of different sit-
> uations . . . this is a very different situation from the first bewildered audition
> of a complicated classical piece . . . the passionate attachment one can form
> [to pop works] are fully as much a function of our own familiarity as of the work
> itself . . . what we listen to is ourselves, our own previous auditions. (Jameson
> 1979, 129–30)   *verification*

In Jameson's comparison, the listening experience of a "complicated classical piece" clearly pinpoints the complex unfolding of the work as the locus
of meaning—and this would seem entirely in keeping with a "structural listening" model. More implicit under this formulation is the suggestion that
listening to classical music is about perceiving an independent and self-
sufficient work that commands our exclusive attention (to master our "bewil-
derment"), whereas the "generic" nature of popular music (the term "piece"
is used by Jameson only to refer to classical music) implies the lack of a self-
sufficient, attention-demanding work. It would almost seem that in listening
to popular music, a subject cannot distinguish between her/himself and the
music—revealing a dangerous pre-Oedipal inability to separate self and
Other. Indeed, Jameson argues that

> in mass culture, repetition effectively volatilizes the original object—the "text,"
> the "work of art"—so that the student of mass culture has no primary object of
> study. . . . Mass culture presents us with a methodological dilemma which the
> conventional habit of positing a stable object of commentary or exegesis in the
> form of a primary text or work is disturbingly unable to focus, let alone to
> resolve. (Jameson 1979, 137–38)

For Jameson, in losing the status of "stable object of commentary," "the
music itself" has vaporized as a locus of meaning in popular music. But his
formulation, which appears to posit a "structural listening" model as a
marker of artistic autonomy and hence cultural value, implies a common
understanding of the nature of a "work." That understanding is implicitly
underpinned by the modernist ideals of artistic autonomy outlined above;
indeed, Jameson himself characterizes the idea of artistic individuality as a
modernist trope.

While the idea of engaging with a musical work may seem to presuppose
an autonomous text (as well as an autonomous listening subject), I would
argue that this is a historically contingent model; it does not allow for cul-

tural forms that break from an ideal of "high art," particularly those that place less emphasis on the creative primacy of a single author of a stable text. *Pace* Jameson, I would argue that critical engagement does not presuppose "high art" repertoires; indeed, as Simon Frith observes,

> people bring similar questions to high and low art, that their pleasures and satisfactions are rooted in similar analytic issues, similar ways of relating what they see or hear to how they think and feel. The differences between high and low emerge because these questions are embedded in different historical and material circumstances, and are therefore framed differently. (Frith 1996, 19)

As we will see below, music videos do not match Jameson's modernist model of autonomy, hence an exploration of music videos must find a different conceptual framework for the interaction between texts and their appraisal.

2.1 Semiotician Umberto Eco has instead argued for an "intention of the text": the text itself, providing clues as to how it "wants" to be read, may present sufficient intentionality to create its own "Ideal Reader" (or perhaps, in the case of music, "Ideal Listener"). This model opens up the interpretative field and might provide a useful alternative to the search for a composer's original intentions.

Italian semiotician and critic Umberto Eco, attempting to work around the need for stable and verifiable authorial subjectivity while still retaining the possibility of predictable signification, focuses on the notion that a text *itself* (rather than its author's intended message) may contain the locus of meaning. "A text," Eco suggests, "as it appears in its linguistic manifestation or surface, represents a chain of expressive devices that must be actualized/deployed by its recipient" (Eco 1998, 50). Furthermore,

> A text is in any case woven up with "white spaces," gaps to be filled . . . because, the more its function is aesthetic rather than explanatory, a text wants to leave the interpretative initiative up to its reader, even if it usually wants to be interpreted within a certain margin of unequivocality. A text wants someone to help make it work. (Eco 1998, 52)

The interpretative process, as Eco depicts it, involves a reader "operating" a text (much as a piece of machinery) so that it will function properly. In order to operate a text successfully, a reader must have a variety of linguistic tools and skills, which Eco refers to as "competences"; these involve vocabulary (both general and specific), understanding of the historical and/or cultural context of the text's "story," knowledge of other texts that are connected to the tradition of the text to be operated, etc. In Eco's terms, a reader who has all the competences required to operate a text successfully can be considered an "Ideal Reader" ("Lettore Modello"). While Eco suggests that each text is created with an Ideal Reader in mind, he also observes that to predict one's Ideal Reader means not only to "hope" that he exists, it means shaping the text so as to create him. A text not only rests upon, but also contributes to the production of a competence. Thus perhaps a text is less lazy, its request to cooperate less liberal than it may want to make us believe. (Eco 1998, 56)

One of the principal ways by which the text shapes the reader's interpretative decisions is by leading the reader to develop a hypothesis about what Eco calls the *topic* of the text:

> The *topic* is a hypothesis that depends on the initiative of the reader, who formulates it in a rather crude way, as a question ("what the hell is this about?") which translates itself into a tentative proposed title ("this is probably about X"). The *topic* is thus a meta-textual instrument that a text can either imply or contain explicitly in the form of *topic* markers, titles, subtitles, guiding expressions. On the basis of the *topic*, the reader will decide to magnify or minimize the semantic properties of the terms at hand, establishing a level of *interpretative coherence*, which we shall call *isotopia*. (Eco 1998, 92)

The reader, in other words, is responsible for establishing a coherent set of guidelines for interpretation of a text (what Eco calls *isotopia*) on the basis of the *topic* (what the reader thinks the text "is about") that the reader has derived from the instructions (implicit or explicit) provided by the text itself. The reader then bases her/his continuing parsing of the text, and decisions to focus on or ignore specific elements (at all levels of structure and content), on the coherent *isotopia*. The text's effect on a reader's negotiation between the *isotopia* and the *topic* is, for Eco, a crucial indication of the construction of an Ideal Reader. For example, Eco suggests that a well-crafted mystery text will attempt to induce its Ideal Reader to overlook crucial semantic clues on first reading, clues that can later be discovered by rereading the text after the reader has discovered the solution.

According to Eco, then, a text "predicts the participation" of its reader and indeed shapes the reader's interpretative decisions; within the text itself are the makings of its Ideal Reader. A text is a "machine" that requires a reader to "help it function," and in its functioning it gives the reader clues to what the next interpretative step should be, thereby anticipating and creating a specific readerly imagination; through these clues, a text can lead its reader to develop a *topic*, a tentative understanding of what the text is "talking about"; a reader then makes further interpretative decisions based on the *topic*, creating in her/his mind a specific coherent scenario of meaning *(isotopia)* that will lead to subsequent decisions to focus on or ignore specific items offered by the text, which will in turn reinforce or hone the *topic* in a sort of hermeneutic circle.

Eco's focus on the "blank spaces" in a work, his perceived need for an ideal recipient (reader/listener) to engage diverse sets of interpretative vocabularies in order to make a work "function," and in general his model of a multifaceted yet coherent *isotopia* seem to approach Subotnik's suggestion of a "stylistic listening" approach. Eco's model might thus provide an interesting paradigm for interpretative work in specific musical repertories. But there is a basic assumption in Eco's model of "intention of the text" that makes it not entirely suitable, as it stands, for the project at hand.

2.2 Eco's discussion still, however, works within the framework of individual communication: a text creates an ideal recipient.

While Eco moves away from authorial intentionality, his interpretative model implies one-to-one communication between a text and its reader. The dialogue between text and reader, and their mutual construction/facilitation, is a private, individual exchange. In Eco's model, locating intentionality on text still relies on the stability and coherence of a text (a text needs to be stable if it is to have intentionality) and of its reader (an individual needs to have a stable subjectivity from which to address a text). Furthermore, Eco's model is still founded on texts that can be read non-linearly—and more interesting texts often "encourage" their readers (in Eco's formulation) to stop and return to previous passages, or to skip ahead, or to read more slowly or more quickly, and otherwise to challenge the linear flow of the written text in order to grasp more subtle aesthetic meanings. Indeed, this non-linear reading of texts is very much akin to the "unpacking" of a musical score, which is then thought of as a fixed "sounded text," within structural listening practices.[3] But since I am interested in interpretative strategies to address musical phenomena that are not easily characterized as "stable texts," and recipients that are often not stable or even systematically self-aware, my task is to take Eco's model in a somewhat different direction.

3.1 Expanding on Eco's lead, this essay explores the idea of the "intention of a musical text" in the context of music videos and MTV. These are complex sources, comprising multiple layers of media and hence authorship.

In moving from a literary to a musical text, the most direct way to translate Eco's notion of the Ideal Reader might seem to be a notion of an "Ideal Listener." Yet the term "listener" is not entirely suited to my purpose, especially in the context of a discussion of music videos, which involve multimedia consumption. Indeed, the notion of "listening" is itself problematic: it implies that the sense of hearing can—or should—be detached from other senses when encountering a multimedia work.[4] For the sake of this discussion, I will use the term Ideal Appraiser, derived from a cross-pollination of Eco's model with Gracyk's notion of "appraisal" as the process of responding to a multimedia work.[5]

Music videos, then, are multimedia works resulting from the intersection of multiple authors and artistic personas. It is perhaps a self-evident point, when dealing with rock/pop repertories, that the author of the lyrics of a rock/pop song is often not the same as the composer of the tune (or, indeed, that different elements of the tune—melody, harmony, orchestration/arrangement—may be contributed by different individuals), and that the lead singer is often yet another individual (not to mention other band members and additional performers, such as dancers, a prominent feature in many pop and hip-hop videos). The songwriters/performers may have control over the video's sound and overall musical structure (videos are, after all, supposed to match "their" song rather closely, though different styles of video do so in a variety of ways, many avoiding or disrupting linear narrative), but directors generally are known (and sought out by performers) for bringing their own specific "look" or visual style to a video. The question of the relative "weight" of visual and sound parameters as perceived by the video appraiser is a tricky one, and for the moment I shall sidestep it, limiting myself to observing that both elements can certainly be appraised simultaneously, even if to varying degrees of consciousness and attention. Ultimately, then, music videos are a prime example of a multimedia work produced by a large number of authors, with differing (possibly competing) expressive/semiotic agendas.[6]

3.2 Music videos are also consumed in ways that differ from Eco's model of detached critical reading, and thus construct their "ideal viewer/listener" (or Ideal Appraiser) through significantly different procedures.

Compounding the complexity of multiple intentionality, music videos are consumed/appraised in a variety of different circumstances, sometimes in their entirety but more often "partially." They can be appraised as songs on radio or CDs, or as videos on MTV, at clubs, or in other venues (for example, retail stores); such encounters are commonly "partial" in that only a portion of the video or song is offered to the appraiser. (We shall discuss the significance of MTV's common use of incomplete videos below.) Hybrid versions of songs, often with visual elements from the video, appear in hit movies and even (in fragmented/altered but recognizable form) in television commercials.

This multiple valence of the music video and its components has strong economic implications, not only in the strictest financial sense, but also in the context of an "economy of pleasure," and this is well expressed in Marxist terms by Andrew Goodwin:

> The essential element of pleasure in viewing the clips must involve more than purely visual pleasure . . . the clips must encompass a delivery of pleasure that relates visuals to the music that is being sold, that provides an experience of

use-value offering a promise of further use-values in the commodity itself (Goodwin 1992, 70–71).

A video must be able to function as a "commercial" for the song with which it is associated, especially since videos do not make up a significant source of income for either the artist or the record company (indeed, record companies tend to consider videos to be unfortunate but necessary expenses, as Goodwin points out). Yet a video cannot serve only that function, since MTV (in selling its commercial time, which can take up as much of 30 percent of each broadcast hour) needs to be able to rely on its viewers' willingness—indeed, eagerness—to watch a video repeatedly (I shall refer to this phenomenon as *iterative* viewing/appraisal), and indeed to tune to the channel in the hopes of seeing a favorite video. Thus, the video must be able to deliver pleasure (and hence signify) in its own right, in a way that *supplements* the song, and must offer meanings that rely on repeated pleasure in the course of successive appraisals. A desirability of iterative consumption (both of the video as a whole and of its primary component, the song) must thus be built into the video's construction of an Ideal Appraiser.

One further characteristic of the genre (which is shared by all time-contingent cultural forms, including film and of course heard—as opposed to score-read—music) is that appraisers cannot interrupt their "reading" of a video to review the meanings of a previous passage, and hence to refine their understanding of the video's *topic*. This immersive condition is in direct contrast to the detached/detachable nature of textual reading; as Eco remarks, "The more complex a text is, its reading is never linear; the reader is forced to look back and re-read the text, perhaps several times, even in some cases beginning from the end" (Eco 1998, 91). Despite the undeniable complexity of a video's layered signification, however, the video appraiser lacks this resource available to Eco's text reader. (While it is possible to pause or rewind a recording, music videos are seldom consumed on videotape.) If a video signified like a complex written text, one would assume that repeated viewings/hearings would be needed in order for appraisers to form a coherent *isotopia*. Indeed, it may well be that the iterative phenomenon of "heavy rotation" (MTV's repeated showing of a video in different time slots, especially in the few weeks following its introduction) is meant to offer the appraising public repeated opportunities to assimilate the information that the video provides. I have speculated elsewhere (see Dell'Antonio 1999, 72–73) that iterative exposure to a text/performance can replace "critically distant" reflection for the purposes of immersion-based critical processes; this may be what MTV is trying to achieve.

But does the appraiser require multiple rehearings/viewings in order to understand a video, or (*pace* Jameson) can videos signify strongly enough to enable the consumer to shape meaning (*topic, isotopia*) the first time around? And how much of the video must be appraised in order for the appraiser to engage the *topic/isotopia* dialectic? We should note here that seeing a video from beginning to end is not a given on MTV: introductions by the network's "video jockeys" (VJs) often overlap with the first few seconds, and on many shows (particularly the popular call-in show *Total Request Live,* on which more below) only portions of videos are shown. The fact that these fragmented versions make up a substantial part of MTV's schedule implies that videos do not require structural integrity—a marker, one would presume, of Horkheimer's "autonomous necessity"—in order to be effectively appraised.

If videos are frequently appraised in versions lacking structural integrity, it would seem that structural appraisal (hence structural listening) is not crucial to the process of understanding music videos. The Ideal Appraiser that music videos envision is not a structural appraiser. But then, Eco is careful to distinguish what he calls the *fabula* of a text (the linear sequence of events that make up its structure) from the *topic* (which is, as we saw above, "what the text is about"). And if the two elements are strongly linked in the textual examples Eco provides (and, certainly, in a structural/formalist notion of musical meaning), they need not be—cannot be, I will argue—in an appraisal of a music video and a concomitant understanding of its *topic.*

Indeed, Goodwin has observed that the "multilayered text" of a popular song (which, following McClary and Walser, he sees as composed of a "stacking up" of different components of social meaning; Goodwin 1992, 94) does not work according to the linear correspondences and connections of realist narrative, and hence cannot be read (we might say appraised) employing the same techniques. This is all the more true of videos, which combine the "meaning stack" of a song with a visual "meaning stack" that can further break down any tendency toward linear narrative progression.[7] This is not to say that videos inherently exemplify Jamesonian assemblages of empty signifiers; as Goodwin has rightly pointed out, the blanket description of MTV as a postmodern phenomenon, and of videos as quintessentially postmodern texts, has relied on mistaken assumptions about the predominance of visual and cinematic components in the structure of music video.[8] All the same, the lack of dependable integrity discourages a structural/teleological appraisal of *fabula* in music videos. Appraisal techniques must turn elsewhere to develop the *topic,* and we shall return to this issue shortly.

One final important issue differentiating the video appraisal process from Eco's model is the thorny question of whether videos are "texts" at all, or whether they should best be understood as recorded performances, and what the distinction might mean for the collective appraiser. "Before trying to make sense of performance as a way of working with a text," suggests Frith, "we should first be sure we understand how performance is different, how it is 'non-textual'. What makes something a performance in the first place?"

(Frith 1996, 204). For our purposes we might ask, to what degree is a music video "performative" and to what degree is it "textual"? Frith cites anthropologist Richard Bauman in observing that "a performance is 'an emergent structure': it comes into being only as it is being performed . . . Bauman [also] suggests that performance is an 'enhancement', involving a heightened 'intensity' of communication: it makes the communicative process itself, the use of language and gesture, the focus of attention" (Frith 1996, 208). "Sincerity" or essential meaning, Frith argues, "cannot be measured by searching for what lies *behind* the performance: if we are moved by a performer we are moved by what we *immediately* hear and see" (215).   *immediacy of performance*

Frith and Bauman's characterization above hinges on immediacy as a necessary component—even a defining trait—of the aesthetic experience of a performance (as opposed to something perceived as a "text").[9] An experience that requires or foregrounds immediacy will necessarily require different strategies for consumption than one that requires distancing or reflection. Of course, immediacy does not preclude awareness (conscious or otherwise) of such structuring aspects as form: after all, listeners always bring a panoply of generic expectations to a musical work, and those expectations can include specific types of structural "milestones." A foregrounding of immediacy does, however, entail an ideal of (at least partial) surprise, a willingness to release the kind of control over the workings of a musical event that is implicit in an ideal of detached structural listening.

If process is foregrounded, focus on text and its completeness is not necessary. Indeed, since completeness of a text can only be assessed through distancing, and performance (as theorized above) gains meaning through immediacy and immersion, assessment of completeness cannot play any role in appraising a performance. The notion of a complete/stable text is thus rejected, or at best marginalized; and as we have speculated in Section 1.2 above, the idea of structural listening seems best suited for—arguably, requires—an identifiable and stable text. Thus, structural listening would seem unsuitable for understanding musical events that can be deemed "performances" rather than "texts."

Frith (1996, 225) suggests that music videos display the characteristics of performance outlined above. It can be argued, however, that videos also display one of the primary characteristics of texts: they are fixed, not variable, and can be recognized (and marketed) as stable entities. If videos are not texts but performances (or, I would argue, text/performance hybrids), and if the most crucial aesthetic aspect of a performance of rock/pop/rap music (and, by extension, the performative aspect of a music video) is its immediacy of signification, and if critical distance is impossible or undesirable when appraising a performance (rather than a text), what other critical options are available?

We might think of this another way, triangulating Eco's textual model

212   ANDREW DELL'ANTONIO

with the notion of structural listening and the distinction between text and performance explored above. If a text calls attention to its unfolding meaning (by asking its reader to arrive at a stable *isotopia* through postulating a *topic*), a performance calls attention to the process of meaning-production (the postulation of the *topic*) itself. If so, a performance is a quintessentially social activity, since the members of the group witnessing a performance are connected by their shared processing of the codes/signs generated by the performance (their shared negotiation between *topic* and *isotopia*), much more self-consciously than solitary readers of the same text can ever be. In other words, the specific message of a performance (and, I would contend with Frith, a music video) is not as crucial as the way the performance/video reinforces understandings about what is collectively meaningful—whether politically, socially, or aesthetically—and how the collective arrives at such meanings. Indeed, the semantic codes that the video text/performance provides to its appraisers may serve (and, as we will see below, frequently do serve) specifically to reinforce a *topic* that is explicitly collective.

The idea of the collective is, indeed, part and parcel of the sensibility surrounding late twentieth-century popular music. As Lawrence Grossberg suggests, "the consumption of rock constructs or expresses a 'community'"; Grossberg connects this with the "authenticity" of hard/folk rock culture, which "assumes that authentic rock depends on its ability to articulate private but common desires, feelings and experiences into a shared public language" (Grossberg 1993, 202). The authenticity of rock depends on permeability between public and private emotions: the boundaries between the individual and the collective are not as clearly drawn as in the modernist paradigm of critical distance. The creative process itself is often portrayed as a collective effort: as Frith observes,

> since the mid-sixties the group (rather than the solo singer) has dominated Anglo-American popular music (at least in terms of male voices), and if such groups more often than not have a "lead" singer we rarely hear his voice completely unaccompanied. We are, that is, accustomed to the idea of a "group voice." (Frith 1996, 201)

If a collective expressive "voice" has long played a role in the "authentic" creative impulse of rock/pop, it is reasonable that this should be so for critical approaches to the repertory as well. Along these lines, Frith suggests that "dancing in public—listening in public—thus seems to be *more* expressive of how we feel about our music, more truthful, than dancing, listening alone" (Frith 1996, 240). Such a construct of authentic experience through collective rather than solitary enjoyment in rock and pop music culture is evident in music videos, which often appeal to collectivity, each genre doing so in a somewhat different way: heavy metal or punk/grunge bands incorporate concert scenes with ecstatic, dancing/moshing/screaming fans; rap videos

reinforcement

authenticity

often have street scenes with the rappers surrounded by dancing fans and/or gesturing, stone-faced homeboys; pop artists incorporate complex choreographed group dance sequences. The video appraiser is encouraged to see her/himself as one of the collective of fans, or perhaps even (by singing/dancing along with the stars) "in sync" with the performers.

I would thus suggest that the critical model that music videos establish is one of collective negotiation; thus the Ideal Appraiser they construct is a collective, not an individual. The *topic/isotopia* of a video is negotiated not according to Eco's one-to-one model of a text and a solitary reader/appraiser, but rather between a group of appraisers who collectively process the semantic information provided by the video; and further, that process of meaning-negotiation (i.e., the collective creation of a *topic*) is assumed to be as crucial as final agreement on a stable set of meanings (or *isotopia*), if not more so. Thus, in working toward a notion of the Ideal Appraiser of music videos, one of the key elements is the breakdown of a single, stable subject position—whether from the standpoint of the video or that of its appraiser.

3.3 Most importantly for this essay, I will argue that the Ideal Appraiser for such texts is not individual but collective: music videos on MTV appear to be meant to be consumed not by an individual but by a group. Indeed, in those occasions in which MTV displays critical reactions to videos, such reactions are collective rather than individual: MTV portrays collectivity and group participation as crucial to the listening/viewing experience.

Collective appraisal is certainly widely portrayed and promoted by the medium that is undeniably most responsible for the dissemination of music videos in America: the Music Television Channel, or MTV.[10] When MTV portrays the process of appraising videos, it always portrays groups, never individuals. Since MTV has a great deal at stake in being seen as "authentic" by its public (that is to say, "authentically" reflecting its public's daily experience; more on this below), its portrayal of video appraisal is quite significant. Though MTV's "authenticity" is of course entirely constructed, the collective listening processes it portrays would seem to be a realistic representation of its public's idea of the video-appraisal process.

I have discussed elsewhere (Dell'Antonio 1999) the collective listening strategies reflected in the first MTV program to embody a collective critical approach to video appraisal, *Beavis & Butt-head* (hereafter B&B). Not long after B&B reached the height of its popularity in the mid-1990s, MTV began introducing a viewer/listener-interactive program based on internet chat technology, *Yack Live.*[11] Yack Live took a number of different forms (most often fans interacting during an interview or other special event with an MTV-sponsored star, but also fan commentary on videos or other MTV events) and was never a regular feature (it would be scheduled for a week, then would change time slot or be discontinued until another special event came along). When paired with music videos, Yack Live resulted in a format remarkably similar to the collective commentary seen in B&B. MTV would announce a time and a specific IRC chat room for its video-based Yack Live, show a number of videos (either from its regular rotation or specially featured videos), and then monitor the chat room and broadcast the dialogue on the chat rooms simultaneously with the videos.[12] While the Yack Live chat was ostensibly about the videos, and a number of the broadcasted comments did indeed reflect on the video's content, the dialogue between the chat participants (sometimes up to fifteen or twenty interweaving individuals) was anything but focused on video commentary. Like B&B, the interlocutors moved freely from specific commentary to sparring/flirting with other "chatters" to commenting on their state of mind. Still, the Yack Live chat was by no means unconnected to the videos: in some sense, the entirety of the exchanges entailed the negotiation of meanings and emotions surrounding the appraisal of a video, instances of an immersion-based collective critical process akin to the one seen in B&B.

Collective critical processes were again at stake in a short-lived MTV show called *Twelve Angry Viewers* (hereafter 12AV), which aired in the period between autumn 1997 and spring 1998. Through a process implicitly portrayed as random, each week MTV chose twelve "jurors" to represent its viewers.[13] Each daily half-hour show presented three videos, each followed by discussion and each juror voting on a 1 to 5 scale; the video that received the most points was declared the day's winner. At the end of each week, jurors voted on the winners of the four previous days, and the weekly winner was put into "heavy rotation" (i.e., MTV pledged to show it on an especially frequent basis) for an unspecified period of time.[14]

While offering an image of the critical process, MTV focused instead on the ostensible results of that process; when jurors cast their votes, they were asked to give only a number, and not a rationale for their choice (though often jurors did provide a one-sentence explanation of their vote). Unlike B&B (which presented short excerpts of each video, thus foregrounding the protagonists' commentary rather than the video), 12AV initially presented videos (almost) in their entirety, perhaps with the ostensible goal of providing the jurors (and the MTV viewership) a full "text" by which to judge the video. In later episodes, as the commentary/discussion portion of the show was increased by one or two minutes, smaller portions of the videos were shown.

Especially interesting for the purposes of this study was MTV's depiction of the critical process in 12AV: during the course of each video, a small but well-visible "picture within the picture" provided the television viewer with a silent image of the 12AV jurors sitting on couches and on the floor in front of the TV (a visual link to the world of B&B, and probably yet another appeal to "real-ness" on the part of MTV, on which more below), appraising the video—and talking among themselves, presumably (?) about the video at hand. The unscripted and overlapping verbal interaction of the jurors during the video was probably considered too potentially disruptive to be overlaid onto the video soundtrack, hence their soundless commentary, which served primarily as an icon of collective critical engagement. Like B&B and the participants in the Yack Live chats, the collective critics of 12AV are shown in the process of verbalizing the critical process during the act of appraisal: once again critical distance is overshadowed by immersion and immediate response.

But MTV seems to have perceived that, by segregating the critical response available for the viewership to hear (the post-video discussion) from the collective critical process (the muted interaction), it risked losing the "authenticity" perceived through interactions in B&B and Yack Live. In later episodes of 12AV, selected jurors' comments were allowed to be heard over the video soundtrack. As MTV increased its deployment of web-based interaction through 1997, not only were MTV viewers encouraged to vote online simultaneously with the jurors, but viewers' comments were sporadically overlaid on the video image as a running text strip, in a clear reference to the Yack Live format. The critical context was made to appear less mediated through interjections of online commentators, since a "chat" context is marked as inherently "spontaneous" in cyberculture. The combination of "live" comments by jurors and online chat participants, overlaid visually and/or aurally on the video that is being judged, was probably meant to create an impression of immediacy and "everyman" participation—despite the fact that the elements of such ostensibly unmediated/spontaneous multimedia interaction were carefully staged by MTV.

It would seem that through 12AV MTV was trying to capitalize on the powerful image of collective critical response, while reining in its potentially dangerous or subversive unpredictability. In foregrounding the voting, the most sterile and quantifiable part of the show, MTV may have been seeking to avoid both distanced critical operations and the kind of prolix interchange, of the "high noise to signal ratio" variety, that characterized the group critical process in B&B and Yack Live. The voting on the show exemplified judgments designed specifically for MTV's purposes: the choice of "hits" for heavy rotation, and the ostensible sanctioning of that choice by "ordinary" viewers. 12AV then is best understood as providing a highly regulated and controlled image of the group critical process, despite its "open discussion" construct. Yet MTV was clearly attempting to exploit a "real" image of collective critical activity, and despite the regimented nature of the show, the possibilities of group critical dynamics were very much a part of its essence; MTV, in encouraging its viewers to imagine the "commercial break" off-camera discussions, opened up a space for a notion of group critical activity. In any case, what is at stake here is not MTV's co-opting of certain aspects of the group critical process to show itself as participating in youth culture for its own commercial gain (which is undoubtedly the case), but the presence and importance of that model as an alternative to a modernist, individual, critically distant process.

The "live" MTV viewer comment as occasional running text strip has survived the cancellation of 12AV: it is a standing feature of the popular daily request show *Total Request Live* (hereafter TRL). To be sure, in TRL the comments by viewers (requesting specific videos) are not "live" but pre-recorded, since requests are taken for an hour prior to the beginning of the show. TRL's construct of the live chat comment is so well engrained in MTV visual rhetoric that it can be entirely orchestrated and still come across as "live"; this is done in part through the use of live cameras outside the MTV studio, where teenage fans are permitted to give five-second lead-in comments to their favorite videos after each video is announced. The "truly live" flavor of the brief fan comment carries over to the "constructedly live" e-mail requests that are overlaid as running text during the video.

The goal of the fan/appraiser who calls or e-mails TRL requesting a video, or who stands outside the studio to make her/his voice heard, is the same as the goal of the juror from 12AV: the placement of a favored video into "heavy rotation," or similar patterns of iterative play. It is significant, I believe, that iteration is portrayed as an ideal through these instances of the collective appraisal process. While specific record companies (and artists) gain by the frequent performance of their videos, MTV has nothing to gain from specific artists' success: its goal is to provide its consumers with an iterative yet continuously changing assortment of "what they like." To be sure, MTV is likely to promote only artists that are socially/economically "acceptable" to what it perceives as its market (no hardcore punk, no country, no lesbian "women's folksong" singers or queercore), though the boundaries of that market are by no means fixed (witness, for example, the continuing expansion of rap and "alternative rock" into the MTV repertory, alongside bubblegum boy and girl groups). Still, MTV viewers are clearly glad to oblige the network with their selections for the videos most worthy of appearing on TRL, so that the notion of iterative play as an ideal seems to be shared by MTV and its public. While the idea that an appraiser wants to have access to a favorite song/video repeatedly over a short span of time is a commonplace in the reception of popular music (and even some "cultivated" repertories, as we will explore below), the immersion implied by such a model is inherently incompatible with the critical distance that must underpin structural listening, since it implies significantly different goals and aesthetic ideals.

Before we go on to speculate on some broader consequences of collective appraisal strategies, let us briefly consider the commonalities in the collective listening process as portrayed by MTV in the examples from B&B, Yack Live, 12AV, and TRL given above:

1. Although MTV makes a show of encouraging intellectual appraisal (through its "discussion" of videos), it also appears to encourage appraisal that is tied to bodily response (perhaps implicitly appealing to a putative higher "reality" of dance and bodily/visceral/somatic effect in rock, a common trope in the understanding of rock/pop authenticity; see Davies 1999).

2. Appraisers' comments tend to focus on the performative aspect, identifying good/bad moments in the band's performance as reflected in the video.

3. Appraisers do indicate an awareness of a potential difference between the aesthetic appraisal of a song and the video associated with the song, and the possibilities that the video's signifying process does not match that of the song (comments such as "the song is great, but the video was boring" were frequent on 12AV).

4. Remarks most frequently address visual aspects, and comments about the sound aspect of a video do not tend to be "musically specific": that is to say, listeners do not generally articulate an awareness of specific events in the sound portion of the video, and they certainly do not indicate a concern with the structure of musical events.

Overall, these interactions seem to indicate attempts at developing a common language that will highlight the most important meanings surrounding a group appraisal of the video.

The non-specificity of the collective process can of course be frustrating to those accustomed to the "clarity" of technical/analytical accounts of musical structure. I would maintain, however, that this apparent "inarticulateness" (for lack of a better word) in no way indicates a lack of sophistication on the part of either the appraisers/critics or the videos they are discussing, but merely a different set of communicative and interpretative priorities. For, as I suggested above, in music video (and pop repertories in general) the process of *topic* postulation/determination may well be more crucial than stability of *isotopia*. Or, as Frith has put it, "the use of language in pop songs has as much to do with establishing the communicative situation as with communicating, and more to do with articulating a feeling than with explaining it" (Frith 1996, 169). This might explain why the collective critical process (as reflected in MTV) is so reluctant to engage in specific explanatory language about the expressive qualities of a video: the immediacy inherent in the collective process resonates strongly with rock/pop's ideal of immediacy, but would seem to discourage the distancing required for the deployment of specific explanatory language. Descriptives may be used in the immersive process of meaning/*topic* formation—indeed, are required if that process is to be collective—but lose their efficacy once the text/performance is removed from the mix. Ultimately, critical distance would be not only undesirable, but indeed lethal to this type of appraisal process.

Turning now briefly from multimedia appraisal to the specific issue of auditory reception, i.e., *listening*—what kind of listening experience does MTV exemplify in the shows discussed above? It is certainly not a detached, critical, structural type of listening. Indeed, since commentary (sometimes from more than one source simultaneously) is overlaid onto the video, adding another layer to the already multilayered text/performance, it is a distracted sort of listening—with a number of other stimuli, both visual and aural, competing for the appraiser's attention. This is of course entirely in keeping with frequent descriptions of both popular music and MTV being used as "background" for other activities.[15] In the context of music videos, music thus "risks" becoming the background at a variety of levels: not only is the listening process merely one component of the broader multimedia appraisal process, but the video appraisal process may itself be only one component of several stimuli demanding the listener's attention.

Overcoming this "danger" of overstimulation by a focus on specific aspects of the sounds connected to the object of appraisal is part and parcel of the "structural listening" model, especially as it applies to pedagogical approaches: the ideal of "active listening"—focusing on "the music itself," often with a structural roadmap, is the mainstay of "music appreciation" textbooks in the USA.[16] But since the appraisal process for music videos occurs in a very different context, one in which (as we have seen) focused attention on the video is not at all the desired effect, we can postulate that the appraisal strategies best suited to a music video can be deployed even if it is in the "background": the Ideal Appraiser for a video can be—perhaps should be—an unfocused appraiser.[17]

We might look at this another way. The collective appraisal process involves a high "noise-to-signal ratio"—that is to say, the interactions between a group of appraisers do not focus solely on the video at hand, but include a variety of other topics that are (more or less directly) related to the appraising process.[18] This critical process is thus not a discrete enterprise, but rather an activity seamlessly integrated into the appraisers' daily life: critical distance is thus not applicable. Furthermore, the process reflects a breakdown of a stable, discrete notion of "music itself": music is one of a wide-ranging group of signifying agents. Given that in the collective process the notion of focusing on just the music in a video is not viable, any "musical specificity" of the commentary is out of the question—in this context, the notion of listening just to the "music itself" doesn't make any sense.

4.1 The idea of a collective listener/reader for a collective text is incompatible with Adorno and Horkheimer's formulations of artistic autonomy or Jameson's ideal of stable subjectivity, but it does seem to mesh with recent theories (such as those of Deleuze and Guattari) that characterize postmodern subject positions as multiple and shifting.

Some examples of accounts of the breakdown of stable subjectivity have been covered above, though mostly in a negative light. Gilles Deleuze and Félix Guattari's arguments are difficult to summarize (this seems to be a purposeful strategy on their part, as they work to incorporate what they see as "postmodern" modes of expression in their style as well as their analyses), but they are considerably more sanguine about the opportunities afforded by the breakdown of the "oedipal" subject (which they see as quintessentially modernist). Their description of the "schizophrenic flow" of postmodern subjectivity appears to resonate with the unpredictability and "unfocused" nature of the collective appraisal process outlined above:

> But through the impasses and the [oedipal] triangles a schizophrenic flow moves, irresistibly . . . a stream of words that do not let themselves be coded, a libido that is too fluid, too viscous: a violence against syntax, a concerted destruction of the signifier, non-sense erected as a flow, polyvocity that returns to haunt all relations. . . . language is no longer defined by what it says, even less by what makes it a signifying thing, but by what causes it to move, to flow, and to explode—desire (Deleuze and Guattari 1977, 133).[19]

Deleuze and Guattari's concept of "pack-formation" also seems to resonate with MTV constructions of group identity:

> The origin of packs is entirely different from that of families and states: they continually work them from within and trouble them from without, with other forms of content, other forms of expression (Deleuze and Guattari 1988, 242).

Deleuze and Guattari theorize that the concept of self-identification as "anomalous" is the catalyst for an individual's entrance into the "pack," and that such identification is based not on specific allegiances, nor on systematic, self-aware individual introspection, but on fluid and loosely-defined desires: "The anomalous is neither an individual nor a species: it has only affects" (Deleuze and Guattari 1988, 244). The pack is characterized by what they define as a "hacceity"—an intersection of collective assemblages. A member of the pack is not a subject, but a potentiality—"something happens to them that they can only get a grip on again by letting go of their ability to say 'I' " (265). Release of self-consciousness is a requirement for an individual to become an effective member of a "pack"—and, I would argue, of a critical appraisal collective.

Deleuze and Guattari view the *process* that individuals undergo in becoming part of a "pack"—a process they refer to as "the becoming"—as more crucial to postmodern subjectivity (if one can still call it that) than the end result. As they observe, each individual can be seen as belonging to several "packs," and each "pack" is defined in relation to an often-undefined "normative majority." The very fluidity of "becoming" brings with it the potential for cultural unpredictability and hence power, despite the inherent marginalization of the pack (which depends on being perceived outside the norm for its very raison d'être).

Deleuze and Guattari's notions of "pack" certainly resonate strongly with the constructs of authenticity through rebellion/marginality that are at the core of rock 'n' roll culture and, hence, MTV's self-image through what Grossberg (1993) has characterized as the appropriation of the "authenticity" of rock culture. Their account of diffusion of ego-focus also fits in with the characterization of popular music and music video as "background" music, that is music that does not occupy a listener/consumer's full attention (we shall return to these notions below).

4.2 Collective listening strategies may be not so much postmodern as non- modernist; their presence and premises certainly call into question an idealization of structural listening as normative practice.

What we have examined so far suggests that the performative texts of music videos are not suited to a model of structural listening, and that collective listening strategies (which, I have argued, show traits of subjectivities and approaches to "objects/phenomena"—texts, performances, etc.—that have been theorized as "postmodern") seem to be (or at least are portrayed as being) uniquely suited to these late twentieth-century multimedia phenomena. Furthermore, Frith argues that incomplete and fragmentary appraisal is fast becoming the norm for all repertories:

> We certainly do now hear music as a *fragmented* and *unstable* object. . . . All music is more often heard now in fragments than completely: we hear slices of Beatles songs and Bach cantatas, quotes from jazz and blues. Such fragmentary listening may have as much to do with—may be particularly suited to—industrialization and urbanization as with recording technology as such. (Frith 1996, 242)

In other words, current social situations contribute to the increasing loss of "completeness" as a criterion for listening to music. Frith's observation is unsettling, however, only if we insist on conceptualizing music as a "text," since texts are inherently incomplete if they are fragmentary; what a text is "about" (its *topic/isotopia*) cannot reliably be established without a complete narrative structure (its *fabula*). But if music can also function as a performance or a text-performance hybrid (as I argue, with Frith, above), then incompleteness is not necessarily an obstacle to the production or understanding of the performance's meanings. Arguably, a music video is about its

↳ again, seek *topic* not *isotopia*

mode of presentation: just a few seconds are enough to establish the coherent system of signs *(isotopia)* that it inhabits, and thus what it is "about" *(topic).* Once the *topic/isotopia* are established, the video's role is to prolong and reiterate those signs, through musical, visual, and (to a much lesser extent) specific textual or structural means. To be sure, there are meanings in most music videos that can be lost if the video is not appraised attentively and/or in its entirety, and the same can be said for popular songs, which create meaning through structural unfolding as well as through immediate signification. However, attentive and thorough appraisal is by no means essential to the *topic/isotopia* of the video/song; otherwise most manifestations of videos/songs, being fragmentary, would be meaningless, powerless to create an Ideal Appraiser—and this is clearly not the case.

But here we come to another quandary: the same could be argued about, say, a Mozart symphony as well. Certain musical gestures or devices in the course of any of Mozart's symphonies provide immediate signification to a listener familiar with eighteenth-century musical conventions, whether by the associative nature of the instrumentation or tone color used, the place of specific harmonic or melodic gestures within normative/accepted practice, irregularity/regularity of adjacent phrases, and so on. We do not need to hear an entire movement to recognize a dominant pedal as a "flag" to specific kinds of events, or to mark a musical idea that features flutes as possibly "pastoral" in character, or to perceive an antecedent/consequent pair as oddly configured, as long as we are familiar with the semiotic codes (whether explicitly "musical" or not) of late eighteenth-century Europe. We cannot, however, focus on the "uniqueness" of a specific Mozartean symphonic movement without listening to it in its entirety—and preferably with the constant attention and focus, not to mention critical distance, that structural listening would seem to require.

Thus, I would argue that only specific, limited repertories—repertories that have traditionally been seen as requiring self-isolation within the collective in order to achieve the goal of critical distance and individualized subjectivity—have demanded a focused (hence non-collective) listening strategy. Or better yet: such a "requirement" of self-isolation may be in no way inherent in the musical work—*pace* Adorno and others who would seek aesthetic worth in organic/internal necessity—but may rather be a construction of a type of subjectivity that requires the "performance" of isolation for its own aesthetic self-validation.[20] And here we are back at the modernist paradigm outlined at the beginning of this essay: a stable, discrete, and complete musical "text" resonates well with a similarly defined ideal of subjectivity on the listener's part; while one could view the sonic experience of the type of musical phenomenon currently regarded as a "stable text"—say, a Beethoven string quartet—as a fluid multimedia negotiation of meanings steeped in immediacy, following the characterization of "performance" in *"collective listening is about negotiation"*

section 3.2 above, models that have chosen structural unfolding as their primary focus have chosen not to do so. Thus the concept of wholeness, uniqueness, and "fixed-ness" of a text may be not only the goal, but arguably—and more fundamentally—the creation of the "structural listening" process.

In other words: the element of the "structural listening" dyad most susceptible to deconstruction may be not the adjective (*pace* Subotnik's tour-de-force), but the gerund: a modernist definition of listening (one that entails focus, uniqueness, and the ability to parse small changes in unique melodic/harmonic configurations over a long span of time) is required for the concept of "structural listening" to even make sense in the first place.[21]

For, assuredly, the fragmented nature of musical/multimedia experience described by Frith above is by no means unique to twentieth-century culture: accounts of eighteenth- and early nineteenth-century appraisal of opera, for example, are remarkably similar. Operas themselves would be heard repeatedly and piecemeal, as audience members came and went based on their favorite performers' stage appearances; popular songs from operas would be printed as broadsheets, sometimes even with different words; and composers would then publish variations on such popular tunes. Interestingly, the work that is seen as launching Schumann's pioneering approach to musical criticism (Chopin's op. 2, which causes Eusebius famously to exclaim "hats off, gentlemen, a genius") is a set of variations on the duet "Là ci darem la mano," from Mozart's *Don Giovanni;* not a "great work of absolute music" but a fetishized excerpt from a popular multimedia show.[22]

If Subotnik's deconstruction of the notion of "structural" listening was an important stage in the reassessment of modernist ideals of musical experience, the above (brief) challenge to the notion of "[attentive] listening" itself (which, as I argue, hinges on modernist notions) may open the way for alternative perspectives on Subotnik's "replete," "stylistic" listening. Structural listening and its requirements (critical distance, stable subjectivity, well-defined object of "music itself," differentiated notion of "listening" as an activity separable from generalized appraisal of multimedia) appear to be best suited to a controllable, already known repertory; the fluidity of developing repertories requires immersion and constant negotiation about what produces meaning. It makes sense that this should be a collective process, because meaning is produced collectively: an individual responding to a text/performance can only place that text/performance in a context of meaning that s/he already has in place. Thus, structural listening can only tell us what we already know about musical meaning; collective listening is about negotiation, and its language must necessarily be tentative and unformed.

This is not to say that the kinds of discourse MTV portrays should be accepted as the most representative versions of collective listening; clearly MTV has a stake in the acceptance of its offerings as valid, and thus any critical engagement must be tempered and controlled, lest it reject portions of MTV's programming that are financially successful for the company. Thus, MTV representations of the collective critical process can probably best be understood as simulating critical processes and appealing to them, rather than transparently reflecting them—all the more so since the high noise-to-signal ratio and gradual development inherent to the collective listening process does not fit a format that seeks to show, comment, and pass judgment on three videos in roughly twenty minutes. Even when collective critical strategies are less mediated by MTV than 1'2AV (as, for example, in the Yack Live chat room conversations), the level of critical observation is relatively low, and one could foresee a more subtle and discerning (dare one say articulate) approach; but the phenomenon of the chat room is still in its infancy, and I would venture that new modes/standards of articulateness will gradually form around this medium.[23] After all, what is articulate to the structural listener (or the academic) may seem inarticulate to those who are participating in the collective listening process, and vice versa.

But finally, we should briefly speculate on the origin and nature of the collective appraisal model: is it a creation of MTV, or is MTV responding to and attempting to shape/develop a broader phenomenon?

5.1 Since the idea of a collective critical process seems to resonate with MTV's public, this raises the question whether MTV has fostered this tendency or responded to it (or possibly both): Gramsci's concept of "organic intellectual" activity will be brought to bear on this issue.

We have explored how MTV has enlisted the internet and its increasing opportunities for virtual reality ("you are really there"), whether real or apparent, to construct a sense of collective participation; such participation is seen as crucial to the image of "authenticity" that the network seeks to project. As Goodwin succinctly puts it, "MTV, like pop music, needs to display its creativity, its ability to change, its refusal to stop moving. It is not just that MTV must be seen as hip and irreverent, but that it must seem always to be hip and irreverent in new ways" (Goodwin 1992, 132). MTV has very good economic reasons for wishing to construct "hipness," and we shall return shortly to the question of whether its "authenticity" can usefully support a genuine collective appraisal process. First, however, a useful observation on the nature of popular culture, and its connection to the concept of "authenticity": Antonio Gramsci, in theorizing on the nature of "folk" and "popular" culture, focuses on the category of songs "written neither by nor for the

social creature

people, but adopted by the people because they conform to the people's way of thinking and feeling." This, Gramsci concludes, is the only truly "popular" type of music, because "what distinguishes popular song, in the context of a nation and its culture, are not its artistic traits, nor its historical roots, but its way of conceiving life and the world, in contrast with 'official' society; in this, and in this alone, can we look for the 'collectivity' of popular song, and of the people themselves (Gramsci 1975, 1:679–80). More important than the "authenticity" of the sources of popular cultural artifacts in the historical past of a specific group, according to Gramsci, are the ways in which those artifacts are perceived by a group to reflect their social/aesthetic position, in contrast to the positions of others, particularly those perceived to be "establishment" figures. Note also Gramsci's focus on the ideally "collective" nature of popular song, which we might usefully compare with Grossberg's characterization of rock culture (see section 3.2 above). We might say: if MTV succeeds in creating a space for the formation of groups that are able collectively to negotiate cultural meanings, then MTV may be operating in a role that Gramsci defined as that of the "organic intellectual": one who does not impose cultural ideals, but acts as a catalyst to organize the cultural ideals of a group.

In describing the role and cultural products of organic intellectuals, Gramsci further suggests that "[the new popular genre] must elaborate that which already exists, whether polemically or otherwise; what matters is that it must sink its roots in the humus of popular culture as it is, with its tastes, tendencies, etc., with its intellectual and moral world, even if it is backwards and conventional" (Gramsci 1975, 3:1822). In other words, the organic intellectual's role is to accept the cultural premises of her/his popular culture, to facilitate its development, and not necessarily to question or resist its premises (as Gramsci puts it, "whether polemically or otherwise"); we shall return to this crucial point below. Eco remarks that Gramsci's model "does not rule out the presence of an educated group of producers and of a mass of consumers; but the relationship becomes dialectical, rather than paternalistic: the former interpret the needs and circumstances of the latter" (Eco 1997, 51). This seems to be exactly the role that MTV is playing: it must be perceived as the authentic mouthpiece and servant of its public, and in a very real sense it is, within the premises of consumer capitalism; and we shall return to this point as well.

It may be paradoxical to talk about Gramscian organic intellectuals operating within late capitalist culture, but what is happening with MTV seems to work along similar lines. Frith observes that "the [record company's] product is laid out for us so as to *invite* assessment. The record company works to define the evaluative grounds, thus ensuring that we make the right judgment" (Frith 1996, 61). Likewise, MTV welcomes the notion of critical process, especially when that process is meant to reinforce a notion of rock 'n' roll "authenticity," on which the network relies for its own authenticity. MTV has thus attempted to depict critical process as dependent on the group/collective nature of "authentic" rock 'n' roll experience.

A constructed version of the Gramscian concept (in Eco's words) of a "dialectical, rather than paternalistic" relationship between the "organic intellectual" producer of culture and the mass consumers seems to be what is at play here. MTV doesn't want to give its consumers what it thinks is good for them, it wants to appear to give them transparently what they want; indeed, it makes a show of asking them what they want, and of showing the consumers' own "authentic" participation in the process. This is to a large extent a construct, but it cannot be completely fictional, otherwise MTV risks losing the perception of "authenticity" on which it founds its legitimacy.

Goodwin has remarked that, since music videos are geared to the success of another product (i.e., hit songs), audiences "become the 'product' to be 'delivered'—to advertisers" (Goodwin 1992, 44); he thus characterizes consumers as pawns in the economic maneuvers between MTV and record companies. Goodwin is especially keen to debunk what he perceives a pernicious notion of "consumer sovereignty" integral to MTV's propaganda (45–47); but his characterization may be overcompensating. Although videos are certainly conceived by the record companies as advertisements for their commodities, MTV has control over how the videos are packaged for appraisal. Because of its need to portray authenticity, MTV creates spaces which, though carefully orchestrated, still provide room for individual listeners' input and creativity, and in any case depict collective critical engagement as an ideal for its audiences. As Frith observes, "[music] producers are seen to 'interfere' in the proper communication of musicians and audience. But this is not necessarily the case: they may, in fact, make that communication possible" (Frith 1996, 62). Likewise, MTV opens a space for the collective critical process, even as it tries to shape it to its economic needs. In any case, while MTV may not be the institution that Gramsci envisioned in his formulation of the organic intellectual (it certainly does not participate in the explicit class struggle that Gramsci advocated), I would suggest that Gramsci's model provides a useful key into the nature of MTV's relationship to the ideal of collective appraisal. While collective appraisal processes are independent of MTV, the network has fostered them in an "organic intellectual" sense inasmuch as they serve both its audience's needs and its own. To be sure, MTV has to walk a fine line between opening up a collective space and limiting the critical enterprise to something it can control or defuse, depending on its economic needs; the network thus reveals the potential of collective criticism, takes advantage of its outward manifestations, but must be careful not to grant its collective critics too much independence or critical latitude.

5.2 MTV's portrayals of collective critical response to music video are undoubtedly shaped by the network's commercial considerations, but they also create spaces for active participation on the part of MTV's public.

Goodwin has mined the social implications of MTV's cultural efforts as "an instance in the shift of power away from public service institutions" and toward "free market institutions." MTV, Goodwin argues, attempts to "restructure the subject-as-citizen (the public service model) along the lines of the subject-as-consumer (the free market model)"; its cultural message "may constitute an ideology to the extent that it implies marketplace solutions to all social problems" (Goodwin 1992, 169). "Politically speaking," Goodwin concludes, "music television must be seen as an ideological phenomenon through its capacity to extend the social relations of the marketplace and erode public service notions of culture" (171). Goodwin is here arguing against an idealization of MTV as embodiment of postmodern culture, locus of free and unbounded signification; and he is absolutely on target in this regard.

But Goodwin's (quasi-)Marxist analysis is not entirely dismissive of MTV as a valid cultural phenomenon; ultimately, its ideology does not seem inherently more pernicious than modernist ideals of artistic autonomy. In a truly schizophrenic fashion, "MTV is . . . simultaneously involved in the incorporation and the promotion of dissent" (Goodwin 1992, 155). All cultural formation and critical process, after all, is based on contexts and frameworks of premises; the fact that MTV does its cultural work on the model of "subject-as-consumer" does not negate the possibilities for effective and significant cultural participation on the part of the MTV viewer. For while Jameson reminds us that

> capitalism systematically dissolves the fabric of all cohesive groups without exception . . . and thereby problematizes aesthetic production and linguistic invention which have their source in group life . . . it is a daydream that [mass culture] could be retransformed, by fiat, miracle, or sheer talent, into what could be called, in its strong form, political art, or in a more general way, that living and authentic culture of which we have virtually lost the memory, so rare an experience it has become. (Jameson 1979, 140)

he then focuses on the "collective experience of marginal pockets of the social life of the world system," and the extent to which they may not have "been fully penetrated by the market and by the commodity system." Jameson points out that "you do not reinvent an access onto political art and authentic cultural production by studding your individual artistic discourse with class and political signals." Rather, class struggle and social/cultural consciousness are "the process whereby a new and organic group constitutes itself, whereby the collective breaks through the reified atomization of capi-

talist social life. At that point, to say that the group exists and that it generates its own specific cultural life and expression, are one and the same"
(Jameson 1979, 140).

Within this quasi-Gramscian formulation, Jameson (from the modernist
perspective we have seen above) would probably assume that an "organic
group" must be self-consciously stable, aware of its own existence (and difference from other groups) and its clearly drawn boundaries. But if we combine Jameson's insight about emerging collective cultural expression with
the fluidity and constructedness of late-capitalist groups theorized by
Deleuze/Guattari and embodied in the collectives portrayed on MTV, then
the image of culturally empowering "organic group formation" is implicit in
the collective listening scenarios suggested above. MTV is certainly trying to
harness the cultural power of the organic groups it fosters, and in many ways
it succeeds in doing so; but its ability to harness is dependent on the "authenticity" (or at least perceived authenticity) of such organic groups in reality.
While the groups created by collective appraisal efforts tend to lack a self-
conscious cultural or political agenda, and indeed frequently lack even a
stable group consciousness, the collective appraising process nevertheless
provides a space for collective cultural negotiations that continuously color
and reshape the appraiser's notions of pleasure and power.[24] — "renegotiation"

Collective, "organic" expression, Jameson continues, "is the third term
missing from my initial picture of the fate of the aesthetic and the cultural
under capitalism; yet no useful purpose is served by speculation on the forms
such a third and authentic type of cultural language might take in situations
which do not yet exist" (Jameson 1979, 140). Some twenty years after Jameson's formulation, perhaps such situations now *do* exist. To be sure, the
notion of "authenticity" of cultural language is now more fluid and renego-
tiable than a more thoroughly modernist notion of authenticity, one requiring stable subject and object positions, would assume. And perhaps, as Jameson himself suggests, this authenticity cannot define itself as entirely separate
from capitalist hegemony. Indeed, Goodwin has rejected a simple Marxist
view that "mass culture is the extreme embodiment of the subjection of culture to the economy; its most important characteristic is that it provides
profit for the producers," pointing out that "few cultural texts are today produced as pure commodities" (Goodwin 1992, 45). It may well be that a presumption of commodity-value underlies all late twentieth-century cultural
products, in a way analogous to the status of representation as the unques-
tioned basis of visual art in the Western tradition from the Middle Ages until
the early twentieth century. But commodity-value does not exclude other values to the appraiser; and in portraying videos/songs as desirable commodities,
MTV must engage with notions of artistic/aesthetic value: videos/songs will be
desirable if they are aesthetically satisfying to the potential appraiser/con-
sumer.[25] MTV must therefore encourage its audience to operate critically, and

must do so in an "authentic" way; any attempts on its part to control the results of the critical process cannot be predictable.

Further, I would argue that with the breakdown of a notion of "attentive listening," the pop song or video can no longer claim stable commodity-status: it becomes a component of a broad and fluid network of cultural meaning. A critical process that assists the breakdown of that stable commodity-status (by focusing critical energy on a fluid process of negotiation, one that does not address a specific object by distancing the listener from the work, but rather involves a group of listeners/appraisers spinning a web of conversation that partly envelops the object) can thwart an ideal of hegemonic cultural/economic control, making MTV (and the music industry) scramble to redefine the very nature of commodities as its public constantly renegotiates collective meanings.

"We have seen," concludes Jameson in an early essay on postmodernism, "that there is a way in which postmodernism replicates or reproduces—reinforces—the logic of consumer capitalism; the more significant question is whether there is also a way in which it resists that logic. But that is a question we must leave open" (Jameson 1983, 125). I would suggest that the arguments above begin to address Jameson's crucial question. The critical approach embodied in collective appraisal strategies may not resist the logic of consumer capitalism outright, but it does appear to have the potential for the formation of effective symbolic resistance, cultural shaping, and social awareness.

5.3 Collective critical processes may therefore well be a viable example of "organic intellectual" practices within late-capitalist culture.

Three parallel and connected concluding paragraphs:

1. While it would be naïve to view MTV as operating from a humanitarian point of view, within its free-market-model and profit-oriented parameters the network does open up a space for critical, evaluative discourse; indeed, it relies on such discourse (usually carefully staged, but necessarily verisimilar) for its "authenticity" and continued legitimacy. In so doing, MTV reflects (and may be assisting in shaping/systematizing) a type of listening process and critical discourse that is not solitary but collective. While MTV's ultimate purpose is to create *purchasing* (rather than critical or aesthetic) collectives, its encouragement/validation of the collective process cannot control the results of that process, whether they be economic, intellectual, aesthetic—or, indeed, social/political. As consumers meet the task of evaluating an increasingly plentiful and diverse spectrum of musical offerings, a significant portion of that process of evaluation seems to have collective (as opposed to

individual) potential, and MTV appears to be facilitating this potential in acting as an "organic intellectual" to its public.

2. The fact that the collective listening process seems to pay insufficient attention to "the music itself" may be frustrating to those accustomed to the specificities of structural listening, but the widespread nature of this type of appraisal strategy (and its likely predominance in many pre-modernist cultural circumstances) might usefully place structural listening as a historically isolated process, rather than a universally "inherent" (or even artistically transcendent) one. Collective listening may thus not be "postmodernist" as much as "non-modernist"; and historical perspectives on the listening/appraisal process (particularly those not tied to nineteenth-century "absolute music" repertories) may provide useful insights on contemporary appraisal strategies, both actual and ideal—and, perhaps, vice versa. Such a reevaluation, as it broadens the picture of differing parameters of what is worthy of attention in the appraisal process, might also encourage us to revisit transhistorical notions of "music itself"—in a way that scholars of non-Western culture have already done with transcultural generalizations.

3. The notion of collective, non-structural appraisal as suggested in this essay would doubtless be substantially strengthened by further research on MTV listeners/viewers' own notion of the appraisal process. Such "virtual fieldwork" would certainly help refine the construct of collective listening/appraising, and probably would reveal cracks in the "authenticity" of MTV's construction of the process; I suspect it would also prove enlightening regarding the listeners/viewers' self-consciousness of the collective critical process. In any case, I believe that the examples discussed above indicate the widespread existence of sophisticated appraisal strategies that are in no way dependent on notions of structural listening. If this is the case, it would certainly behoove music scholars to participate in the shaping of a critically articulate language to describe these strategies, at the risk of losing the opportunity to connect with discourse surrounding some of the most vibrant music-related phenomena of our time.

NOTES

I would like to thank Patrick McCreless, James Buhler, and the students in my Fall 1999 graduate seminar at the University of Texas for their crucial feedback on preliminary versions of this essay.

1. For a more extensive discussion of Subotnik's characterization of "structural listening," see the introduction to this volume.

2. I will use the term "appraisal" to describe the process of experiencing multimedia, since the separate terms "listening" and "viewing" are inadequate to the task. Theodore Gracyk recently postulated an important distinction between stages of "appraisal" and "evaluation" in the listening process, with particular reference to

popular music; "evaluation" in Gracyk's terms implies an intellectual value judgment, and comes at a second stage, after the experience of "appraisal" of an event, which— though certainly colored by stylistic expectations—is essentially an aesthetic rather than an intellectual experience. See Gracyk 1999.

3. I would like to thank Nicholas Cook for pointing out this connection.

4. Or, indeed, even an ostensibly "purely musical" work. We shall return to this point in section 4.2 below, in suggesting that the notion of "structural listening" may create specific aesthetic ideals not only through the first of its two defining terms, but perhaps more importantly through the second. See also the introduction and Elisabeth Le Guin's essay in this volume.

5. See also note 2.

6. A more extensive discussion of notions of "authorship" in popular music can be found in Brackett 2000, 14–17.

7. Even when the imagery in a video "tells a story" that is not present in the text of the associated song, and even when that story is ostensibly linear, the *fabula* of the story is almost always intertwined with direct non-*fabula* references to the song (through instrumental solos, lip-syncing, etc.) that work against a strictly linear understanding of the video's *topic*.

8. Goodwin is absolutely right in rejecting "the analysis of music television as a postmodern text" (Goodwin 1992, 154), though his Jamesonian definition of postmodernism rules out some facets of postmodern theory that can usefully be applied to aspects of music videos and MTV programming in general; see below, and a further discussion of this in Dell'Antonio 1999, 76–77.

9. Gracyk (1999), in his discussion of what he considers the two stages of listening experience—appraisal and evaluation—makes a useful link between aesthetic immediacy and appraisal; see also note 2 above.

10. As several critics have observed (see, for example, Goodwin 1992, 30), MTV has attempted to define itself as coterminous with music video culture; while this is by no means the case, since videos are shown in a variety of other circumstances— the BET and CMT channels (not to mention VH-1, MTV's "adult" affiliate) in the USA, MuchMusic in Canada, and several local/regional channels, let alone in clubs, stores, and other venues where the videos are employed as part of the sonic space— MTV's influence has certainly been hegemonic. I would thus argue that an analysis of MTV's portrayal of collective critical process is crucial to an understanding of the reception and appraisal of music videos.

11. For a slightly different angle on *Yack Live*, see Dell'Antonio 1999.

12. Since MTV explicitly reserved the right to edit out any comments that were "offensive," there was a time lag of a few seconds between the posting of the chat room comments and their broadcast on MTV.

13. Juries tended to be racially mixed and gender-balanced, and consisted primarily of individuals between sixteen and twenty-four years of age; the first name, age, and favorite music or home town of each juror were provided at the beginning of each show, perhaps to reinforce the construct of the juror as an "average" MTV viewer and to encourage the audience to identify with specific jurors who matched their age/sex/ethnicity/musical preference.

14. Toward the end of the show's run, special twists were added to the criteria for

selection and voting. For example, one week the jurors voted for the "worst ever," with the winner to be taken *off* MTV rotation; on another instance, viewers mothers were recruited as jurors.

15. E. Ann Kaplan, in her groundbreaking study of MTV, connects the notion of "musical background" with the collective appraisal experience in her account of studies of teenage habits: "The experience [of watching MTV] is then often a group one, people responding loudly to their likes and dislikes as part of the fun. Often, however, the program provides the background for casual partying rather than being watched concentratedly by teenagers." She goes on to remark that "MTV is 'consumed' in a variety of settings, ranging from the lounge or cafeteria of the college student center . . . to the dance club scene . . . to the large department store" (Kaplan 1987, 20). The clear distinction that she draws between concentrated watching and casual partying is, I believe, an artificial dichotomy: rather, the collective appraisal process is likely to involve a continuum of attention span, from occasional focused moments to complete disregard, on the part of each member of the collective. This type of "unfocused" appraisal is by no means limited to contemporary pop music contexts; see note 21 and section 4.2 below.

16. Three recently updated examples include Holoman's *Masterworks,* Yudkin's *Understanding Music,* and Kerman/Tomlinson's *Listen;* "listening guides" in these textbooks are predicated first and foremost on structure, and opening chapters stress the importance of focused, undistracted listening.

17. Before we deplore such lack of focus, it might be worthwhile to point out that the idea of combining music and text (common in the West since at least Aristophanes) implies parallel and simultaneous—and hence "unfocused" (cross-eyed?)— appraisal strategies, one for the sounds, and one for the words. This may indeed be why structural listening is so frequently invoked as most congenial to untexted music . . . and the fact that this type of music makes up a minority of even nineteenth-century "art" repertories (not to mention earlier or later repertories) has not prevented the idealization of the structural listening paradigm.

18. This is evident especially in Yack Live and B&B, since the discussion in 12AV is more regimented, but it also surfaces in the latter.

19. For additional discussion of Deleuze and Guattari's "de-Oedipalized/anti-Oedipal" model and its application to the collective critical process in a specific MTV show, see Dell'Antonio 1999, *passim.*

20. An excellent unpacking of the lasting influence of the modernist/late Romantic notion of self-isolation as a requirement for a "high art" experience can be found in Small 1998, esp. 39 ff.

21. The very fact that this technique needs to be carefully taught (through "music appreciation" courses) to individuals who otherwise very capably appraise multimedia events that have significant musical components should give us pause about its suitability for understanding of a broad range of musical phenomena.

22. For more on Schumann's criticism as a parallel to collective listening/critical strategies, see Dell'Antonio 1999, especially 75 ff.

23. Historians of science have speculated that periods of empirical "scarcity" (or "sloppiness") and/or apparent incoherence are characteristic of conceptual or scientific paradigm shifts; see, for example, Feyerabend 1978, 10–15 and *passim.* With

specific reference to musical issues, see Carl Dahlhaus's discussion of the concept of "New Music" in Dahlhaus 1987b, 1–13.

24. Robert Walser phrased a similar point well in his analysis of the socio-political import of Prince as "gender/culture-bender": "If [Prince] seems to lack the social relevance of self-consciously 'political' artists, it is because he is a rhetorician who deals with aspects of social intercourse that seem—perhaps *must* seem—most private and natural. To engage, disrupt, and rearticulate those affective engagements can be as consequential as any more overt struggle over signification or ideology" (Walser 1994, 87). A collective appraisal of a Prince video could well result in renegotiation of what are acceptable/effective erotic images (whether visual or sonic) for the members of the group, thereby perhaps significantly changing the appraisers' attitudes toward behavior formerly considered "deviant," with concomitant social consequences.

25. I believe it is irrelevant to speculate whether videos can be "aesthetically satisfying" within the modernist standards of artistic autonomy discussed above. With Frith (1996, 19), I am defining aesthetics broadly, tying it to the notion of pleasure/gratification/satisfaction that videos and pop songs unquestionably create for their public.

EIGHT

One Bar in Eight

Debussy and the Death of Description

ELISABETH LE GUIN

It starts, appropriately enough for Debussy, with a dream. The way I remember it now, some years after dreaming it: I was interviewing to be hired by a congregation of a church as their minister. This interview was really a sort of audition, in that I was to give a sample sermon. It took place in a paneled room with mullioned windows, a very solemn and official place, containing a large table surrounded by chairs—like a seminar room. Various church elders were in the chairs; I was at the head of the table. I felt discomfort because I am not a religious person; was I a charlatan to attempt this? But the unsureness dissolved in a sudden perception of what I would say. I began, in this dream, to describe a dream. I knew with total certainty that the act of describing this dream would become, if I did it right, profoundly sacred, and that my listeners would have no trouble recognizing it as such. I had only to make my description completely apt, entire, so that nothing was not described, and nothing said that did not participate in the transport of this image and experience. The words had only—only!—to perfectly match their object, and I would have achieved the sacred.

> The image in the dream-within-a-dream was of a white horse, grazing on bright green grass, sloping slightly toward the point of view, which was some distance above the plane of the ground. Some yards beyond the white horse, the ground sloped away steeply, so that a crest or ridge line appeared behind him; beyond that, indeterminate distance. The sky was blue but shot with cloudiness or mistiness. In front of the grazing horse was a small pond, surrounded by the vivid green, reflecting the whitened blueness of the sky. The horse was a somewhat heavy older animal. It grazed quietly.

I have tried more than once, as above, to recapitulate the act of description that I performed in that dream. I cannot do so, will never remember the exact words; but I recall vividly the triumphant sense that my description *was capable* of becoming perfect, the growing, exultant sense that, if I but chose my words with enough attention, I could equal creation through description. It is in this memory, and in the faith in description that underlies it, that this essay had its genesis.

In his letters, reviews, and essays Debussy exhibits a strong and entertaining character, parts of which—the sarcasm, the love of ellipsis and allusion—are familiar through association with his music, and other parts of which—the vehemence, the occasional sloppiness—come as quite a surprise. On few topics is that vehemence more consistently on display than in his opinions on reception, and most especially on any receptive practice that might partake of the analytic or academic. The strain is a familiar one:

Du goût (S.I.M., 15/2/13)

La Portia du *Marchand de Venise* parle d'une musique que tout être port en soi . . . «Malheur, dit-elle, à qui ne l'entend pas . . . » Paroles admirables, sur lesquelles devraient méditer ceux qui, avant d'écouter ce qui chante en leurs âmes, se préoccupent de savoir la formule qui les servira le mieux. Ou, très ingénieux, juxtaposent des mesures, tristes comme des petits cubes. Musique qui sent la table et la pantoufle . . . Méfions-nous de l'*écriture*. Travail de taupe, où nous finissons par réduire la beauté vivante des sons à une opération où, péniblement, deux et deux font quatre. . . . (Debussy 1971, 223)

On taste

Portia in The Merchant of Venice speaks of a music that everyone carries within: "The man that hath no music in himself . . . let no such man be trusted." Admirable words, and a necessary meditation for those who, before listening to that which sings within their souls, become preoccupied with the formula that will serve them the best, or who, very ingeniously, juxtapose measures, sad like little cubes. Such music smells of the table and of house slippers. Let us distrust writing. Moles' work, where we end up by reducing the living beauty of sounds to a sum where, laboriously, two and two make four.

There are only a very few places in which Debussy's critical statements keep better pace with the complexity of his musical thinking, by suggesting something more challenging than a retreat from description and analysis. One is the famous remark, "Search for the discipline within freedom!" This was directed at writers *of,* not *about,* music, but it is most intriguing when musicologically appropriated. Another, longer statement is directed toward the listener:

Du respect dans l'art (S.I.M., 12/12)

En verité, nous regardons souvent très mal—les paysages qui ne sont pas célèbres en savent quelque chose et jusqu'où peut aller la fantaisie des appréciations—nous entendons peut-être plus mal encore?

Ainsi restons persuadés qu'il y a des personnes très honorables qui n'entendent qu'une mesure sur huit . . . — cette arithmétique n'est pas infaillible, elle doit même varier avec chaque individu, — il est donc naturel qu'à la fin d'un morceau il leur manque des mesures et que leur compte ne soit pas juste! Ce manque est difficile à avouer, à moins d'employer cette ruse habituelle qui consiste à dire, l'air préoccupé : «J'ai besoin d'entendre cela plusieurs fois . . . » Rien n'est plus faux! Quand on entend bien la musique — écartons l'entraînement, les études appropriées — on entend tout de suite, ce qu'il faut entendre. Le reste n'est qu'une affaire de milieu, ou d'influence extérieure. (Debussy 1971, 216)

Of respect in art

In truth, we often see very poorly—landscapes that are not celebrated know something about how and where our fantasy of appreciation goes. Do we perhaps listen even more poorly?

Thus we remain persuaded that there are very honorable people who hear but one bar in eight. This arithmetic is not infallible, it must vary for every individual, but it is only natural that at the end of the piece they will be missing some measures, and that their summing-up will not be correct! This failure is difficult to admit, except by means of that habitual ruse that consists of saying, with a preoccupied air, "I need to hear that several times." Nothing is more false! When one really listens to music—let us set aside training or appropriate study—one hears at once what should be heard. The rest is nothing but a matter of environment and exterior influence.

This statement, "When one really listens to music . . . one hears at once what should be heard," is exasperatingly breezy. It does rather seem to be sloppy rhetoric, for he asserts the opposite elsewhere; writing a decade earlier about Dukas's difficult piano sonata, Debussy had acknowledged, with apparent approval, that such remote and rigorous music demanded being played "over and over again at the piano," while in a 1914 interview conducted by Calvocoressi, he is paraphrased as saying, "To believe that one can judge a work of art at first hearing is the strangest and most dangerous of delusions."[1] Nonetheless I want to explore here the ways in which, taken seriously, this statement points to a kind of trope in musical reception, in which aural experience is approached through analogy to the visual mode. Debussy's music encourages this tendency particularly seductively, and in the process asks contradictory things of us that are still in need of sorting out.

The piece on which I chose to begin this exploration was the song "Soupir," first of the *Trois Poèmes de Stéphane Mallarmé* of 1913—music as aphoristic and gnomic as any he produced, and, as such, a pretty unwise choice; but, as Debussy may well have intended, I was needled by his challenge, and wished to put both him and myself to the test. At the same time, there is some bet-hedging in such a choice, for this piece is also a poem, and a poem's existence might reasonably be expected to tether the auditory experience to some kind of semantic one. However, disentangling the knot with which the music and semantics are tied is always fraught, and here exceptionally so, Mallarmé and Debussy being each so dedicated to the confounding of denotational relationships.

THE POEM

A tracing-through and demonstration of the various possibilities and realizations for this music's relationship to this poem—tone painting, mood setting, symbolism, subversion—could easily consume the rest of this essay, and in so doing represent a turning aside from "hearing at once," into an engagement with writing. What I propose to do here is to introduce the poem and point the way to a *listening* familiarity with it as a spoken event—one intended to approximate the degree of familiarity that Debussy's 1913 audience would, by and large, have had. Thus the relationship to the poem that I wish to establish for this experiment is deliberately inexplicit, one in which the poem forms an implicit, half-articulate frame of sound-meaning for subsequent listening.

Soupir

Mon âme vers ton front où rêve, ô calme soeur,
Un automne jonché de taches de rousseur,
Et vers le ciel errant de ton oeil angélique
Monte, comme dans un jardin mélancolique,
Fidèle, un blanc jet d'eau soupire vers l'Azur!
Vers l'Azur attendri d'un Octobre pâle et pur
Qui mire aux grands bassins sa langueur infinie
Et laisse, sur l'eau morte où la fauve agonie
Des feuilles erre au vent et creuse un froid sillon,
Se traîner le soleil jaune d'un long rayon.

Sigh

My soul toward your brow, where dreams, oh calm sister,
An autumn scattered with freckles,
And toward the errant heaven of your angelic eye,
Mounts, as in a melancholy garden,
Faithful, a white fountain sighs toward the azure!
Toward the tender azure of an October pale and pure
That mirrors in the great basins its infinite langour
And lets, on the dead water where the fawn agony
Of leaves strays with the wind and ploughs a cold furrow,
The yellow sun be trailed by a long ray.

The act that will be of most importance here will be to speak the poem aloud, preferably many times, savoring it; this act assumes a special importance for the English-speaking reader with less than excellent French (a group in which I belong). Some of Mallarmé's resonances—the rhymes, the other similarities of timbre from line to line ("ton front . . . automne jonché . . . Monte," "langueur . . . Laisse")—can be heard and felt in the mouth this way. Others—homonyms and assonances with absent words that do not appear on the page, but whose possibility haloes the heard text with other, unrealized, imaginary meanings—are surely lost. Speaking the poem is a good way to get some sense of Mallarmé's syntactical extensions, the stretched and torqued constructions that put the poem into tension with the traditional alexandrine, or twelve-syllable line (another imaginary resonance, lost on most English-speakers, since syllabic meters do not really function in English)—and into a very exaggerated tension with any sort of normal sentence structure. Note, for instance, how the main verb ("monte") of the first statement does not appear until the beginning of the fourth line, when it has already been loaded down with two complex and delicate descriptive clauses; and, mirroring the mirroring evoked in the text, how the object of the second statement ("un long rayon") is separated by another active and evocative descriptive ellipsis from its verb ("laisse"). One may become aware of a slow rising motion (the speaker's gaze, the fountains, vague expectation), in the first half of the poem, followed by an equally slow subsidence into cool nostalgia (the autumn, abandonment, a setting sun) the second. In my translation I have attempted to reproduce both Mallarmé's peculiar syntax, and to use as many cognates as possible, in order to retrieve, at some remove, these tensions and resonances (while, inevitably, losing the rhymes). However, the Anglophone's relation to the poem's language as soundscape is in this context not wholly disadvantageous: for such a listener, French will tend to lose its transparency and become a sonic object, no longer fully semantic, impenetrable but for the beautiful shadings of vowel sound, so challenging and sensuous to the foreign palate: further along the continuum from poetry to music.

TERMS OF THE EXPERIMENT

Although I wanted to take Debussy at his word by restricting my hearings to that which was audible "at once," it did not seem feasible to me, for purposes of an essay, to restrict myself to a single hearing of this song. My compromise had to depart from Debussy's Rousseau-like apostrophe, "Let us distrust *writing*." Instead I chose—reasonably enough, or so I thought—to distrust reading: it became the particular and central *modus* of this experiment that I not resort to the use of a score. As it evolved, this meant not just an eschewal of reading, but of seeing; since live performances of "Soupir" were not to be had during the period of my experiment, my engagement with the piece consisted entirely of listening to it over a sound system. From this primary exclusion of the visual came yet further exclusions of "environment and exterior influences": in particular, any direct tactile or executional relationship to the music (the twitching of fingers, holding/releasing of breath, or tensing of vocal cords in sympathy, such as one would experience subliminally in a watched performance) was much reduced. There is little doubt that so severely disembodied a listening would have seemed bizarre to Debussy. However, it permitted a close examination of the possibility of having a *purely auditory* experience.[2]

There were two exceptions to my regime of exclusion: I had, as I have already noted and recommended, some acquaintance with the poetry beforehand; and I did take notes for each listening,[3] since I could not extend the distrust of writing so far as to abolish this habit; it would also have abolished this essay.

THE SONG

From the very first moments of "Soupir": a low chord, arpeggiated on the piano leisurely in time and widely in interval: it sounds cool, "neutral," architectural. And then, oh triumph of many years of hard-won ear-training! a framework kicks in: I think, "That chord starts somewhere around low E," and internally I "see" a bass stave, on which the E and the ensuing pitches "write" themselves.[4] I think, "Ah, it sounds neutral because I can 'see' that it is made of stacked-up fifths." Eschewing the physical score has not prevented me from creating a virtual one and mentally annotating it.

I try another time, with the admonition in place: avoid thinking about pitch, since it is the aspect of listening most freighted by the academic conventions Debussy deplores; concentrate on other things—time, timbre, register, articulation.

I can still "allow" the coolness, the spaciousness, I think. They are colored by a brassiness in the piano's low register on this recording that is peculiarly attractive. A little later, the singer (Hugues Cuenod)[5] makes some plangent vowel sounds (I am especially fond of the three different sounds taken by the vowel "i" in *infinie*), which are a source of pleasure to me, subliminally evoking the peculiar sensations that arise in my American palate and throat when I try to pronounce French. (Here, it seems, I invoke a virtual, participatory body.) Vocal timbres seem in every way apposite to piano timbre: warm, immediate, utterly personal, intrinsically different from it; the idea of the singer producing the "same" pitch as the piano (or of participating in the "same" chord with it) seems superficial, artificial. The interest and the character of timbres seems to inhere almost entirely in their differences, which rise to my attention at moments of transition or contrast between them, and then recede again. My awareness of these moments takes a kind of binary form, "Different"—"Not different," which proves extremely resistant to linear or cumulative interpretation; I find it nearly impossible to hear or surmise structures of timbral resemblance or referentiality across longer stretches of the music.

Nevertheless, earlier listenings do begin to make a kind of text for the later ones—a "score" of what to expect when, based on perceptual and interpretive moments that I find especially pleasurable. They are pleasurable in themselves, but also because I crave their momentary qualities of connection, their adherence to an expected sequence of events, their participation, perhaps, in a plan. I begin to wait, every time, for a lovely third-related shift (harmonic in the piano, registral in the voice) at *fidèle* (enjoying my perception of its smooth instability as a rather subversive piece of word painting,) and the exquisite synaesthetic mimesis on *rayon,* its long, loss-tinged stretch under the mind's eye becoming, so effortlessly, a long, desolate duration to the ear.

Similarly, I worry at the places where my sense of the poem collides with Debussy's. I don't hear things I want to hear, especially the long rising-to-falling, inbreath-to-outbreath motion of the poem, either registrally or in terms of any cumulation-to-release of energy. Mallarmé's exquisitely self-conscious turning point at "Vers" is overrun, in Debussy's setting, by the subdued momentum of a throbbing short–long rhythm in the piano part. I also hear things that I don't want to hear: Debussy's reintroduction of the opening gestures in the piano at the very end seem like an irrelevant feint at closure.

Interspersed with these perceptions and questions, all of which strike me as "promising," are others—many, a majority in fact—that are maddeningly jejune. While I can retain memorable events, like those mentioned above, from listening to listening, my real-time listening concentration, unmoored from the visual referents of score or performers, proves shockingly ill-trained in following any single "promising" feature consistently, systematically, through a single listening session. Invariably I get "distracted." I can "hear what I ought to hear," or rather, what I as a musicologist think I ought to hear—that is, interesting and subtle features of the music, my stock in trade—quite immediately, but I have immense difficulty maintaining them as an auditional stance. I never do "pin down" any places where Debussy precisely recreated or metamorphosed timbres from earlier in the piece, although I sense that he does both. I lose these glimmers of recognition quickly to other equally immediate, equally urgent perceptions, to some of which it now pains me to admit ownership (a really shining example: "The music helps me understand the mood of the words!") The immediacy of timbre is firmly linked to momentariness, temporariness; my auditional memory for it is exceedingly weak. The experience is like nothing so much as my novice attempts at meditation, in which my attention wanders, again and again and again, from its object; but with the added vexation of my knowing I am supposed to be far from a novice at listening to music. I am acutely aware of how well I fit the bill of Debussy's "honorable people who hear but one bar in eight," that awareness (and the chagrin it causes me) becoming, in fact, one of the chief points of continuity between listenings; I worry and worry at certain vague but compelling matters, like timbral recurrence and metamorphosis, like vocal-register-in-relation-to-surrounding-harmony, over successive listenings, and the worry becomes part of my "score," in the unhappy sense of a score I am trying to settle.

The desire for something to look at is acute: I want a means to winnow these wayward perceptions, confirm the "good" ones, dismiss the embarrassing ones, and salve my musicological ego in the process. I want a sense of how to shape and interpret heard experience that acknowledges that experience's immediacies; and I look to historical context for guidance.

SEEKING A CONTEXT FOR THIS EXPERIMENT

Debussy's presumption of an immediate listening seems to be modeled on the synoptic gaze, the instantaneous, complete taking-in of a visual experience. As such, it is scarcely an idea peculiar to Debussy; it has more the character of a cultural obsession with what I might call the synoptic fallacy. Fallacy, because it is not difficult to demonstrate that synopsis does not actually work in the reception of visual art objects, let alone in other kinds of art. In a classic essay, Etienne Souriau reminds us of how we actually use time in visual reception:

> One must see . . . the movement of the spectator around the statue or the architectural monument as a plastic or view-absorbing execution, which unfolds in order the various aspects which are held within the physical frame, and which are the aesthetic reason for that frame as it was planned.
>
> Are there profound and basic differences between this "plastic execution" and a musical performance? In a musical, theatrical or choreographic work, the order of successive presentation is set, constant, precisely measured and determined. In painting, sculpture, or architecture, this order is not determined: the spectator is [at least relatively] free. (Souriau 1958, 123–24)

Souriau's spectator is given certain executional options at certain times and exercises delimited choices among them. His musician is plainly playing off a score; a more precise musical counterpart to the visual process would be to an improvising performer, or perhaps a listener, for both of whom synopsis perpetually unravels into process.

Yet by calling it "fallacy" and pointing out its unraveling, I do not mean thereby to discard or discredit the concept of synopsis—to the contrary: fallacies can turn out to be prodigiously fruitful tools for interpretation, as long as one remains open to the possibility that what ends up getting interpreted may not be what one set out to prove! For one thing, I think there may be some argument to be made for the operation of synopsis as we encounter it on the level of biological survival. Humans can take in a great deal of complex information very quickly indeed by a single glance, or even a peripheral "take," especially when the object of the glance is another human; we see, more or less instantly, a great deal more about others than we are generally called upon to make conscious. This is also true of certain auditory information, especially timbre (and the combinations of timbre with pitch), ambience, and the micro-temporal operations of articulation, and again, especially when what is being heard is another human. Tone of voice, breathing, delivery all give us far more instantaneous information than we generally think about: one has only to reflect on how automatically and how accurately we gauge sex, age, body size, state of mind, state of health, ethnic/cultural background, social class (these last two verging into vocabulary), the type of space (indoor, outdoor, large, crowded . . .) from which we are being addressed: all this and more, in the first five words a stranger speaks to us through the small and distorting microphone of the telephone. Such timbral/ambient/articulational perception seems to be inherently symbolic or referential; all of these momentary perceptions point "outward," toward concrete signifieds—people, places, emotions, old memories. In a musical context, they will consequently tend to exceed the boundaries of what a piece of music is usually considered to be.

In music the positing of a synoptic model can represent a way of flash-freezing the fluid nature of temporalized perception, thereby making experience into an object, and thereby also rendering it available to description. Thus not only a fallacy but a conundrum, for what has happened to immediacy in this process? Debussy himself was certainly aware of this difficulty:

Concerts Colonne—Société des nouveaux concerts (S.I.M., 1/11/13)

[L]a musique est précisément l'art qui est le plus près de la nature, celui qui lui tend le piège le plus subtil. Malgré leurs prétentions de traducteurs-assermentés, les peintres et les sculpteurs ne peuvent nous donner de la beauté de l'univers qu'une interprétation assez libre et toujours fragmentaire. Ils ne saisissent et ne fixent qu'un seul de ses aspects, un seul de ses instants: seuls, les musiciens ont le privilège de capter tout le poésie de la nuit et du jour, de la terre et du ciel, d'en reconstituer l'atmosphère et d'en rythmer l'immense palpitation. (Debussy 1971, 239–40)

[M]usic is precisely the art that is closest to nature, and which conceals the most subtle trap. In spite of their pretensions as sworn interpreters, painters and sculptors are unable to give us an interpretation of the beauty of the universe that is anything but quite free, and always fragmentary. They can only seize or fix upon one of its aspects, one of its instants: but musicians have the privilege of capturing all the poetry of the night and day, of the earth and sky, of reconstituting its atmosphere and giving rhythm to its immense palpitation.

Here Debussy evades consideration of the arts of the shadow-play and of cinematography, nascent in Paris during his prime, and said to be a source of fascination to him.[6] The cinema, a facsimile of continuity created through the extremely rapid sequencing of innumerable synoptic moments, was certainly a new way for the visual artist to give "rhythm to [the] immense palpitation" of experience. In the passage above, Debussy offers music as a kind of cinematic alternative to the "fragmentary" synoptic process; but the listener gets no advice about how to go about capturing the poetry so encoded, and remains in danger of appreciating (perhaps) one immense palpitation in eight.

If, as I have suggested, by synoptically "appreciating" or "capturing" the motion of music through time is meant a process of rendering it susceptible to description, then it is a contemporary of Debussy who cast the most serious doubt on the possibility of this venture. Through his books and his public lectures at the Collège de France, Henri Bergson had by 1913 established a popular reputation unusual for a professional philosopher in any day or age. This was built in part upon his considerations of the nature of time as a perceptual rather than a conceptual field, and in particular his idea of *durée,* duration. Bergsonian duration is a rejection of the Newtonian idea of time as analogous to space, that is, a "repetitious, homogeneous, paradoxically static" (Gunter 1983, xxi) neutral field, in which temporal experiences take place: an idea that is essentially a figure–ground separation, and as such, markedly visualistic. This separation was collapsed by Bergson, in an effort— one which he was to refine and labor over his entire life—to make the embodied experience of time the arbiter of the concepts and language we use in assessing it. Bergson did not live to write exhaustively or systematically about music, but in one of his best-known passages he used musical reception as a central metaphor for true durational awareness:

Pure duration is the form which the succession of our conscious states assumes when our ego lets itself live, when it refrains from separating its present state from its former states. For this purpose it need not be entirely absorbed in the passing sensation or idea: for then, on the contrary, it would no longer endure. Nor need it forget its former states: it is enough that, in recalling these states, it does not set them alongside its actual state as one point alongside another, but forms both the past and the present states into an organic whole, as happens when we recall the notes of a tune, melting, so to speak, into one another. Might it not be said that, even if these notes succeed one another, yet we perceive them in one another, and that their totality may be compared to a living being whose parts, although distinct, permeate one another just because they are so closely connected? The proof is that, if we interrupt the rhythm by dwelling longer than is right on one note of the tune, it is not its exaggerated length, as length, which will warn us of our mistake, but the qualitative change thereby caused in the whole of the musical phrase.[7]

The reception of music is here presented as a kind of temporalized organicism: the field of attention is attenuated across the duration of a "tune." (Bergson's unspecified tune, with its organic coherence, would seem to hail from some time between 1770 and 1870; he does not address the question of whether something more disjunct (like "Soupir") could be heard in this way, nor whether such hearing is possible over a span of time that is longer than a tune—say, a song consisting of a handful of tunes or discrete melodic gestures, lasting about two and a half minutes.) This invocation of musical reception as an icon of something organic gets Bergson into just the sort of trouble one might expect, in that he positions the organic as a version of the natural: outside of the realm of the explainable, even the articulable.

In Bergson's view, cinematographical innovations in visual continuity were an approximation, but only a poor one, of the exquisitely "musical" fluidity of real durational perception. "Whether we would think becoming, or express it, or even perceive it, we hardly do anything else than set going a kind of cinematograph inside us. . . . Of the altogether practical nature of this operation there is no possible doubt" (Bergson 1983, 306). "Practical" here is a pejorative. Practical it is, because human beings will persist in the illusion of "supposing that we can think the unstable by means of the stable, the moving by means of the immobile" (273). But ideal it is not.

> [W]ith these successive states . . . you will never reconstitute movement. Call them *qualities, forms, positions,* or *intentions,* as the case may be, multiply the number of them as you will, let the interval between two consecutive states be infinitely small: before the intervening movement you will always experience the disappointment of the child who tries by clapping his hands together to crush the smoke (Bergson 1983, 308).

Bergson's work labors uphill against the human reliance on the inevitable stabilities and immobilities of words. Not only mistrusting analysis and description, he ends up effectively disallowing language as any kind of acceptable bearer of meaning—a bad position for a philosopher to be in.[8]

Bergson's understanding of language is interesting, however, in its invocation of kinesthesis; his concept of a "motor-diagram," evolved by human beings as they learn to use language, makes very clear some of the neural and muscular pathways by which the heard may become the understood.[9] Of course similar pathways evolve as humans learn to use music; I have mentioned the involuntary responses of my palate and throat to the vocal sounds on my recordings. If I were a pianist, doubtless many more elements in the "motor diagram" would emerge. But I am not a pianist, and they do not, which is a demonstration of the extremely contingent usefulness of kinesthetic models for an interpretation of listening. The subtle inclusions and sympathies of kinesthetic response arise in direct proportion to the physical familiarity of the listener with the instruments being heard (and they multiply hugely if that instrument is seen). While it would seem that kinesthetic listening has a kind of primacy, and that the visualistic, synoptic response arises only in the absence of any reliable kinesthetic referent, the latter situation is bound to be the more frequent for almost every listener.

Despite the self-conscious sonorousness of his poetry, and the copious references to music in his critical and theoretical writings, Mallarmé himself is a problematic source of real, practicable guidance in listening. He does write from a listener's standpoint; but what he calls Music is *not* music as most listeners understand it, but a labile metaphorical construct. Listening, as an act of wresting coherent experience from the rude data of sounds, serves as Mallarmé's chief metaphor for poetic creation, the act of wresting poetry from the rude data of experience. The continuum from awareness to attention to *poiesis* is described as a Melodic Line; our intimations of the connectedness of disparate events as Harmony. This metaphor offers us some beautiful images for what it is we, as listeners, and even as particularly Debussyan listeners, are doing; but there are two fundamental problems with using Mallarméan "music" to help us toward an appropriately Debussyan listening praxis. One is that Mallarmé, like Bergson, sees little value, little "charm," in description:

> Les monuments, la mer, la face humaine, dans leur plénitude, natifs, conservent une vertu autrement attrayante que ne les voilera une description, évocation dites, *allusion* je sais, *suggestion* . . .[10]

> Monuments, the sea, the human face, in their native plenitude, retain a virtue that charms differently than that revealed in a description; call it evocation, or *allusion, suggestion.*

And then there is the little issue of silence. This perfected metaphorical Music simply must not trouble us with any messy, non-denotational sounds:

> [C]e n'est pas sonorités élémentaires par les cuivres, les cordes, les bois, indéniablement mais de l'intellectuelle parole à son apogée que doit avec plénitude et évidence, résulter, en tant que l'ensemble des rapports existant dans tout, la Musique (Mallarmé 1985, 278).

> [I]t is undeniably not the elementary sonorities of brass, strings, woodwinds, but of the intellectual word at its apogee that must result, with plenitude and evidence, as the combination of connections existing in everything, in Music.

All of these writers on music condemn description. Description is, after all, an essentially Enlightenment act, and as such, more than a hundred years out of date in 1913; with Debussy we are already generations into the artistic and critical cultivation of the Romantically indescribable. Why, then, make such heavy weather of an anachronistic critical process? If one were not to so insist on the availability of receptive experience to description, this "crisis" would evaporate. But of course, insist I do, furiously, doggedly, and of necessity. While description may not be everyone's epistemological mooring, as the opening of this essay shows it to be for me, I do firmly hold it to be mandatory on the part of anyone who is serious about making sense of the experience of art: with musicology's modest pretensions to science come certain unavoidable obligations to Enlightenment practices and values, of which description is the linchpin.

Perhaps not surprisingly, some of the most helpful thinking and writing on this crisis comes from the French Enlightenment's own endless discursive anxiety over it. Synopsis as a kind of epitome of visuality, visuality as a kind of epitome of unmediated (and therefore genuine or inarguable) experience, and appearance as that quality of the object which summons the whole complex in the viewer, are a central concern of eighteenth-century French aesthetics and criticism. This concern spills over from art into music criticism, driving the numerous and overlapping musical *Querelles*. Critics and pamphleteers worry and worry at the nature of music's immediacy, at determining where that operates and how it works; and typically, these exegeses of music as a signifying art take visuality as their model and starting point. Rousseau in the *Essay on the Origin of Languages* (Rousseau n.d. [1754]) calls the instantaneous visual language of gesture the "most vigorous," and locates it as the primary language. He even uses this to explain the power of narrative, as a *cumulation* of apparitions or tableaux, which "strike a redoubled blow" to the senses, producing a more emotionally and morally intense effect than that possible through the single glance. (One has to wonder what Rousseau would have made of the "redoubled blows" of the cinema.)

The frequent insistence in the *Encyclopédie* that music must paint, not just things, but *sentiments,* can be read as a kind of evolution toward an understanding of music as expressive rather than "merely" representational; by these lights, the sophisticated composer, the painter of sentiments, paints not only toward what we see, but what we think and feel in the seeing of it. However, this seems to be simply a relocation of the synoptic moment, rather than a supersession of it, from the plane of figural to that of emotional recognition. In his considerations of the act of seeing and of recognition, Diderot asserts that

> [Q]u'on n'est affecté, dans les premiers instants de la vision, que d'une multitude de sensations confuses qui ne se débrouillent qu'avec le temps et par la réflexion habituelle sur ce qui se passe en nous . . .[11]

> [O]ne is affected, in the first instants of vision, by a multitude of confused sensations, which untangle themselves only with time and by our habitual reflection on that which passes in us.

Thus, as part of this relocation, he weds reflection to synopsis. However, immediate judgments of taste and feeling are still possible, indeed they are inevitable; subsequent reflection, the "descent into oneself," serves the necessary function of grounding them in reason. Thus the fundamental affective and effective business of music, as of any art, is still one of "painting," of accomplishing apparitions, tableaux—Diderot called them "hieroglyphs"—within the listener. These tableaux, not of things, but of feelings, then require reflective unpacking and analysis in order to attain their meaning. Diderot's famous acknowledgement of this process reads like an elegant lament:

> Autre chose est l'état de notre âme; autre chose, le compte que nous en rendons, soit à nous-même, soit aux autres; autre chose, la sensation totale et instantanée de cet état; autre chose, l'attention successive et détaillée que nous sommes forcés d'y donner pour l'analyser, la manifester, et nous faire entendre. Notre âme est un tableau mouvant, d'après lequel nous peignons sans cesse: nous employons bien du temps à le rendre avec fidelité: mais il existe en entier, et tout é la fois: l'esprit ne va pas à pas comptés comme l'expression. Le pinceau n'exécute qu'à la longue ce que l'œil du peintre embrasse tout d'un coup.[12]

> The state of our soul is one thing; another, the account we make of it, whether to ourselves or to others; another, the total and instantaneous sensation of that state; yet another, the successive and detailed attention we are forced to pay in analyzing it, manifesting it, and making ourselves understood. Our soul is a moving tableau, after which we paint without ceasing; we spend much time in rendering it with fidelity: but it exists, entire, all at once: the spirit does not move step by step, as does its expression. The paintbrush can only execute at length that which the eye of the painter embraces in an instant.

The art historian Michael Fried has explored at length the preoccupation of eighteenth-century painters with images of this very process. Jean-Baptiste Greuze is merely the best-known of the many who depicted scholars and maidens and patriarchs (and, of course, artists) absorbed in their various objects of contemplation; these images are themselves only appearances, icons, even fetishes of the reflective process, of "spending much time." Diderot's *Salons,* the essays in which he treats of the biannual exhibitions at the Louvre (and in which he lionized Greuze during the 1760s) are among the great monuments of this act of "successive and detailed attention" that grounds the descriptive art. They are also a site of its crisis, for no matter how lucid, sensitive, and perceptive the prose, transparency is never achieved. In fact, at a fairly early point, its very vividness serves to move description away from its object and make it an independent act, at best parallel to the thing described, sometimes freely diverging from it in flights of visualistic fancy intended to incite readers into their own independent, sympathetic envisioning of the absent canvas. In Norman Bryson's words, "[T]he image itself is no longer made to emanate from the information supplied by the writing, but on the contrary writing is only the score by which the reader's perceptual apparatus must realise [the image]" (Bryson 1981, 189).

This kind of description unpacks the visualizing, concretizing, freeze-frame synoptic process, and "musicifies" reception through description, determining sequence and duration (and even content!) of what is "seen." Such readerly reconstitution of the art object is, as Bryson suggests, really a kind of performance, the description really a kind of score. It functions just as well in musicological description as in art-historical, and we take it for granted as a basic performative mode for reading literature in our discipline. (Souriau's account of listening, quoted above, fits the reception of such descriptions much more aptly than it does the first-hand reception of the music described.) How many of the readers of this essay, after all, listened to the Debussy song *as* they read my accounts of it? Is transparency really ever the object here?

His own realization that the pursuit of descriptional transparency had led him full-tilt into fiction and persuasion caused Diderot, in his later writings, to retreat from description in moral dismay.[13] Among those in the ensuing century who were most fruitfully to take up the challenge was another contemporary of Bergson's and of Debussy's, Edmund Husserl. Husserl's principal strategy for the rendering of perception into the conceptual currency of language is what he calls the *epochê,* or "bracketing," of perceptions. This maneuver is exceptionally easy to misunderstand and misuse; in particular, some followers of Husserl have made it serve as an expedient exclusionary gambit whereby inconvenient facts, such as social and political contexts, may be deliberately omitted from a critical stance. However, in its ideal (and rather idealistic) form, the *epochê* allows, even mandates, *any* and *all* contingent phenomena in the assessment of experience; they must only be approached with infinite attention and caution as to their nature and source *as perceptions,* and as to their inflection through, or possible origins in, beliefs, convictions, associations, etc., etc. Any assumptions we make about these perceptions automatically become subject to the same scrutiny. This is not a disallowal, but a radical defamiliarization, of experience. An experience so regarded, "plays . . . the role of 'transcendental clue' to the typical infinite multiplicities of possible *cogitationes* . . . that, in a possible synthesis, bear [it] within them . . . " (Husserl 1960, 50). In this view, the phenomenon—in our case, the musical work as heard—is a *clue* to the range of its possible appearances within the hearer, which can be further teased forth by processes such as memory, association, and reflection.

Ideally, the vagaries and interplays of memory and attention exercised by the engaged listener, manifesting as a kaleidoscope of *topoi*—and, not incidentally, as my apparently helpless drifting from one immediacy to the next, from "promising" to "dumb" perceptions and back again—should all be given the benefit of a full and passionate Husserlian attention. To write of the agency of the listener in this case means finding out, tracing through, explaining what might have been brought to bear on the listening experience at *any given moment*—the likely (or not so likely, or utterly idiosyncratic) "melodic paths," as Souriau calls them, or the Lacanian "signifying chains" elegantly invoked by Katherine Bergeron (1994, 136)—of memory and association.

Is there *any* way to delimit and regulate this descriptive task? Proust's *éminence grise* gives this question its apprehensive cast. To actually do an *epochê* for even one momentary phenomenon, musical or otherwise, would lead to a nearly infinite regression of association—and yes, one can indeed envision the magnificent descriptive voyage thus summoned, *eight volumes* set in motion by an experience not musical but gustatory, the flavor of a madeleine crumbled in *tisane,* through which at long last a sufficiently textured and nuanced account of experience, situated in a delicate recreation of the conditions of one man's receptive subjectivity, emerges. The time it takes to write or read such descriptions is obviously grossly disproportionate to the time it took to have the experiences described; even more so than Diderot anticipated. This price for retaining description is a steep, in fact an unpayable one; certainly neither I nor my readers have the patience for anything like a Proustian response to Debussy's "Soupir." There is fuel for apprehension, too, in the tendency of such description to wander far indeed from its original object. The musical work-concept is threatened with utter dissipation. In a musicological description, we habitually use the visuality of the score, its obvious object-hood, in order to prevent excessive wandering and keep memory and association ontologically anchored.

Is any useful unity indicated, or even just suggested, across the fractures and prohibitions of my account of "Soupir"? Most definitely, there is the unifying, habitual, constant experience of text-making—denied a visual text, I make a text of expectation (fulfilled or denied), or, growing from expectations, judgments (good or bad); I find myself structuring experience as figure–ground, over and over again. This experiential unity, however, is not peculiar to this song: I would do it with any complex piece of music listened to in this way. Specificity is much harder. "Soupir" points, possibly, toward the beginnings of a novel understanding of timbre. The song's subtlety in this regard suggests that timbral meaning is perceptually constituted through transitions, contrasts with preceding/proceedings, moments of change from/to. If this is so, it would be sameness or identity—that which we often constitute as "unity"—that would be the neutral background; expression and meaning would arise from what is essentially a sequence of minute surprises, the direction and referentiality of which would lie very largely in the listener's own private store of memory and association. But there can be no denying that I am left, in the end, with an unfinished monument, a descriptional torso. Visual reference to a score would at least have allowed a comforting illusion here of "having accounted for every bar"; its prohibition forces me to confront the fact that I am bold to consider myself able to account for even one in eight.

For some months after reaching this point in this project I could not finish this essay; I struggled miserably with a sense of failure and futility. I imagined Debussy watching my struggles from Elysium with a sardonic eye, as if to say: the more fool she, to take my challenge literally. I pondered how Diderot, the finest describer of us all, evolved his art into a deft and cynical repudiation of itself, giving it human form in the disturbingly indescribable Nephew of Rameau, personification of the absurd; absurd, which literally, etymologically, means "from deafness." Only in the generous-minded pragmatism of Baudelaire, in his essay on the painter and caricaturist Constantin Guys, did I feel I could find, if not closure, at least a stopping place. Baudelaire suggests that the unresolvable tension in which I found myself is

> un duel entre la volonté de tout voir, de ne rien oublier, et la faculté de la mémoire qui a pris l'habitude d'absorber vivement la couleur générale et la silhouette, l'arabesque du contour.[14]

> a duel between the will to see everything and forget nothing, and the faculty of memory, which has formed the habit of absorbing vividly the general color, the silhouette, the arabesque of contour.

Baudelaire spends the first part of this essay praising Guys's ability to capture and render the fleeting, volatile play of visual sensation, characterizing it in one place as a return to a childlike way of seeing, and in another as a kind of artistic inebriation with immediacy: Guys is, in other words, a master synopsist. Not until late in the essay does Baudelaire reveal that Guys painted always after the fact, always by memory. He goes further, to declare that this is the ideal mode for producing all art, and all accounts of art: for in his view, memory is a purifying and controlling influence, the dividing line between an indiscriminate inventory of impressions (he uses the terms "myope" and "de bureaucrate") and something true, vivid, valuable.

> Ainsi, M.G., traduisant fidèlement ses propres impressions, marque avec une énergie instinctive les points culminants ou lumineux d'un objet (ils peuvent être culminants ou lumineux au point de vue dramatique,) ou ses principales caractéristiques, quelquefois même avec une exagération utile pour la mémoire humaine; et l'imagination du spectateur, subissant à son tour cette mnémonique si despotique, voit avec netteté l'impression produite par les

choses sur l'esprit de M.G. Le spectateur est ici le traducteur d'une traduction toujours claire et enivrante. (Baudelaire 1949, 122)

Thus, M.[onsieur] G.[uys], faithfully translating his own impressions, with instinctive energy marks the high or luminous points of an object (they may be high or luminous from a dramatic point of view) or its principal characteristics, sometimes the same thing as an exaggeration useful to human memory; and the imagination of the spectator, submitting in turn to this despotic mnemonic, sees clearly the impression produced by objects on the spirit of M.G. Here the spectator is the translator of an always clear and seductive translation.

If I accept this ethos of the caricaturist, then everything valuable about my description hinges on *which bar* (or gesture or timbre or rhythm or personal association) *of the eight* (or eight hundred or eight hundred thousand that inhabit the phenomenal sphere of even a short piece like "Soupir") *gets described.* As a critic, I have a positive obligation to make the selection, not only accepting but rejoicing in its incompleteness: according to Baudelaire, complete description is not just impossible (and impossibly pedantic), it is fundamentally unsuited to how people think, and remember, and understand.

Le beau est fait d'un élément éternel, invariable, dont la quantité est excessivement difficil à déterminer, et d'un élément relatif, circonstantiel, qui sera, si l'on veut, tour à tour ou tout ensemble, l'époque, la mode, la morale, la passion. Sans ce second élément, qui est comme l'enveloppe amusante, titillante, apéritive, du divin gâteau, le premier élément serait indigestible, inappréciable, non adapté et non appropriée à la nature humaine (Baudelaire 1949, 122).

Beauty is made of an eternal, invariable element, the quantity of which is excessively hard to determine; and of a relative, circumstantial element, which may be, as one wishes, turn by turn or all together, the epoch, fashion, morals, passion. Without this second element, which is like the amusing, titillating envelope, the aperitif, a heavenly little cake, the first element will remain indigestible, inappreciable, neither adapted nor appropriate to human nature.

And so partiality, in both senses, reigns. Did I ever really think it could be otherwise? Only in my dreams. Yet I do wonder about Debussy, whose arch wryness about the inefficient listening of "honorable people" seems to mask a real, Diderotic regret, an insuperably melancholy longing for the unity of interpretation with experience; perhaps he too is a victim of "the will to see everything and forget nothing."

NOTES

1. This interview appeared in English in *The Etude*, vol. 32, no. 6 (1914), 407; reprinted in Debussy 1977.
2. In his recent work on Debussy's *Faune*, David Code argues very persuasively that "the piece must be read as well as heard," as there are too many perceptual and

associative slippages for it to be rightly considered as a purely heard object; he suggests that in fact Debussy did not locate the full existence of that work in real-time listening (David Code, "Parting the Veil of Debussy's *Voiles*," unpublished paper delivered at the meeting of the International Musicological Society, Leuven, Belgium, August 2002). This may well be true of the Mallarmé songs too, but it is the capacity of the listener to bring visual or other associative experience to bear upon the act of listening, *while* listening, that I am interested in here.

3. Although I strove to do this in "real time," I succumbed twice to the temptation to pause the recording in the middle of a song in order to get a reaction down on paper.

4. It turns out to be an E♭—I peeked at the score after writing this essay. (I do not have perfect pitch.)

5. Of the several recordings I used for this essay, I came to prefer Cuenod's, and listened to it the most. It is "Hugues Cuenod chante Debussy," with Martin Isepp, piano, Nimbus Records NI 5231, 1979/1990. (Cuenod was born in 1902; the occasional frailty and variability of his septuagenarian voice heightens the distinction of its timbre from that of the piano, and does not permit the listener to lose touch with its human origin.)

6. See Smith 1973, 61. Along with other evidence of this, Smith quotes Debussy's remark in a letter to Varèse: "J'aime les images presque autant que la musique" (I love images almost as much as music).

7. Marcel 1958, 144, quoting p. 100 of the Pogson translation of Bergson's *Time and Free Will*.

8. It is amazing that a thinker so profoundly inimical to language as Bergson proves himself to be should have won the Nobel Prize for literature, as he did in 1927.

9. Bergson 1959, esp. 100–117.

10. Mallarmé 1985, 276; Mallarmé acknowledges this passage as a quote from his own "La musique et les lettres."

11. Diderot 1875, 1:320, "Lettre sur les aveugles."

12. Ibid., 1:369, "Lettre sur les sourds et muets."

13. A fine account of Diderot's centrality to the project and problematics of description can be found in chapters 6 and 7 of Bryson's (1981) magisterial work of the critical imagination.

14. Baudelaire 1949, 122. I am most grateful to Katherine Bergeron for drawing my attention to this article.

NINE

The Return of the Aesthetic
Musical Formalism and Its Place
in Political Critique

MARTIN SCHERZINGER

A few rungs down. One level of education, itself a very high one, has been reached when man gets beyond superstitious and religious concepts and fears and, for example, no longer believes in the heavenly angels or original sin, and has stopped talking about the soul's salvation. Once he is at this level of liberation, he must still make a last intense effort to overcome metaphysics. Then, however, a retrograde movement is necessary; he must understand both the historical and the psychological justification in metaphysical ideas. He must recognize how mankind's greatest advancement came from them and how, if one did not take this retrograde step, one would rob oneself of mankind's finest achievements.

FRIEDRICH NIETZSCHE, *Human All Too Human*

INTRODUCTION: TURTLES, TIGERS, TROUT

In the late twentieth century, the landscape of musicology witnessed many new cultural and historicist approaches to music. These approaches challenge the institutionalized priorities of a field of studies that tended to reflect a formalist emphasis on the self-referential aesthetic autonomy of music and its independence from other forms of social discourse. The new critical stance has produced a heightened awareness of the ideological dimensions of the latter "purely aesthetic" paradigm and a renewed interest in the heterogeneous and much contested cultural arena that is its condition of possibility. Various traditionally excluded categories, such as race, class, gender, sexuality, and so on, became legitimate topics for musicological debate, and a renewed faith in the political relevance of musicological writing was instituted. Thus, the turn to cultural critique brought a new agenda to the academic study of music that sets out to contest the status quo, effect positive social change, and resist negative social change.

This essay shares a deep concern for the social and political issues raised by this critique, but it argues for the importance of aesthetic values and formal characteristics specific to musical texts. While this theme seems to take on an antagonistic quality in these times, I hope it will become clear that standing as the opposition to the opposition of orthodoxies does not mean standing as the *enemy* of that opposition. Indeed, far from dismissing the new musicological writings I criticize below, this project is an effort to take in new directions the debate these writings have made possible. Moreover, by rejecting the widespread turn against the aesthetic, I do not want to isolate music from everyday life and then buttress that isolation in terms of universal and eternal ideas; nor do I aim to defend or redeem music theory and analysis as it is generally practiced today. Indeed, most theory and analysis, conceiving its terrain of investigation in wholly abstract and hermetic terms, is a genuine impediment to the development of political interpretation. The rigorous critique of such detached formalism has played a significant role in forging a socially responsible and politically concerned musicological praxis. What follows is an effort to offer a third possibility between, on the one hand, an apolitical analytic practice and, on the other hand, an anti-analytic political practice. While there is a risk of aesthetic escapism or narrow idealism whenever music asserts itself independent, this is not inevitable. By broadening our historical sense of what aesthetics at its best meant, we might once again imaginatively grasp the radical particularity of musical experience, which in turn can resist the control of totalizing concepts and sedimented beliefs about it. On the other hand, the impact that aesthetic elaborations on music can have on the sociopolitical scene is complex and multifaceted, and I want to include this kind of emancipatory figuration of the aesthetic as but *one* option among many for imaginative political intervention in the world. Indeed, I will speculate on specific ways that, via close formal analysis, reflections on the purely aesthetic aspects of music may productively address social and political matters in very diverse music-cultural settings. In particular, I will offer examples of how various formal music analyses can alleviate concrete political difficulties in these different social contexts.

Let me begin with a brief critique of the ideological exclusions effected by the kind of musicological discourse that tends to read musical production in social or political terms, rather than according to the formal categories of music analysis. I will argue in two ways: First, I will suggest that, caught in the throes of a variety of cultural and historicist studies, musical interpretation risks reading right through the musical text as if it was a mere representation of the social. The resistance in contemporary musicological writing to the aesthetic autonomy of the musical work (understood as a self-enclosed and internally consistent formal unity) thereby risks erecting an equally self-enclosed system of relations between world and work. That is, the social interpretation of music risks simply transposing those attributes formerly associated with musical form onto the world and then reading them as if they were a genuinely historical or sociological approach to the musical object. In this process, the music as such is in danger of disappearing against a general background of social determination, and, in the absence of any dialectical antithesis to that social network, the possibility of productive autonomy and effective resistance wanes.

Paradoxically, the new musicology was launched in the name of a historical and social inquiry (that insists on subordinating the musical text to its function within a broader social context) precisely to resist its naturalized ideological function. But the idea that historicizing (or contextualizing) musicological inquiry functions as a panacea to the ideology of the "purely musical" is equally based on error. When Daniel Chua writes, "To write a history of absolute music is to write against it," he also creates a lack of interest in the independent formal dimensions of historical inquiry—its absolutist hold on the "absolute" music under investigation no less than its promise of absolution from that music's ideological curse (Chua 1999, 7). Just as Fredric Jameson's call to "Always historicize!" is menaced by his observation that history "is inaccessible to us except in textual form, and . . . our approach to it and to the Real itself necessarily passes through its prior textualization" (1981, 35), so too is the rush to historicize (or socially contextualize) musicological inquiry substantially complicated by the fact that historical and social content too is patterned by an aesthetic form. In short, getting rid of formalism in music studies does not get rid of the problem of form.

The second point I want to make is that the new musicological insight that music's aesthetic autonomy is a cultural convention (or invention) seems to have implied a lack of importance and significance for close music analysis in general. Of course this does not follow. In fact, it is only possible to elevate the social world (or, conversely, the musical work) as the determining factor of musical experience when world and work are construed antithetically. In this construal, the dialectical relations between them dwindle and musical "formalism" becomes falsely understood as (what Theodor Adorno might call) a "self-identical" repressive practice. While it is true that all close analysis of music cannot not close down various options for debate, it is not true that such analyses (elaborated *as if* the music were autonomous) cannot open up other options. Susan McClary's observation that the "purely musical" should be granted no metaphysical independence because of its intensely ideological legacy overlooks the possibility that metaphysics may be strategically harnessed to allay political problems in the social world. On the nature of musical processes as they figure in her academic project, she writes, "No metaphysics—just cultural practice. Nothing but turtles. All the way down" (2000, 4). The turtles are a reference to an old legend about the foundations of the world. In the story, a holy man explained to a disciple that "the earth sits on the back of a huge tiger, which stands on the flanks of an enormous elephant, and so on. When the cosmological series reached a giant turtle, the sage paused. His enraptured pupil—believing he had arrived finally at ultimate truth—exclaimed, 'So the universe rests on that turtle!' 'Oh, no,' replied his mentor. 'From there it's turtles all the way down' " (1).

But, contra McClary, the wisdom of the tale may not be that the world rests on many, many turtles (a.k.a. "cultural practices") instead of only one, but that the sage cannot quite say this. The sage's pause marks the limit (or what Gayatri Spivak might call the "perhaps-structure") of all knowledge, and the statement about turtles, framed as a negation of the youth's hasty conclusion, marks the eternal return of the same that haunts all efforts to determine knowledge of the world once and for all. The point is that the world only becomes "turtles all the way down" when the desire for knowledge becomes absolute; when *becoming* becomes a world-picture. So, not only does McClary's text elevate the moment that the sage utters his most empty formalism, but it overlooks the beautiful tiger (and the elephant) upon whose backs we are hanging in dreams. After all, how beneficial to life, how beautiful, is the giant turtle upon whom our perspective is narrowed to endless turtles? And in what darkened waters does it swim?

In musical terms, what I am saying is that the observation that all musical processes (including "purely musical" ones) are so many cultural conventions is a preamble to knowledge passing as a conclusion. This observation does not register the irreducible metaphysical step required to institute any form of political commitment; still less does it register the role that those musical processes that do not take themselves to be reducible to cultural practice might play in these commitments. According to Friedrich Nietzsche, after overcoming metaphysics, the possibility of advancing depends on a "retrograde movement" (1986, 27). That is, to inhibit the maelstrom of radical skepticism from becoming an absolute formula, an imaginative leap of faith is required. I want to advance a series of faithful leaps (or retrograde musicological movements) that idealize music as a purely aesthetic phenomenon, but that simultaneously rein back its imaginative flight, like a trout on a line, to the project of productive political intervention and social upliftment in the social world.

To sum up, in this paper I want, first, to elaborate various means of resisting the ideological closure and programmatic constraint of recent trends in musicology—especially those that emphasize social and political issues over close reading and other formal techniques associated with musical analysis; and second, to elaborate new kinds of closure and constraint produced by music analysis that may be politically beneficial in various quarters. Let me turn now to a more sustained critique of the new musicology. To avoid reducing this remarkably rich field of discourse to a checklist of essential features, I will launch my critique of it in the context of a particularly impressive, indeed exemplary, case of new musicological writing, namely the work of Rose Rosengard Subotnik. In fact, Subotnik's awareness of the dialectical relation between work and world confounds the simplistic distinctions between these two realms to which I have alluded. Also, she recognizes the necessity of a moment of faith in all scholarly discourse and thereby reduces the essentialized methodological grip of the metaphorics of "cultural practice." It is hoped, therefore, that my critique of Subotnik's quite complex position has implications beyond the context of her project.

THE PROBLEM OF "STRUCTURAL LISTENING"

In *Deconstructive Variations: Music and Reason in Western Society,* Subotnik raises the question of the political, social, and moral significance of music scholarship with an interest in "improv[ing]," or "changing the conditions of" society (1996, 50). By investigating and assessing the "social and moral significance of the values discerned in music" (171), she hopes to "develop a new paradigm for the relationship between musical responsibility and society" (173). Broadly speaking, the imagined social improvements hinge on a kind of liberal pluralism that will accommodate "a variety of perspectives" on various scholarly assertions (65); where different "schools of thought can flourish in a constant and creative tension with each other" (61); and where the "dogmas and value judgments that separate us into particularized subcultures are swept away" (59). In the chapter "How can Chopin's A-Major Prelude be Deconstructed?", Subotnik elaborates two incompatible readings of the prelude neither one of which should be "more forcefully encourage[d]" (143). Deconstruction is introduced as a safeguard against foundationalism in the following way: Because Derridean *différance* insists on "the irreducible distance between initial and subsequent meanings," our claims to objective knowledge are disconcerted (56). Thus, as a persistent reminder of the limits of our knowledge—which is implicated in our "moral certainties" (172)—deconstruction "keeps us honest"; it "encourages our integrity as critics" (56).

At the same time, Subotnik resists relativism all-the-way-down (associated with this construal of deconstruction) by insisting, with E. D. Hirsch, on "honoring the value, no matter how unattainable the realization, of attempts at reconstructing original [authorial] intention" (69). Indeed, such "good faith efforts" condition the "very possibility of human communication" (69). Subotnik then advances a method that may begin to recapture such an "[original] source of signification" via the concept of "stylistic listening" (169–70). Applied specifically to the terrain of twentieth-century music, her argument "suggests that only something akin to 'stylistic listening' would permit contemporary listeners to exercise any prerogatives they might have as cultural insiders" (170). So, "emic" access to a source of signification, while "unrecoverable" in the robust sense, is best approximated in the context of stylistic listening (168).

In contrast, another kind of listening that seems to be inherently out of sync with the cultural inside is posited as politically reactionary in general. This way of hearing is called "structural listening." This essentially formalist way of listening is defined as "a method which concentrates attention primarily on the formal relationships established over the course of a single composition" (148). Subotnik carefully exposes the limits of this modality and finally subordinates it to the broader category of stylistic listening. Indeed, the "method" of structural listening, as the "primary paradigm for listening, cannot define much of a positive role for society"; by itself it "turns out to be socially divisive"; "limits the benefits of musical education"; advances, by implication, "ideological deception", and "selfishly refuses to participate in the discourse of society" (170–71). Structural listening is thus both epistemologically flawed (by failing, for instance, to confront the "irreducibility of style, both in its concrete physicality and in the ever-changing face it presents to new contexts of interpretation" [169]) and politically conservative (by, for instance, "beg[ging] off its social responsibilities" [175]).

My critical reflections on Subotnik's argument to follow come out of a growing skepticism about the distinction that such a focus makes between "structural" and "non-structural" listening. It seems to me that this kind of argument does less to undercut than to underscore the opposition, and that it essentially accepts formalism's hermetic claims, instead of configuring the business of analysis and close reading *as* social. This opposition is then hierarchized, with "stylistic listening" as the master-word, so that "structural listening" cannot impose itself on the interpretation of music. In Jacques Derrida's terms, the opposition has become a violent hierarchy in which one term controls the other both logically and axiologically. At best then, Subotnik's text reads "structural listening" as if it were not material but transparent, as if it were a mere instance of "stylistic listening." That is its limit. I want to argue against this asymmetrically bifurcated way of describing musical listening, and I will do so on deconstructive grounds. What follows is an attempt to reconfigure the similarities and contrasts between deconstruction and different approaches to the study of music in the academy today. My argument will take a simple shuttling strategy: First, I will show that Subotnik's reading of deconstruction is limited and perhaps even undermining of some basic poststructuralist insights. Second, I will show that certain practices of music analysis paradoxically share basic ground with deconstruction. This I will do through a comparison of the work of (1) Jacques Derrida and David Lewin, and (2) Ernesto Laclau and Benjamin Boretz. Following that, I will return to the critique of new musicological uses of poststructuralism, this time via a close reading of David Schwarz's elaborations on musical hearing in the context of French psychoanalytic categories. It is hoped that this back-and-forth argument will begin to complicate the network of relations between formal music analysis, anti-formalist musicology, and poststructuralism. Following that, I will offer perspectives on the way these fields of discourse intersect with politics and strategies for the progressive use of formal analysis.

THE FORMALISM/DECONSTRUCTION NEXUS

Like Subotnik, I am interested in the politics of musical formalism, but unlike Subotnik, I do not want to make a case for or against its place in the study of music based on unfettered epistemological grounds. Facts are probably theory-laden—selected, organized, hierarchized, formalized, narrativized—and theories probably instantiate ethical values that are founded on political commitments. This is why the question of the ethico-political can supplement the gap upon which the factual rests. I want now to raise some questions about Subotnik's text, and then to compare the practice of deconstruction with the work of specific music theorists. This comparison will set the stage for various proposals for the politically strategic use of musical formalism.

Subotnik's text raises many more questions than I have time to address here. For example, has "structural listening" perhaps been so narrowly defined in her text that it loses all applicability; that it does not capture the concrete practice of formalism in our discipline? Concomitantly, has "stylistic listening" been so broadly defined that it loses all specificity? Do two incompatible readings of a musical text amount to a "deconstruction" of that text? Or is this more like two different interpretative *commitments*? Also, does Derridean deconstruction encourage the liberal pluralism endorsed by Subotnik? Can one derive from purely deconstructive premises a democratic politics? At this point, it is worth introducing a second reading of deconstruction: one that involves less an embrace of the tolerant coexistence of different readings and more the experience of a structural undecidability; one whose irreducible undecidability is less the result of some empirical imperfection (or the "unrecoverable" emic access to the "source of signification" (1996, 169)) and more the result of a trace of contingency lodged within the logic of any structure (at its origin); and one through which no specific political program can be advanced. With both Subotnik's reading and this second reading of deconstruction in mind, I will now examine some of the relations that deconstruction has to some types of musical formalism. In both cases, I want to note, first, the similarities (too often overlooked) between a kind of 'open' formal analysis and the values that Subotnik upholds; and second, the similarities (also generally overlooked) between such analysis and Derridean deconstruction.

The first obvious point is that, like Nietzsche, who in his Preface to *Daybreak* asks us "to read slowly, deeply, looking cautiously before and after, with reservations, with doors left open, with delicate eyes and fingers" (1997, 5), Derrida urges us to read closely by arguing that certain important differences "come . . . to light only under a microscope, a divine microscope capable of perceiving delicate sculptures on the scales of reptiles" (1997, 62). But more specifically, I can think of two accounts, corresponding to the two construals of deconstruction mentioned above, that share unexpected affinities with the practice of formal music analysis. First, the work of David Lewin, a musician and mathematician who consolidated the field of set theory in music studies and who is sometimes regarded as a preeminent formalist in the domain of music scholarship, can be considered from the perspective of the first construal. In Subotnik's terms, this is a perspective that rejects "narrowly . . . 'fixed' musical structures" (1996, 173) and concerns itself with the "diverse, unstable, and open-ended . . . multitude of contexts in which music defines itself" (175).

On David Lewin and Jacques Derrida

In his article "Music Theory, Phenomenology, and Modes of Perception," David Lewin is interested in examining with some precision the variety of formal perceptions that are generated by musical events (1986, 327–92). He reacts, in step with Subotnik, against the view of art (especially musical art) "as something 'given' and 'there'" upon which the expert interpreter "exercis[es] mechanical skills" (378). To allay this kind of problem, Lewin draws to our attention "the need for studies in *the poetics of analysis*" (382). Resisting musical interpretation that claims to exhaust the subject through formal closure, he builds into his analyses a variety of phenomenal time-spans (or "occupational contexts") that build "a different family of mental constructs for perceiving . . . passage[s] of [musical] time" without assuming that these time-systems are functionally isomorphic (359). This leads him to musical reflections that fall outside the logic and grasp of the kind of either/or methodological commitment that wants to fix the meaning of a musical event irreducibly. With reference to Schubert's song *Morgengruß*, Lewin says:

> By saying, "the harmony of measure 12 is" . . . , we are already falsely constraining our musical perceptions by implicitly asserting that there is *one* phenomenological object called "*the* harmony of measure 12," and we are also constraining our perceptions by saying of this object that it "*is*," putting it as *one* location in *one* present-tense system that renders falsely coextensive a number of different times. (Lewin 1986, 358)

Lewin surmises that the temptation to place musical things in unique spatial locations is "prompted by the unique vertical coordinate for the . . . notehead-point on the Euclidean/Cartesian score-plane" (360). Indeed, succumbing to this temptation by rendering conclusive analytic verdicts strikes him as "fantastically wrong" (359).

To dramatize the point, Lewin paradoxically begins his analysis by narrowing the focus on the contents of measure 12 *as if* they could be spatialized in a Euclidean/Cartesian way. This is where the argument becomes deconstructive. In Derrida's scheme, dissemination/*différance* interrupts any identity of a term or concept to itself, or any homogeneity of a term/concept within itself. By marking the detour/supplement through which a concept comes to meaningfulness, *différance* submerges the concept in a signifying chain that lies beyond the immediate context of that concept. Hence, deconstruction reveals the differential structure of the concept, which is no longer only itself in itself. It becomes a conceptual effect, a nominal accretion produced by a complex interweaving of signifiers; in short, it becomes a concept-metaphor. Likewise, Lewin insists that even the apparently simple perception that engages measure 12 of *Morgengruß* "in its own context" (1986, 346) necessarily involves contexts that "lie outside of the time of the entire musical performance" (332)—socio-cultural forces, or what Lewin calls "a long historical/cultural shadow" (342) that make this perception possible. At its most self-evident then, measure 12 might sound something like a measure of g^6 harmony, with a D in the upper voice. Quite different things emerge when we hear the measure in more extensive contexts. The fact of a "density of attacks in the accompaniment" (347), with one (but only one) attack on every eighth-note beat, or the fact of lying in a high register, is noticed only in relation to "what-[is]-notice[d]-elsewhere" (347); in this case the opening eleven measures, which contrast in these respects. Like Derrida in his discussion of *différance,* Lewin calls these absent presences "retensions"—when they project "remembered past times" (329)—and "protensions"—when they project "future expectations into present consciousness" (329). The latter are not to be equated with traditional conceptions of "expectation" or "implication" because, as he explains, "[i]n the traditional view, [the implied] perception . . . 'has not yet happened' at [the time of the event under investigation] , but we 'expect' it, perhaps with a certain probability or entropy value" (323). For Lewin, in contrast, the said perception "*does actually happen*" (332) at that time. Like Derrida's figuration of the differing/deferring of *différance,* measure 12 is thus shot through with temporality within the perception of its "present." Thus, like Derrida's sign, measure 12 is dynamically divided with itself. In short, the "being" of measure 12 is inflected with "time."

Remaining in the context of retention, Lewin advances a second perception of measure 12 in terms of its tonal function. The dominant prolongation that we have at hand in the three measures leading up to it furnishes measure 12 with the sound of a challenge, one that denies the dominant its "leading-tone function in a context that otherwise clearly prolongs 'dominant' sensations" (1986, 348). This perception obviously flies in the face of the phrase boundary at measure 11, which encourages hearing measure 12 as a beginning and so in terms of protensions. Now, in conjunction with measure 13, measure 12 sounds like "d minor is being tonicized," and involves constructing a D-minor tonic somewhere in protension, perhaps around measure 14 (349). But, once this perception opens up to previous measures, another perception comes into play, one that *denies* the perception of a confusing blues-inflected dominant. Importantly, for Lewin, the denial is itself regarded as substantially perceptual and ultimately as aesthetically relevant. This is why he resists falsely dichotomizing the musical perceptual field, and asserts as a rule of thumb for analysis: "mistrust anything that tells you not to explore an aural impression you have once formed" (359). Instead of "trying to deny and suppress various of our perceptual phenomena," Lewin advocates a multi-capillaried approach that takes changes of mind seriously (359). Ultimately, an ideal analysis will want to sustain a variety of perceptions formed in differently determined connections, however incompatible these perceptions seem to be with one another.

The perception that denies the dominant function of measure 12 because of holding a D-minor tonic in protension yields a second perception that connects D minor-in-waiting with the fleetingly tonicized D-minor harmony in measure 8, suggesting an elaboration or expansion of that tonicization. The temporal context for this perception includes measure 8-in-retention and measure 14-in-protension. Another perception of these events involves an effort to make sense of the tonicization of D minor in the context of the prolonged dominant in measures 9–11. Lewin contends that, partly because of the melodic D_5 that is prolonged throughout this span, one expects a return to dominant harmony following the tonicization of D minor. The G-minor 6th chord under this perception is rendered "completely *forwards*-looking, inflecting a subsequent (protensive) d minor harmony; in *this* perception, the g minor chord has no direct prolongational relation to the dominant harmony that precedes it" (350–51). The denial mentioned above is reinforced; indeed, the blues-perception is virtually annihilated. Lewin then reads the ensuing sounds of measure 14 as an inverted and chromatically inflected D-minor chord with a passing seventh instead of as merely an F-minor triad. Thus we expect C_5 and $A\flat$ in the bass, *dissonant* in the context of D-minor tonality, to resolve downwards to $B\flat_4$ and G_3 respectively. But another perception, engendered by the same temporal context, has different expectations, because it is oriented to hearing sequential patterns instead of maintaining D-minor harmony. This hearing, encouraged by the recognition that measure 14 has the same intervallic structure as measure 12, thus projects a iv^6–V progression in "c minor" (352). Notice that this perception again involves a denial of the previous perception. And yet, because the last two perceptions involve coextensive segments, Lewin draws on Rameau's idea of *double emploi* to show how the same sound signifies a kind of f and d chord at once. For Lewin, traditional temporal parlance is not adequate to capture these distinctions because it assumes that a single event can emerge only within a single temporal frame. When the events of measure 15 confirm the sequential reading, a new connection is established with the A♭ in the bass in measure 9 (the former possibly an expanded recapitulation of m. 9) and the span from measures 9 to 15 sounds like an elaboration of dominant harmony in C major instead of C minor. This permits us to revisit the blues-perception of G minor once again, albeit from a different phenomenological space and time. In other words, it is not that we rehabilitate this perception, because, as Lewin says, it is "not necessarily 'really' dead," even if some perceptions took it that way.

For Lewin, the point is to hear the musical work as a complex structure of interrelationships, weaving different threads of perceptual meaning in different temporalities. Elsewhere he draws on Edmund Husserl's distinction between understanding the work as "*Gegebenheit* and *Dasein*" instead of as "*Sinn* and *Anwesenheit*," as "*given* and *there* (regardless of the temporal situatedness of the listener), not just *sensible* and *present*" (1986, 375). Although they are described in a style quite remote from Derrida, Lewin's irreducibly temporalized perceptions approximate the workings of Derrida's deconstructive phenomenological inquiries, especially his discussion of the sign's *temporization* (or the becoming-time-of space)—a notion that he also borrows from Husserl.[1] At the very least, Lewin's project resembles that of Derrida in the terms that Subotnik interprets the latter. It is wholly compatible with Subotnik's general description of an ideal way of listening. That is, while it might eschew the radical polyvalence of a genuine deconstruction (if only because of the conceptual limits it places on its "poetic" apparatus or the certainty with which it regards the horizons of the work), Lewin's analysis resists "fixing" musical structures (in the narrow manner that Subotnik associates with "structural listening") and precisely concerns itself with the "diverse, unstable, and open-ended . . . multitude of contexts in which music defines itself" that characterize "stylistic listening" (1996, 173; 175). I could also make the point that Lewin, like Derrida, asserts a kind of linguistic component for his model of listening, which irreducibly enmeshes these perceptions in socio-cultural forces that exceed the work's temporal enclosures. However, it should suffice here to note that, far from constraining the terms of listening in a pedantically technical vocabulary, Lewin puts a high premium on the task of raising perceptual possibilities, or even inventing categories of musical listening.

The general point I am trying to make is that Derrida, a crucial philosophical underpinning for the new critical musicology, shares various premises with Lewin, whose work is sometimes identified as formalist. In a commentary to *Music and Text: Critical Inquiries*, Hayden White, for example, writes that Lewin's reading of a phrase in Mozart's *Figaro* is "a rigorously formalist analysis of the score," which ignores an "ideological analysis of the extent to which it participates in or resists complicity with the dominant structure of social relationships, class and gender roles especially, of the historical moment in which they were composed" (in Scher 1992, 311; 313). Without denying that Lewin bypasses this order of social issues in his analyses, it is important to recognize that his *transformational* stance, which redefines various theoretical ideas in terms that are shot through with temporality (past and future elements) in the moment they are thought on the basis of the present, has important (if unexpected) affinities with deconstruction.[2] This kind of musical experience is thus constituted as a complex structure of transformational weaving, an interlacing that permits different threads of (what Joseph Dubiel might call) "sense" to tie up in different ways.[3] It is a musical system that closely resembles the non-representational model for language proposed by Derrida, and thus signals at least a simulative kinship between deconstruction and a close analytic listening. It might even be argued that Lewin's manner of close listening supplements the gap upon which our language to describe that listening rests. In other words, the omnitemporalized musical experience resists absorption into the discourse (with its spatializing tendencies) used to describe it. Thus, music, like dissemination, multiplies a non-finite number of semantic effects, which in turn breaks down a certain limit of the music/text, or at least prohibits an exhaustive checklist of its signifieds.

Perhaps the parallel between Derrida and Lewin, while unnoticed in new musicological writings, should not be that surprising. It is worth remembering, for example, that Derrida's philosophical perspectives are genealogically linked to nineteenth-century German metaphysical reflections precisely on the figure of music. This historical linkage further argues against construing music-formal and deconstructive premises antithetically. Since the invention of aesthetics in the eighteenth century philosophers have long taken music as a paradigm case for asserting a realm that is beyond the reach of linguistic signification and implicated instead in an ineffable higher truth about the workings of the world. Whether this interest took the form of Wilhelm Heinrich Wackenroder's idealism (in which music occupied a pure angelic domain independent of the actual world), or Arthur Schopenhauer's endlessly striving Will (to which music bore the closest of all possible analogies), or Nietzsche's Dionysian strain (which represented the rapturous musical frenzy that destroyed the veils of *maya* and freed us from norms, images, rules, and restraint), or Søren Kierkegaard's analysis of the absolutely musical (which best exemplified the highly erotic striving of the pure unmediated life force), music frequently served as a discursive site for speculation on the limits of philosophy, knowledge, and meaning. A central metaphor for that which resisted epistemological certainty, music in philosophical discourse functioned as a kind of discourse of the unsayable par excellence.[4]

Less apparent today is the way this kind of theorizing of fundamental negativity (which came out of German metaphysics) has impacted the current French philosophical, psychoanalytic, and literary-theoretical scene. While the explicit reference to music has receded in most poststructuralist writings, the form of the inquiry has not changed much. Like the older figure of music, the operations of deconstruction, for example, mark what is semantically slippery, and puzzle the divide between hardened historical oppositions. Coming out of the Hegelian principle of non-identity, what counts as meaning in the deconstructive account includes what is not said, what is silenced out of discourse, and that which impedes narrative coherence. Still, despite the general evacuation of thought about the purely musical, the metaphor of music is never far away in these later writings. In his description of the sound of the operatic voice, for instance, Roland Barthes isolates that which imposes a limit on predicative language as the "grain of the voice," the visceral materiality that escapes linguistic significance (Barthes 1985, 267–77). Julia Kristeva too points to the musical basis of a non-representational theory of language—one in which the "tone" and the "rhythm" of the pure signifier reverberates as if in musical space (Eagleton 1983, 188). And Derrida works out his notion of the *supplement*—the negatively privileged term that marks a semantic excess that cannot be subsumed into the discourse under investigation—in the context of Jean Jacques Rousseau's consideration of melody and speech in the *Essai sur l'origine de langue* (Derrida 1976, 141–64).

This rather complicated path in the history of philosophy via German metaphysics to poststructuralist French theory (to use shorthands) ought to disconcert both the view that thought about music somehow lags behind the recent theoretical developments in postmodernism, critical theory, and cultural studies, and the view that music figured as pure sounding forms in motion, precisely the discourse lacking significance, is somehow the antithesis of these developments. Broadly speaking, their historical affinities are more prominent than their differences. This is not to say that writers on music today are generally aware of music's influence on poststructuralism. On the contrary, the lack of historical perspective has frequently favored the view that music's aesthetic autonomy signals an unanchored (other-worldly) realm absolutely free of social considerations, instead of that it signals a resistance to a saturating taxonomy of its themes in the social world. As a result, certain forms of music theory that share a basic preoccupation with poststructuralist premises are routinely read as disengaged formalisms. It is this mistaken reading that I am trying to challenge here. Let me give another example.

On Benjamin Boretz and Ernesto Laclau

The thought of Benjamin Boretz (another apparent arch-formalist) can be productively compared with the second construal of deconstruction outlined above. Recall that this construal was less concerned with multiple readings of a musical passage (or linguistic text) and more concerned with showing how close reflection on some concept issues forth an encounter with the concept's wholly intimate other. Thus Boretz's reflections on the concept of "rhythm," say, can be shown to share a kinship with Derrida's reflections on "friendship" or Ernesto Laclau's reflections on "toleration".[5] Arguably, Boretz's work amounts to a deconstruction of the concept-metaphor under scrutiny. Again, this argues against contrasting deconstruction with formal musical analysis too vividly. Perhaps the radical decontextualization of the concept-metaphor under deconstructive scrutiny is itself a kind of formal musical activity—a suspension of a certain context in order to elaborate the conditions of the concept-metaphor's possibility and thus also to open up the logical horizon of its possibility. Let me explain.

In "Deconstruction, Pragmatism, Hegemony," Laclau is interested in thinking about the category of "toleration" as it might matter in the context of a radical democracy (1996, 47–67); in "In Quest of the Rhythmic Genius," Boretz is interested in thinking about the category of "rhythm" as it might matter in a work of Stravinsky (1971, 149–55). Both proceed by examining the conditions of possibility (and thus of impossibility as well) of the respective categories, starting with an effort to ground the categories in themselves. Both arguments proceed in a manner that resembles the early arguments of Hegel's *Phenomenology of Spirit*, by following a kind of *to-know-is-to-say* logic. That is, by taking the content-less categories at their word, as exhaustive or self-sufficient, these writers show how the intuitive content of these concepts is out of kilter with what they turn out to be when they are reflected upon or brought to articulation. For both, this attempt confronts them with two vanishing points. First, to be closed in themselves, these concepts must exclude that which is their other: on the one hand "intolerance," and, on the other, "non-rhythmic strata" (such as pitch or timbre) (Laclau 1996, 50; Boretz 1971, 151).

If the definition of toleration is taken as abstractly self-sufficient, Laclau argues, it would be logically possible to have a situation in which one "accepts tolerating the intolerant beyond a certain limit, one could end up with the installation of an entirely intolerant society under the auspices of toleration" (1996, 50). Absolute toleration, that is, can logically become intolerance. Alternatively, if the definition of "rhythm" is taken that way, it would be logically possible to infer the same rhythmic genius to a string of thirty-two equally-spaced metronome ticks as to the chord-repeating opening of Stravinsky's "Dance of the Adolescents" in his *Rite of Spring*. That is, if the (identical) pattern of attack points were the sole determinant of musical "rhythm," there would be no telling these examples apart.

On the other hand, it is plausible to think that other principles—not provided by the notions of "toleration" or of "rhythm" in themselves—can capture the necessary discriminations in these examples. This would solve the problem of what should and should not be tolerated with an appeal to some kind of limiting claim, perhaps a normative principle; and of what counts as a " 'transcription of the *[Sacre]* passage . . . with respect to 'preserving the rhythm,' " (Boretz 1971, 150) with an appeal to various limiting functional events in the non-rhythmic auditory dimensions of the piece. Boretz demonstrates how the rhythmic quality of any musical passage is inevitably beholden to aspects of timbre, dynamics, registral locutions and dispersions, polyphony, modes of articulation, concepts of pitch relation, tonal function, and extramusical predisposition. So, if these categories are to avoid the situation (issued forth by a self-grounded definition) of becoming their opposite, we must appeal to independent, or *supplemental,* contents that functionally guide our understanding of them. Both writers provisionally reverse the priority of the pure concepts and these seemingly infelicitous contents: the prior identification of supplemental normative criteria would disambiguate what should and should not be tolerated; and the prior identification of functionally significant non-durational events would specify which durations are relevant to a rhythm.

But this structural dependence on events outside of the categories' felicitous denotation confronts each writer with a second vanishing point: Laclau asserts that the terrain dividing the tolerable from the intolerable has been qualitatively transformed into one between "the morally acceptable and the morally unacceptable" (1996, 51). Thus grounding toleration "in a norm or content different from itself dissolves it as a meaningful category" (51). Likewise Boretz claims that grounding rhythm in non-rhythmic dimensions "deprives rhythm of its independent status as a musical stratum," and the concept ends up denying "the very intuition on which it is principally founded and by which it is principally motivated" (1971, 153).

Now, for both writers, this seeming deadlock also points to a solution, albeit not of the Hegelian sort. Laclau argues that, from the point of view of the content, toleration is meaningful only insofar as one accepts that which one finds morally disagreeable. Why should this matter? Perhaps because one has a political interest in a society that can cope with a certain degree of internal differentiation. From the point of view of the concept itself, toleration cannot be entirely without limit because of the necessary relation tolerance has to intolerance. That is, intolerance conditions the possibility and the impossibility of tolerance—it is an inevitable accomplice. Again the grounds for deciding what is and is not tolerant is a matter of political commitment: a "radical democrat" might want to cope with more differences than a supporter of the "moral majority" would (Laclau 1996, 51). Indeed, the struggle concerning the contents of toleration in any given society is made possible by the very lack of a necessary content in the term.

Boretz argues slightly differently: from the point of view of the content, rhythm is meaningful only insofar as it "subsum[es] every dimensional and inter-dimensional substructure" of the music under investigation (1971, 154). Why should this matter? Perhaps because one has a musical interest in a rhythmic theory that can cope with a certain degree of internal differentiation between different inter-dimensional settings. From the point of view of the concept itself, rhythm cannot be a mere matter of "timelength pattern[s] exhibited by an (auditory) succession" because of the necessary relation this has to any auditory event whatever (1971, 150). Again, the grounds for deciding what is and is not pertinently rhythmic is a matter of musical commitment: one theorist might want to say that rhythm is the least systematic of parameters, irreducibly contingent on particularities like pitch, polyphony, concepts of harmony, and extramusical predispositions, while another may want to say that not so many of these factors count in a discussion of rhythm itself. Perhaps the former orientation also prefers to focus on particular instances of rhythmic activity while the latter prefers the context of a general theory. Indeed, the debate concerning the contents of rhythm in any music-theoretical community is made possible by the very lack of a necessary content in the term.

The point of this comparison is to show that Boretz and Laclau share the same basic argumentative strategy. Both read deconstructively: a category of thought is placed under context-free investigation precisely in order to identify the conditioning grounds of its emergence. Both achieve this by way of a kind of Freudian "talking cure" that insists on articulating, or bringing to linguistic expression, the meaning of the concept. This illuminates the inadequate handle the expression seems to have on what the term takes itself to be. Where the line dividing the poles of the term and its opposite is drawn, is (speaking in terms of the duality itself) logically undecidable. (The opposition turns out to be more basic than either of its poles in itself; indeed the duality is the undecidable ground of possibility for both terms.) Finally, both accounts want to resist a general abstract theory of the respective concepts and to open the horizon of possibility for their coming to mean.

This is where the aesthetic imagination of music analysis can be productively set against the largely demystifying work of the new critically-oriented musicology. Indeed, the mere presence of poststructuralist premises in musicological discourse does not assure that these are productively implemented. Sometimes musicologists who explicitly reckon with such premises even close down their imaginative horizons. One might expect, for example, that a psychoanalytic inquiry into the subject of listening—whether this focuses on the listening subject or on the subjection of/through listening—would

make much of the extra-linguistic dimensions associated with the unconscious. As a continual activity of sliding signifiers whose exact meanings (signifieds) are beyond reach, Jacques Lacan's model of the unconscious, say,
can be said to have historical links to an essentially musical one. However, in
his book *Listening Subjects: Music, Psychoanalysis, Culture,* David Schwarz
approaches the subject in a surprisingly reductive way. Instead of figuring the
terrain of the absolutely musical as analogous to the movements of the
unconscious per se, his musical analyses, which for the most part are
beholden to texted music, usually take the argumentative form of some or
other musical "representation" of a Lacanian process. Let me demonstrate
this paradoxical problem.

On David Schwarz and Jacques Lacan

In an analysis that innovatively intersects the writings of Lacan and Heinrich
Schenker, Schwarz examines Schubert's "Der Doppelgänger" and "Ihr Bild"
from the cycle *Schwanengesang.* The analysis employs the categories of mirror misrecognition, the uncanny, and the drive. For example, in "Der Doppelgänger" the narrator's confrontation with his own double in the second
stanza is analyzed in terms of the psychoanalytic gaze. Lacan's concept of the
gaze *(regard)* is shaped by Sartre's claims in *Being and Nothingness* that "my
fundamental connection with the Other-as-subject must be able to be
referred back to my permanent possibility of *being seen* by the Other" (1992,
256–57). The gaze identifies the subject as essentially a "given-to-be-seen" (in
Lee 1990, 157). In other words, to grasp subjectivity outside of myself entails
the reality of being looked at. Lacan makes this Sartrean goal explicit:
"What we have to circumscribe . . . is the pre-existence of the gaze—I see
only from one point, but in my existence I am looked at from all sides" (in
Lee 1990, 156). Yet the gaze is not substantially tied to the actual presence
of another object or subject manifesting the gaze; in fact, it is "invisible" and
anonymous. Like the role of *Das Man* (the They) in Heidegger's *Being and
Time,* Lacan's gaze is the outside structuring activity—"the Other watching
me"—that lays down the conditioning grounds of the subject's existence.

According to Schwarz, "the musical signifier of the gaze [in "Der Doppelgänger"] is the pitch class F♯, which is ubiquitous in the music," while "the
musical signifier of recognition is the pitch class G as upper neighbor to F♯"
(1997, 66). It is true that the climactic G2 in measure 43 articulates the
"eig'ne Gestalt" with which the narrator is ultimately faced, but it is less clear
why the repeated F♯s signify the structure of the gaze. In Schenkerian terms,
the way in which F♯ elaborates scale degree 5 projects a kind of fixation or
stasis; an inability to unhinge the vocal line from its opening repetitions. Tex-
tually, this seems to conjure first the stillness of the night in which the poem
is launched, and second, a hitherto still latent inertia of obsession and

melancholy. Like the house at which he is staring, the narrator (still) finds himself standing "auf dem selben Platz" ("in the same place") in Heinrich Heine's poem. Harmonic activity is kept to a minimum and the melodic line circles tirelessly around F♯1. Finally in measure 25, the melody begins on a note other than F♯1. This is the moment in which another person enters the scene: the moment in the text plausibly suggestive of the drama of the gaze. This is the stanza in which the melodic line is unhinged from its repetitiousness and becomes energized in an upward sweep into measure 42. Thus, far from "signifying the gaze," F♯ seems to signal a kind of brooding stasis that *precedes* the imagined presence of another. And this presence is felt precisely by departing from F♯.

Given the social emphasis on the structuring activity of the gaze, it may be inappropriate to explain this romantic experience of a double in these terms. While the registral sweep from measure 25 to measure 41 ultimately settles on the pitches F♯ and G again, as if to lay bare the structure of the narrator's fixation, the process seems more narcissistic than social. After all, the gaze of the narrator's double is diverted (staring at the sky), while the Lacanian gaze is directed at the subject from a multitude of perspectives. More importantly, can the Lacanian gaze appropriately *be signified* by a pitch class? If the gaze is a kind of presentiment that lies behind conscious experience, the effect of which is manifested in that experience without itself being readily accessible to consciousness, can it be experienced through this repeated note? Or is F♯ a *representation* of the gaze? If so, why is the invisible and inaccessible gaze represented by that which is ubiquitous and compulsively repetitious, by the sound that is closest and clearest to our ears?

The problem with Schwarz's "representational" stance here and elsewhere in the book is that it does not bear the weight of the post-Freudian psychoanalytic apparatus at all levels of argument. Thus, while psychoanalysis in recent literary theory has served to disengage from interpretations of literary works as "expressions," "representations," or "reflections" of reality (understanding them instead as forms of production that effect a way of perceiving the world), Schwarz recapitulates the form of the former interpretations even if the "reality" his Schubert songs "represent" has been replaced by the real, the drive, or the gaze. It is as if these psychoanalytic modalities had already been established (thus functioning as the argument's signified) and the music was a representation (or signifier) of them. This pattern of thought, a site of desire all of its own, pervades the book.

In the discussion of "Der Doppelgänger," for example, Schwarz asserts that "E minor is the music's *objet a*, the signifier of the music's irreducible alterity" (1997, 70). In the discussion of Primus's cover version of Peter Gabriel's song "Intruder," a "listening gaze," whereby "the music [is] listening to us," is evoked "through the pounding bass guitar and percussion that accompanies the text throughout, sounding just on our side of the listening

plane" (1997, 97). Elsewhere, in a portion of Diamanda Galas's *Plague Mass,*
"B-flat signifies . . . the abjection of the voice stripped of its signifying function" (156). Thus the *objet a,* the gaze, and the abject are all positively elaborated by some musical sound: the suggested tonality of E minor, the pounding of a guitar and drums, and the note B♭ respectively. Strictly speaking, this
is not theoretically possible. The *objet a,* for instance, which by Slavoj Žižek's
account "is not a positive entity existing in space . . . [but] . . . ultimately
nothing but a certain *curvature of the space itself* which causes us to make a
bend precisely when we want to get directly to the object" (in Schwarz 1997,
160), exceeds signification; its presence is experienced only in the negative
form of its consequences.

Perhaps one interesting implication of Schwarz's positive account of the
objet a is the suggestion that the very act of hinting at a modulation somehow
elaborates a certain curvature of musical space. Thus a musical passage's *objet
a* is partly revealed when it seems to behave as if under the influence of a new
key without actually stating it. This suggestion is tantalizing and may be worth
exploring. In "Ihr Bild," for example, there is an interesting moment, deeply
embedded within the narrator's vision of the beloved's seemingly living
expressions, where the music seems to swerve from the possibility of changing mode. To begin with, the music contrasts stark octaves in B-flat minor of
"Ich stand in dunklen Träumen und starrt' ihr Bildniss an" ("I stood in deep
dreams and stared at her picture") with the naive, warm and obedient
chorale harmonization in the parallel major of "und das geliebte Antlitz
heimlich zu leben begann" ("and the beloved image secretly began to live"),
and so sets up a modal opposition between the quiet stasis of dream-like staring, on the one hand, and the exquisite satisfaction of secret fantasy, on the
other. But, unlike its minor counterpart, the major-mode material reveals a
vulnerability to inflection by the minor throughout the piece. In measures
10 and 12, for instance, the chromatic A♭ briefly reflects the mode of contrast
in phrases that are otherwise candidly in B-flat major. (In measure 10, the A♭
relates to C minor—to which triad it moves in measures 10–11—and in measure 12 it relates to E-flat major.) When the turn to (B-flat) minor becomes
more pronounced in measures 15–16 (as the beloved's lips appear to move),
the music turns out to be really becoming (G-flat) major. No longer even
noticing the fantastical dimension of what he sees, the narrator is drawn still
deeper into the object of contemplation: "Um ihre Lippen zog sich ein
Lächeln wunderbar" ("around her lips appeared a wonderful smile").

It is in the next phrase that the music seems to swerve away from becoming minor once more. On the last beat of measure 20, a chromatic passing
tone in the bass produces a ♭iv chord in G-flat minor, but it is denied any consequence. It is as if, after eluding the turn to (B-flat) minor in previous measures by elaborating G-flat major, the analogous possibility that minor can
haunt major in a different key as well must be repressed to sustain the secret

phantasmic activity. The passage continues in G-flat major, as if nothing had happened, by imitating measures 18–19 almost exactly. At this point, the narrator's vision has been enfolded by another layer of unreality; he begins to probe the imagined reason for the beloved's imagined tears—"und wie von Wehmutsthränen erglänzte ihr Augenpaar" (and, as if with tears of sorrow, her eyes shone). The point is that, while the previous phrase (mm. 15–18) takes seriously the possibility of changing mode, this one (mm. 19–22) represses it, and so betrays the desire to hold onto the major mode at all costs. Of course, G-flat major is more closely related to B-flat minor than it is to B-flat major, which (despite the music's efforts to avoid the sound of it) predestines the return of the minor to some extent. Also, the moment G-flat major seems to slip away in measure 20 (with a major-to-minor subdominant progression partly analogous to mm. 10 and 12), the chromatically descending bass line (E♭, E♭♭, D♭) also juxtaposes the enharmonic equivalents of the major and minor thirds of B-flat. And the fragility of this sustained fantasy (supported by a failure to modulate, by the haunting proximity of B-flat minor, and by faint references to both versions of the B-flat triad) is revealed in the next gestures (mm. 23–24) when the music is roughly yanked back to B-flat minor and the narrator finds himself reflecting on his own fixated condition once more.[6] This swerve away from the option of modulating may be figured in terms of a kind of musical bend away from the reality of one's condition on account of desire, a kind of paradoxical *objet a*. This is not to say the C-flat minor triad, for example, *represents* the *objet a*, but that the failure to change mode in its presence discloses the dimensions of that desire.

This kind of approach to the psychoanalytic dimensions of music could be broadened to include all musical moments (not only not-modulating ones) that reflect something out of sync with (what McClary might call) the "conventional wisdom" of a piece of music (2000, 1–31). By swerving from the music's syntactic or stylistic norms, the particular musical expression dialectically challenges the control of those normative generalities within which the piece operates. This is why the "representational" stance in *Listening Subjects* is problematic. It tends to disengage from such dialectical considerations and to analyze music's relation to psychoanalysis by way of one-to-one mappings. To take a paradoxical example from the analysis of Diamanda Galas, how does a note "*signify*" the abjection that "erases boundaries among . . . signifying categories" (Schwarz 1997, 157)? The traditional roles of music and language have been dramatically reversed here. Schwarz grants music the power to signify and represent in positive terms that which eludes signification, while linguistic signifiers are caught in a kind of musical sliding. So, while Lacan's model of language inherits the lineaments of the nineteenth-century philosophical figuration of music, Schwarz's "Lacanian" hearing of music inherits the lineaments of a pre-Lacanian model of language. The discourse traditionally lacking significance signifies and the tra-

272   MARTIN SCHERZINGER

ditionally signifying discourse becomes pure movement. The priorities have been reversed with frequently paradoxical results.

A second problem with the "representational" stance is the way the analyses often uphold a passive view of the psychodynamics at work. If musical processes *represent* psychoanalytic ones, they cannot move beyond them, mark *their* limits, or offer a space for radical contingency. This is troubling, if only because the work of art for Heidegger, Derrida, Lacan, and Kristeva (not to mention the musical work for Wackenroder, Schopenhauer, Nietzsche, and Kierkegaard) is endowed with just this rupturing potential. For Lacan, for example, painting provides a way out of the alienation of the gaze. By resisting the gaze through the intervention of the "real" in painting, the viewer is able to accept the subjectifying effect of the gaze and thus be freed from his/her search for satisfaction through fantasy. In contrast, Schwarz's music mainly *subjects*. His music is passively linked to some or other self-identical psychoanalytic dynamic: Schubert's "Der Doppelgänger" is a "musical representation of the . . . Lacanian enjoyment *[jouissance]*" (Schwartz 1997, 69), Peter Gabriel's "Intruder" "represents the . . . language-bound fantasy of power" (93–94), Diamanda Galas's cries and declamations are "representations of abjection" (160), and so on. Unless the analyses can be moved out of the logic of "representation" nothing else is foreseeable.

IMMANENTISM, IMAGINATION, AND POLITICS

Let me now suggest another distinction instead between, on the one hand, a "structural" listening (or a "stylistic" listening for that matter) that entails a notion of arrest, of limiting an interpretation, and, on the other, a "structural" (or again "stylistic") listening that opens doors of imaginative possibility. The first analytic orientation would yield an interpretation of music that is eternally firm, rendered immobile by a kind of self-announced, wholly immanent meaning. By "immanent" I mean an account in which everything that is analytically relevant persists within the system under investigation. Such an interpretation would recognize neither a disjuncture between what the musical event means and its *happening* nor any appeal to independent criteria. Perhaps a certain reading of Schenkerian analysis, one that reduces the *Urlinie* to some kind of essence; or perhaps a certain kind of set-theoretical reading, that hears various pitch-class sets as fixed (as nameable sonorities whatever their context) would count as such a limiting kind of approach. Perhaps, even, the technical language of music analysis generally, uninterested as it seems to be in permitting terms from ordinary language into its discourse, places music analysis in the domain of immanence, practically by definition. But, first, is this outer sign (the use of this language alone) enough to clinch the charge that this is a case of immobilizing our listening? I think the cases of Lewin and Boretz suggest that it is not always enough. Second, does the problem of immanence also haunt accounts that go beyond (what Subotnik calls) the "internal configuration" of the musical text (1991, 244)? I think the cases of Subotnik and Schwarz suggest that it can do so. Moreover, when we speak of hearing tonal music in terms of cognitive archetypes, for example, or when we speak about the conventional dimensions of music-making as already established and fixed, we risk immanentism. Subotnik, for example, renders "the common musical logic or well-established set[s] of convention" as "irrefutable" fact instead of as negotiable determinant (1991, 245). What I am suggesting is that we can build neat formalist circuits with hybridized language as well, maybe even more believable ones.

The second orientation for listening, the "opening-possibility" sort, is one that widens the horizon of musical meaning by marking various moments of musical undecidability. This approach would give rise to new perspectives and new ways of organizing musical sounds and their possible intersections with social meanings. At the same time, it would resist meanings whose unity is determined by the totalizing tendency (however grammatically fragmented and diverse its terminology may seem) that structures the multiplicity of the text.

With this distinction between analytic orientations in mind, my argument is now going to take an unexpected turn. While I prefer the latter imaginative and open-ended orientation, I want to argue that, even though both are highly relevant to aspects of the political, *neither of these ways of listening is inherently more politically or socially beneficial than the other.* In fact, I think that assessing the political use to which ways of listening or methods of musicological study can be put entails, first, an explicit formulation of the political problem that is disturbing one (at least in the background of one's work), and, second, a program that puts the former in service of the latter. To quote Derrida on the *Politics of Friendship:* "If the political is to exist, one must know who everyone is, who is a friend and who is an enemy, and this knowing is not in the mode of theoretical knowledge but in one of *practical identification*" (1997, 116). Now, even while this choosing of friends and enemies turns out to be a *mad* practice—a decision in the experience of the undecidable (radically unpredictable, radically contingent)—we are obliged to identify the contexts that factually limit structural undecidability if we want to institute political commitments.[7]

Now, I also think that *both* ways of listening I have just outlined ("immanentist" and "imaginative") can be, and often are, put in political service. Let me demonstrate this with examples. First, let me mention two examples of how a rigidly structural analysis of the immanentist and pedantically "limiting" sort can yield ideas that can be put to politically *progressive* use.

Example 1: By taking seriously Schoenberg's call for due attention to the abstract musical "idea," as well as Adorno's praise for Schoenberg's "negation of all facades" (in Subotnik, 1996, 150; 162), a music analysis of the music of Webern (explicitly linked to Schoenberg throughout Subotnik's text) that counterintuitively ignores aspects of "color," "medium," and "affect" (aspects of "stylistic listening"), and, in the domain of the brazenly "structural" alone, may issue forth a radical critique of gender hierarchy. The link between Webern's musical material and the then prevalent discourse of "inversion" suggests that the former was elaborating, however implicitly, an androgynous musical ideal. In Webern's terms, the new music's preoccupation with formal symmetries was an effort to transcend the gendered dualism of major and minor that culminated in an ungendered atonal musical space.[8] In short, reducing the music to its autotelic inner structural symmetries can contribute to imagining the institution of gender parity in the social world.

Example 2: By comparing the harmonic language, structurally speaking, of Shona *mbira dza vadzimu* music of Zimbabwe with the *nyanga* panpipe music of the Nyungwe of Mozambique or the kalimba and panpipe music of the VhaVhenda of South Africa, a musical analysis may show cultural resonances between these "tribal" groupings that traverse the political border of their respective modern nation-states. Thus, excavating various structural affinities in music can assist in rewriting the past in terms of a shared, instead of an irreducibly divided, history of southern Africa. In light of the legacy of colonial investments in the invention of tribalism in southern Africa, this music-analytic dogmatism can therefore challenge another, more virulent, dogmatism.[9] In short, the strategic mobilization of starkly closed musical structures can contribute to the freeing up of post-colonial social space.

Second, let me mention two examples of how a structural analysis—now of the imaginative and "opening" sort—might equally yield ideas that can be put to politically progressive use.

Example 1: By marking for consciousness that which is contingent and particular (or inherently multiple and undecidable) in music of the canon, close music analysis may disturb the unitary conception of the Western canon figured as a cumulative-evolutionary narrative. For instance, if an analysis of Beethoven's Violin Concerto is startled by the radical peculiarity of the D♯s that interrupt the respectable tonal behavior (in D major) of the first movement in measures 10 and 12, instead of with the way the movement's *Urlinie* realizes a latent world-historical trajectory, then Beethoven's organic connection to Perotin, Machaut, Josquin, Monteverdi, and Bach cannot be taken with too much confidence.[10] More generally, by resisting the reductive, predictive, and generalizing tendency of immanentist music analysis, imaginative close listening can encourage a social consciousness not wholly absorbed by (what Georg Lukács calls) the "reification" of capitalist rationality.[11] In other words, the imagination can supplement the gap upon which social conventions are founded, and thus contribute to the devolution of power in the political world. This is why Murray Krieger insists that the aesthetic "can have its revenge upon ideology by revealing a power to complicate that is also a power to undermine" (in Clark 2000, 1).

Example 2: By analyzing, for example, the perceptually beriddling (indeed undecidable) harmonic and rhythmic patterning of Zimbabwean mbira music, we may be, first, opening institutional space for African music's contribution to international musicological definitions and debates, and, second, staking a claim on the canon (globally conceived) for music in the marginalized world. First, the close analytic examination of African music's temporalities can revise our understanding of perceptions of meter and rhythm *in general*. In this way, imaginative analysis may help to *Africanize* those (Western) theories that go as universal. Second, the close analytic examination of African harmony can demonstrate aesthetic complexities that may encourage canonizing the music outside of the foreclosed categories of "world music."[12] This in turn can contribute to the structural uplifting of African music in global modernity.[13] Perhaps structural listening can therefore help some of us hear value where we heard none before. (Or does the supposition that structural listening, for example, is irreducibly *not* "applicable to music that falls outside the canon" [Subotnik 1996, 158] answer to another need—one that will not grant African music an unmarked entry into global modernity?)[14]

I am trying to say that there are political reasons for not turning musical formalism into a kind of Correct Consciousness taboo in the domain of cultural politics on the left. If it is true, as Subotnik maintains, that structural listening yields an "impression of objectivity," "a unifying principle [that] establish[es] the internal 'necessity' of a structure as tantamount to a guarantee of musical *value*" (1996, 158–9, italics mine) then why, in the wake of this knowledge, do we choose to turn away from structural listening instead of using its evident power to assign value to strategically reconstellate culture in terms that we prefer? Nietzsche's insight that we continue to hold on to certain truths and values even after they are shown to be based on error or on values that we do not agree with, makes me worry about giving up the compelling territory of structural listening just because some musicologists believe it is based on values they do not uphold. Rephrased in more recent parlance, just because the emotional investments and the hopes that people have are the result of what Laclau calls a "complex discursive-hegemonic construction" (1996, 63), and not the expression of an *a prioristic* essence, is no argument against their validity. If *this* scenario is right, then it will not do for us to *either* celebrate structural listening as upholding some criterion of truth *or* to recoil from its ideology in alarm. While it is true that formal approaches to the study of music are but interpretations, it is worth remembering that the McClary-like negation of all metaphysics, for example, which casts us forever out of the Eden of unmediated truth, is also an interpretation. And while it is true that formal approaches to the study of music inevitably close down various other approaches, it is worth remembering that such closure is a necessary condition for the openings it proffers. As Nietzsche writes in *Daybreak,* "One blinds some birds to make others sing more beautifully" (1997, 41). Let the structural riddles multiply! After all, if Nietzsche could hold *good* and *evil* to be gradations on a continuum, to be refinements of one another, how few risks must our musicology be taking to channel *ways of hearing* into irreducible opposites? How advantageous to life is the "Beyond" we imagine of "structural listening"?

NOTES

1. On *temporization,* see Derrida 1986, 1–28.
2. On "transformation," see Lewin 1987 and 1993.
3. On musical "sense," see Dubiel 1992.
4. On the "unsayable," see Budick and Iser 1989.
5. Boretz 1971, 149–55; Derrida 1997; Laclau 1996, 47–67.
6. It is important to point out that hearing this moment as a swerve away from the opportunity to modulate depends on noticing mm. 15–18 as yielding to that possibility. This, to my mind, is what distinguishes the chromatic inflection in m. 20 from those in mm. 10 and 12. Only after hearing the move to the contrasting key succeed in the previous phrase does the one in mm. 19–22 feel like an evasion. On the other hand, the tenuousness of the B-flat major music (embedded in the key of B-flat minor) makes it sound like the return of the octaves in m. 25 is all too due. I would like to thank Joseph Dubiel for prompting me to refine my analysis of "Ihr Bild."
7. Like those supplemental criteria that unexpectedly encroach upon the concept-metaphors of "friendship," "toleration," and "rhythm," the political efficacy of a chosen modality of listening to music is not logically entailed in that modality.
8. On the gendered history of major and minor and its undoing in the new music, see Webern 1975, 28; 37; 43; For an extended analysis of these relations, see Scherzinger 1997.
9. On the invention of tribalism in this part of the world, see Ranger 1985.
10. On the peculiarities of the D♯s in Beethoven's Violin Concerto and its connection to the practice of music analysis, see Dubiel 1996, 26–50.
11. On "reification," see Lukács 1971. On predictive and generalizing conceits in music theory, see Maus 1993.
12. On the strategic canonization of African music, see Scherzinger 2001.
13. By focusing on harmony instead of rhythm, this kind of analytic work might also demythologize the shorthand view that African music is predominantly "rhythmic." On the invention of African rhythm, see Agawu 1995.
14. Of course, Subotnik's critique is concerned with legitimating non-canonic

music and not with marginalizing it further (as I suggest here). My point is that legitimation cannot be achieved through the critique of an institutionally accepted method, but only—and then only *perhaps*—through a strategic use of the sanctioned method. Therefore, the critique of a method (on grounds of its exclusionary "inapplicability" elsewhere) paradoxically produces a lack of interest in its progressive potential.

AFTERWORD

Toward the Next Paradigm of Musical Scholarship

ROSE ROSENGARD SUBOTNIK

IN LOVING MEMORY OF MY MOTHER, BRUNA HAZAN ROSENGARD
(OCTOBER 17, 1909–JANUARY 1, 2004)

> *I want them to water-ski*
> *across the surface of a poem*
> *waving at the author's name on the shore.*
>
> *But all they want to do*
> *is tie the poem to a chair with rope*
> *and torture a confession out of it.*
>
> *They begin beating it with a hose*
> *to find out what it really means.*
>
> BILLY COLLINS, *"Introduction to Poetry"*

I can't cry over the Ecstasy of St. Francis, *or any other painting. I have joined the ranks of the tearless. Like other art historians, I am fascinated by the pictures I study, but I don't let them upset my mental balance. It's all right for a picture to be challenging, but I don't think of pictures as dangerous: when I look at an image it doesn't occur to me that it might ruin my composure, or alter the way I think, or change my mind about myself. There is no risk, no harm in looking. . . .*

Each idea from a book is like a little tranquilizer, making the picture easier to see by taking the rough edges off of experience. Once, it seemed there was nothing between me and the Ecstasy of St. Francis *but a foot or two of empty air. Now it's like peering between the shelves in a library: somewhere back there, beyond the wall of books, is the painting I am still trying to see. . . .*
[T]he picture no longer . . . matters to my life, only to my work.

> JAMES ELKINS, *Pictures and Tears*

Not to be able to distinguish the noble from the deplorable is morally obtuse. In the wake of Sept. 11 we may want, finally, to get beyond sentimental complacency about art. Art is not blameless. Art can inflict harm. The Taliban know that. It's about time we learned.

> RICHARD TARUSKIN, *"Music's Dangers and the Case for Control"*

The biggest block to sensuous enjoyment may simply be the strange painfulness that many of us feel when our minds are not occupied.

> JON SPAYDE, *"Born Sensuous"*

*The cultural prognostication biz is kaput. . . . [I]f it's a fool's errand to guess how a
war will change . . . the culture, that's only half of the equation. The other, overlooked
half—though just as impossible to guess—is how the culture will eventually change
the war. In America, our take on our previous wars keeps changing. . . . The way any
war looks to its veterans may be unrecognizable to cultural consumers a generation
hence.*

FRANK RICH, *"Close Reading"*

Diagnosing the present is a lot like predicting the future, only riskier. Both
require the deciphering of clues laid down in the past. Both require the passage of time for an assessment of their accuracy. But tellers of the future
(including astrologers, weather forecasters, and economists) are frequently
absolved of their miscalculations; everyone understands that although such
people look toward the future, they cannot actually see it. Diagnosticians, by
contrast, look toward the past, asking not only where we are but also how we
got there. Working with their backs to those of us who come after, they distract us from realizing that they, too, could not see the future. We forget how
different the present looked in its own time, to its own viewers; and we fault
those viewers for failing to imagine a future perspective (our perspective)
from which their miscalculations would seem so evident (and so avoidable).
Limitations are harder to forgive in a diagnosis than in a prognosis.

My notion of structural listening first took shape in late 1985, in the draft-
ing of an essay I had been commissioned to write under the title of "The
Challenge of Contemporary Music."[1] My reaction to this title, which I suspect surprised the editor who chose it, was to try to diagnose some of the reasons that the twentieth-century music most admired by academic scholars
and composers during the 1970s and 1980s had so little resonance for most
of the people—by which I mean Americans—I knew. When I decided a year
later to expand my discussion of structural listening into an entire article,[2]
the object of my intended diagnosis grew with it. On one level, I continued
probing the social isolation of twentieth-century art music by tracing references to structural values in writings by Schoenberg and Stravinsky,[3] the pair
whose perceived polarity had shaped so much twentieth-century composition, especially in the academy. On another level, I wanted to understand
how values of structural listening could play a dominant role in traditions as
divergent as Adorno's critical oeuvre, with its roots in Continentalist philosophy and German musical thought, and analytic music theory, with its affinities for what I had elsewhere called "Anglo-American empiricism."[4]

Both of those traditions had had an enormous impact on my own musical career, the former on my scholarship, the latter on my education more

generally. And the more I grappled with the notion of structural listening, the more acutely I sensed troubles in the musical world I inhabited. Why, in spite of my affection and admiration for my professors, had so much of my graduate training struck me as irrelevant?[5] Why did I so often resist reading scholarly articles on music? Why had my discovery of a gripping musical thinker, Adorno, endangered my survival as a musicologist?[6] Slowest to emerge, and hardest to confront, was this question: what in almost forty years of serious musical study had overlaid my childhood love of classical music with such burdensome feelings of anxiety and obligation?[7]

By itself, the notion of structural listening was not a sufficient answer to any of these questions. But using dialectic to tease out something I called "style" (which included sound and rhetoric[8]) from something I called structure helped me to identify certain things I wanted to incorporate into the study of music. On one side, I wanted thinking about music to intersect not just occasionally but constantly with the most exciting issues available to the mind: defining the good in life (moral philosophy and social theory) and in art (criticism and aesthetic theory). On the other side, I wanted to find ways of engaging with music that permitted me to say something valuable about a piece without invariably needing first to achieve mastery over every element of its formal detail. Most of all, I think, I was desperate for a norm of writing about music that centered on good and exciting uses of the English language, uses that banished technical signs to the extent possible and referred those remaining not, at least in the first instance, to scores or complex diagrams but to ideas in the writing itself. For me, at least, it was important to encounter such writing on a regular basis in order to sustain the intensity not only of my thinking about music but also of my feelings for the music I was thinking about.

Today it seems obvious that what lay at the heart of my essay on structural listening was a desire to diagnose the defects of a reigning scholarly paradigm so as to help make way for its replacement. But although I used the term "paradigm" in that essay (e.g. p. 173), and although Thomas Kuhn, who coined the usage, had published his *Structure of Scientific Revolutions* twenty-six years before my essay appeared, the term and its associated concept had nothing like the currency in the 1980s that they have today. Nor is that the only difference worth noting between the language and assumptions of the time in which I wrote that essay and the time in which I write now. Many of the differences that in retrospect seem most salient are essentially changes in style, changes no doubt connected to some broader changes, which I have analyzed elsewhere, in our conception of humanistic scholarship, from an enterprise grounded on foundational principles to an enterprise guided by an aesthetic sensibility.[9] Other differences are due, more simply, to intervening advances in research.

Thus on the one hand, the image I just used, of employing dialectic to "tease" one concept out of another, is today a commonplace; several of the contributors to this volume use it. In 1986, however, references to dialectic in English-language musical scholarship were distinctly uncommon, and the sensibility behind our current usage of the verb "tease" was probably not yet in existence. And at that time, on the other hand, after ten years of study, I was still making my way very slowly through the thicket of Adorno's musical writings. Even now, when young musical scholars have far more access to Adorno, few command an unimpeded view of his entire intellectual land-scape. Back then, most English-speaking musicologists experienced Adorno's terrain as a virtual wilderness, through which we hacked our way, one painstaking idea at a time.

Even more striking is the change in the status of poststructuralism. In the 1980s, Derrida and deconstruction, though old hat in American English departments, were still barely visible in American musicology.[10] My own familiarity with poststructuralism was less than a year old at the time I set out to write my essay on structural listening; the idea of including the term "deconstruction" in my title occurred to me only after the essay had gone through several drafts. Since that time, musical scholarship has assimilated the primary, or at least secondary, sources of poststructuralism, which have in turn profoundly affected its style. Today, indeed, the deconstructive mode of thinking permeates not only the entire academy but also everyday life. For evidence of this ubiquity one need look no further than the editorial pages of American newspapers where, after the catastrophe of September 11, 2001, variants of the following assertion turned up repeatedly: If we fight back against our enemies by [depriving suspects of their civil rights, turning our neighbors into objects of prejudice, accepting our government's policies uncritically, etc.], then we render ourselves indistinguishable from those we fight, and the enemy has already won. Twenty-five years ago, the punch line of this assertion—formulated in countless editorials, columns, and letters to the editor in 2001 as a surprising and sophisticated moral—might well have packed the sizzle of an ironic twist. Today that punch line carries little more charge than the fizzling current of a cliché.

Our culture's practice in deconstruction has honed our skill, to use Martin Scherzinger's felicitous terms, at "undercut[ting] [rather] than under-scor[ing] . . . opposition[s]" (above, p. 257). It has also made us expert at spotting a deconstruction that stops short of fully disarming a binary distinction. If the intended target of such a deconstruction is itself an ideology committed to boundaries and distinctions, then we can charge that deconstruction, in the manner of the September 11th cliché, with committing the very offense it attacks. Three contributors to the present volume in effect level this charge at my essay on structural listening. Tamara Levitz does so explicitly in advocating "an approach to listening in which structure is not opposed to history, meaning, or style, as Subotnik proposes, but [is] rather itself understood as immanently historically meaningful" (above, p. 71).

Joseph Dubiel does so without ever mentioning me, in his objection to an overly "restrictive" definition of " 'structure' as order" along with his suggestion that " 'structural' listening" is to be defined, if at all, not "by any characteristic of . . . *listening*" but rather "as a certain way of *thinking about* listening."[11] And Scherzinger levels this criticism at me several times, for example via his linkage of my work with the underscoring rather than the undercutting of oppositions, or in his suggestion that "the problem of immanence . . . haunt[s] accounts [such as Subotnik's] that go beyond (what Subotnik calls) 'the internal configuration' of the musical text."[12]

The thrust of these deconstructive objections is undoubtedly correct. Although I do believe (with Scherzinger's concurrence [above, pp. 255–56]) that I brought to my analysis of structural listening a well-developed dialectical sensibility, and that this sensibility allowed me to provide a useful analysis of autonomous structure as a sub-category of style, I readily acknowledge that I did not have the capacity in the 1980s to delimit structure to a degree compatible with a twenty-first-century deconstructive ethos.

Though hiding behind a time lapse does not tell the whole story. Whether or not the limitation I describe is a function of having matured under a different configuration of paradigms than did the contributors to this book, the truth is that even now, with a better understanding of my past limitations, I would resist yielding completely to a more up-to-date ethos. For one thing, such a capitulation might force me into positions I do not hold even now concerning the notion and the value of structural listening itself. The deconstructive objections to my critique of structural listening amount to a conflation of my critique with the concepts I criticize, all under the rubric of a (somewhat enlarged) notion of structural listening.[13] In effect, some scholars now view my critique of structural listening as itself a version of structural listening, with the result that it is not always clear whether their attacks on the notion of structural listening actually support or reject my critique of that notion. The paradoxes of deconstruction preclude any simple certainty that the enemy of one's enemy is one's friend!

But even if we do lump together my critique and its objects as older notions of structural listening, those notions had a useful, and perhaps salutary, conceptual firmness. However much we may have progressed beyond defining "structural" listening in ways that make it clearly distinguishable from other modes of listening, the notion retains considerable force on just that older level, a force demonstrated by the essays in this very book. Whether they expand it, or attack it, or fall back on it by default, these essays do not, by and large, move beyond an ability to imagine what a discrete mode of structural listening might be. In many instances, the conceivability of such a mode is precisely what allows the critics of that mode to lay out their arguments with confidence and gives those arguments their point. To disavow my role in perpetuating such a mode of structural listening might, in a small way, hasten the arrival of a day when we can no longer imagine such a notion of listening. I have no interest in such a day. My original essay made clear the value I attached to structural modes of listening even as I pleaded for the enlargement of musical study through the development of other modes.[14] I have not changed my mind on this matter.

Nor would I want, through disavowing a discrete mode of listening, to encourage, if only in a small way, the disintegration of scholarly confidence into unfocused subtlety. Beyond structural listening itself, I have ideological reasons for resisting a complete (post)modernization of outlook: as strongly as I support the nurturing of an aesthetic sensibility in scholarship, I am not comfortable with the prospect of losing all the strengths and priorities of the older, foundationalist paradigms. To put it in personal terms, if once I felt hopelessly (i.e., unemployably) ahead of American musicology in my penchant for dialectical thinking, now I am content to bring up the rear by defining oppositions in a way that allows for the integrity of each component. When Martin Scherzinger proposes a dichotomy between "an embrace of the tolerant coexistence of different readings" and "a structural undecidability . . . [resulting from] a trace of contingency lodged within the logic of any structure (at its origin),"[15] he is making a distinction between what he sees as my ideological position and a more current ideology to which he subscribes. Whatever the political possibilities of these positions, the former one, the one he attributes to me, is clearly compatible with traditional (prepostmodern) notions of liberalism. And although I would argue that my essay in fact makes allowance for Scherzinger's own position, that is, for a structural rather than a merely historical or contingent gap in the processes of communication,[16] I would acknowledge that traditional liberalism remains my position, even today.

The relationship between one's time and one's intellectual convictions is always worth reconsidering. I cannot protect those elements of my structural listening essay that seem outdated to a new generation from being read, at least in part, as evidence of my failure to imagine myself out of the present in 1986. Still, I hope that these elements will also be considered, at least in part, at face value. For in addition to arising in ignorance of a future that is now here, these elements also constitute an ideological position that I worked out when I was fully adult. What has changed in fifteen years is the genealogy I would ascribe to that position. Today, the ideological values underlying my essay on structural listening seem traceable less to the dialectical philosophy of Adorno, the primary subject of that essay, than to the liberalism of Leonard Meyer, in whose honor the essay was written.

Having now, through confession of my diagnostic sins, purchased absolution for those I may commit in making a prognosis, I have an enviable opportunity, in this afterword, to venture one or two predictions about the shape that American musical scholarship will take in the coming decade. The opportunity is doubly enviable because Andrew Dell'Antonio, in bringing together nine such diverse and original examples of new musical thinking, has provided an unusually rich basis for thinking about the future.

If it is fair to say that the present collection offers a window into the formation of a new paradigm for musical scholarship, which I shall henceforth call the "Next Paradigm," one prediction seems safe: that new paradigm will not concern itself, at least in the way I envisioned, with what I once called "stylistic listening." To the extent that the New Musicology, in its early stages, wanted an alternative to Structural Listening, it probably shared my vision of that alternative as a different sort of listening. Exponents of the Next Paradigm, as represented by the contributors to this volume, share the impatience of the New Musicology with old models of Structural Listening;[17] but with few exceptions, and those are largely illusory, the alternative they propose is not simply some different sort of listening. In this connection it may be useful to remark that the New Musicology has already become a target of frequent criticism in this collection. But it is even more important to note that representatives of music theory and analysis—formally oriented practices—may well be, in their various ways, the most outspoken critics of Structural Listening in this volume. Not one defends the concept.

This is not to deny a tone of defensiveness perceptible at times in essays concerned with music theory. This tone puzzled me for a while, until I realized that the negative elements in my critique of Structural Listening might have struck a nerve among scholars dedicated to formal analysis. Such scholars might even have seen my essay as part of a New Musicological onslaught on the very survival of their field. My slowness to draw these conclusions should not be taken as evidence of disingenuousness (or, I hope, stupidity) on my part. Nothing could have been farther from my thoughts in the mid-1980s than the idea that music theory might one day be an endangered species of scholarship. Though my essay on Structural Listening dealt with issues important to music theory, I gave little thought to theorists while I was writing it; the scholars I wanted to reach were musicologists. For the most part, I took musicology and music theory for essentially unconnected enterprises at that time, as they had been at Columbia University when I studied there in the 1960s.[18] Dell'Antonio's inclusion of theorists in this collection as well as the willingness of those theorists to participate in it are both signs that the Next Paradigm will involve convergences between musicology and music theory on many issues. The common aspects of the alternatives offered in this volume to Structural Listening are a case in point.

When Fred Maus makes his elegant diagnosis of traditional music theory as itself a kind of defense mechanism, he stresses not only the potentially overwhelming power of music but also the lengths to which analysis typically

goes to contain that power; in effect he presents the middle and late twentieth-century paradigm of theory as an attempt at total control.[19] In pointing
beyond that paradigm toward a new alternative based on "a tense, complex
relation of shared agency and responsibility," that is, toward a "positive
model of shared creation,"[20] Maus invokes two themes that underlie the reaction to Structural Listening of just about every writer in this collection. The
first, which I have already identified in connection with criticism of my own
work, is the need for musical scholars to collapse philosophical distinctions
between seemingly opposed concepts. The other is the need for musical
scholars to renounce mastery as a goal, or, for that matter, even as a virtue.
Both can be related to sensibilities as well as anxieties that were barely evident at the time I wrote my Structural Listening essay.

Of the first theme, good evidence is provided by the orientation of so
many essays in this collection away from the scrutiny of objects, and toward
reflection on the processes of analysis and interpretation themselves. Maus
himself, for instance, is primarily concerned not with the ways in which theorists analyze music but with the imagery in which they couch their analyses.
Paul Attinello's argument is designed to transform itself into an extended
meditation on the uses of self-reflexiveness in scholarship along with the
problems generated by such usage.[21] Mitchell Morris is at pains to think out
the kinds of conditions under which we could interpret music ethically. Each
of these enterprises can be described as developing a self-reflexive scholarly
tendency that I believe first emerged clearly with the New Musicology: the
shifting of focus away from the signified to the signifier.[22] At its best, this shift
can be associated with the refinement of a certain aesthetic sort of honesty,
whereby the scholar's constant self-scrutiny raises his or her sensitivity to any
false move.

Indeed, even granting that the title of this collection encourages certain
priorities and concerns, most of the essays here suggest a growing preoccupation among musicologists and music theorists alike with the act of listening itself; and concomitantly, an inclination not to disregard musical structures so much as to reconfigure all analysis of music within a larger analysis
of listening. This movement toward listening is most explicit in the sharply
contrasting, finely wrought efforts of Dubiel and Elisabeth Le Guin to distill
in its essence something like a bravely and exquisitely honest phenomenology of listening. That project quintessentializes the resistance to binary distinctions that clarifies, in turn, why the Next Paradigm does not simply
replace Structural Listening with some other type of listening. Subtly disas-
sembling and reassembling, teasing out and conflating components within
the experience of listening, these two authors do in an especially direct way
what most of their fellow contributors do in a variety of ways. They make it
more difficult for us to place definitional barriers around the notion of
"structure," and thereby to configure our own work as a hierarchy of clean

oppositions: between listening and structure on one level; between Structural and Nonstructural (say Stylistic) Listening on another; and to some extent, though more problematically, between experience and analysis on yet another.

The few exceptions that might be noted to this tendency are in large part, as I hinted earlier, more illusory than actual. Both Robert Fink and Tamara Levitz center their respective essays on the analysis of one specific musical work, and at that a canonical masterwork: Beethoven's Ninth Symphony in Fink's case; in Levitz's case, Stravinsky's *Rite of Spring*. No one, however, could mistake either of these essays for an exercise in structural analysis as practiced by the Old Musicology. The engine that drives Fink's essay, which pays every bit as much attention as Maus's does to the analyst's verbal imagery, is precisely the determination to undermine the mind-set that posits impassable barriers between "'music itself'" and interpretation, that is, between structure and hermeneutics.[23]

Levitz is in some ways more of a genuine exception. Philosophically she opposes binary thinking; and she severely criticizes Richard Taruskin for what amounts to the false resolution of a binary, that is, for his failure to acknowledge a contradiction between his "[campaign] to reintegrate ideological critique into the traditional discourse of music theory" and the grounding of his own analysis on a "'structural' theoretical approach."[24] Yet more perhaps than any other essay in this volume except Scherzinger's, Levitz's illustrates how difficult it is even for critics of binary oppositions to escape them.

One of Derrida's great insights, in formulating deconstruction, was into the inextricable dependence of argument on the language of positions it opposes. Scherzinger illustrates this inextricability when he opposes thinkers who are trapped by binaries to thinkers who undercut binaries. Here the deconstructionist imagery of infinite regress rears its familiar head. Similarly, what Levitz opposes to boundaries within the old theory and practice of Structural Listening is to some extent just another bounded concept of structure, expanded to incorporate, in admirably examined detail, the traditionally neglected parameter of dance. The whole point of Levitz's emphasis on dance can be read as a rebuke of older notions of structure for their narrowness. To put it another way, the very force with which Levitz and Scherzinger distance themselves from my binary conception of Structural Listening renders them dependent on that conception as a foil for their own arguments. And that dependence links them, oddly enough, with Dell'Antonio as in some ways the most direct heirs in this collection to my essay on structural listening.

Dell'Antonio, of course, sets out openly to build on the foundations of that essay, not to question them. In this, as in so many capacities (starting with the organization of this volume), Dell'Antonio is for me the disciple of whom every scholar dreams—the one who takes up where one has left off and goes someplace unimagined and far better.[25] On one level, he seems the biggest exception of all to the movement I have been charting in the Next Paradigm, away from my own binary thinking. Far from fleeing binary oppositions, Dell'Antonio's essay seems to revel in them: what makes his study so ingenious is precisely his ability to analyze a new cultural practice, watching MTV, by finding persuasive binary opposites to one after another of the elements I once defined in Structural Listening.[26]

On another level, however, Dell'Antonio's argument moves in the opposite direction of Scherzinger's and Levitz's. Whereas they renounce binary oppositions only to become caught up in them, Dell'Antonio's seeming embrace of those oppositions ends in his undercutting them. In shifting his attention from the canon to MTV, Dell'Antonio does not stop at suggesting that different musical objects invite different modes of listening. He further proposes that modes of listening essentially create their objects (p. 222); in making this proposal, he performs exactly the sort of anti-binary operation that typifies this collection of essays: he turns the analysis of music into a deconstruction of listening.

What Dell'Antonio conjures up here is the image of a quasi-Heisenberg effect, whereby changes in the act of listening unavoidably alter our definitions of what we listen to. This entire collection made me think in many contexts of such an image, as when Maus implies, in the final section of his essay, that recognizing the dynamics in current analysis might alter the demands we make on our musical culture (pp. 38–39); when Morris suggests that our moral sense may precondition what we define as structurally satisfying (p. 51); or when Scherzinger quotes Žižek's definition of an object as "a certain *curvature of the space itself* which causes us to make a bend precisely when we want to get directly to the object" (p. 270; italics Žižek's).

Levitz, too, evokes this image in the sense that her method of analysis not only expands the object she makes available but also alters the character of that object. For in moving from the fixed notation of a score to the historically and structurally more fluid domain of choreography, Levitz forces attention to the many aspects of music that cannot be fixed in a single, definitive form or traced to a single, controlling author (see below, note 27). In a sense this amounts to saying that she insists on infusing structural parameters with social ones, thereby rejecting a binary opposition between the two. Of the decision to fold society into analysis, which tempts every contributor to this collection except Dubiel, I regret I do not have the space here to say more. More immediately relevant, in any case, is the extent to which Levitz's turn toward indeterminate aspects of music—whether these involve the unrecorded movements of dancers or conflicting claims within an artistic collaboration—dovetails with the second principal theme that I have noted in this collection: the distrust and rejection of mastery as a goal, or even as a virtue.

On no topic discussed in this volume is there greater unanimity: every contributor casts doubt, at some level, on the possibility and value of mastery as a concept within the framework of studying music. Here, perhaps, is a common link to my criticism of Structural Listening, where many of the priorities I question, including a preoccupation with formal unity and an advocacy of stern formal attentiveness, have an affinity to ideals of mastery. In some instances in the present collection, writers reject the conception of the musical composition, even in the art tradition, as the outcome of a master's power to exercise total control. Levitz, as I have just indicated, presents the *Rite of Spring* as the often contingent product of a collaboration.[27] Attinello starts his essay with the implication that some works are better understood in terms of "violence, chaos, and attempts to stretch human perception" than as "experiments in organization, transformation, and sound."[28] Dubiel proposes viewing a Bach prelude as a configuration in which loose ends, such as an unrealized modulation, are not necessarily tied up by the conclusion.[29] In a similar move, Fink argues for hearing the Ninth Symphony as a work in which Beethoven acknowledges—or tries violently to conceal—his impotence to exert total formal control over his own material.[30]

More to be expected, no doubt, are denials of mastery in popular pieces, such as Dell'Antonio's observation that "[music] videos do not require structural integrity . . . in order to be effectively appraised" (p. 210). Still, what Dell'Antonio's formulation makes especially clear is the difficulty of wholly separating concepts of mastery within any musical work from attitudes about the acts of listening and judging. And indeed, one can argue that the turn away, in this volume, from associating musical works with mastery reflects the larger turn toward scholarly self-reflexiveness and, with it, a growing willingness to acknowledge a whole range of limitations—creative, theoretical, epistemological—to which composers and critics alike are subject.

Several contributors to this volume place particular emphasis on limitations that preclude any observer from attaining global command of a terrain. Attinello, for example, posits clear boundaries around our "window of understanding," outside of which lie things "we simply cannot [stretch far enough to] grasp" (or "would prefer not to understand") (p. 167). And Morris, denying that morality can be grounded on abstract, universal grounds, cautions that "understanding . . . the ethical import of listening" requires processes of specification; and that "the kinds of projects that grow from . . . this specification attempt to accommodate such variance that any statement will necessarily be incomplete."[31]

Not surprisingly, rejections of mastery are most often aimed in this book at specifically musical modes of reception: at listening, analysis, and criticism. Scherzinger articulates this rejection by referring to the unlimited semiotic dynamics set in motion by a composition.[32] Maus likewise, though in very different terms, locates a force against analytical mastery within music itself, which "has an invasive aspect, a way of dissolving a listener's control" (p. 31). Going on, as I noted earlier, to characterize musical analysis as a defense mechanism, whereby the theorist can attempt to appropriate control for the listener, Maus at the same time proposes a new model of music theory in which the listener would no longer desire complete control.[33] Dubiel's entire essay pursues a definition of hearing that "does not involve recovering every bit of detail that I can see (or think I see) in the notation. . . . Hearing something," he continues, "responding to it intensely and relevantly—may not involve mastering it."[34] Dell'Antonio complements his own dismissal of structural integrity as an internal requisite for music videos with an even more emphatic denial of what amounts to mastery as a precondition for listening competently to videos.[35] Citing Simon Frith as a source for the assertion that "incomplete and fragmentary appraisal is fast becoming the norm for all repertories," Dell'Antonio goes on to argue, in effect, that if performance (as opposed to a score) is taken as the fundamental condition of music, "then incompleteness is not necessarily an obstacle to the production or understanding of . . . meaning."[36] Le Guin sums up the position on mastery concisely and eloquently in her penultimate observation, "And so partiality, in both senses, reigns," though she alone, among all the contributors, conveys a tone of regret, as in her closing allusion to "an insuperably melancholy longing for the unity of interpretation with experience."[37]

"Unity of interpretation with experience" is surely the unspoken object within any notion of critical or analytic mastery: it is precisely what these, and any, scholars give up on when they renounce the claim to mastery.[38] Implicit in Le Guin's expression of regret is the acknowledgment of a discrepancy that preoccupies most of the writers in this volume: an imbalance between what we experience when we listen to music and the language through which we grapple with that experience. All of those concerned with this issue concede the inadequacy of any words we might choose, however carefully, to convey that experience in its fullness and specificity. At least two, Fink and Attinello, link this inadequacy to an ancient category that has enjoyed a widespread revival in recent decades, the sublime.[39] Both of these authors use the notion of the sublime to designate a situation in which artistic form points toward a violence of content that exceeds the powers of form to represent it.[40] In varying ways each author also suggests the extent to which analysis and criticism, when honestly confronting the sublime in art, will themselves encounter head-on the hardships of trying to capture a whirlwind in words.

But interpretive hardships of this kind are by no means limited to music of the sublime, or to the writings that address such music. As these and other contributors to this volume again and again make clear, the difficulties of articulating the inarticulable are construed within the Next Paradigm as the condition that underlies all writing about music. Scherzinger, for example, concedes those difficulties directly in his reference to "the gap upon which our language to describe . . . listening rests" as well as in his witty designation of certain efforts to transcend that gap as "a kind of Freudian 'talking cure' " (pp. 263 and 267). Dubiel invokes those difficulties both in his rejection of a one-to-one correlation between "a music-structural proposition" and the "audible" and in his insistence on "some articulable relationship between analysis and hearing" as the standard for analytical validity: the very strength of his insistence suggests how easily one may fall short of this standard.[41]

What emerges from these numerous invocations of semiotic inadequacies, difficulties, and gaps is the sense that the Next Paradigm is being shaped, in part, by doubts, and even a pervasive anxiety, about the status and future of writing. On one level the question being raised is this: in writing about music, what can one say that is valuable and true? The ongoing shift I cited earlier, from foundationalist principles to aesthetic sensibilities as a standard for appraising scholarship, has decreased the possibility of answering this question with authority; and the erosion of authority raises grounds for doubt, in turn, about the general importance of one's own work. When Dubiel advocates, for instance, that "the main value of [one's] analyses . . . be something like responsiveness,"[42] what warranty can he offer that the scholar's responses will have a claim on anyone else? Is his casual afterthought, that "a related value is frankness," intended to provide such a warranty? Is frankness sufficiently rigorous to prevent the collapse of the individual into the solipsistic? Le Guin and Attinello explicitly raise the specter of a merely private scholarly writing: Le Guin as an inherent danger in attempts at wholly conscious listening, without reference to scores;[43] Attinello in his ingenious suggestion that practice in self-reflexive writing might help us in our writing to distinguish "the generalizable or the communicable from the private or the contingent, from . . . more personal or accidental memories and wishes" (p. 171).

But beyond these specific and individualized worries lies a question about writing with larger and more ominous implications: rather than "What is it possible to write about music?" the question becomes, "Is it any longer possible to write about music at all?" Dell'Antonio goes a fair distance toward arguing that as new conditions of musical life take hold, writing may be superseded. Acknowledging the "apparent 'inarticulateness' " of typical responses to music videos, he goes on to observe that the "immediacy" evoked by music videos "discourage[s] the distancing required for the deployment of specific explanatory language," adding that the descriptive language involved in such responses loses its efficacy once the video is over.[44] What is at stake in questions about the prospects of writing under the Next

Paradigm is not just the legitimacy of any individual scholar's work but the future of musical scholarship itself. For young scholars in particular, that is cause for anxiety indeed.

My nerve in predicting the directions that musical scholarship may take does not extend to calculating odds on the survival of humanistic scholarship as a profession. But I will venture this much: the best way to protect the status of writing as scholarly paradigms change is for scholars to produce excellent new writing. It is my strong conviction that each of the essays in this collection meets that high standard. In concluding this afterword, I would like to dwell briefly on two that arouse in me much optimism about the future of musical scholarship, the first by Robert Fink, the second by Elisabeth Le Guin. Each is a tour de force: although both explicitly renounce the kinds of control that once informed standards of mastery, each displays a virtuosity that recalls old-fashioned ideals of richness in art. For each draws into its frame an ever-widening view of the past. One thereby closes, in a very satisfying manner, a circle in recent musicology. The other, which overwhelms us with the unexpectedness of its form, makes us want to rush headlong into the surprises of the future.

By no means the least appealing quality of Fink's essay is its suggestion of chivalry. Setting out to redress years of vilification directed at Susan McClary,[45] Fink mounts a rescue mission that has us sitting on the edge of our seats. There is a delicious pleasure in watching Fink knock off McClary's attackers. When he steps forth at the end to top McClary's accusation of rape with his own of murder, the susceptible reader may be tempted to swoon.[46]

The larger significance of Fink's success, however, comes from the utter persuasiveness of his brilliantly planned defense. No essay in this collection offers a more seamless or effective merger of hermeneutic interpretation with structural analysis. One would be hard pressed to find a better demonstration anywhere of how to make rigorous metaphorical sense out of formal relationships; so compelling is Fink's interpretation of the Beethoven Ninth that it just about succeeds in melting one's [my] resistance to reading about sharps and flats. By bringing in two centuries' worth of critical responses to the Ninth, and the theories underlying them, Fink gives his account of McClary historical authority while shining a torch on the context of McClary's critique itself.

Especially fascinating is the aesthetic conundrum that Fink embeds at the center of his enterprise, which he labels "Beethoven's 'aesthetics of failure.'"[47] This conundrum itself has something of an illustrious history. Mozart addressed one version of it in his famous dictum that even the most violent of passions must be presented in a musically pleasing way.[48] Schumann addressed another in his suggestion that the "[reign of] disorderly confusion" in the Finale of Berlioz's *Symphonie fantastique* is "only fitting for an infernal wedding";[49] and Tovey still another in his complaint about

French composers who seem to look on Berlioz's errors as the basis for a new style of composition.[50] Adorno hinted at yet another in his distinction between the socially induced "fissures and fractures" in a composition and "those [that] are attributable merely to the subjective inadequacy of the individual composer."[51] Reduced to its essentials, the conundrum amounts to this: how do we decide when disorder in music is legitimate?

By tying disruptions in Beethoven's Ninth Symphony to a cave-in of the formally controllable, Fink establishes the soundness of McClary's critique, on both musical and ideological grounds, and he confirms its importance. Fink is right to argue that McClary's confrontation of disturbance in a revered masterpiece presents us not with a sacrilege but with an opportunity. Her work enables us to gauge the full range of effects that can be exerted by art, including danger and violence, conjured up so wonderfully by Fink's candid-camera shot of Furtwängler and Goebbels at the Beethoven Ninth.[52]

Fink's announcement, at the outset of his essay, that he never took McClary's formulation as "an attack on Beethoven himself" (p. 110) quickened my pulse, for it at once brought to my own mind Edward Lowinsky's long-ago warning that I would come to rue a limitation I had imputed to Beethoven.[53] So it was with something of thrill that I came upon a direct quote, toward the end of Fink's essay, of the very remark that had once raised Lowinsky's hackles (p. 145). In choosing to quote this particular sentence from my work, Fink convinced me utterly of his sound historical instincts. He had drawn exactly the line that I would have drawn from my work to Susan's; and he thereby closed a circle between where she and I are today, on opposite coasts facing Fink's paradigm, and where we were thirty years ago, together in Chicago facing Lowinsky's.

Le Guin's achievement is of an order I have not encountered elsewhere. Like Fink's article, it never mentions my essay on structural listening; indeed it does not mention me at all. And yet I can think of no work that I would be happier to count in my legacy, no matter how distant or attenuated the connection. The originality of Le Guin's essay is so ferocious that it has an extraordinary enlivening effect. Reading it, I had much the same sensation that one might have in the first, scoreless hearing of an exciting new piece: holding my breath with each surprise, unable at any moment to anticipate where I was going, I had the sensation at every moment not of reading Le Guin's essay but of writing it. Even now, many months after I read it for the first time, just thinking about her essay makes me feel more intelligent.

What is there to say about an essay that manages to condense three hundred years of French art and thought into the bubble of a single musical experiment? For one thing, that the essay itself seems very French: in its choice of artists and thinkers; in its attachment to the Enlightenment; in the elegant simplicity of its experiment; in its projection of a visuality so vivid that one seems to read the essay to the accompaniment of an unfurling visual "soundtrack"; in its ability, within a remarkably few pages, to conjure up the spirit of Proust's great experiment. Or of Descartes'. Le Guin's way of undercutting the distinction between listener and object is to examine her own mind as she listens to Debussy's song "Soupir."[54] What she finds in her mind is an entire (French) world; how far is this from the *cogito*? Here, if anywhere, in this homage to French thinking processes, is a binary alternative to the turgid, score-driven following of Germanic symphonic structures!

Yet if in fact this experiment took shape, at one time, as a response to Structural Listening, it has transformed itself into an almost incomparably different sort of enterprise. Setting out to provide its readers with something as close as possible to an account of raw, unprepared, scoreless listening, this essay at once clarifies the virtual impossibility of separating raw hearing from verbal reflection. Very quickly it becomes an extended, rigorous rumination on the difficulties of writing about music—an inquiry, if you will, into the relationship between hearing sounds and choosing words. What Le Guin pins down, through her excursions into French literature, painting, and philosophy, is the almost unavoidably verbal character, with attendant consequences, of any attempt to capture the essence of a specific musical experience.

Turning the relationship between word and sound first this way, then that, Le Guin almost has us believing that all of French history was invented solely to answer her own question: how can we translate the experience of hearing music into words? Through charting the answers of one great Frenchman after another, she offers a probing analysis of what we do and think when we listen, while simultaneously conducting a seminar in French cultural history.

A few tools in her analysis are particularly useful. One, noted in her title, is description, her capsule history of which is alone worth the price of this entire book. Where Dubiel's phenomenology set "audible relevance" as a requirement for verbal analysis (p. 187), Le Guin's non-negotiable standard is description: "[A]nyone who is serious about making sense of the experience of art . . . [has] certain unavoidable obligations to Enlightenment practices and values, of which description is the linchpin" (p. 245). The paradox of description, she concludes, is that all the powers of its reasonableness cannot render it adequate to experience. Description is the function that confirms the insuperable insufficiency of writing; Enlightenment description gave way to "the Romantically indescribable."[55] Diderot himself, Le Guin tells us, who had presided over the glory days of description, was forced to abandon it once he understood its essential fictionality (p. 247); long before the twentieth century, it seems, Diderot had a clear glimpse of postmodernist epistemology. To retain any role for description thereafter entailed paying a Proustian—one might almost say Faustian—price: of all the images in this collection, none is more compelling than Le Guin's allusion to the elephantine disproportion of Proust's words, grown to eight volumes before it approached sufficiency to the chain of experiences set off by one bite into a cookie (p. 248).

Another tool is (the fallacy of) the synoptic gaze or capture, a concept that helps us to understand the fictions through which we transform multiple experiences into the illusion of one fixed image.[56] "[S]ynoptically 'appreciating' or 'capturing' the motion of music through time [means] a process of rendering it susceptible to description" (p. 242). Combining the synoptic illusion with still other conceptual tools, such as Husserl's bracketing, Le Guin goes a long way toward suggesting how our actual notions of the "engaged listener" may not match our preconceptions thereof (preconceptions that could include, I imagine, the Structural Listener).[57] By her account, "[W]rit[ing] of the agency of the [engaged] listener . . . [might mean] finding out, tracing through, explaining what might have been brought to bear on the listening experience at *any given moment*" (p. 248; italics hers).

This formulation has resonance in many directions. One paradoxical correlate is a Germanic world of overdetermination, as represented by the motivic web surrounding Wagner's characters as well as by the sources of Freudian dreams. But overdetermination is not limited to Germans; Proust's "nearly infinite regression of association" surely provides a classic instance (p. 248). For our own purposes, however, what is most important about this formulation is its apparent role in a new paradigm of how to analyze our listening experiences and, finally, of how to write about music. "[M]emory, association, and reflection," Le Guin observes, can all help us "tease[ ] forth" the "musical work as heard" (p. 247). Tempered by various disciplining factors—Le Guin mentions two possibilities, the restrictiveness of the visual score and the selectivity of Baudelaire's "memory"[58]—the rigorous non-linear process she describes might well replace efforts to engage in structural listening.[59] It might even constitute the paradigm underlying her own essay.

No contributor to this volume is more attuned than Le Guin to the long odds against writing anything true or valuable about music. In one guise or another she is constantly mentioning the problem. "[N]o matter how lucid, sensitive and perceptive the prose," she says at one point, "transparency is never achieved" (p. 246). Or again, Bergson's conception of musical reception lies "outside of the realm of the explainable, even the articulable" (p. 243). Note her own discouragement toward the end of her essay: "Specificity is much harder. . . . I am left, in the end, with an unfinished monument, a descriptional torso. . . . I am bold to consider myself able to account for even one [bar] in eight" (pp. 248–49).

And yet like Dell'Antonio in quite a different context (p. 220), Le Guin adds one other element to the paradigm she constructs for writing about music: performance. The "kind of description [that] unpacks the visualizing, concretizing, freeze-frame synoptic process, and 'musicifies' reception through description," she writes, amounts to "a readerly reconstitution of the art object . . . [which is] really a kind of performance" (p. 247). If Le Guin's essay exemplifies the new paradigm she is developing for writing about music, then writing about music is far from an insoluble problem. Le Guin's essay is not merely a performance; it is a bravura performance.

Although this essay makes no mention of Structural Listening, the underlying relationship does, in the end, seem clear: Le Guin has thought long and hard about the structuring of listening. I am pleased to have given her an occasion to present a piece of scholarship well beyond my own capabilities. The same holds true for the other essays as well. Each contributor to this collection has paid me the courtesy of using my essay on Structural Listening in some way as a point of departure for work I could neither have done nor imagined. Together they have given all of us in the older generation an incomparable gift: a mountaintop from which we can imagine, at least, that we see the future. And however much these young scholars may worry about the prospects for writing about music, their own accomplishments, as represented in this volume, are the best reassurance they could provide. The Next Paradigm of musical scholarship is in good hands.[60]

NOTES

Epigraphs: (1) Collins 2001, 16 ("Introduction to Poetry"); (2) Elkins 2001, x; 90–91; 92; (3) Taruskin 2001, 36; (4) Jon Spayde, "Born Sensuous: A User's Guide to Rediscovering Your Senses," *UTNE Reader* (November–December 2001), quoted by Leslie Brokaw, "Literary Life," *Boston Globe,* 19 December 2001: C:3; (5) Frank Rich, "Close Reading: On the Cultural Battlefields," *New York Times Magazine,* 23 December 2001, 19.

1. By Philip Alperson (who also chose the title), for his 1987 collection of essays by philosophers on music. Because of some unresolved editing problems in that version of my essay, I direct readers to the corrected and revised version in Subotnik 1991, 265–93. The discussion of structural listening appears in the latter version on pp. 277–83.

2. "Toward a Deconstruction of Structural Listening: A Critique of Schoenberg, Adorno, and Stravinsky." The first version of this article appeared in a Festschrift for Leonard Meyer (Narmour and Solie 1988, 87–122). For a brief account of how this essay originated, see Subotnik 1996, xxxii–xxxiii; see also below, note 18. The version to which this afterword will refer, cited hereafter as "Subotnik 1996, 'Structural Listening,' " is the revised version that appears in Subotnik 1996, 148–76.

3. The authorship of Stravinsky's *Poetics* has never seemed in doubt to me. It is a well-established tradition of ghostwriting that the work belongs to the public claimant, not to the private writer. In terms of this tradition, Alexis Roland-Manuel has no more claim to the *Poetics* than does Alex Haley to *The Autobiography of Malcolm X.*

4. On Anglo-American empiricism see "The Role of Ideology in the Study of Western Music," in Subotnik 1991, 3–14. The widespread influence of Schenker's and Schoenberg's theories confounds, of course, any clean or thoroughgoing division between Germanic and Anglo-American schools of musical thought, except perhaps

to the extent that English-speaking theorists distance themselves from Schenker's metaphysics or Schoenberg's bent for reflection.

5. It felt irrelevant, that is, not to a career in musicology but to what I had imagined would be the life of the mind. I felt this even at Columbia, where I had the chance to take fascinating courses with Edward Lippman in the Music Department and Richard Kuhns and Albert Hofstadter in the Philosophy Department as well as the life-changing cross-disciplinary doctoral seminar given by Jacques Barzun and Lionel Trilling. I doubt I would have lasted in most other musicology programs at that time.

6. For an extended analysis of the intellectual excitement generated after 1960 by writers of scholarly musical criticism, including Joseph Kerman and Charles Rosen as well as Adorno, see Subotnik 2002, 236–45.

7. On notions of obligation see Joseph Dubiel: "[I]t is important that I avoid any sense of obligation to listen to, or for, the particular facts the analysis manages to mention" (above, p. 198); and Elisabeth Le Guin: "I can 'hear what I ought to hear,' or rather, what as a musicologist I think I ought to hear" (above, p. 239).

8. For my definition of rhetoric see my essay "The Cultural Message of Musical Semiology: Some Thoughts on Music, Language, and Criticism Since the Enlightenment," in Subotnik 1991, 181–82.

9. See Subotnik 2003. My perception of an intellectual movement toward the aesthetic began to develop some years ago. See, for example, Subotnik 1996: "How Could Chopin's A-Major Prelude be Deconstructed," 238–39 (note 96); and "The Closing of the American Dream?," pp. 200 and 206.

10. It is worth recalling that Carolyn Abbate, who published *Unsung Voices* in 1991 and is today the doyenne of English-language musical semiotics, was not among those invited to the 1988 Dartmouth Conference entitled "The Musical and Verbal Arts: Interactions."

11. Joseph Dubiel, pp. 174 (restrictive), 175 (order), and 173 (thinking). Italics are his. Though Dubiel emphasizes "the possible discrepancy between an attribution of 'structure' and the experience, presumably *of* this 'structure,' that the attribution is meant to account for" (p. 187), this discrepancy seems to allow for a subtle incorporation of the notion of structure into the very definition of listening. Such an undercutting of difference would be unavailable to any mode of attention, which I assume includes my own version of structural listening, that seemed content to assume a "one-to-one . . . correlat[ion]" between analyzed structure and experienced structure (p. 187). Note in the phrases cited here Dubiel's characteristic inclusion of scare quotes to flag uses of "structure" and "structural" that do not have his approval; and see below, notes 13 and 41.

12. Scherzinger, p. 257 and p. 273, respectively. Relevant also to this line of criticism is Scherzinger's "skepticism about the distinction . . . between 'structural' and 'non-structural' listening" (p. 257); and his placement of the term "structural listening" in scare quotes, say, in the passage just cited or at the head of the section that begins on p. 256. See also below, notes 13 and 17.

13. See above, notes 11 and 12, and below, note 17.

14. See especially Subotnik 1996, "Structural Listening," 171–72.

15. Scherzinger, p. 258. See also below, note 24.

16. See especially Subotnik 1996, "Structural Listening," 168–69, where I suggest that "overtones of intervening knowledge and experience" are "essential [even

within a single culture] to the very possibility of communication." By contrast, Scherzinger (p. 258) stresses my emphasis on historical and contingent gaps.

17. Henceforth, the use of capital letters in the terms "Structural Listening" and "Stylistic Listening" will signify reference to those terms as used in Subotnik 1996, "Structural Listening." Such usages may include objects as well as processes, in contexts of defining or of criticizing either mode. See also above, notes 12 and 13.

18. Paradoxically, of course, Leonard Meyer, for whom I wrote "Structural Listening," was himself not only nominally a theorist but also the colleague for whom I, as a musicologist, felt the greatest intellectual affinity when I taught at the University of Chicago. But Meyer was altogether a maverick: incapable of confining himself within a single discipline (or of producing a dull idea), he was the one analyst on whom readers could always count, even in the years of the driest formalism, to keep them off-balance and interested. In developing my essay for his Festschrift (see above, note 2), I thought of Meyer neither as a theorist nor as an anti-theorist—much less as a target for criticism—but rather as a pioneering humanist who had eluded the pitfalls of Structural Listening and found a way to read music closely without severing it from emotion or meaning. In that sense, I have long considered him the father of the New Musicology at its best; in its fusion of musicological concerns with those of theory (in more than one sense), his work also seems seminal to what I am analyzing here as "the Next Paradigm."

19. See Fred Everett Maus, especially pp. 38–39.

20. Maus, p. 39. Although Maus refers explicitly here to the relationships between composers and performers and between performers and audiences, he also implies that under certain conditions, and at least with certain kinds of music, the same sort of model might be applied to the analysis of music.

21. See especially Attinello, pp. 171–72.

22. See Subotnik 2002, 247–50; also Subotnik 2003, 25–26. Of interest in this connection may be various images of art in Adorno's *Aesthetic Theory* suggestive of signifiers without signifieds. See, for example, the following passages in Adorno 1998: "Subjective experience contributes images that are not images *of* something" [italics his] (86); "Artworks bear expression not where they communicate the subject, but rather where they reverberate with the protohistory of subjectivity, of ensoulment" (112–13); "[Artworks] are the form of knowledge that is not knowledge of an object" (347); and especially the following observation, with its closing invocation of the Kantian sublime: "What speaks out of [art, through its nondiscursive language] is truly its subject insofar as it indeed speaks out of it rather than being something depicted by it. The title of the incomparable final piece of Schumann's *Scenes from Childhood*, 'The Poet Speaks,' one of the earliest models of expressionist music, takes cognizance of this. But the aesthetic subject is probably unrepresentable" (168); etc. Such images are powerful and complex though they should not be taken as evidence that Adorno countenances the absolution of artistic criticism from responsibility for the world beyond art; I consider this aspect of Adorno's thought in Subotnik 2002, 249–50. See also below, notes 39 and 55 on the sublime.

23. See Robert Fink, especially p. 112, where he defines a specific metaphorical interpretation "not [as] a distraction from form . . . but [as] a powerful analytical key to just those formal questions it was thought to displace"; also pp. 124–25 on van den Toorn.

24. The terms of this sentence are brought together from Levitz, p. 74. Her presentation of Taruskin seems to me, in spite of itself, to confirm the value of the dialectic that Taruskin in effect proposes between structure and social analysis. Taruskin strikes me as right to insist that his "claim [about Stravinsky] is just one of many possible claims" (Mitchinson 2001, 39); in the same way, Levitz's core evidence of the Chosen One's independence—the Chosen One's use of "specific gestures" choreographed "note for note" (p. 85) to the music—could as well be read as evidence for the character's lack of independence, that is, for her status as puppet, or even slave, in relation to Stravinsky's music. Though perhaps my making these suggestions merely confirms that Taruskin and I are both stuck in Scherzinger's earlier stage of deconstruction, the liberal stage, wherein we lean toward conceding the coexistence of discrete interpretations; see above, note 15.

25. Andrew Dell'Antonio's review of my second book, *Deconstructive Variations* (Subotnik 1996), demands special appreciation in this regard (see Dell'Antonio 1998). If one wanted to make the case against a structural gap in the communication between writer and reader, that review would provide a splendid piece of evidence. Reading it, I had the sensation that Dell'Antonio had thought his way into my brain, understanding my aims, concerns, and priorities from the inside out, exactly as I had hoped they would be understood—and then synthesized and articulated them in ways that I could not have done myself. The generosity of his willingness to understand me on my own terms was unqualified and rare; I don't know, obviously, if those qualities played a role when *Notes* chose this piece in 2000 for its Eva Judd O'Meara Award (annual award for best review published in *Notes*).

26. One additional binary that Dell'Antonio does not specify but nevertheless strongly suggests is an opposition between Adorno, as associated with structural listening, and Walter Benjamin, whose notion of distraction (Benjamin 1969, 239–40) bears such close affinities to the kinds of attention Dell'Antonio reports as directed at MTV.

27. See especially Levitz, p. 98: "[The] historically contingent work [of Stravinsky, Nijinsky, and Piltz] demonstrated the limitation of any project that tried to define *Le Sacre* as an expression of an objective spirit, essentialist politics, or of pure reason based on structural listening." Also worth mentioning in this connection is the negative force of collaboration that Levitz invokes in her memorable image of Adorno and Taruskin as figures who have "donned the bearskins and joined the elders, to sit in the circle with Stravinsky and watch the Chosen One dance herself to death" (p. 79).

28. Attinello (p. 154). See also p. 170 for his use of a quote from the psychologist Louis Sass to the effect that "some . . . statements . . . may . . . be attempts . . . to express concerns that are just too all-encompassing or too abstract to be stated in clear and specific terms, even by the most clear-minded of speakers"; and pp. 168–69 for his questioning of "rigor."

29. See especially Dubiel, p. 193, where he rejects the notion that "nothing in a great piece is allowed to be lost," and his advocacy for the C-sharp minor Prelude in Book I of Bach's *Well-Tempered Clavier* as "in many ways a looser and more obscure composition than it initially seemed it was going to be" (p. 193).

30. See Fink, e.g. p. 125, on situations where "beautifying criticism's defensive focus on formal innovation ('new rules of the game' [a term taken from Lyotard]) would provide little protection, since the collapse of the masterwork's 'organic' form

would be precisely the issue"; and p. 130 for his characterization of the start of the recapitulation in the first movement of Beethoven's Ninth as "a violent acting out covering up a more fundamental formal impotence." See also p. 112, where he introduces his notion of "Beethoven's 'aesthetics of failure' "; and below, notes 47 and 50.

31. On rejection of universals, see Morris, p. 67; for the quotations see Morris, p. 58.

32. See Scherzinger, p. 263: "[M]usic . . . multiplies a non-finite number of semantic effects, which in turn break down a certain limit of the music/text, or at least prohibit an exhaustive checklist of its signifieds."

33. See Maus, pp. 37–38, on attempts to reverse control, and pp. 35–39, on a sado-masochistic model of listening, beginning, perhaps, with the sentence "This is starting to sound kinky."

34. See Dubiel, pp. 186 and 187. See also p. 198: "I've been talking about some musical percepts that don't carry the connotations of intellectual mastery."

35. See Dell'Antonio, e.g. p. 220, on " 'background' music," which "does not occupy a listener/consumer's full attention"; and p. 218, on the "Ideal Appraiser for a video" as "unfocused."

36. Dell'Antonio, p. 220. On the postmodernist turn in music from score to performance as a paradigm see Subotnik 1993 and Subotnik 2003.

37. Le Guin, p. 250. The last phrase is immediately preceded by a reference to "a real, Diderotic regret."

38. Thereby, in a sense, reintroducing binary distinctions into an epistemological pattern of infinite regress.

39. Beginning on p. 111, Fink structures his essay to a significant extent on Lyotard's distinction between the modern and the postmodern sublime. Attinello sets up his use of the sublime in his discussion of Rilke; see pp. 155 and 156. Le Guin in effect points to the notion of the sublime when noting that Enlightenment description was replaced by "the Romantically indescribable" (p. 245). An important musical analysis of the sublime appears in Adorno 1998, 196–99. See also above, note 22, and below, note 55.

40. On violence see, e.g. Fink, pp. 142–46, moving from McClary through the Reign of Terror and Furtwängler; and Attinello, p. 162, on the attempt of certain modern music "to blow the world apart."

41. Dubiel, pp. 187 and 175. On the latter point see also p. 187 on Dubiel's "strict interest in holding theoretical propositions to a standard of audible relevance [although] the ways of meeting this standard are meant to be multiple, even beyond anticipation." See also above, note 11.

42. See Dubiel, p. 198, for this argument and the following reference to "frankness."

43. See Le Guin, pp. 248–49: "[E]xpression and meaning would arise from what is essentially a sequence of minute surprises, the direction and referentiality of which would lie very largely in the listener's own private store of memory and association." See also below, note 58.

44. See Dell'Antonio, p. 217. Of importance to his line of reasoning is the argument he quotes (p. 217) from Simon Frith, that " 'the use of language in pop songs has . . . more to do with articulating a feeling than with explaining it.' "

45. The low point, which Fink does not mention, probably came when the *Reader's Digest* featured an item about McClary in its "That's Outrageous" column, contrasting the prestige of her MacArthur award against the scandal of her Beethoven criticism. I saw this item but cannot say in what year or issue.

46. See Fink, p. 146: "Insofar as the celebration of an ideal society actually *sounds like* a murder to us as listeners ('bludgeoning the piece to death' [see quote from McClary, Fink, p. 142]), it flirts with the collapse of societal order, as it flirts with the collapse of the musical form through which that order is embodied in sound" [italics his].

47. Fink, p. 112 and pp. 129–41. See also above, note 30.

48. From Mozart's letter of 26 September 1781 to his father, explaining his approach to Osmin's music in *The Abduction from the Seraglio:* "[P]assions, whether violent or not, must never be expressed in such a way as to excite disgust, and . . . music, even in the most terrible situations, must never offend the ear, but must please the hearer, or in other words must never cease to be *music*" [italics Mozart's]. See Anderson 1938, 1144. From Mozart's formulation, I have derived the term "Osmin's paradox," which I often use in class as a shorthand label for the conundrum I am describing here, in all of its various guises.

49. Schumann 1835, 234. See also Schumann's notion, in the same essay, that the "undistinguished" melodic character of Berlioz's *idée fixe* is suitable for representing "a persistent, tormenting idea," and that Berlioz "could not have succeeded better" through any other sort of melody "in depicting something monotonous and maddening" (242).

50. Tovey 1939, 44: "The canonizers (including the cleverest of all French academicians, Saint-Saëns) seem almost to wish to institute Berlioz's harmonic weaknesses into doctrines for the future." This formulation is not unrelated to Lyotard's concept, cited in Fink, pp. 124–25, that beautifying strategies of criticism solve disruptions in order by calling them "'new rules of the game.'" See above, note 30.

51. Adorno 1976, 63 ("Classes and Strata"). I discuss Adorno's treatment of compositional flaws in Subotnik 1997, 139.

52. See Fink, p. 145. David Josephson has kindly called my attention to the videotape *Great Conductors of the Third Reich* (produced by Stefan Zucher [New York: Bel Canto Society, c. 1997]). One clip shows Furtwängler conducting the closing sections of Beethoven's Ninth at a concert celebrating Hitler's birthday, on April 20, 1942. As the music ends and the applause begins, one sees Goebbels walk to the foot of the stage and Furtwängler lean down to accept his handshake. Josephson, a first-class historian and an expert on the exile of Jewish musicians from Nazi Germany, sees evident distaste in Furtwängler's bearing at this moment. But whether or not one shares Josephson's reading, one cannot miss seeing in this film the ease with which the music of the *Ode to Joy* serves the Nazi agenda on such an occasion. On page 7 of "Music in the Third Reich," the booklet that accompanies the *Great Conductors* video, Frederic Spotts notes that "The [Ninth] Symphony was a musical fixture on such celebratory occasions as Hitler's birthday." And indeed, the Furtwängler clip gives way immediately to another clip showing the close of the Beethoven Ninth, this one conducted by Hans Knappertsbusch, at a Nazi-sponsored occasion that took place either in 1942 or in April, 1943.

53. I recount the incident in Subotnik 1991, xv. The remarks Lowinsky questioned appear in the same source, 33–34.

54. The first of the *Trois Poèmes de Stéphane Mallarmé* (1913).

55. Le Guin, p. 245. The affinities of this notion to that of the sublime are obvious; see above, note 39 and also note 22.

56. See Le Guin, pp. 240–42.

57. See Le Guin, p. 248.

58. See Le Guin, pp. 249–50. Worth comparing, in this context, is the line of thought that takes Adorno from a consideration of the "process of internalization, to which music as a self-deliverance from the external world of objects owes its very origin," and of the "active experience of music [as consisting] in . . . an imagination that does justice to the matter" to a consideration of the possible benefits of "teaching . . . listeners truly to 'read' music, to enable them to appropriate musical texts in silence, in pure imagination" (Adorno 1976, 133–34). See also above, note 43.

59. The shift suggested here seems strongly related to a shift I discuss elsewhere, from structural explanations of compositions to genealogical explanations of the contexts, experiences, and other music absorbed into the process of composition. See Subotnik 2003, 24–25.

60. I wish here to express my regret that the shape these remarks took eventually excluded a number of topics I had initially hoped to address. Had I found a way to include them, I would have made considerably more references to essays in this volume. Among those topics, and the scholars involved, were these: analysis of the concept of self or subject (Maus, Morris, Attinello, Dell'Antonio); relation of musical scholarship to political or social analysis (Morris, Levitz, Dell'Antonio, Scherzinger); emphasis on the presence or absence of visual elements, including notions of the gaze and scoreless listening (Maus, Levitz, Dubiel, Le Guin, Scherzinger); and genealogical or dialogic modes of hearing and criticism (Morris, Levitz, Dell'Antonio; see above, note 59). Above all I regret having to renounce an extended discussion of ways in which the study of music is affected by the relationship of cognitive and moral concerns. Many philosophical issues have interested me over the years; but this difficult and unwieldy relationship has been a steady preoccupation, bordering on an obsession, that lies at the heart of almost every bit of writing I have done. Had I figured out how to focus here on the relationship of the cognitive and the moral to the aesthetic, the star of my afterword would have been Mitchell Morris, whose essay in this collection picks up that gauntlet and (to Americanize my sports metaphor) runs with it. If Dell'Antonio has inherited my structural listening legacy, Morris, the only one of the nine contributors who actually studied with me, has graciously presented himself in his essay as my philosophical heir.

BIBLIOGRAPHY

Acocella, Joan. 1987. "Photo Call with Nijinsky: The Circle and the Center." *Ballet Review* 14, no. 4:49–71.

———. 1991. "Nijinsky/Nijinska Revivals: The Rite Stuff." *Art in America* 79:128.

Acocella, Joan, and Lynn Garafola. 1991. "Introduction." In *André Levinson on Dance: Writings from Paris in the Twenties,* edited by Joan Acocella and Lynn Garafola. Hanover: Wesleyan University Press.

Acocella, Joan, Lynn Garafola, and Jonnie Green. 1992. "*The Rite of Spring* Considered as a Nineteenth-Century Ballet." *Ballet Review* 20:68–71.

Adair, Christy. 1992. *Women and Dance: Sylphs and Sirens.* New York: New York University Press.

Adorno, Theodor W. 1975. "Missverständnisse." *Melos* 17, no. 3 (1950). In *Gesammelte Schriften,* edited by Rolf Tiedemann, vol. 12. Frankfurt am Main: Suhrkamp.

———. 1976. *Introduction to the Sociology of Music* [1962]. Translated by E. B. Ashton. New York: Seabury (Continuum).

———. 1978. *Philosophie der neuen Musik.* Frankfurt am Main: Suhrkamp.

———. 1986. "What National Socialism has Done to the Arts." In *Gesammelte Schriften,* edited by Rolf Tiedemann, vol. 20/2. Frankfurt am Main: Suhrkamp.

———. 1997. "Stravinsky: Ein dialektisches Bild"; *Quasi una fantasia* (1963). In *Gesammelte Schriften* 16, edited by Rolf Tiedemann. Frankfurt am Main: Suhrkamp, 1978. Translated by Rodney Livingstone. New York: Verso.

———. 1998. *Aesthetic Theory.* Translated and edited by Robert Hullot-Kentor. Minneapolis: University of Minnesota Press.

Agawu, Kofi. 1993. "Does Music Theory Need Musicology?" *Current Musicology* 53:189–98.

———. 1995. "The Invention of 'African Rhythm.' " *Journal of the American Musicological Society* 48:380–95.

Allanbrook, Wye Jamison. 1983. *Rhythmic Gesture in Mozart: Le Nozze di Figaro and Don Giovanni.* Chicago: University of Chicago Press.

Alperson, Philip, ed. 1987. *What Is Music? An Introduction to the Philosophy of Music.* New York: Haven.

Anderson, Emily, ed. and trans. 1938. *The Letters of Mozart and His Family,* vol. 3. London: Macmillan.

Asaf'yev, Boris. 1982. *A Book about Stravinsky.* Translated by Richard F. French, introduction by Robert Craft. Michigan: UMI Press.

Attali, Jacques. 1985. *Noise: The Political Economy of Music.* Translated by Brian Massumi. Minneapolis: University of Minnesota Press.

Attinello, Paul. 1995. "Performance and/or Shame: A Mosaic of Gay (and Other) Perceptions." *repercussions* 4, no. 2:97–130.

Barkin, Elaine. 1979a. "Arnold Schoenberg's Opus 19/6." *In Theory Only* 4, no. 8:18–26.

———. 1979b. "play it AS it lays." *Perspectives of New Music* 17, no. 2:17–24.

Barthes, Roland. 1985. "The Grain of the Voice." In *The Responsibility of Forms: Critical Essays on Music, Art, and Representation.* New York: Hill and Wang.

Bataille, Jacques. 1986. *Erotism: Death and Sensuality.* Translated by Mary Dalwood. San Francisco: City Lights Books.

Baudelaire, Charles. 1949. "Le peintre et la vie moderne" (ca. 1860). In *Selected Critical Studies of Baudelaire,* ed. D. Parmée. Cambridge: Cambridge University Press.

Benjamin, Jessica. 1988. *The Bonds of Love: Psychoanalysis, Feminism, and the Problem of Domination.* New York: Pantheon Books.

Benjamin, Walter. 1969. "The Work of Art in the Age of Mechanical Reproduction" (1936). In *Illuminations,* ed. Hannah Arendt, trans. Harry Zohn, 217–51. New York: Schocken Books.

———. 1979. *One-Way Street and Other Writings.* Translated by Edmund Jephcott and Kingsley Shorter. London: Verso.

Benjamin, William E. 1981. "Schenker's Theory and the Future of Music." *Journal of Music Theory* 25, no. 1:155–73.

———. 1999. "Schenker's Theory and Virgil's Construction of the World." *Theory and Practice* 24:107–16.

Berg, Shelley. 1988. Le Sacre du printemps: *Seven Productions from Nijinsky to Martha Graham.* Theater and Dramatic Studies, no. 48. Ann Arbor: UMI Research Press.

Bergeron, Katherine. 1994. "The Echo, the Cry, the Death of Lovers." *19th-Century Music* 18, no. 2, 136–51.

Berghaus, Günter. 1993. "Dance and the Futurist Woman: The Work of Valentine de Saint-Point." *Dance Research* 11, no. 2: 27–41.

Bergson, Henri. 1959. *Matter and Memory* [1908]. Translated by N. M. Paul and W. S. Palmer. Garden City, N.Y.: Doubleday & Co.

———. 1983. *Creative Evolution* [1911]. Translated by Arthur Mitchell. Lanham, M.D.: University Press of America.

Bollas, Christopher. 1987. *The Shadow of the Object: Psychoanalysis of the Unthought Known.* New York: Columbia University Press.

Boretz, Benjamin. 1971. "In Quest of the Rhythmic Genius." *Perspectives of New Music* 9:149–55.

Boulez, Pierre. 1966. "Stravinsky demeure." In *Relevés d' apprenti,* ed. Paule Thévenin. Paris: Éditions du Seuil.

Brackett, David. 2000. *Analyzing Popular Music*. Berkeley: University of California Press.

Brandstetter, Gabriele. 1995. *Tanz-Lektüren: Körperbilder und Raumfiguren der Avant-garde*. Frankfurt am Main: Fischer.

———. 1998. "Ritual as Scene and Discourse: Art and Science around 1900 as Exemplified by *Le Sacre du printemps*." *The World of Music* 40, no. 1:37–59.

Brett, Philip. 1994. "Musicality, Essentialism, and the Closet." In Brett, Wood, and Thomas 1994.

———. 1997. "Piano Four-Hands: Schubert and the Performance of Gay Male Desire." *19th-Century Music* 21, no. 2:149–76.

Brett, Philip, Elizabeth Wood, and Gary C. Thomas, eds. 1994. *Queering the Pitch: The New Gay and Lesbian Musicology*. New York: Routledge.

Bryson, Norman. 1981. *Word and Image: French Painting of the Ancien Régime*. Cambridge: Cambridge University Press.

Budick, Sanford, and Wolfgang Iser, eds. 1989. *Languages of the Unsayable: The Play of Negativity in Literature and Literary Theory*. New York: Columbia University Press.

Bullard, Trumann. 1971. "The First Performance of Igor Stravinsky's *Sacre du Printemps*." Ph.D. diss., University of Rochester.

Burke, Edmund. 1757. *Philosophical Enquiry into the Origin of our Ideas of the Sublime and the Beautiful*. Harvard Classics, vol. 24, pt. 2 (1909–14). New York: P. F. Collier & Son Co.

Burnham, Scott. 1995. *Beethoven Hero*. Princeton: Princeton University Press.

Califia, Pat. 1988. *Macho Sluts*. Los Angeles: Alyson Publications.

Canudo, Ricciardo. 1914. "Manifeste de l'art cérébriste." *Montjoie* 1–2.

Chennevière, Daniel. 1914. "La musique chorégraphique." *Montjoie* 1–2.

Chua, Daniel. 1999. *Absolute Music and the Construction of Meaning*. Cambridge: Cambridge University Press.

Clark, Michael P., ed. 2000. *Revenge of the Aesthetic: The Place of Literature in Theory Today*. Berkeley: University of California Press.

Cody, Gabrielle. 1998. "Woman, Man, Dog, Tree: Two Decades of Intimate and Monumental Bodies in Pina Bausch's Tanztheater." *Drama Review* 42, no. 2.

Collins, Billy. 2001. *Sailing Alone around the Room*. New York: Random House.

Collins, Randall. 1999. *The Sociology of Philosophies*. Cambridge, Mass.: Harvard University Press.

Cone, Edward T., ed. 1971. *Fantastic Symphony* by Hector Berlioz. Norton Critical Scores. New York: Norton.

———. 1974. *The Composer's Voice*. Berkeley: University of California Press.

———. 1982. "Schubert's Promissory Note: An Exercise in Musical Hermeneutics." *19th-Century Music* 5, no. 3:233–41.

———. 1989. "Three Ways of Reading a Detective Story—or a Brahms Intermezzo." In *Music: A View from Delft*, ed. Robert Morgan. Chicago: University of Chicago Press.

Cook, Nicholas. 1988. *Analyzing Musical Multimedia*. Oxford: Clarendon Press.

———. 1993. *Beethoven: Symphony No. 9*. Cambridge Music Handbooks. Cambridge: Cambridge University Press.

———. 2001. "Between Process and Product: Music and/as Performance." *Music The-*

ory Online 7, no. 2 (April). http://www.societymusictheory.org/issues/mto. 01.7.2/mto.01.7.2.cook.html.

Cook, Nicholas, and Mark Everist, eds. 1999. *Rethinking Music.* Oxford: Oxford University Press.

Copeland, Roger, and Marshall Cohen, eds. 1983. *What is Dance? Readings in Theory and Criticism.* Oxford: Oxford University Press.

Craft, Robert. 1988. "The Rite: Counterpoint and Choreography." *The Musical Times* 129, no. 1742:171–76.

Curtis, Liane. 2000. "The Sexual Politics of Teaching Mozart's Don Giovanni." *The National Women's Studies Association Journal* 12:119–42.

Cusick, Suzanne G. 1994. "On a Lesbian Relation with Music: A Serious Effort Not to Think Straight." In Brett, Wood, and Thomas 1994.

———. 1999. "Gender, Musicology, and Feminism." In Cook and Everist 1999.

Cyr, Louis. 1982. "*Le Sacre du printemps:* Petite histoire d'une grande partition." In *Stravinsky: Études et témoignages,* ed. François Lesure. Paris: Éditions Jean-Claude Lattes.

———. 1986. "Writing *The Rite* Right." In *Confronting Stravinsky: Man, Musician, and Modernist,* ed. Jann Pasler. Berkeley: University of California Press.

Dahlhaus, Carl. 1987a. "Das Problem der 'höheren Kritik': Adornos Polemik gegen Strawinsky." *Neue Zeitschrift für Musik* 148, no. 5:9–15.

———. 1987b. " 'New Music' as a Historical Category." In *Schoenberg and the New Music,* trans. Derrick Puffett and Alfred Clayton. Cambridge: Cambridge University Press.

Davies, Stephen. 1999. "Rock versus Classical Music." *Journal of Aesthetics and Art Criticism* 57:193–204.

DeBellis, Mark. 1995. *Music and Conceptualization.* Cambridge: Cambridge University Press.

Debussy, Claude. 1971. *Monsieur Croche et autres écrits.* Edited by François Lesure. Saint-Amand: Éditions Gallimard.

———. 1977. *Debussy on Music.* Translated and edited by Richard Langham Smith. New York: Knopf.

Deleuze, Gilles, and Félix Guattari. 1977. *Anti-Oedipus: Capitalism and Schizophrenia.* Translated by Robert Hurley, Mark Seem, and Helen R. Zone. New York: Viking.

———. 1988. *A Thousand Plateaus: Capitalism and Schizophrenia.* Translated by Brian Massumi. London: Athlone.

Dell'Antonio, Andrew. 1998. Review of Subotnik 1996. *Music Library Association Notes* 54:894–97.

———. 1999. "Florestan and Butt-head: A Glimpse into Postmodern Music Criticism." *American Music* 17:65–86.

Denby, Erwin. 1977. "Notes on Nijinsky's Photographs." In *Nijinsky, Pavlova, Duncan* [1946], ed. Paul Magriel. New York: Da Capo.

Dennis, Christopher J. 1998. *Adorno's "Philosophie der neuen Musik."* Studies in the History and Interpretation of Music, vol. 58. Lewiston, N.Y.: Edwin Mellen Press.

Derrida, Jacques. 1976. *Of Grammatology.* Translated by Gayatri Chakravorty Spivak. Baltimore and London: Johns Hopkins University Press.

———. 1986. *Margins of Philosophy.* Translated by Alan Bass. Chicago: University of Chicago Press.

————. 1997. *Politics of Friendship*. Translated by George Collins. London and New York: Verso.

Diderot, Denis. 1875. *Œuvres complètes de Diderot, revue sur les éditions originales*. Edited by J. Assézat. Paris: Garnier.

Docherty, Thomas. 1993. *Postmodernism: A Reader.* New York: Columbia University Press.

Downes, Olin. 1935. *Symphonic Masterpieces.* New York: Dial Press.

Dubiel, Joseph. 1990. " 'When You are a Beethoven': Kinds of Rules in Schenker's *Counterpoint.*" *Journal of Music Theory* 34, no. 2:291–302.

————. 1992. "Senses of Sensemaking." *Perspectives of New Music* 30, no. 1:210–21.

————. 1996. "Hearing, Remembering, Cold Storage, Purism, Evidence, and Attitude Adjustment." *Current Musicology* 60–61:26–50.

————. 1997. "On Getting Deconstructed." *Music Theory Online* 2.2 (March 1996); reprinted in *Journal of Musicology* 15, no. 3:308–15.

————. 1999. "Composer, Theorist, Composer/Theorist." In Cook and Everist 1999.

————. 2000. "Analysis, Description, and What Really Happens." *Music Theory Online* 6, no. 3. Followed by a Response by Allen Forte, Dubiel's Reply to Allen Forte, and another Response by Forte; also by a number of relevant messages on *mto-talk.*

Dupuy, Dominique. 1995. "Entrer en notation: motus volant, scripta manent." In *La memòria de la dansa: Colloqui Internacional d'Historiadors de la Dansa, Barcelona, 27–30 Octubre de 1994*. Paris: A.E.H.D.

Eagleton, Terry. 1983. *Literary Theory: An Introduction.* Oxford: Blackwell.

Easton, Dossie, and Catherine A. Liszt. 1995. *The Bottoming Book, or, How to Get Terrible Things Done to You by Wonderful People.* San Francisco: Greenery Press.

Eco, Umberto. 1990. *I limiti dell'interpretazione.* Milan: Bompiani.

————. 1997. *Apocalittici e integrati: comunicazioni di massa e teorie della cultura di massa.* Milan: Bompiani. Original edition, Milan: Bompiani, 1964.

————. 1998. *Lector in fabula: la cooperazione interpretativa nei testi letterari.* Milan: Bompiani. Original edition, Milan: Bompiani, 1979.

Elkins, James. 2001. *Pictures and Tears: A History of People Who Have Cried in Front of Paintings.* New York and London: Routledge.

Elterlein, Ernst v. (pseud. Ernst Gottschald). 1853. *Beethoven's Symphonien nach ihrem idealen Behalt.* 3d ed. Dresden: Brauer, 1870.

Epstein, David. 1979. *Beyond Orpheus: Studies in Musical Structure.* Cambridge, Mass.: MIT Press.

————. 1990. "Brahms and the Mechanisms of Motion." In *Brahms Studies: Analytical and Historical Perspectives,* ed. George S. Bozarth. Oxford: Clarendon Press.

Ernest, Gustave. 1920. *Beethoven.* Berlin: Bondi.

Feyerabend, Paul. 1978. *Against Method.* London: Verso. Original edition, London: Humanities Press, 1975.

Fink, Robert. 1994. "Arrows of Desire: Long Range Linear Structure and the Transformation of Musical Energy." Ph.D. diss., University of California at Berkeley.

————. 1998. "Desire, Repression, and Brahms's First Symphony." In *Music/Ideology: Resisting the Aesthetic,* ed. Adam Krims. Amsterdam: OPA.

————. 1999a. "Going Flat: Post Hierarchical Music Theory and the Musical Surface." In Cook and Everist 1999.

————. 1999b. " 'Rigoroso (= 126)': *Le Sacre du printemps* and the Forging of a Modernist Performing Style." *Journal of the American Musicological Society* 52:299–362.

Forte, Allen. 1977. "Schenker's Conception of Musical Structure." In *Readings in Schenker Analysis and Other Approaches,* ed. Maury Yeston. New Haven: Yale University Press.

————. 1978. *The Harmonic Organization of "The Rite of Spring."* New Haven: Yale University Press.

Franko, Mark. 1995. *Dancing Modernism/Performing Politics.* Bloomington, Ind.: Indiana University Press.

Freud, Anna. 1966. *The Ego and the Mechanisms of Defense.* Translated by Cecil Baines with later revisions. New York: International Universities Press, 1966.

Freud, Sigmund. 1961. *Beyond the Pleasure Principle.* Translated by James Strachey. New York: W. W. Norton.

————. 1963. *General Psychological Theory: Papers on Metapsychology.* Edited by Philip Rieff. New York: Collier Books.

Frith, Simon. 1996. *Performing Rites: On the Value of Popular Music.* Cambridge, Mass.: Harvard University Press.

Garafola, Lynn. 1989. *Diaghilev's Ballets Russes.* Oxford: Oxford University Press.

————. 1999. "Reconfiguring the Sexes." In *The Ballets Russes and Its World,* ed. Lynn Garafola and Nancy and Norman Baer. New Haven: Yale University Press.

Gay, Peter. 1988. *Freud: A Life for Our Time.* New York: Doubleday.

Giertz, Gernot. 1975. *Kultus ohne Götter: Emile Jaques-Dalcroze und Adophe Appia.* Münchener Universitätsschriften 4. Munich: Kitzinger.

Gilmore, Bob. 1995. "Changing the Metaphor: Ratio Models of Musical Pitch in the Work of Harry Partch, Ben Johnston, and James Tenney." *Perspectives of New Music* 33:458–503.

Goehr, Lydia. 1999. Review of Roger Scruton, *The Aesthetics of Music. Journal of the American Musicological Society* 52:398–409.

Goldberg, Marianne. 1989. "Artifice and Authenticity: Gender Scenarios in Pina Bausch's Dance Theatre." *Women and Performance* 4, no. 2.

Goodwin, Andrew. 1992. *Dancing in the Distraction Factory.* Minneapolis: University of Minnesota Press.

Gracyk, Theodore. 1999. "Valuing and Evaluating Popular Music." *Journal of Aesthetics and Art Criticism* 57:205–20.

Gramsci, Antonio. 1975. *Quaderni del carcere.* 3 vols. Edited by Valentino Gerratana. Turin: Einaudi.

Griepenkerl, Robert Wolfgang. 1838. *Das Musikfest oder die Beethovener.* Leipzig. Quoted by Dieter Rexroth in *Ludwig van Beethoven Sinfonie Nr. 9,* ed. Rexroth. Pocket score. Mainz: B. Schott's Söhne, 1979.

Grossberg, Lawrence. 1993. "The Media Economy of Rock Culture: Cinema, Postmodernity and Authenticity." In *Sound and Vision: The Music Video Reader,* ed. Simon Frith, Andrew Goodwin, and Laurence Grossberg. London: Routledge.

Grove, George. 1884. *Beethoven's Nine Symphonies.* Boston, Mass.: Ellis.

————. 1896. *Beethoven and His Nine Symphonies.* 3d ed. London: Novello, 1898.

Guck, Marion A. 1993. "Taking Notice: A Response to Kendall Walton." *Journal of Musicology* 11, no. 1:45–51.

————. 1994. "Analytical Fictions." *Music Theory Spectrum* 16, no. 2:217–30.

————. 1997. "Music Loving, or, the Relationship with the Piece." *Journal of Musicology* 15, no. 3:343–52.

Gunter, Pete. 1983. "Introduction." In Henri Bergson, *Creative Evolution* (1911). Translated by Arthur Mitchell. Lanham, Md.: University Press of America.

Hanly, Margaret Ann Fitzpatrick, ed. 1995. *Essential Papers on Masochism*. New York: New York University Press.

Hanslick, Eduard. 1982. "Vom Musikalisch-Schönen." In *Vom Musikalisch-Schönen, Aufsätze, Musikkritiken,* ed. Klaus Mehner. Leipzig: Reklam.

Hargrave, Susan Lee. 1985. "The Choreographic Innovations of Vaslav Nijinsky: Towards a Dance-Theatre." Thesis, Université du Québec à Montréal.

Hart, Lynda. 1998. *Between the Body and the Flesh: Performing Sadomasochism*. New York: Columbia University Press.

Hill, Peter. 2000. *Stravinsky: "The Rite of Spring"* Cambridge: Cambridge University Press.

Hirata, Catherine Costello. 1996. "The Sounds of the Sounds Themselves: Analyzing the Early Music of Morton Feldman." *Perspectives of New Music* 34, no. 1:6–27.

————. 2002. "Analyzing the Music of Morton Feldman." Ph.D. diss., Columbia University.

Hodeir, André. 1961. *Since Debussy: A View of Contemporary Music*. Translated by Noel Burch. New York: Grove Press.

Hodson, Millicent. 1980. "A la recherche du *Sacre* de Nijinski." Issue on Ballet: Danse, *l'Avant scène* 3.

————. 1986. "Ritual Design in the New Dance: Nijinsky's Choreographic Method." *Dance Research* 4, no. 1.

————. 1987. "*Sacre:* Searching for Nijinsky's Chosen One." *Ballet Review* 15/3.

————. 1996. *Nijinsky's Crime against Grace: Reconstruction Score of the Original Choreography for* Le Sacre du Printemps. Stuyvesant, NY: Pendragon Press.

Hopkins, Antony. 1981. *The Nine Symphonies of Beethoven*. London: Scolar Press.

Horkheimer, Max. 1972. *Critical Theory*. Translated by Matthew J. O'Connell. New York: Seabury.

Horkheimer, Max, and Theodor Adorno. 1991. *The Dialectic of Enlightenment* [1944]. Translated by John Cumming. New York: Continuum.

Hugo, Valentine. 1971. *Nijinsky on Stage*. London: Studio Vista.

Hull, Kenneth Ross. 1989. "Brahms the Allusive: Extra-Compositional Reference in the Instrumental Music of Johannes Brahms." Ph.D. diss., Princeton University.

Husserl, Edmund. 1960. *Cartesian Meditations*. Translated by Dorion Cairns. The Hague: M. Nijhoff.

Jahn, Otto. 1882. *Life of Mozart*. Translated by Pauline P. Townsend. New York: E. F. Kalmus.

Jameson, Fredric. 1979. "Reification and Utopia in Mass Culture." *Social Text* 1.

————. 1981. *The Political Unconscious: Narrative as a Socially Symbolic Act*. Ithaca, N.Y.: Cornell University Press.

————. 1983. "Postmodernism and Consumer Society." In *The Anti-Aesthetic: Essays on Postmodern Culture,* ed. Hal Foster. Port Townsend, Wash.: Bay Press.

Jameux, Dominique. 1990. "Le *Sacre du printemps:* modernité, archaïsme." In Le Sacre du printemps *de Nijinsky,* les carnets du Théâtre des Champs-Élysées. Paris: Théâtre des Champs-Élysées.

Jaques-Dalcroze, Emile, ed. 1912/1913. *Der Rhythmus: Ein Jahrbuch* I and II. Hellerau: Hellerauer Verlag.

———. 1912. *The Eurhythmics of Jaques-Dalcroze*. London: Constable & Company.

———. 1965. *Le rythme, la musique et l' éducation*. Lausanne: Foetisch Frères.

Jeschke, Claudia, Ursel Berger, and Birgit Zeidler, eds. 1997. *Spiegelungen: Die Ballet Russes und die Künste*. Berlin: Verlag Vorwerk 8.

Joseph, Charles M. 1999. "Diaghilev and Stravinsky." In *The Ballets Russes and Its World*, ed. Lynn Garafola and Nancy and Norman Baer. New Haven: Yale University Press.

Kaplan, E. Ann. 1987. *Rocking around the Clock: Music Television, Postmodernism, and Consumer Culture*. New York: Methuen.

Kerman, Joseph. 1980. "How We Got into Analysis, and How to Get Out." *Critical Inquiry* 7:311–31.

———. 1988. "Taking the Fifth." In *Das musikalische Kunstwerk: Festschrift Carl Dahlhaus zum 60. Geburtstag*, ed. Hermann Danuser, Helga de la Motte-Haber, Silke Leopold, and Norbert Miller, 484–90. Regensburg: Laaber.

Kindermann, William. 1985. "Beethoven's Symbol for the Deity in the *Missa Solemnis* and the Ninth Symphony." *19th Century Music* 9, no. 2:102–18.

Kingsbury, Henry. 1988. *Music, Talent, and Performance: A Conservatory Cultural System*. Philadelphia: Temple University Press.

Kirstein, Lincoln. 1976. *Nijinsky Dancing*. New York: Knopf.

Knapp, Raymond. 1997. *Brahms and the Challenge of the Symphony*. Stuyvesant, N.Y.: Pendragon Press

———. Forthcoming. "Utopian Agendas: Variation, Allusion, and Referential Meaning in Brahms' Symphonies." In *Brahms Studies,* ed. David Brodbeck, vol. 3. Lincoln: University of Nebraska Press.

Komar, Arthur, ed. 1971. *Dichterliebe: An Authoritative Score; Historical Background; Essays in Analysis; Views and Comments*. New York: W. W. Norton.

Koozin, Timothy. 1999. "On Metaphor, Technology, and Schenkerian Analysis." *Music Theory Online* 5, no. 3.

Kopelson, Kevin. 1997. *The Queer Afterlife of Vaslav Nijinsky*. Stanford: Stanford University Press.

Krasovskaya, Vera. 1971. *Russian Ballet Theatre at the Beginning of the 20th Century*. Vol. 1, *The Choreographers*. Leningrad: Isskustvo.

———. 1979. *Nijinsky*. Translated by John E. Bowlt. New York: Schirmer.

Kretzschmar, Hermann. 1886. *Führer durch den Konzertsaal*. 4th ed. Leipzig: Breitkopf & Härtel, 1913.

Kuhn, Thomas. 1962. *The Structure of Scientific Revolutions*. Chicago: University of Chicago Press.

Kundera, Milan. 1991. "Improvisation en hommage à Stravinski." *L'infini* 36.

Lacan, Jacques. 1977. *Écrits: A Selection*. Translated by Alan Sheridan. New York: W. W. Norton.

Laclau, Ernesto. 1996. "Deconstruction, Pragmatism, Hegemony." In *Deconstruction and Pragmatism,* ed. Chantalle Mouffe. London and New York: Routledge.

Lang, Paul Henry. 1971. *Critic at the Opera*. New York: W. W. Norton.

Launay, Isabelle. 1993. "A la recherche d'une danse moderne: Étude sur les écrits de Rudolf Laban et de Mary Wigman." Ph.D. diss., Université-Paris VIII (Saint-Denis).

le Huray, Peter. 1979. "Music in Eighteenth- and Early Nineteenth-Century Aesthetics." *Proceedings of the Royal Musical Association* 40:90–99.

le Huray, Peter, and James Day, eds. 1981. *Music in Eighteenth- and Early Nineteenth-Century Aesthetics.* Cambridge: Cambridge University Press.

Lee, Jonathan Scott. 1990. *Jacques Lacan.* Boston: Twayne Publishers.

Lesure, François. 1980. Le Sacre du printemps: *Dossier de Presse.* Geneva: Minkoff.

———. 1990. "L'accueil parisien du *Sacre.*" In Le Sacre du printemps *de Nijinsky,* les carnets du Théâtre des Champs-Élysées. Paris: Théâtre des Champs-Élysées.

Levitz, Tamara. 2001. "In the Footsteps of Eurydice: Jaques-Dalcroze's Staging of Gluck's *Orpheus und Eurydice* in Hellerau, Germany, 1912." *Echo* 3, no. 2. http://www.humnet.ucla.edu/echo/volume3-issue 2/levitz/levitz1.html.

Lewin, David. 1982–83. "Transformational Techniques in Atonal and Other Music Theories." *Perspectives of New Music* 21, nos. 1–2:312–71.

———. 1986. "Music Theory, Phenomenology, and Modes of Perception." *Music Perception* 3, no. 4:327–392.

———. 1987. *Generalized Musical Intervals and Transformations.* New Haven: Yale University Press.

———. 1993. *Musical Form and Transformation: Four Analytic Essays.* New Haven: Yale University Press.

Lukács, Georg. 1971. *History and Class Consciousness: Studies in Marxist Dialectics.* Translated by Rodney Livingstone. Cambridge, Mass.: MIT Press.

Lyotard, Jean-François. 1984. *The Postmodern Condition: A Report on Knowledge.* Translated by Geoff Bennington and Brian Massumi. Minneapolis: University of Minnesota Press.

———. 1992. "Réponse à la question: qu'est-ce que le postmodernisme?" *Critique* 419 (April 1982). Translated by Régis Durand and reprinted as "Answering the Question: What is Postmodernism?", in *The Post-Modern Reader,* ed. Charles Jencks. New York: St. Martin's Press.

MacIntyre, Alasdair. 1984. *After Virtue: A Study in Moral Theory.* Second Edition. Notre Dame, Ind.: University of Notre Dame Press.

———. 1988. *Whose Justice? Which Rationality?* Notre Dame, Ind.: University of Notre Dame Press.

———. 1994. "Nietzsche or Aristotle?" In Giovanna Borradori, *The American Philosopher: Conversations with Quine, Davidson, Putnam, Nozick, Danto, Rorty, Cavell, MacIntyre, and Kuhn.* Translated by Rosanna Crocitto. Chicago: University of Chicago Press.

Mallarmé, Stéphane. 1985. "Crise de vers." In *Œuvres,* ed. Yves-Alain Favre. Paris, Garnier.

Manning, Susan. 1991. "German *Rites:* A History of *Le Sacre du Printemps* on the German Stage." *Dance Chronicle* 14, no. 2.

Marcel, Gabriel. 1958. "Bergsonism in Music" [1925]. In *Reflections on Art: A Source Book of Writings by Artists, Critics, and Philosophers,* ed. Suzanne Langer. New York: Oxford University Press.

Martinson, Harry. 1999. *Aniara: A Review of Man in Time and Space.* Translated by Leif Sjöberg and Stephen Klass. Brownsville, Ore.: Story Line Press.

Marx, Adolph Bernhard. 1859. *Beethoven Leben und Schaffen.* Berlin: Janke.

Maus, Fred Everett. 1988. "Music as Drama." *Music Theory Spectrum* 10:56–73.

————. 1991. "Music as Narrative." *Indiana Theory Review* 12:1–34.
————. 1992. "Hanslick's Animism." *Journal of Musicology* 10, no. 3:273–92.
————. 1993. "Masculine Discourse in Music Theory." *Perspectives of New Music* 31, no. 2:264–93.
————. 1996. "Love Stories." *repercussions* 4, no. 2:86–96.
McClary, Susan. 1987. "Getting Down Off the Beanstalk." *Minnesota Composer's Forum Newsletter* (February 1987). Reprinted in McClary 1991.
————. 1991. *Feminine Endings: Music, Gender, and Sexuality.* Minneapolis: University of Minnesota Press.
————. 2000. *Conventional Wisdom: The Content of Musical Form.* Berkeley: University of California Press.
McClary, Susan, and Robert Walser. 1990. "Start Making Sense! Musicology Wrestles with Rock." In *On Record: Rock, Pop and the Written Word,* ed. Simon Frith and Andrew Goodwin. New York: Pantheon.
McMylor, Peter. 1994. *Alasdair MacIntyre: Critic of Modernity.* London: Routledge.
McNeil, Jean, trans. 1989. *Masochism.* New York: Zone Books.
Meyer, Leonard. 1967. *Music, the Arts, and Ideas.* Chicago: University of Chicago Press.
Miller, William Ian. 1997. *The Anatomy of Disgust.* Cambridge, Mass.: Harvard University Press.
Mitchinson, Paul. 2001. "Settling Scores: Richard Taruskin Explores the Dark Side of Music." *Lingua Franca* 11, no. 5 (July/August): 34–43.
Morris, Mitchell. 1992. "On Gaily Reading Music." *repercussions* 1, no. 1:48–64.
————. 1995. "Admiring the Countess Geschwitz." In *En Travesti: Women, Gender Subversion, Opera,* ed. Corinne E. Blackmur and Patricia Juliana Smith. New York: Columbia University Press.
————. 1998. "Musical Eroticism and the Transcendent Strain: The Work of Alexander Skryabin, 1898–1908." Ph.D. diss., University of California at Berkeley.
————. 1999. "It's Raining Men: The Weather Girls, Gay Subjectivity, and the Erotics of Insatiability." In *Audible Traces: Gender, Identity, and Music,* ed. Elaine Barkin and Lydia Hamessley. Zurich and Los Angeles: Carciofoli Verlagshaus.
Narmour, Eugene, and Ruth Solie, eds. 1988. *Explorations in Music, the Arts, and Ideas: Essays in Honor of Leonard B. Meyer.* Stuyvesant, N.Y.: Pendragon Press.
Nef, Karl. 1928. *Die Neun Sinfonien Beethovens.* Leipzig: Breitkopf & Härtel.
Nietzsche, Friedrich Wilhelm. 1974. *The Gay Science (with a Prelude in Rhymes and an Appendix in Songs).* Translated by Walter Kaufmann. New York: Vintage Books.
————. 1980. *On the Advantage and Disadvantage of History for Life.* Translated by Peter Preuss. Indianapolis and Cambridge: Hackett Publishing Company.
————. 1986. *Human All Too Human: A Book for Free Spirits.* Translated by Marion Faber and Steven Lehmann. Lincoln and London: University of Nebraska Press.
————. 1989a. *Beyond Good and Evil: A Prelude to the Philosophy of the Future.* Translated by Walter Kaufmann. New York: Vintage.
————. 1989b. *On the Genealogy of Morals* and *Ecce Homo.* Translated by Walter Kaufmann and R. J. Hollingdale. New York: Vintage Books.
————. 1997. *Daybreak: Thoughts on the Prejudices of Morality.* Translated by R. J. Hollingdale. Cambridge: Cambridge University Press.
Nijinska, Bronislava. 1992. *Bronislava Nijinska: Early Memoirs.* Translated and edited by Irina Nijinska and Jean Rawlinson. Durham: Duke University Press.

Nijinsky, Vaslav. 1995. *The Diary of Vaslav Nijinsky.* Unexpurgated edition, ed. Joan Acocella, trans. Kyril Fitzlyon. New York: Farrar, Straus and Giroux.

Noyes, John K. 1997. *The Mastery of Submission: Inventions of Masochism.* Ithaca, N.Y.: Cornell University Press.

Nyman, Michael. 1999. *Experimental Music: Cage and Beyond.* London and New York: Macmillan, 1974. Reprint, Cambridge: Cambridge University Press.

Odom, Selma. 1997. "Nijinsky in Hellerau." In *Spiegelungen: Die Ballets Russes und die Künste,* ed. Claudia Jeschke, Ursel Berger, and Birgit Zeidler. Berlin: Verlag Vorwerk 8.

Ostwald, Peter. 1991. *Vaslav Nijinsky: A Leap into Madness.* New York: Carol Publishing Group.

Paddison, Max. 1993. *Adorno's Aesthetics of Music.* Cambridge: Cambridge University Press.

Pasler, Jann. 1981. "Debussy, Stravinsky and the Ballets Russes: The Emergence of a New Musical Logic." Ph.D. diss., University of Chicago.

Pirrotta, Nino. 1994. *Don Giovanni's Progress: A Rake Goes to the Opera.* Translated by Harris S. Saunders, Jr. New York: Marsilio.

Postel du Mas, Vivian. 1914. "Les caractères géométriques du danseur moderne." *Montjoie* 1–2.

Praz, Mario. 1970. *The Romantic Agony.* Translated by Angus Davidson. 2d ed. Oxford: Oxford University Press.

Rambert, Marie. 1972. *Quicksilver.* London: Macmillan.

Ramsey, Burt. 1995. *The Male Dancer: Bodies, Spectacle, Sexualities.* London: Routledge.

Ranger, Terence. 1985. *The Invention of Tribalism in Zimbabwe.* Gweru, Harare, Gokomere: Mambo Press.

Reich, Steve. 1987. "Notes." In his *Early Works: Come Out/Piano Phase/Clapping Music/It's Gonna Rain.* New York: Elektra/Nonesuch 9 79169–2.

Rich, Adrienne. 1973. *Diving into the Wreck.* New York: W. W. Norton.

Richards, I. A. 1964. *Practical Criticism, a Study of Literary Judgment.* New York: Harcourt, Brace.

Ricoeur, Paul. 1986. *Lectures on Ideology and Utopia.* Edited by George H. Taylor. New York: Columbia University Press.

Riemann, Hugo. 1880s? *Concert Program w/Analysis.* Unpub.

———. 1889. *Grundriß der Kompositionslehre (Musikalische Formenlehre),* Vol. I. Berlin: Hesse.

Riezler, Walter. 1936. *Beethoven.* Berlin: Atlantis.

Rilke, Rainer Maria. 1984. *Selected Poetry.* Translated by Stephen Mitchell. New York: Vintage/Random House.

Rink, John. 1999. "Opposition and Integration in the Piano Music." In *The Cambridge Companion to Brahms,* ed. Michael Musgrave. Cambridge: Cambridge University Press.

Rivières, Jacques. 1947. *Nouvelles études.* Paris: Gallimard.

Rolland, Romain. 1941. *Beethoven: Les Grandes Époques créatrices,* Vol. 4 (La Cathédrale Interrompue), 1 (La Neuvième Symphonie). Paris: Sahler, 1943.

Rosen, Charles. 1972. *The Classical Style.* New York: W. W. Norton.

Rousseau, Jean-Jacques. Undated. *Essai sur l'origine des langues* (1754). Edited by Pierre-Yves Bourdil. Paris: L'École.

Rubin, Andrew, and Nigel Gibson, eds. 2002. *Adorno: A Critical Reader.* Oxford: Black-well.

Said, Edward W. 1991. *Musical Elaborations.* New York: Columbia University Press.

Saint-Point, Valentine de. 1914. "La Metachorie." *Montjoie* 1–2.

Sartre, Jean-Paul. 1992. *Being and Nothingness: A Phenomenological Essay on Ontology.* Translated by Hazel E. Barnes. New York: Washington Square Press.

Sass, Louis. 1992. *Madness and Modernism: Insanity in the Light of Modern Art, Literature and Thought.* New York: Basic Books.

Satin, Leslie. 1990. "Valentine de Saint-Point." *Dance Research Journal* 22, no. 1:1–12.

Sauer, Wilhelm. 1958. *Beethoven und das Wesen in der Musik.* Berlin: Hesse.

Savran, David. 1998. *Taking it like a Man: White Masculinity, Masochism, and Contemporary American Culture.* Princeton: Princeton University Press.

Schenker, Heinrich. 1912. *Beethovens Neunte Sinfonie.* Leipzig. Vienna: Universal-Edition.

———. 1979. *Free Composition.* Edited and translated by Ernst Oster. New York: Macmillan.

———. 1992. *Beethoven's Ninth Symphony.* Edited and translated by John Rothgeb. New Haven: Yale University Press.

Scher, Steven Paul, ed. 1992. *Music and Text: Critical Inquiries.* Cambridge: Cambridge University Press.

Scherzinger, Martin. 1997. "Anton Webern and the Concept of Symmetrical Inversion: A Reconsideration on the Terrain of Gender." *repercussions* 6, no. 2:63–147.

———. 2001. "Negotiating the Music Theory/African Music Nexus: A Political Critique of Ethnomusicological Anti-Formalism and a Strategic Analysis of the Harmonic Patterning of the Shona Mbira Song Nyamaropa." *Perspectives of New Music* 39. no. 1:5–117.

Schoenberg, Arnold. 1978. *Theory of Harmony.* Translated by Roy E. Carter. Berkeley: University of California Press.

———. 1984a. "New Music: My Music." In *Style and Idea: Selected Writings of Arnold Schoenberg,* ed. Leonard Stein. Berkeley: University of California Press.

———. 1984b. "On the Question of Modern Composition Teaching." In *Style and Idea.*

Schumann, Robert. 1835. "A Symphony by Berlioz." In Cone 1971, 220–48.

Schwarz, David. 1997. *Listening Subjects: Music, Psychoanalysis, Culture.* Durham, N.C. and London: Duke University Press.

Sedgwick, Eve Kosofsky. 1990. *Epistemology of the Closet.* Berkeley: University of California Press.

———. 1993. *Tendencies.* Durham, N.C.: Duke University Press.

Small, Christopher. 1998. *Musicking: The Meanings of Performing and Listening.* Hanover, N.H.: Wesleyan University Press/University Press of New England.

Smith, Richard Langham. 1973. "Debussy and the Art of the Cinema." *Music & Letters* 54:61–70.

Snarrenberg, Robert. 1994. "Competing Myths: The American Abandonment of Schenker's Organicism." In *Theory, Analysis, and Meaning in Music,* ed. Anthony Pople. Cambridge: Cambridge University Press.

———. 1997. *Schenker's Interpretive Practice.* Cambridge: Cambridge University Press.

Solie, Ruth. 1988. "Beethoven as Secular Humanist." In Narmour and Solie 1988.

Sontag, Susan. 1966. *Against Interpretation.* New York: Delta.

Souriau, Etienne. 1958. "Time in the Plastic Arts." In *Reflections on Art: A Source Book of Writings by Artists, Critics, and Philosophers,* ed. Suzanne Langer. New York: Oxford University Press.

Spivak, Gayatri Chakravorty. 1976. "Preface." In Jacques Derrida, *Of Grammatology,* trans. Gayatri Chakravorty Spivak. Baltimore and London: Johns Hopkins University Press.

Stanciu-Reiss, Françoise. 1957. *Nijinsky ou la Grace: Ésthétique et psychologie.* Paris: Plon.

Steinbeck, Dietrich. 1987. *Mary Wigmans Choreographisches Skizzenbuch 1930–1961.* Berlin: Edition Hentrich.

Stoller, Robert J. 1991. *Pain and Passion: A Psychoanalyst Explores the World of S&M.* New York: Plenum Press.

Stravinsky, Igor. 1935. *Chroniques de ma vie,* vol. 1. Paris: Les Éditions Denoël et Steele.

———. 1962. *An Autobiography.* New York: W. W. Norton.

———. 1969. *"The Rite of Spring": Sketches 1911–1913.* Facsimile reproductions from the manuscript. Nevers: Boosey & Hawkes.

———. 1970. *Poetics of Music (In the Form of Six Lessons)* [c. 1942]. Translated by Arthur Knodel and Ingolf Dahl. Cambridge, Mass.: Harvard University Press.

———. 1984. *Selected Correspondence,* vol. 2. Edited by Robert Craft. New York: Knopf.

Stravinsky, Igor, and Robert Craft. 1962. *Expositions and Developments.* New York: Doubleday.

Stravinsky, Vera, and Robert Craft, eds. 1978. *Stravinsky in Pictures and Documents.* London: Hutchinson.

Strickland, Edward. 1993. *Minimalism: Origins.* Bloomington and Indianapolis: Indiana University Press.

Subotnik, Rose Rosengard. 1991. *Developing Variations: Style and Ideology in Western Music.* Minneapolis: University of Minnesota Press.

———. 1993. Review of Edward Said, *Musical Elaborations. Journal of the American Musicological Society* 46:476–85.

———. 1996. *Deconstructive Variations: Music and Reason in Western Society.* Minneapolis: University of Minnesota Press.

———. 1997. Review of Max Paddison, *Adorno's Aesthetics of Music. Journal of the Royal Musical Association* 122, Part 1:133–47.

———. 2002. "Adorno and the New Musicology." In Rubin and Gibson 2002, 234–54.

———. 2003. "Foundationalist vs. Aesthetic: A Cost-Benefit Analysis of the Changing Musicological Paradigm." in *Rethinking Interpretive Traditions in Musicology.* Proceedings of the International Conference at Tel Aviv University, Department of Musicology, 6–10 June 1999. Edited by Shai Burstyn and Zohar Eitan. *Orbis Musicae* 13:15–29.

Taruskin, Richard. 1988a. "The Pastness of the Present and the Presence of the Past." In *Authenticity and Early Music: A Symposium,* ed. Nicholas Kenyon. Oxford: Oxford University Press.

———. 1988b. Letter to the editor. *Musical Times* 129, no. 1746.

———. 1989. "Resisting the Ninth." *19th-Century Music* 12:241–56.

———. 1992. "She Do the Ring in Different Voices [Review of Carolyn Abbate, *Unsung Voices*]." *Cambridge Opera Journal* 4:187–97.

———. 1993. "Back to Whom? Neoclassicism as Ideology." *19th-Century Music* 16:286–302.

———. 1995. "A Myth of the Twentieth Century: *The Rite of Spring*, the Tradition of the New, and 'The Music Itself.' " *Modernism/Modernity* 2:1–26.

———. 1996. *Stravinsky and the Russian Traditions.* 2 vols. Berkeley: University of California Press.

———. 1997. *Defining Russia Musically: Historical and Hermeneutical Essays.* Princeton: Princeton University Press.

———. 2001. "Music's Dangers and the Case for Control." *New York Times*, December 9, 2001, Section 2:1, 36.

Taylor, Charles. 1989. *Sources of the Self: The Making of the Modern Identity.* Cambridge, Mass.: Harvard University Press.

Tovey, Donald Francis. 1935. *Essays in Musical Analysis II (Symphonies, Variations and Orchestral Polyphony).* London: Oxford University Press.

———. 1939. "Berlioz: Symphonie fantastique, Op. 14." In *Essays in Musical Analysis VI (Supplementary Essays, Glossaries and Index)*, 44–50. London: Oxford University Press.

Treitler, Leo. 1980. "History, Criticism, and Beethoven's Ninth Symphony." Reprinted in Treitler 1989.

———. 1982. " 'To Worship that Celestial Sound': Motives for Analysis." *Journal of Musicology* 1:524–58.

———. 1989. *Music and the Historical Imagination.* Cambridge, Mass.: Harvard University Press.

———. 1993. "Gender and Other Dualities of Music History." In *Musicology and Difference: Gender and Sexuality in Scholarship*, ed. Ruth Solie. Berkeley: University of California Press.

van den Toorn, Pieter C. 1987. *Stravinsky and "The Rite of Spring": The Beginnings of a Musical Language.* Oxford: Oxford University Press.

———. 1991. "Politics, Feminism, and Contemporary Music Theory." *Journal of Musicology* 9/3:1–37. Revised and reprinted in van den Toorn 1995.

———. 1995. *Music, Politics, and the Academy.* Berkeley: University of California Press.

Varilio, Paul. 1994. "Gravitational Space." In *Traces of Dance: Drawings and Notations of Choreographers*, ed. Laurence Louppe. Paris: Éditions Dis Voir.

Wagner, Richard. 1846. "Bericht über die Aufführung der neunten Symphonie von Beethoven im Jahre 1846, nebst Programm dazu." In *Richard Wagners Gesammelte Schriften und Dichtungen*, Band II, 56–58. 2d ed., Leipzig: Siegel's, 1887.

———. 1873. "The Rendering of Beethoven's Ninth Symphony." In *Prose Works V*, trans. Ellis, 231–53. London, 1898.

Wallace, Robin. 1986. *Beethoven's Critics: Aesthetic Dilemmas and Resolutions during his Lifetime.* Cambridge: Cambridge University Press.

Walser, Robert. 1994. "Prince as Queer Poststructuralist." *Popular Music and Society* 18, no. 2:79–89.

Walton, Kendall. 1990. *Mimesis as Make-Believe: On the Foundations of the Representational Arts.* Cambridge, Mass.: Harvard University Press.

———. 1993. "Understanding Humor and Understanding Music." *Journal of Musicology* 11, no. 1:32–44.

Webern, Anton. 1975. *The Path to the New Music.* Translated by Willi Reich. London: Universal.

Weingartner, Felix. 1907. *On the Performance of Beethoven's Symphonies.* Translated by Edward Crosland. London: Breitkopf & Härtel.

Werckmeister, Otto. 1981. *Versuche über Paul Klee.* Frankfurt am Main: Syndikat.

————. 1989. *The Making of Paul Klee's Career: 1914–1920.* Chicago: University of Chicago Press.

Whittall, Arnold. 1982. "Music Analysis as Human Science? *Le Sacre du Printemps* in Theory and Practice." *Music Analysis* 1, no. 1:33–54.

Williams, Christopher A. 1993. "Of Canons and Contexts: Toward a Historiography of Twentieth-Century Music." *repercussions* 2, no. 1:31–74.

Witkin, Robert W. 1998. *Adorno on Music.* London: Routledge.

Žižek, Slavoj. 1991a. *For They Know not what They Do: Enjoyment as a Political Factor.* London and New York: Verso.

————. 1991b. *Looking Awry: An Introduction to Jacques Lacan through Popular Culture.* Cambridge, Mass.: MIT Press.

CONTRIBUTORS

Paul Attinello is Lecturer at the University of Newcastle-upon-Tyne. He has published on high modernism and queer studies in the *Journal of Musicological Research*, *Musik-Konzepte*, *Musica/Realtà*, *MLA Notes*, the revised *New Grove*, and several collections. He created the Newsletter of the Gay & Lesbian Study Group of the American Musicological Society, editing its first three volumes, and contributed to *Queering the Pitch: The New Lesbian & Gay Musicology* (Routledge, 1994). Current projects include a monograph on Darmstadt composers, a book on music about AIDS, and books on Meredith Monk and Gerhard Stäbler.

Andrew Dell'Antonio is Associate Professor of Musicology at the University of Texas, Austin. He has published on early modern instrumental music, Monteverdi historiography, and Beavis & Butt-Head. Following a year as Mellon Fellow at the Harvard–Villa I Tatti Center for Italian Renaissance Studies, he is working on a broad study of the changing role of listening as a spiritual-aesthetic practice in seventeenth-century Italy.

Joseph Dubiel is Associate Professor of Music at Columbia University, teaching composition and theory. He has received the SMT Young Scholar Award, a Guggenheim Fellowship for composition, and other awards, and has co-edited *Perspectives of New Music*. His vocal and chamber music is recorded on Centaur, and his writing is published in the collection *Rethinking Music,* and in *Perspectives, Journal of Music Theory, Journal of Musicology,* and other journals.

Robert Fink is Associate Professor of Musicology at the University of California, Los Angeles. His work has appeared in the *Journal of the American Musicological Society, Nineteenth-Century Music, American Music, Modernism/Modernity, ECHO: A Music-Centered Journal,* and the collection *Rethinking Music.* He is the author of *Repeating Ourselves* (University of California Press, 2005), a study of American minimal music as a cultural practice.

Elisabeth Le Guin received a doctorate in historical musicology at Berkeley in 1997, and currently teaches in that discipline at UCLA. Her academic interests are eclectic—she has published on Luigi Boccherini, the subject of her dissertation (online, in *ECHO: A Music-Centered Journal* [1999]; in *Revista de Musicología* [2004]; and forthcoming in 2005 as *Boccherini's Body: An Essay in Carnal Musicology* [California]); on New Age music (in *repercussions* and in the *New York Times*); and on the relations between seventeenth-century horse training and music-making (in forthcoming collections on information theory and on Early Modern horsemanship). All are connected by an over-arching interest in music as an embodied practice, grounded in her experience as one of the foremost Baroque cellists in the United States.

Tamara Levitz is Associate Professor of Musicology at the University of California, Los Angeles. She specializes in musical modernism in Europe and the Americas, and has published on the Weimar Republic, American experimentalism, Stravinsky, early John Cage, Kurt Weill, Yoko Ono, the discipline of musicology, and popular music of the 1960s. She is currently working on a book on "visualized music"—collaborative projects of music and dance in Europe and the Americas between the wars.

Fred Everett Maus is Associate Professor of Music Theory at the University of Virginia. His research interests include theory and analysis, gender and sexuality, popular music, aesthetics, dramatic and narrative aspects of instrumental music. He has published in the *Journal of Aesthetics and Art Criticism, Popular Music, repercussions,* and *Perspectives of New Music;* and in the collections *Rethinking Music, Performance and Authenticity in the Arts.* He was a founding member of the editorial board of *Women and Music,* and co-director and co-chair of the program committee, for the conference Feminist Theory and Music 4.

Mitchell Morris is Assistant Professor of Musicology at the University of California, Los Angeles. He has published essays on gay men and opera, disco and progressive rock, musical ethics, and contemporary music in journals such as *repercussions* and *American Music* as well as in collections such as *Musicology and Difference, En travesti,* and *Audible Traces.* He is currently preparing a book entitled *The Persistence of Sentiment: Essays on Pop Music in the 70s* and at work on a project entitled *Echo of Wilderness: Music, Nature, and Nation in the United States, 1880–1945.*

Martin Scherzinger is a composer and Assistant Professor of Musicology and Theory at the Eastman School of Music. He has published in *Music Analysis, Yearbook of Traditional Music, Current Musicology, Perspectives of New Music, South*

African Journal of Musicology, Disclosure: A Journal of Philosophy and Theory, Journal of the Royal Musical Association, Indiana Theory Review, and in various collections. Recently he was awarded a Mellon ACLS Fellowship and an outstanding publication award from the Society for Music Theory (2002).

Rose Rosengard Subotnik is Professor of Music at Brown University. Both of her books were published by the University of Minnesota Press in Minneapolis: *Developing Variations: Style and Ideology in Western Music* (1991); and *Deconstructive Variations: Music and Reason in Western Society* (1996). Past fellowships include a Fulbright Scholarship to Vienna, a Guggenheim Fellowship, an ACLS Fellowship, and a Howard Fellowship. Her areas of specialization are music and critical theory (with particular emphasis on Adorno), American musical theater and song, and opera.

INDEX

Abbate, Carolyn, 297n10
The absolute, 48, 263
Acocella, Joan, 82, 104n58
Adair, Christy, 98
Adorno, Theodor W.: on Beethoven, *Missa Solemnis*, 144–45; on Beethoven, Ninth Symphony, 144; on Beethoven's late style, 144, 145; on compositional flaws, 301n51; Continental philosophy of, 280; on dance, 73, 77, 78, 100n23; dialectical philosophy of, 284; on disorder in music, 293; immanent criticism of, 75; on internalization, 302n58; Marxism of, 70, 79; on musical autonomy, 202, 218; on musical consciousness, 99n14; on musical value, 70; on music reading, 3; patriarchal views of, 121; *Philosophie der neuen Musik*, 73, 75, 100nn23–24; on popular music, 203; on rationality, 50; on Schoenberg, 273–74; on Stravinsky, *Sacre du Printemps*, 9, 72, 73–80, 85–86, 88, 105n67; and structural listening, 2, 47, 70, 75, 202; on subjectivity, 73, 74, 100n16; Subotnik on, 144, 145, 280, 281, 282; theory of permanent regression, 99n15; on Viennese School, 88
Aesthetics: of capitalism, 226; cognitive aspects of, 302n60; of failure, 112, 292, 300n31; French, 245; immediacy in, 9, 211; intellectual movement toward, 281, 297n9; late twentieth-century, 252–53; modernist, 203; moral aspects of,

302n60; of musical autonomy, 254, 264; of musical formalism, 253; postmodern, 7; of the sublime, 111
Agawu, Kofi, 99n12
Agency: in composition, 23; intelligibility in, 56; intention in, 55–56; in musical production, 42n25; in music theory, 15–16, 19; in sadomasochism, 39
Allanbrook, Wye Jamison, 33
Alperson, Philip, 296n1
Androgyny, 166
Angels: in postmodernism, 158–62; in Rilke's poetry, 155, 157, 170
Appraisers, ideal, 207, 213, 218, 221. *See also* Collective appraisal
Aristotle: on catharsis, 65; concept of virtue, 52, 53, 55; metaphysical biology of, 53
Art: Debussy on, 241–42; Enlightenment concept of, 47; form *versus* content in, 3; high and low, 205; nondiscursive language of, 298n22; political, 226; respect in, 234–35
Art plastique, 102n42, 104n57; *Sacre du Printemps* (Stravinsky) as, 80–84
Art works: autonomy of, 2, 12, 203; irreproducibility of, 203; purpose of, 12n2
Attali, Jacques, 145–46
Authenticity: in collective appraisal, 223; of MTV, 213, 224–25, 228, 229; in popular music, 204; through rebellion, 220; of rock culture, 220; of Stravinsky, *Sacre du Printemps*, 79

Bryson, Norman, 247
Burke, Edmund: on the beautiful, 112; on
the sublime, 112–13
Bussotti, Sylvano, 169

Cage, John, 169
Canudo, Ricciotto, 83, 102n42
Capitalism: aesthetic production under, 226;
and postmodernism, 228; rationality of,
274–75; social life under, 226–27
Chopin, Frédéric, 222
Choreography: fluid nature of, 288; of Nijinsky, 7, 8, 10, 78, 80–87, 91, 93–98,
101n27, 103nn51,55. *See also* Dance
Chua, Daniel, 254
Cinema, 245; Bergson on, 243; capital investment in, 203; synoptic moments in,
242
Class struggle, 226
Collective appraisal, 220; authenticity in,
223; in *Beavis & Butt-head*, 213–16; in
capitalist culture, 228–29; in listening,
203, 213, 229, 230n9; on MTV, 213–18,
223, 231n15; of music videos, 202, 203,
212, 213, 217, 289; "noise-to-signal ratio"
in, 218, 223. *See also* Appraisers, ideal
Collins, Randall, 44, 45
Composers: contract with listeners, 2; ethical
positions of, 46; homosexual, 169–70;
intentionality of, 187; relationship with
performers, 298n20
Composition: agency in, 23; aggressive, 37;
as empirical activity, 48; genealogical
explanations of, 302n59; imaginary, 30,
41n14; structural explanations of,
302n59; universal validity of, 49
Cone, Edward T., 7; on agency, 38; *The Composer's Voice*, 23–27, 30–36, 38, 40nn7–9;
on control, 38, 40nn7–8; on listening, 34;
on musical seduction, 31–34; on personae, 42n22; "Schubert's Promissory
Note," 31, 41n18
Congress of Vienna, 143
Control: analytical discourse of, 7; in psychoanalysis, 22; scientific metaphors of, 6;
and submission, 7; and subordination,
18–19. *See also* Domination; Mastery
Control, musical, 40n7; Forte on, 18–19, 30;
in music theory, 18–19, 21, 286, 292
Cook, Nicholas, 98n2, 106n84; on
Beethoven, Ninth Symphony, 19, 140, 143

Creativity: Barraqué on, 160; and destruc-
tion, 159; listener in, 201, 202; on MTV,
223; sublimation of, 163
Creely, Robert, 62
Cuenod, Hugues, 238, 251n5
Culture: capitalist, 224, 228–29; commercial,
203–4; moralistic sensibility of, 161; pub-
lic service notions of, 226
Culture, mass, 204; criticism of, 203; Gramsci
on, 223–24; Marxist view of, 204; resis-
tance to, 224
Culture, rock, 212, 224; authenticity of, 220
Curtis, Liane, 41n19
Cusick, Suzanne, 38, 42n21, 109, 110; "On a
Lesbian Relation with Music," 42n25; on
transgender intersubjectivity, 149n3

Dadaism, poetry of, 157
Dahlhaus, Carl, 101n24; on "New Music,"
232n23
Dance: abstract, 102n42; Adorno on, 73, 77,
78, 100n23; gender identity in, 102n41;
meaning through, 71; as mimesis, 84;
New Wave, 66; Nijinsky on, 104n66; as
plastique animé, 83, 97; ritual, 102n40;
Taruskin on, 79. *See also* Choreography
Darmstadt school, 6, 169
Davies, Maxwell, 155, 156, 162; First Symphony, 161
Debussy, Claude, 233; on images, 251n6; and
Jaques-Dalcroze, 107n89; on listening, 235,
237, 240, 244, 250; on musical reception,
234, 235; *Prélude à l'après-midi d'un faune*,
250n2; on respect in art, 234–35; "Soupir,"
235–40, 248, 251–55; on taste, 234; on
visual art, 241–42; on writing, 234, 237
Deconstruction: Derridean, 258, 262; Laclau
on, 265, 266–67; liberal stage of, 299n24;
of *Morgengruß*, 259–62; and musical formalism, 258–72; in musicology, 256, 257;
of structural listening, 202, 283; transformational aspects of, 263
Deleuze, Gilles, 169, 170, 202; "Coldness and
Cruelty," 43n26; on oedipal subject,
231n19; on pack formation, 219–20; on
subject positions, 219
Derrida, Jacques, 257, 262, 272; on *différance*,
260; on friendship, 265; and German
metaphysics, 263; on language, 263, 287;
Politics of Friendship, 273; on reading,
258–59; on *supplement*, 264

Reznor, Trent, 64; musical poetics of, 65–66; music videos of, 65
Rhetoric, musical, 281, 297n8
Rhythm: concept of, 267; non-rhythmic dimensions of, 266; in Stravinsky, 88, 90–91, 265
Rich, Adrienne, 130; "The Ninth Symphony of Beethoven Understood at Last as a Sexual Message," 141, 142–43, 147
Rich, Frank, 280
Riemann, Hugo: on Beethoven, 118, 124; *Grundriß der Kompositionslehre*, 115; and Schenker, 124, 149n6
Rilke, Rainer Maria, 154, 300n39; angels in poetry of, 155, 157, 170; *Duino Elegies*, 155, 157; *Sonnets to Orpheus*, 155
Rimbaud, Arthur, 69n20
Rivières, Jacques, 84, 96
Rock music: authenticity of, 225; avant-garde, 66; culture of, 212, 220, 224
Rodin, Auguste, 83
Roerich, Nicholas, 76, 79, 82, 95, 100n17; *The Call of the Sun*, 85; and Russian totems, 103n57
Roland-Manuel, Alexis, 296n3
Rolland, Romain, 118–19
Romanticism: the indescribable in, 245, 294, 300n39; and Industrial music, 66; musical sublime in, 112; as nascent modernism, 124
Rosen, Charles, 42n21, 297n6
Rothstein, Edward, 148n1
Rousseau, Jean Jacques: *Essai sur l'origine des langues*, 245, 264

Sacher-Masoch, Leopold von: *Venus in Furs*, 43n26, 123
Sade, Marquis de, 145
Sadomasochism, 35–36; agency in, 39; feminist thought on, 42n24; Freud on, 42n22; in listening, 300n33; power relations in, 7, 36; roles in, 36, 38–39, 42n21; of the sublime, 122
Saint-Point, Valentine de, 83
Saint-Saëns, Camille, 301n50
Sartre, Jean Paul: *Being and Nothingness*, 268
Sass, Louis, 170, 299n28
Sauer, Wilhelm, 119; patriarchal views of, 121
Schenker, Heinrich, 13–22; and the absolute, 48; *Beethovens Neunte Sinfonie*, 148; on

Beethoven, Ninth Symphony, 114, 115–16, 123, 137, 138, 149nn6–7, 151–52n25; conception of musical structure, 13; conception of musical time, 17; fantasy recompositions of, 30; on *Fernhören*, 28; graphic analyses of, 13, 29; influence of, 296n4; as listener, 28; Kerman on, 120–21; on middleground, 29, 41nn10,12; motivic thought of, 18; organicism of, 120, 123; on Riemann, 124; as role model, 14; on Schumann, 16–22; Schwarz on, 268; *Urlinie* of, 272
Schoenberg, Arnold, 193; Adorno on, 273–74; on Bach, 200n10; Boulez on, 88; influence of, 296n4; in musical canon, 90; on musical idea, 273; on musical meaning, 3; *Six Little Piano Pieces*, 187–92; and structural listening, 2, 47, 70, 202; structural values of, 280; use of dissonance, 73; and Webern, 274
Schopenhauer, Arthur, 272
Schubert, Franz: *Der Doppelgänger*, 268–70; homosexuality of, 46; *Ihr Bild*, 268–71; *Morgengruß*, 259–62; *Schwanengesang*, 268
Schumann, Robert: *Aus meinen Thranen spriessen*, 16–22; *Dichterliebe*, 16, 21, 50; musical criticism of, 11, 222, 231n22; *Scenes from Childhood*, 298n22; Schenker on, 16–22; on Berlioz, *Symphonie fantastique*, 292–93
Schwarz, David: *Listening Subjects*, 268, 271; on Schenker, 268
Science: modernist valuing of, 5; paradigm shifts in, 231n23
Scores, musical: reading of, 3, 26–27, 28, 29, 250n2; visual reference to, 249
Scriabin, Aleksandr Nikolayevich, 100n17
Sedgwick, Eve Kosofsky, 68n12
Seduction, musical, 31–34; resistance to, 33
Self: analysis of concept, 302n60; dialogical constitution of, 56; false, 25; isolation of, 231n20; in modernism, 50, 54; narrative constitution of, 53, 56; and Other, 204; in Stravinsky, *Sacre du Printemps*, 78
Semantics, musical, 236, 300n32
Sensuality: of modernist music, 156, 163; sadomasochistic, 7
Serialism, 165, 166, 169
Set theory, 259, 272
Sexuality, and musical experience, 31–34

van den Toorn, Pieter C.: on Beethoven, Ninth Symphony, 114, 127–29, 138; on McClary, 123, 124–25, 146; *Music, Politics, and the Academy,* 99n12, 146; on Nijinsky, 101n32, 103n55; on Stravinsky, *Sacre du Printemps,* 5, 72, 81, 88, 90–92, 94

Vieillermoz, Émile, 84

Violence: in modernist music, 156; musical representation of, 63, 67; sonic, 154; in Stravinsky, *Sacre du Printemps,* 82; in the sublime, 290

Virtue: Aristotelian, 52, 53, 55; Christian, 52; in classical thought, 52; conflicts in, 55; Homeric, 52, 53; social configuration of, 54–55

Virtue, musical, 7, 11, 58–59, 66; embodiment of, 8–9; institutions of, 55; in structural listening, 57

Vision, Diderot on, 245–46

Wackenroder, Wilhelm Heinrich, 263, 272

Wagner, Richard, 295; on Beethoven, Ninth Symphony, 117, 123; technique of, 180; *Tristan Prelude,* 61, 176–84

Walser, Robert, 210, 232n24

Walton, Kendall, 41n13, 199n1

Webern, Anton: structural listening to, 274

Wedekind, Frank, 122–23, 151n19

Werckmeister, Otto, 158, 159

Wigman, Mary: choreography of, 93, 98, 106n81

Williams, William Carlos, 62

Woolf, Virginia, 171

Writing: insufficiency of, 294; as performance, 162–63

Yack Live (MTV), 213–16, 223, 230nn11–12

Yudkin, Jeremy: *Understanding Music,* 231n16

Žižek, Slavoj, 4–5, 7, 10, 11, 288

Text:	10/12 Baskerville
Display:	Baskerville
Compositor:	Binghamton Valley Composition
Music Setter:	Mansfield Music-Graphics
Printer and Binder:	Maple Vail Manufacturing Group